MOONKNIGHT

TOO TOUGH TO DIE

Mercenary Marc Spector died and was reborn in the shadow of Khonshu, the Egyptian god of the moon. Spector became M
the Fist of Khonshu, to fight evil. Through his Midnight Mission, he is the defender of all those who travel at

MOON KNIGHT

Moon Knight's ally Terry revealed himself to be the villainous Zodiac in disguise and the secret mastermind
a series of recent attacks. Zodiac blew up the Midnight Mission and badly injured Moon Knight. Before he could
Hunter's Moon, the rival Fist of Khonshu, intervened. Zodiac escaped, but with the support of his new
friends and neighbors, Moon Knight remains committed to carrying on his mission.

TOO TOUGH TO DIE

JED MacKAY
WRITER

#7-12

FEDERICO SABBATINI (#7) & **ALESSANDRO CAPPUCCIO** (#8-12)
ARTISTS

RACHELLE ROSENBERG
COLOR ARTIST

VC's CORY PETIT
LETTERER

CORY SMITH & **RACHELLE ROSENBERG** (#7-11) AND **STEPHEN SEGOVIA** & **RACHELLE ROSENBERG**
COVER ART

MARTIN BIRO
ASSISTANT EDITOR

ANNALISE BISSA
ASSOCIATE EDITOR

TOM BREVOORT
EDITOR

DEVIL'S REIGN: MOON KNIGHT #1

FEDERICO SABBATINI
ARTIST

LEE LOUGHRIDGE
COLOR ARTIST

VC's CORY PETIT
LETTERER

ROD REIS
COVER ART

MARTIN BIRO
EDITOR

COLLECTION EDITOR **DANIEL KIRCHHOFFER**
ASSISTANT MANAGING EDITOR **MAIA LOY**
ASSOCIATE MANAGER, TALENT RELATIONS **LISA MONTALBANO**
DIRECTOR, PRODUCTION & SPECIAL PROJECTS **JENNIFER GRÜNWALD**
VP PRODUCTION & SPECIAL PROJECTS **JEFF YOUNGQUIST**
BOOK DESIGNERS **ADAM DEL RE** WITH **STACIE ZUCKER**
SVP PRINT, SALES & MARKETING **DAVID GABRIEL**
EDITOR IN CHIEF **C.B. CEBULSKI**

MOON KNIGHT VOL. 2: TOO TOUGH TO DIE. Contains material originally published in magazine form as MOON KNIGHT (2021) #7-12 and DEVIL'S REIGN: MOON KNIGHT (2022) #1. First printing 2022.
3111-7. Published by MARVEL WORLDWIDE, INC., a subsidiary of MARVEL ENTERTAINMENT, LLC. OFFICE OF PUBLICATION: 1290 Avenue of the Americas, New York, NY 10104.
EIGE, Chief Creative Officer; DAN BUCKLEY, President, Marvel Entertainment; DAVID BOGART, Associate Publisher & SVP of Talent Affairs; TOM BREVOORT, VP, Executive Editor; NICK LOWE, Executive Ed
igital Publishing; DAVID GABRIEL, VP of Print & Digital Publishing; SVEN LARSEN, VP of Licensed Publishing; MARK ANNUNZIATO, VP of Planning & Forecasting; JEFF YOUNGQUIST, VP of Production & Spe
ORALES, Director of Publishing Operations; DAN EDINGTON, Director of Editorial Operations; RICKEY PURDIN, Director of Talent Relations; JENNIFER GRÜNWALD, Director of Production & Special Projec
roduction Manager; STAN LEE, Chairman Emeritus. For information regarding advertising in Marvel Comics or on Marvel.com, please contact Vit DeBellis, Custom Solutions & Integrated Advertising Mana
arvel.com. For Marvel subscription inquiries, please call 888-511-5480. **Manufactured between 7/15/2022 and 8/16/2022 by SEAWAY PRINTING, GREEN BAY, WI, USA.**

0 9 8 7 6 5 4 3 2 1

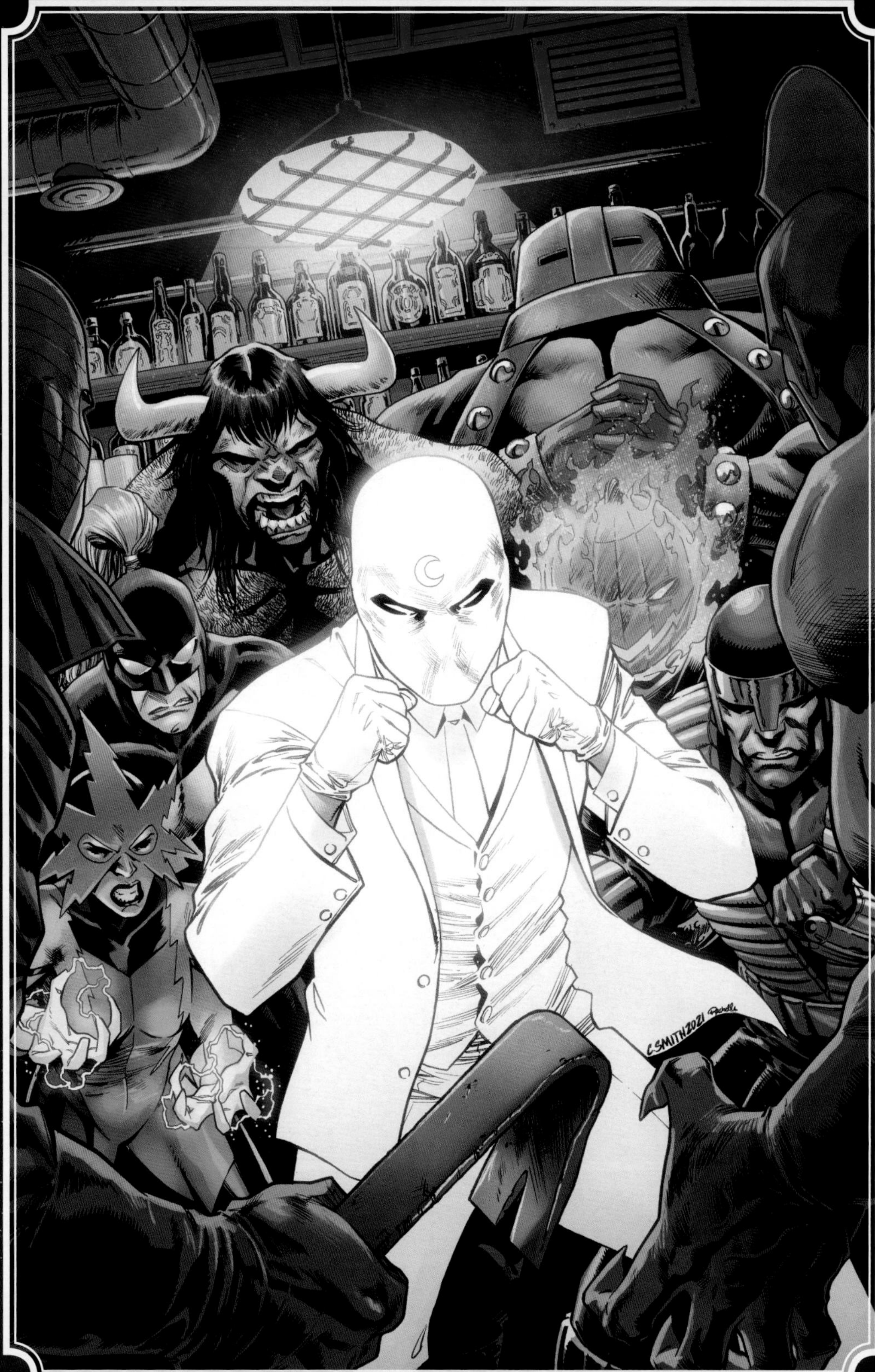
C.SMITH2021

7 HEADHUNTERS

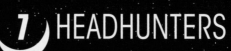

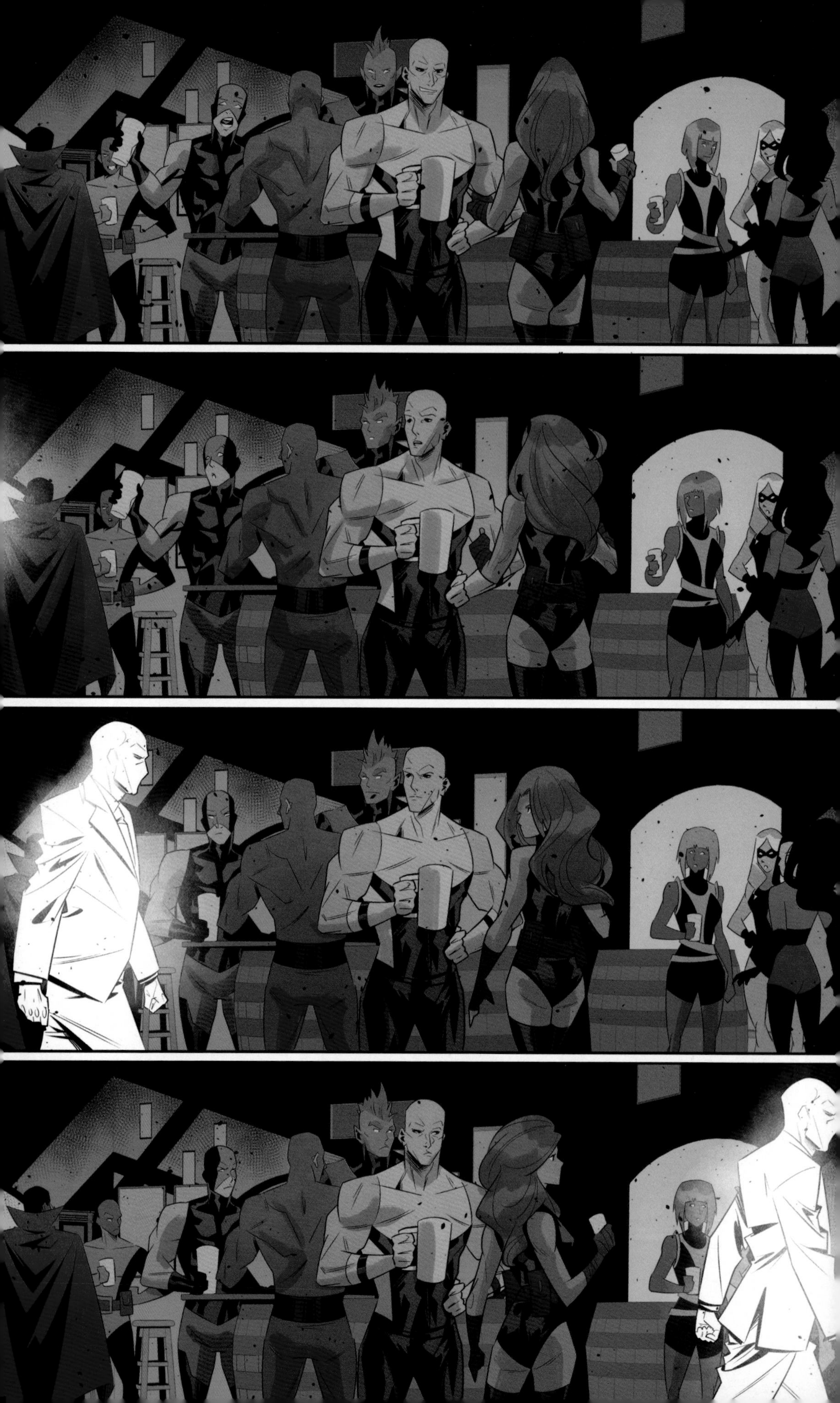

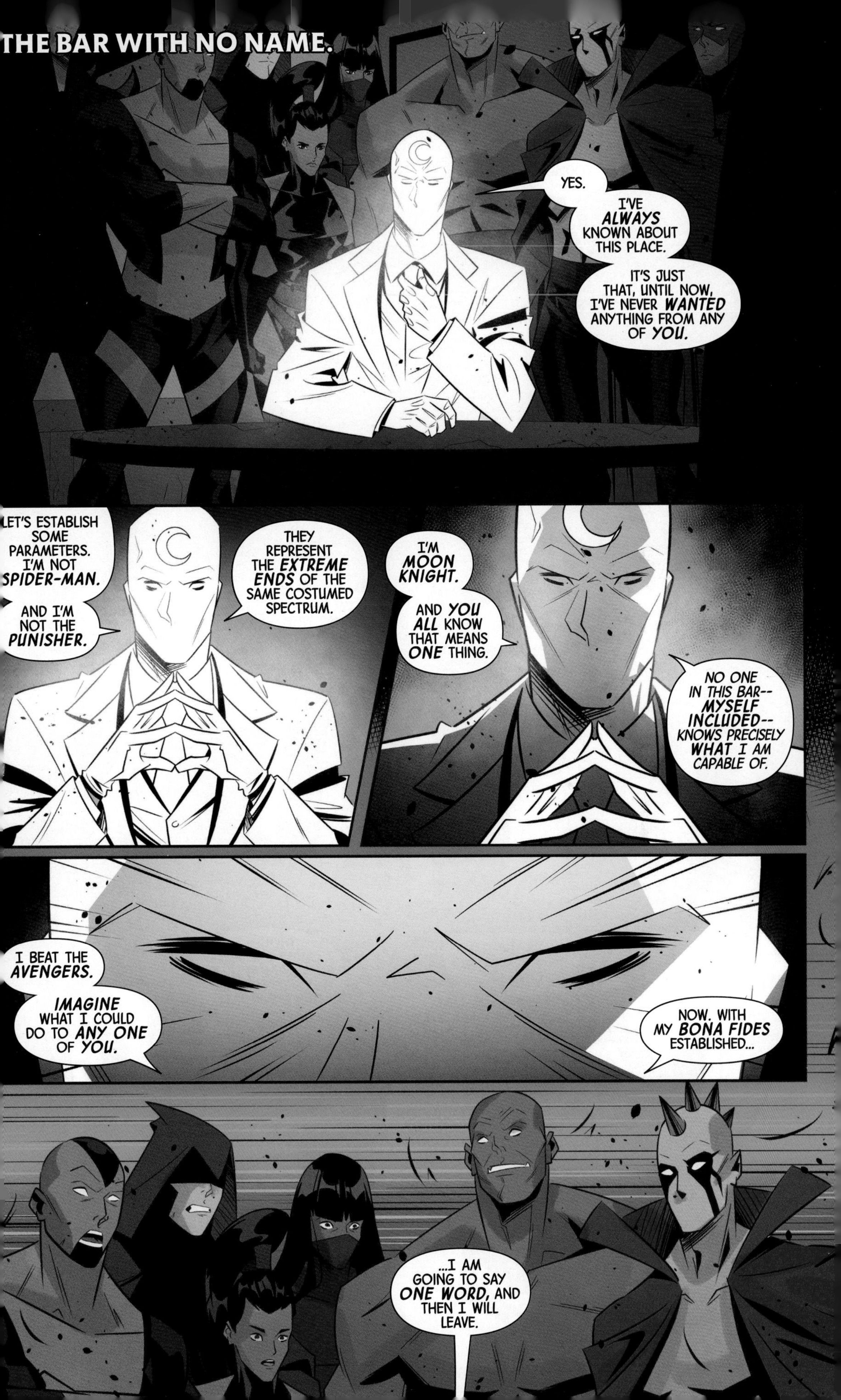
THE BAR WITH NO NAME.
YES.
I'VE ALWAYS KNOWN ABOUT THIS PLACE.
IT'S JUST THAT, UNTIL NOW, I'VE NEVER WANTED ANYTHING FROM ANY OF YOU.
LET'S ESTABLISH SOME PARAMETERS. I'M NOT SPIDER-MAN.
AND I'M NOT THE PUNISHER.
THEY REPRESENT THE EXTREME ENDS OF THE SAME COSTUMED SPECTRUM.
I'M MOON KNIGHT.
AND YOU ALL KNOW THAT MEANS ONE THING.
NO ONE IN THIS BAR-- MYSELF INCLUDED-- KNOWS PRECISELY WHAT I AM CAPABLE OF.
I BEAT THE AVENGERS.
IMAGINE WHAT I COULD DO TO ANY ONE OF YOU.
NOW, WITH MY BONA FIDES ESTABLISHED...
...I AM GOING TO SAY ONE WORD, AND THEN I WILL LEAVE.

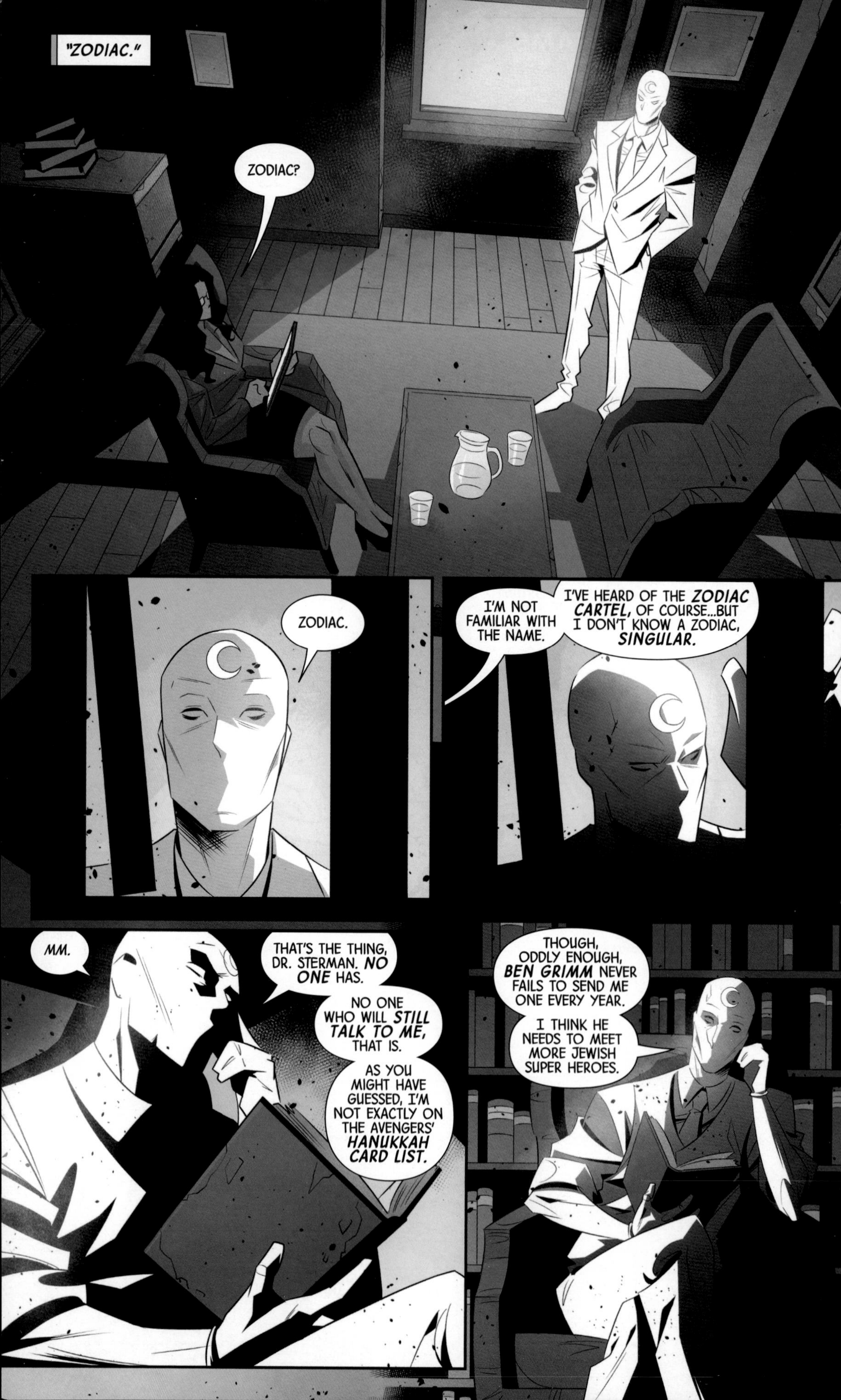
"ZODIAC."
ZODIAC?
ZODIAC.
I'M NOT FAMILIAR WITH THE NAME.
I'VE HEARD OF THE ZODIAC CARTEL, OF COURSE...BUT I DON'T KNOW A ZODIAC, SINGULAR.
MM.
THAT'S THE THING, DR. STERMAN. NO ONE HAS.
NO ONE WHO WILL STILL TALK TO ME, THAT IS.
AS YOU MIGHT HAVE GUESSED, I'M NOT EXACTLY ON THE AVENGERS' HANUKKAH CARD LIST.
THOUGH, ODDLY ENOUGH, BEN GRIMM NEVER FAILS TO SEND ME ONE EVERY YEAR.
I THINK HE NEEDS TO MEET MORE JEWISH SUPER HEROES.

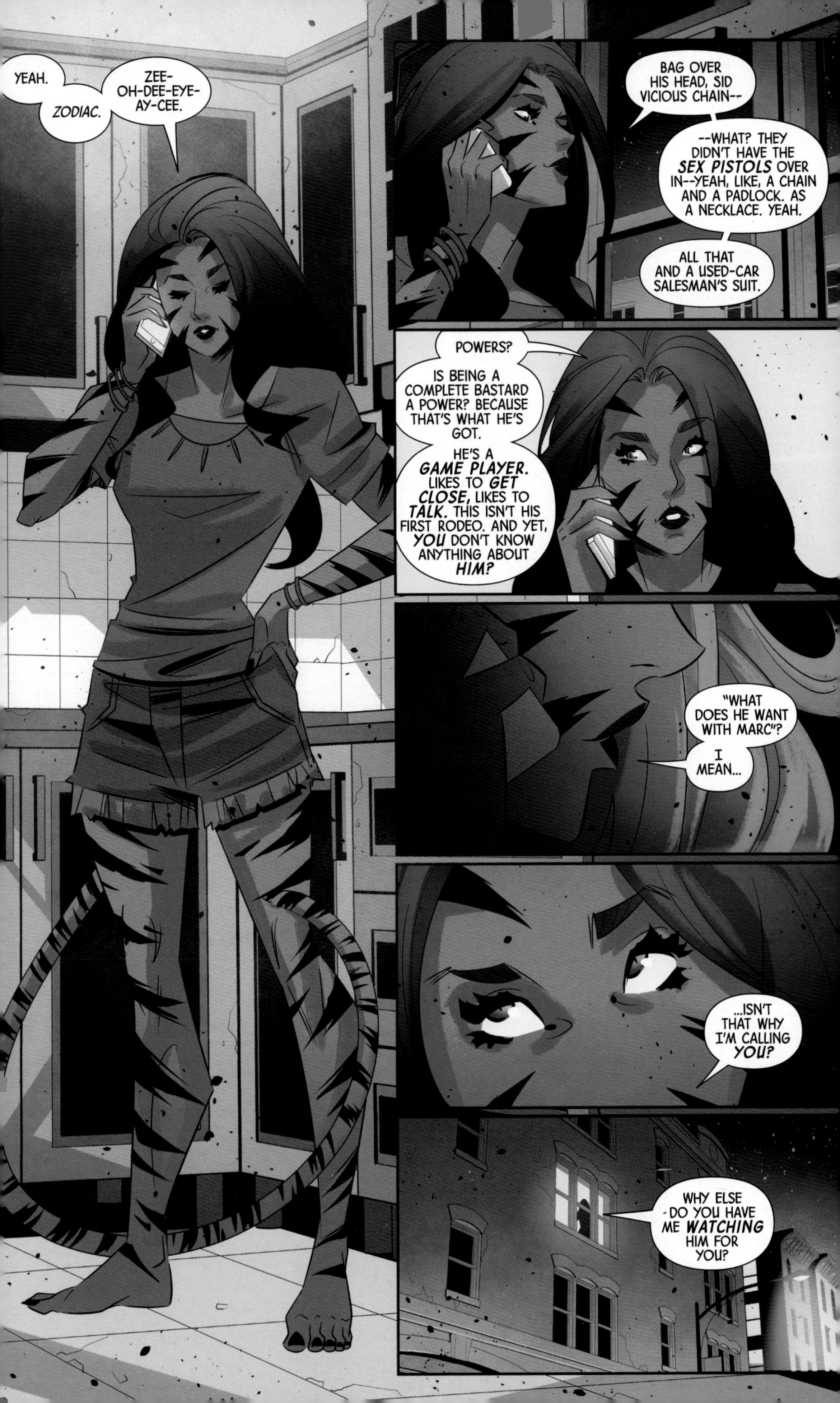

YEAH.
ZODIAC.
ZEE-OH-DEE-EYE-AY-CEE.
BAG OVER HIS HEAD, SID VICIOUS CHAIN--
--WHAT? THEY DIDN'T HAVE THE SEX PISTOLS OVER IN--YEAH, LIKE, A CHAIN AND A PADLOCK. AS A NECKLACE. YEAH.
ALL THAT AND A USED-CAR SALESMAN'S SUIT.
POWERS?
IS BEING A COMPLETE BASTARD A POWER? BECAUSE THAT'S WHAT HE'S GOT.
HE'S A GAME PLAYER. LIKES TO GET CLOSE, LIKES TO TALK. THIS ISN'T HIS FIRST RODEO. AND YET, YOU DON'T KNOW ANYTHING ABOUT HIM?
"WHAT DOES HE WANT WITH MARC"?
I MEAN...
...ISN'T THAT WHY I'M CALLING YOU?
WHY ELSE DO YOU HAVE ME WATCHING HIM FOR YOU?

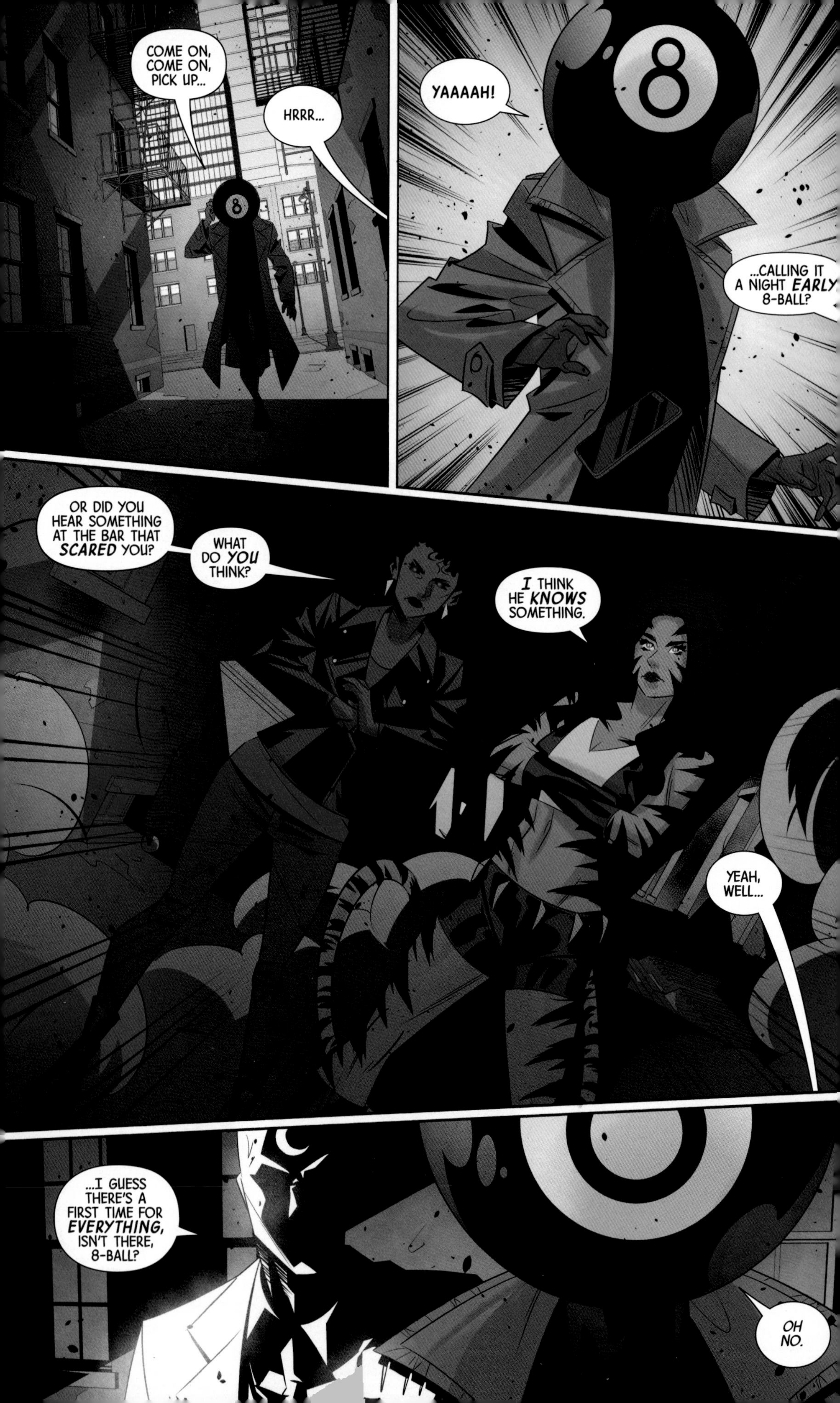
COME ON, COME ON, PICK UP...
HRRR...
YAAAAH!
...CALLING IT A NIGHT EARLY, 8-BALL?
OR DID YOU HEAR SOMETHING AT THE BAR THAT SCARED YOU?
WHAT DO YOU THINK?
I THINK HE KNOWS SOMETHING.
YEAH, WELL...
...I GUESS THERE'S A FIRST TIME FOR EVERYTHING, ISN'T THERE, 8-BALL?
OH NO.

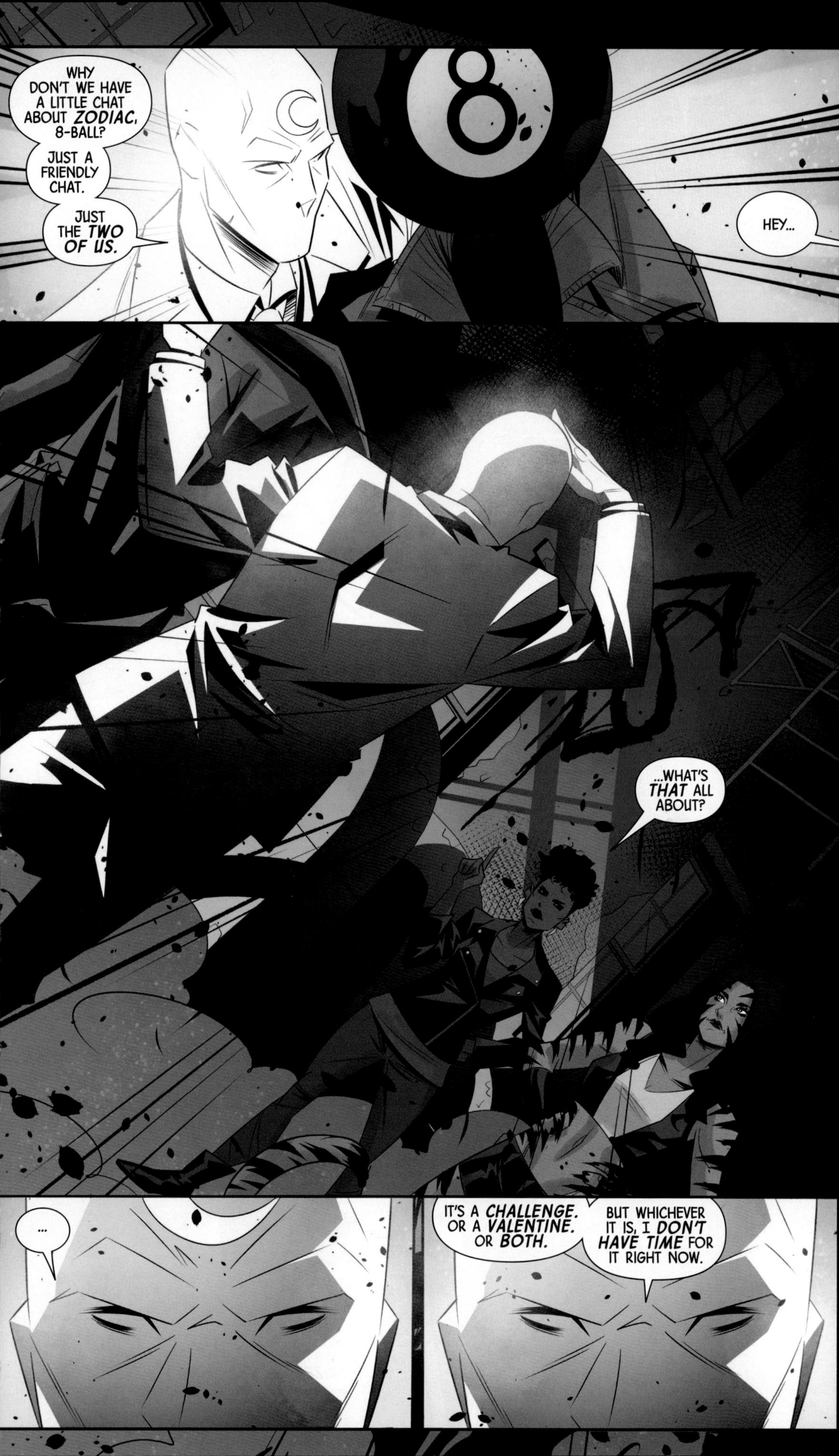
WHY DON'T WE HAVE A LITTLE CHAT ABOUT ZODIAC, 8-BALL?
JUST A FRIENDLY CHAT.
JUST THE TWO OF US.
HEY...
...WHAT'S THAT ALL ABOUT?
...
IT'S A CHALLENGE. OR A VALENTINE. OR BOTH.
BUT WHICHEVER IT IS, I DON'T HAVE TIME FOR IT RIGHT NOW.

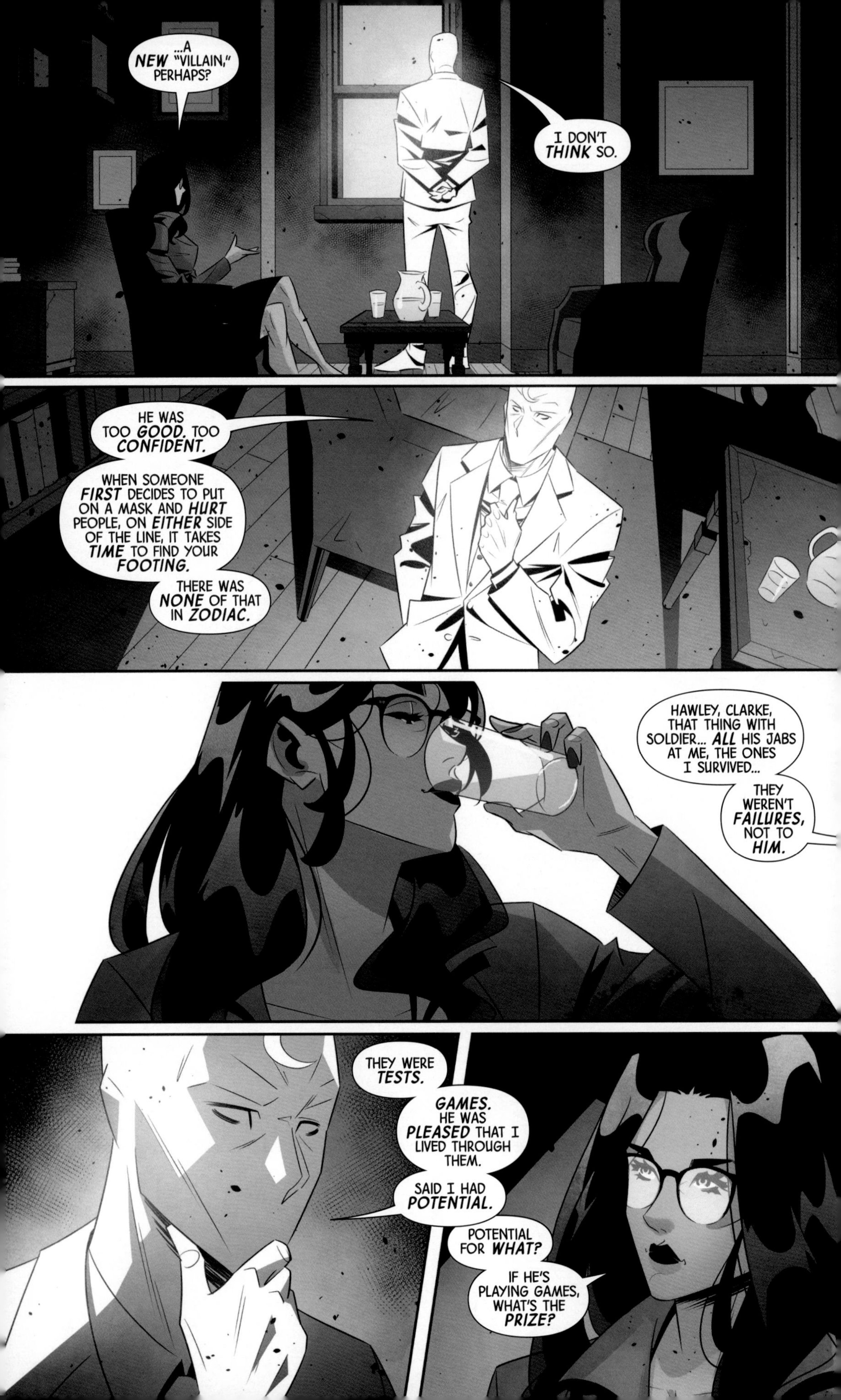

...A NEW "VILLAIN," PERHAPS?
I DON'T THINK SO.
HE WAS TOO GOOD. TOO CONFIDENT.
WHEN SOMEONE FIRST DECIDES TO PUT ON A MASK AND HURT PEOPLE, ON EITHER SIDE OF THE LINE, IT TAKES TIME TO FIND YOUR FOOTING.
THERE WAS NONE OF THAT IN ZODIAC.
HAWLEY, CLARKE, THAT THING WITH SOLDIER... ALL HIS JABS AT ME, THE ONES I SURVIVED...
THEY WEREN'T FAILURES, NOT TO HIM.
THEY WERE TESTS.
GAMES. HE WAS PLEASED THAT I LIVED THROUGH THEM.
SAID I HAD POTENTIAL.
POTENTIAL FOR WHAT?
IF HE'S PLAYING GAMES, WHAT'S THE PRIZE?

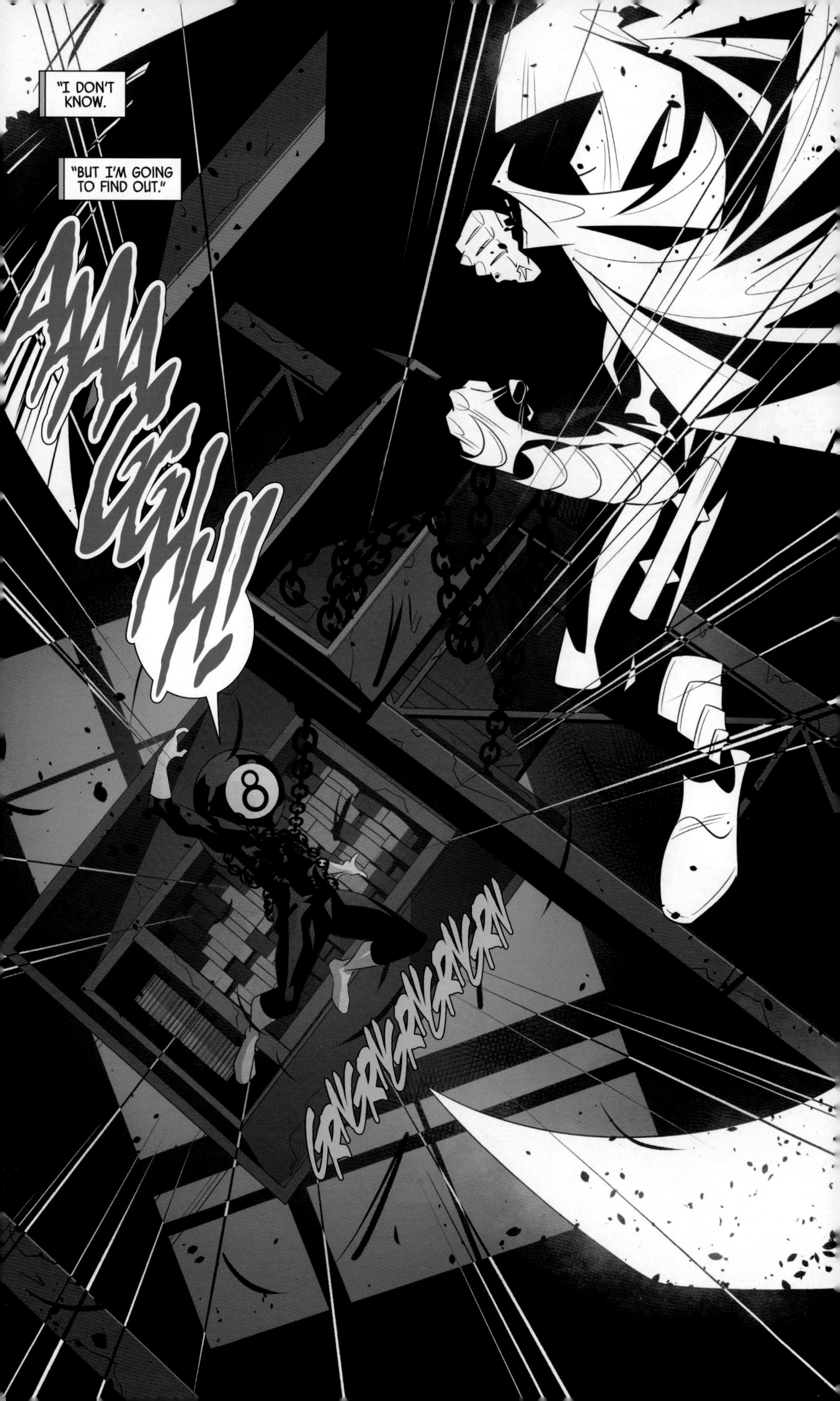
"I DON'T KNOW.
"BUT I'M GOING TO FIND OUT."
AAAUGGH!
GRNGRNGRNGRNGRN

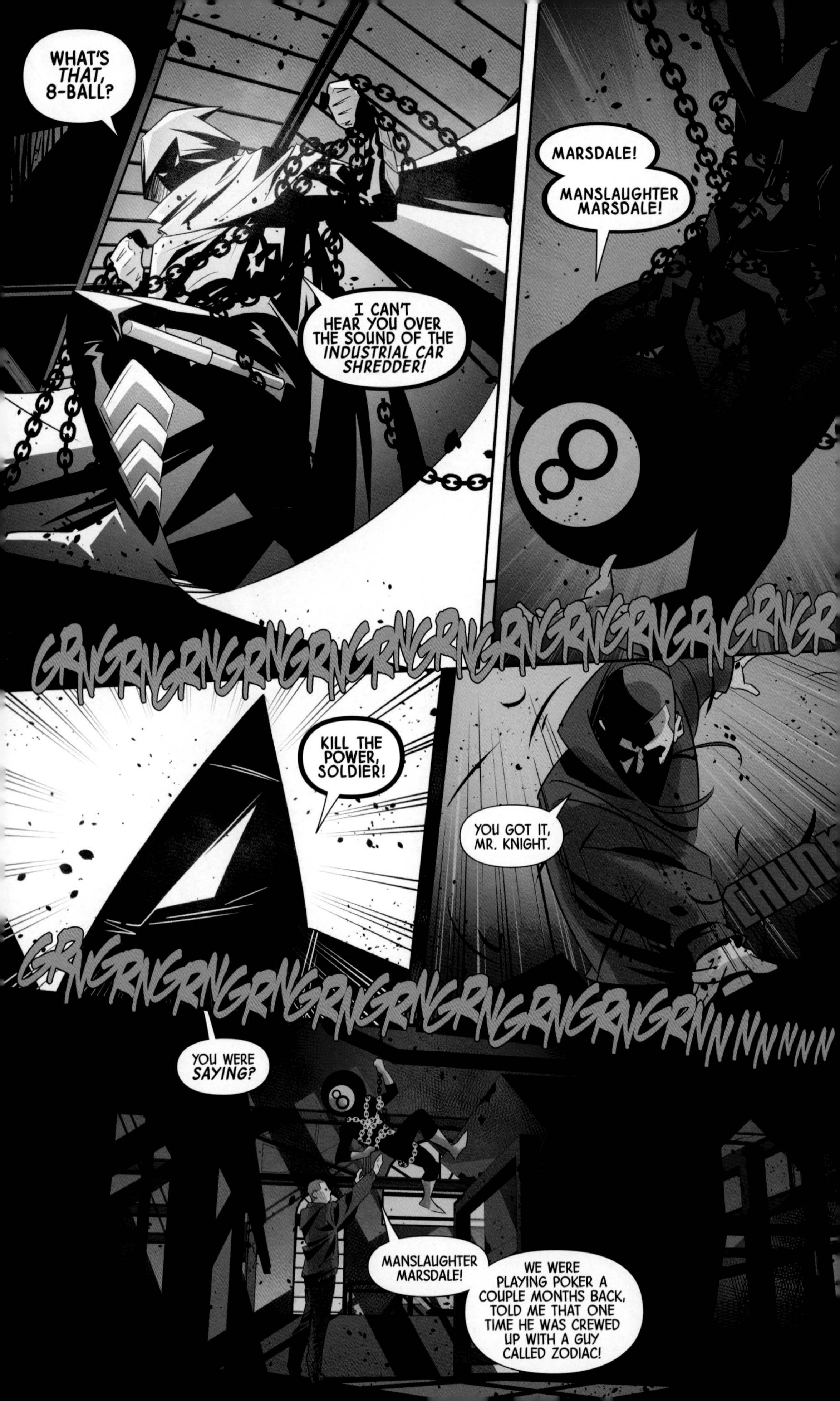

WHAT'S *THAT,* 8-BALL?
MARSDALE!
MANSLAUGHTER MARSDALE!
I CAN'T HEAR YOU OVER THE SOUND OF THE *INDUSTRIAL CAR SHREDDER!*
GRNGRNGRNGRNGRNGRNGRNGRNGRNGRNGRNGRNGRNGRNGRNGRNGR
KILL THE POWER, SOLDIER!
YOU GOT IT, MR. KNIGHT.
GRNGRNGRNGRNGRNGRNGRNGRNGRNGRNGRNGRNGRNGRNNNNNNN
YOU WERE *SAYING?*
MANSLAUGHTER MARSDALE!
WE WERE PLAYING POKER A COUPLE MONTHS BACK, TOLD ME THAT ONE TIME HE WAS CREWED UP WITH A GUY CALLED ZODIAC!

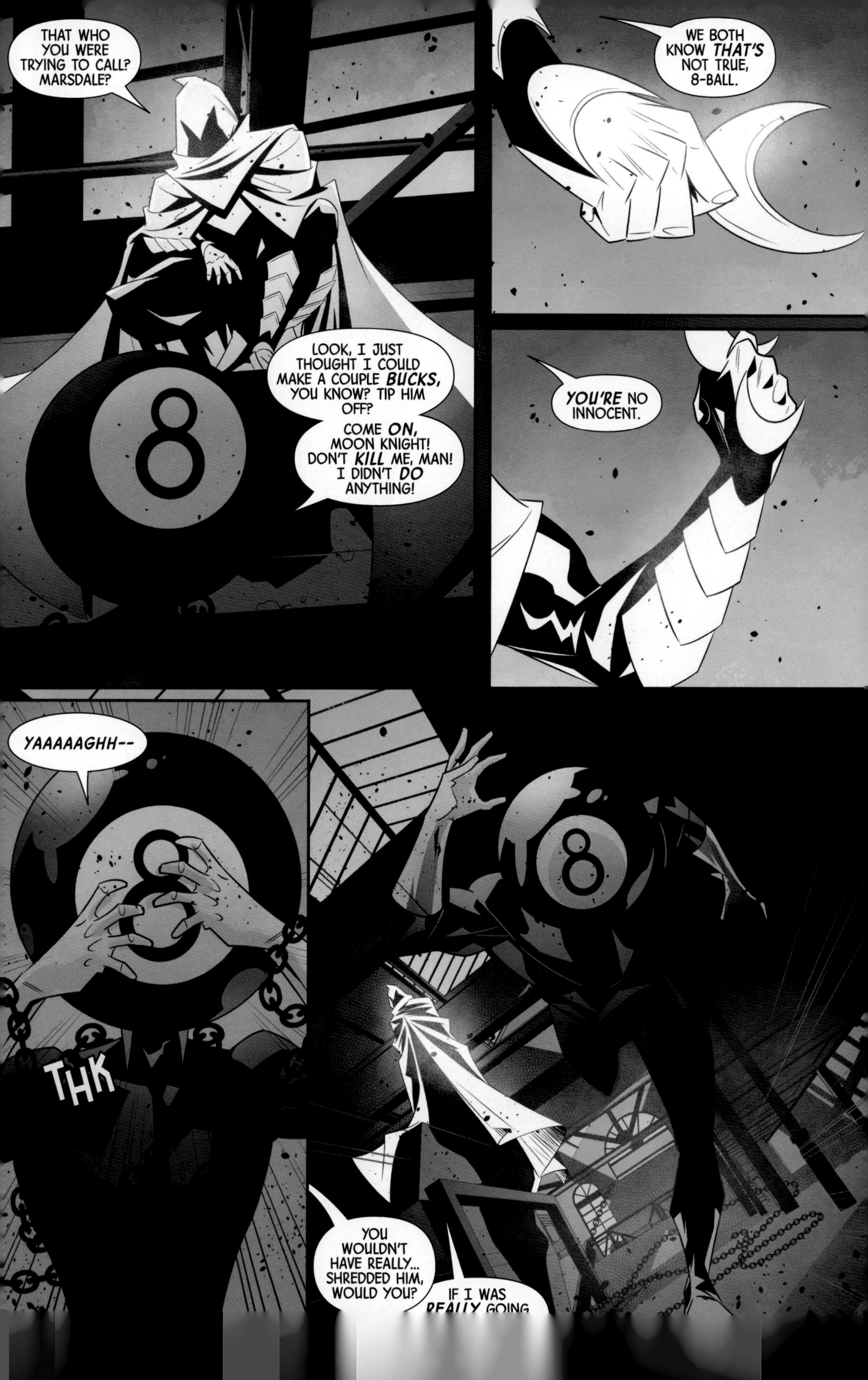

THAT WHO YOU WERE TRYING TO CALL? MARSDALE?
WE BOTH KNOW *THAT'S* NOT TRUE, 8-BALL.
LOOK, I JUST THOUGHT I COULD MAKE A COUPLE *BUCKS*, YOU KNOW? TIP HIM OFF?
COME *ON*, MOON KNIGHT! DON'T *KILL* ME, MAN! I DIDN'T *DO* ANYTHING!
YOU'RE NO INNOCENT.
YAAAAAGHH--
THK
YOU WOULDN'T HAVE REALLY... SHREDDED HIM, WOULD YOU?
IF I WAS

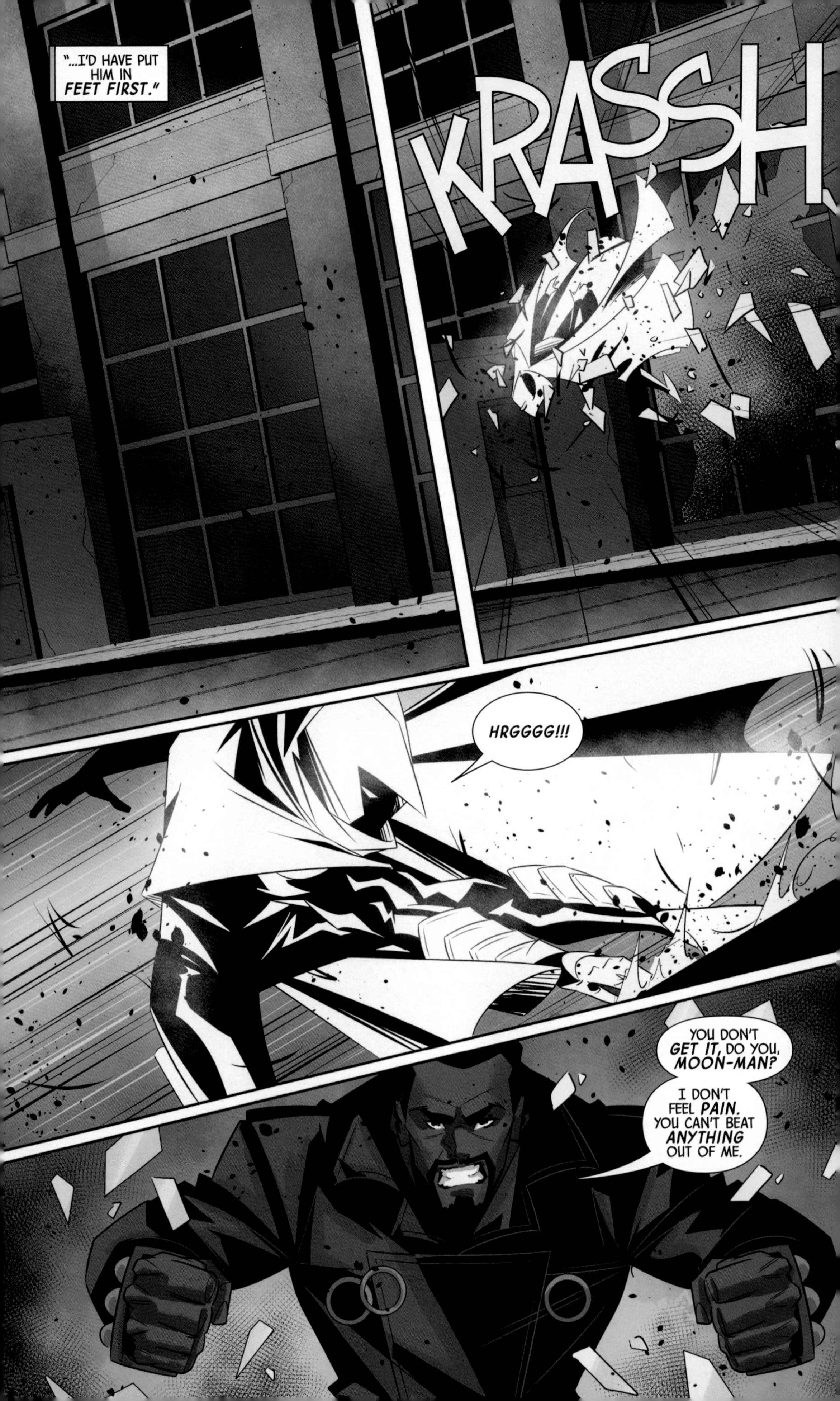
"...I'D HAVE PUT HIM IN FEET FIRST."
KRASSH
HRGGGG!!!
YOU DON'T GET IT, DO YOU, MOON-MAN?
I DON'T FEEL PAIN. YOU CAN'T BEAT ANYTHING OUT OF ME.

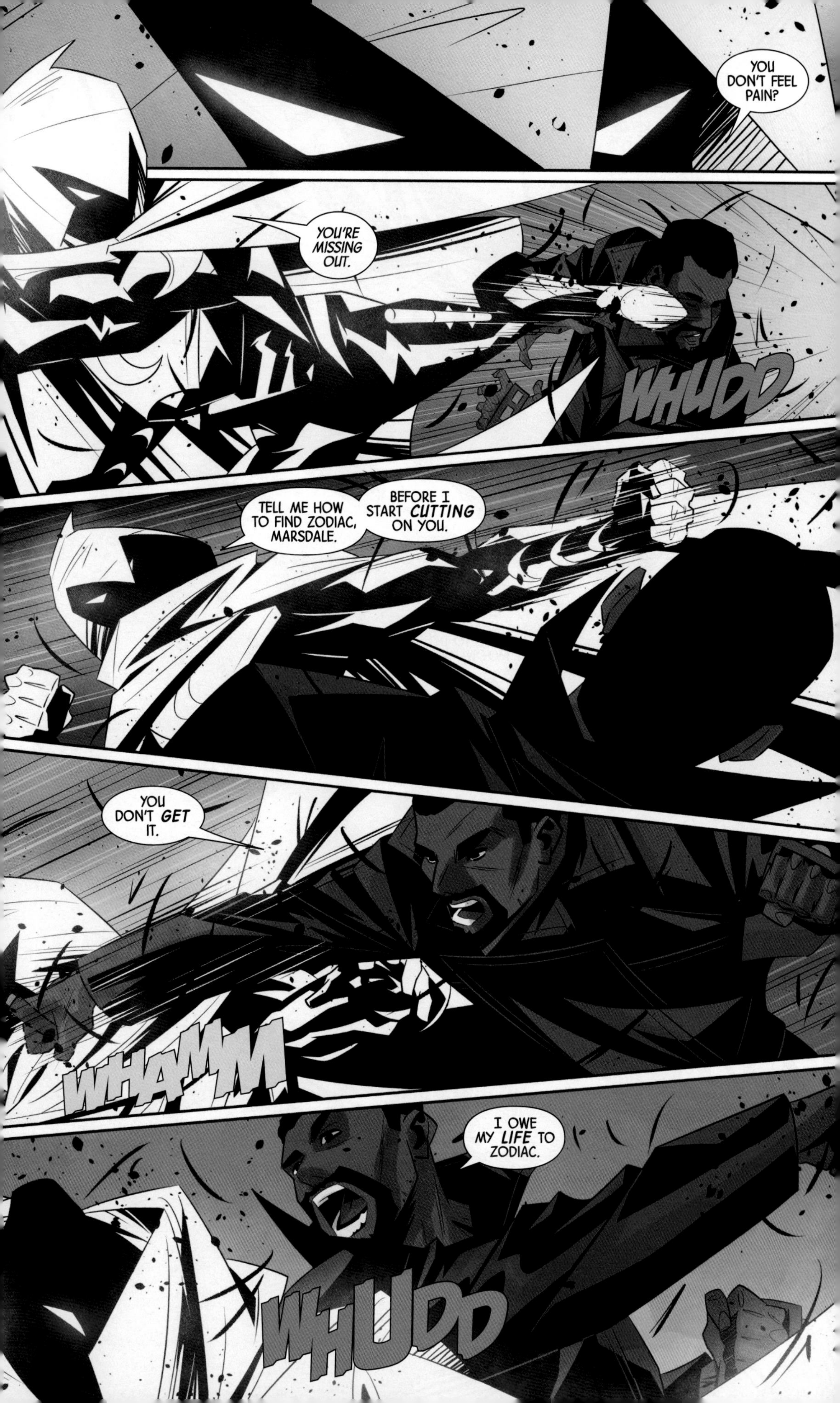
YOU DON'T FEEL PAIN?
YOU'RE MISSING OUT.
WHUDD
TELL ME HOW TO FIND ZODIAC, MARSDALE.
BEFORE I START *CUTTING* ON YOU.
YOU DON'T *GET* IT.
WHAMM
I OWE MY *LIFE* TO ZODIAC.
WHUDD

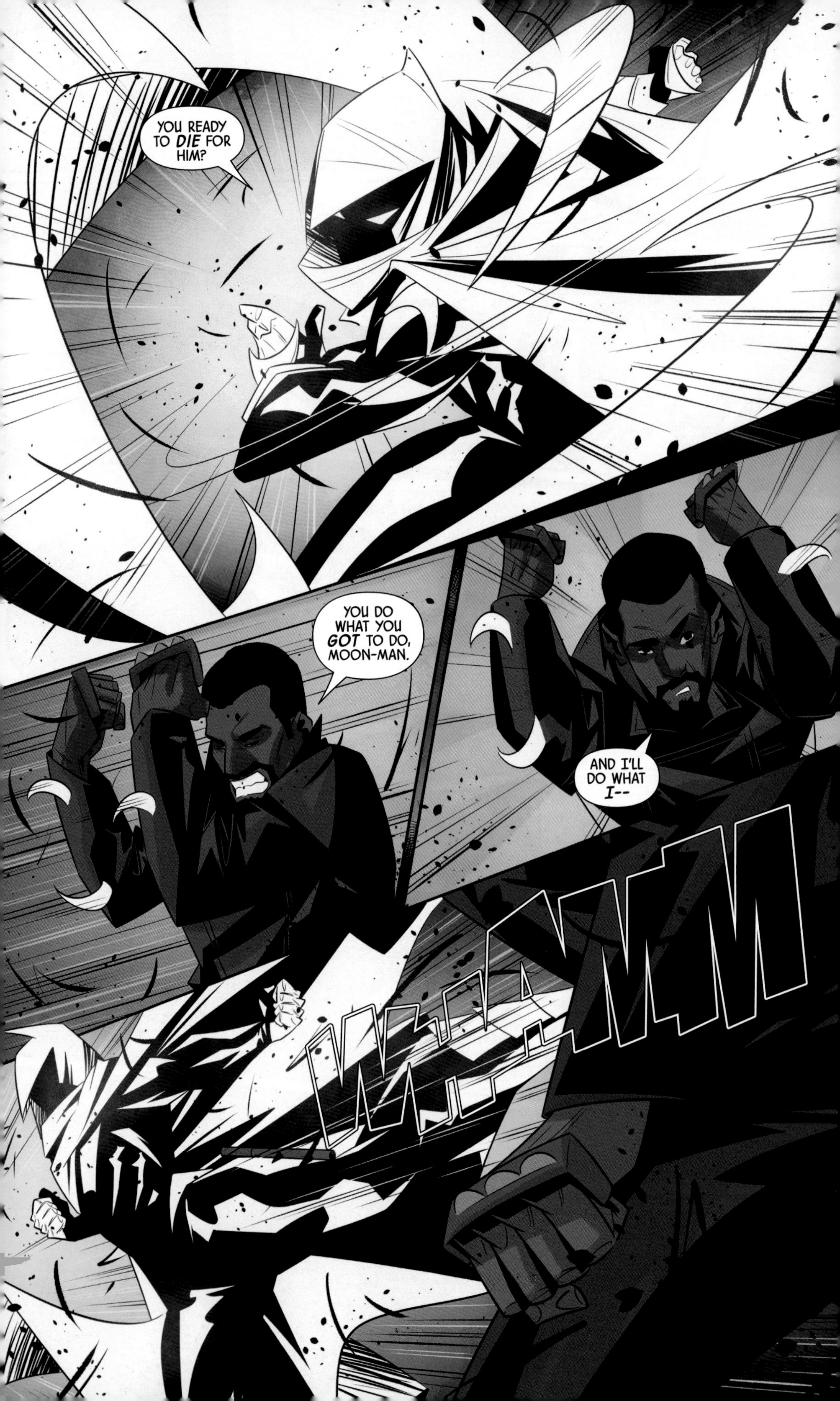
YOU READY TO DIE FOR HIM?
YOU DO WHAT YOU GOT TO DO, MOON-MAN.
AND I'LL DO WHAT I--
WHAMM

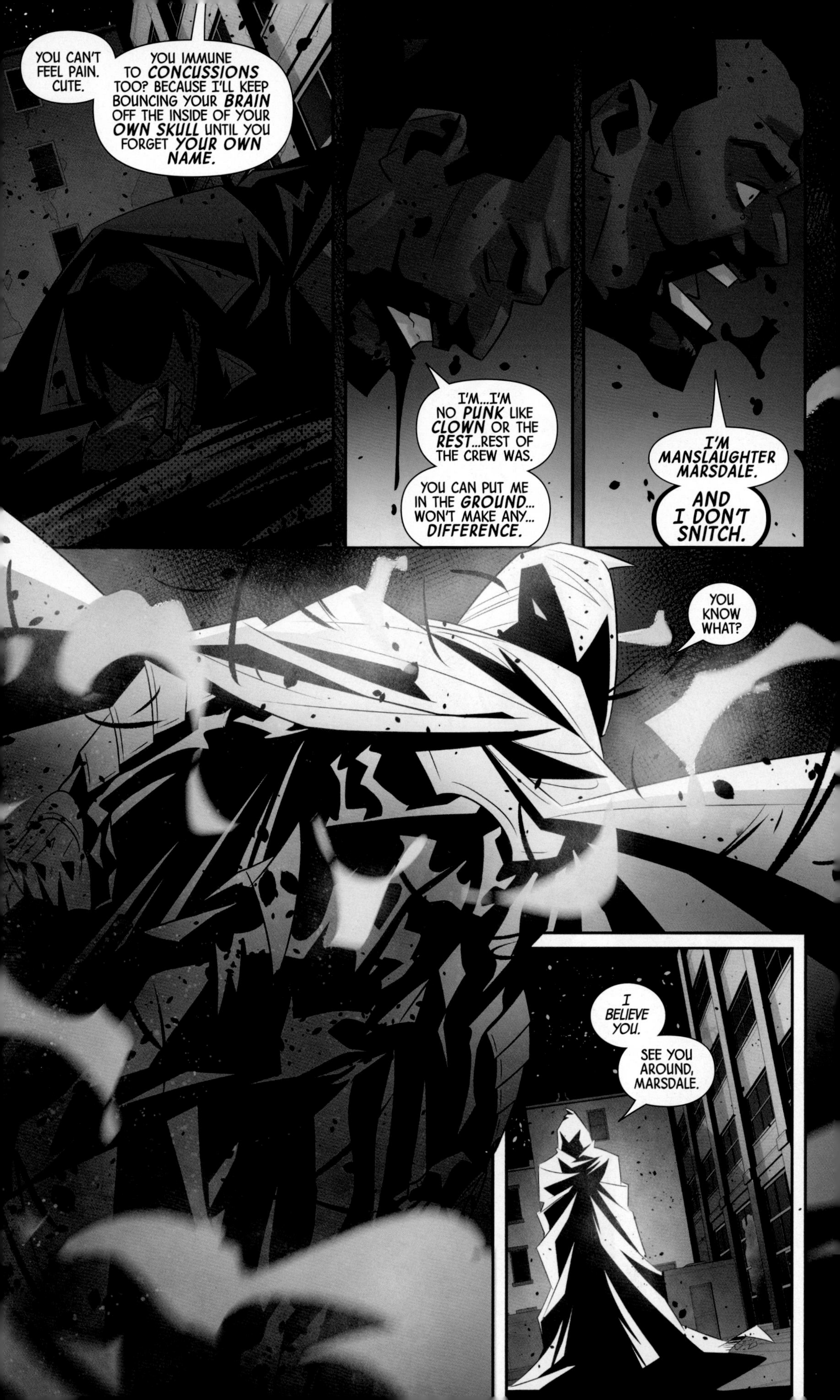

YOU CAN'T FEEL PAIN. CUTE.
YOU IMMUNE TO CONCUSSIONS TOO? BECAUSE I'LL KEEP BOUNCING YOUR BRAIN OFF THE INSIDE OF YOUR OWN SKULL UNTIL YOU FORGET YOUR OWN NAME.
I'M...I'M NO PUNK LIKE CLOWN OR THE REST...REST OF THE CREW WAS.
YOU CAN PUT ME IN THE GROUND... WON'T MAKE ANY... DIFFERENCE.
I'M MANSLAUGHTER MARSDALE.
AND I DON'T SNITCH.
YOU KNOW WHAT?
I BELIEVE YOU.
SEE YOU AROUND, MARSDALE.

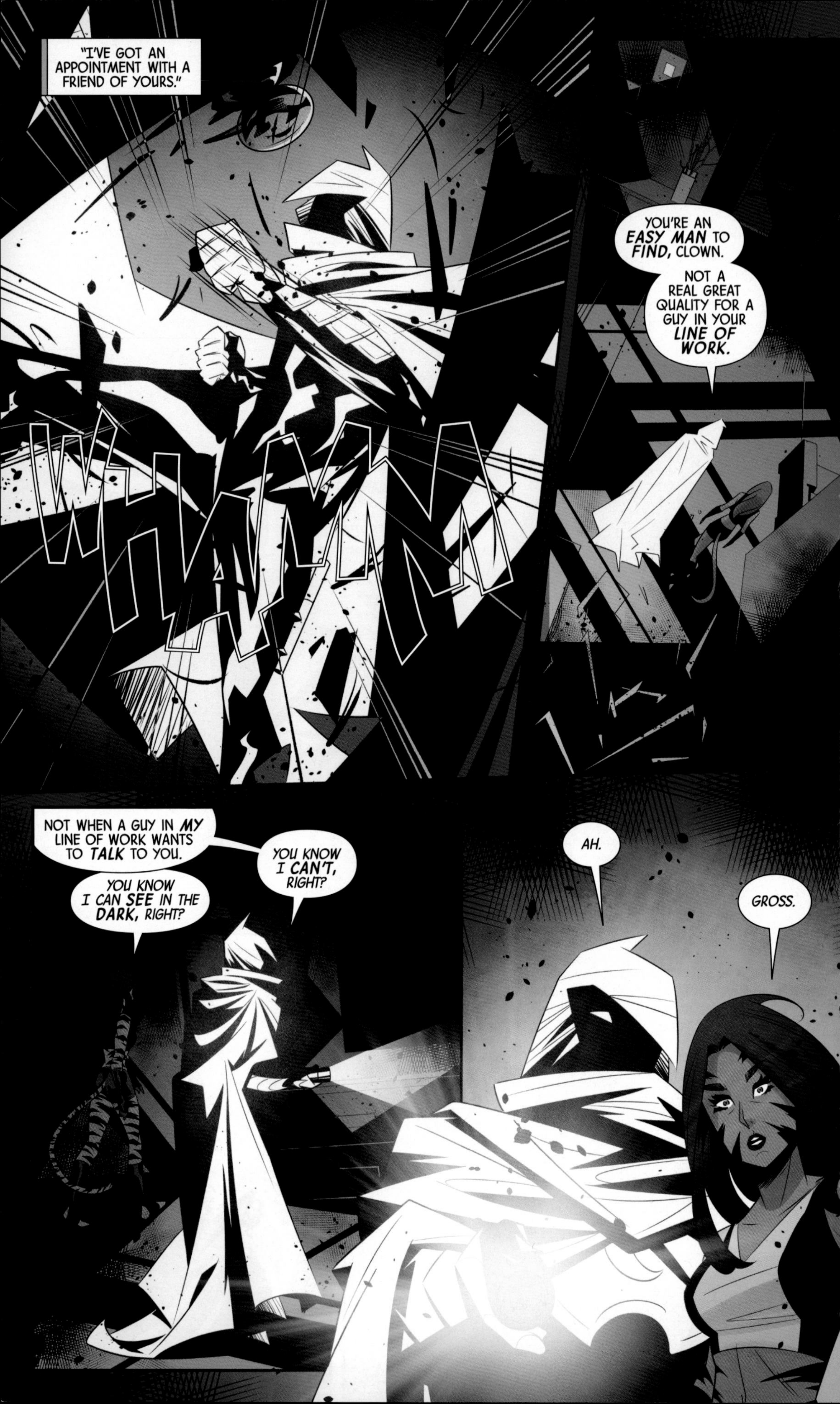
"I'VE GOT AN APPOINTMENT WITH A FRIEND OF YOURS."
WHAMM
YOU'RE AN EASY MAN TO FIND, CLOWN.
NOT A REAL GREAT QUALITY FOR A GUY IN YOUR LINE OF WORK.
NOT WHEN A GUY IN MY LINE OF WORK WANTS TO TALK TO YOU.
YOU KNOW I CAN'T, RIGHT?
YOU KNOW I CAN SEE IN THE DARK, RIGHT?
AH.
GROSS.

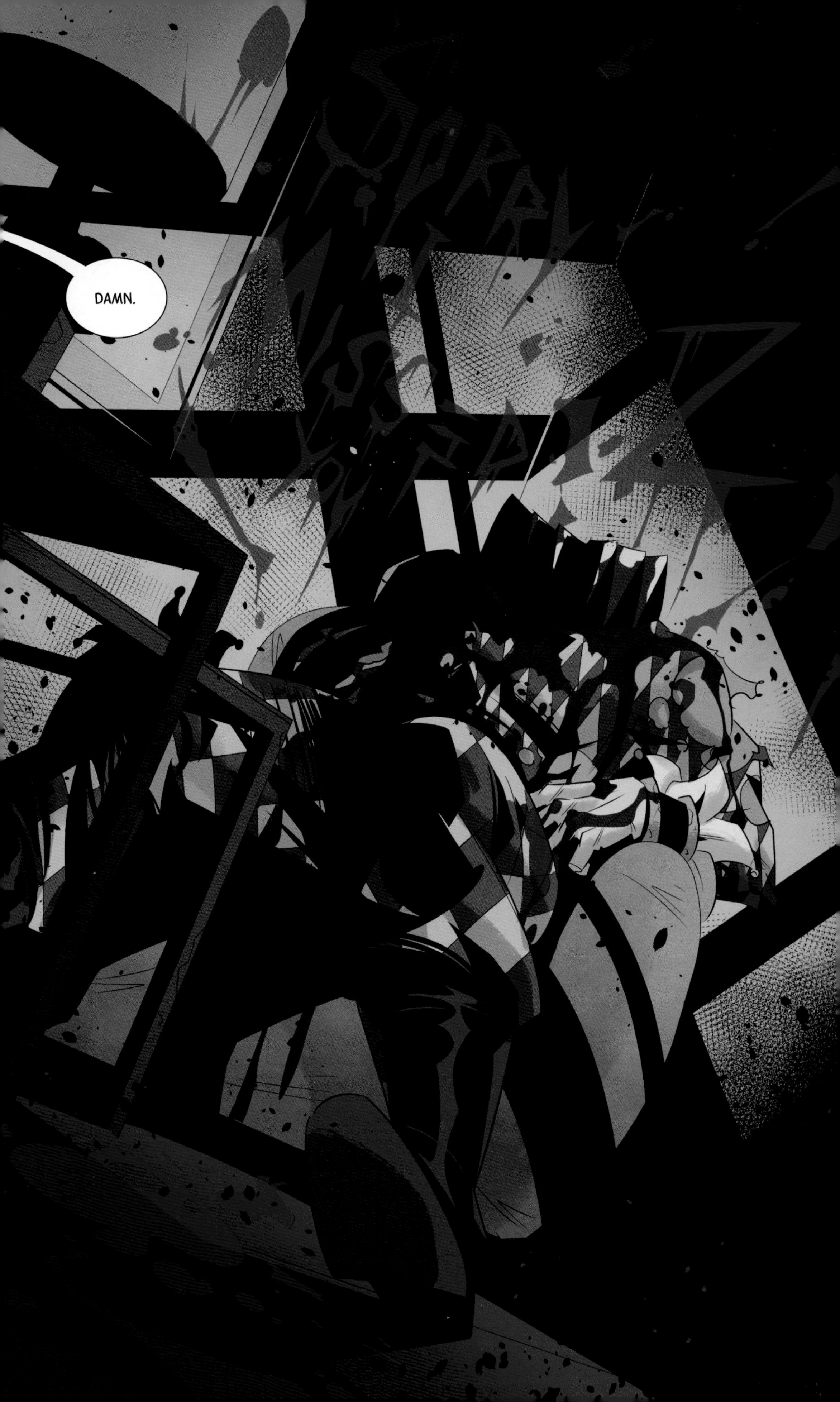
DAMN.

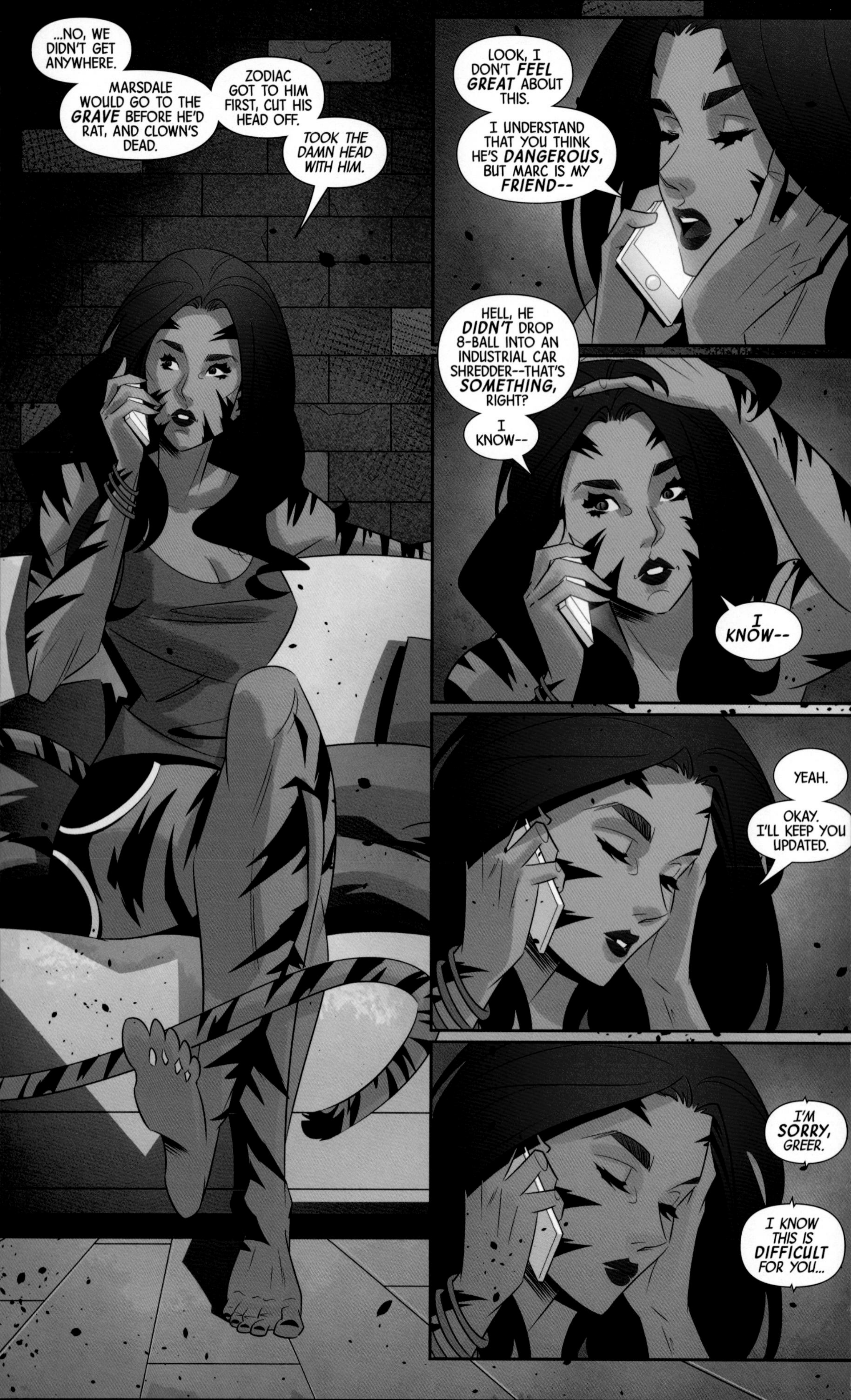

...NO, WE DIDN'T GET ANYWHERE.
MARSDALE WOULD GO TO THE GRAVE BEFORE HE'D RAT, AND CLOWN'S DEAD.
ZODIAC GOT TO HIM FIRST, CUT HIS HEAD OFF.
TOOK THE DAMN HEAD WITH HIM.
LOOK, I DON'T FEEL GREAT ABOUT THIS.
I UNDERSTAND THAT YOU THINK HE'S DANGEROUS, BUT MARC IS MY FRIEND--
HELL, HE DIDN'T DROP 8-BALL INTO AN INDUSTRIAL CAR SHREDDER--THAT'S SOMETHING, RIGHT?
I KNOW--
I KNOW--
YEAH.
OKAY. I'LL KEEP YOU UPDATED.
I'M SORRY, GREER.
I KNOW THIS IS DIFFICULT FOR YOU...

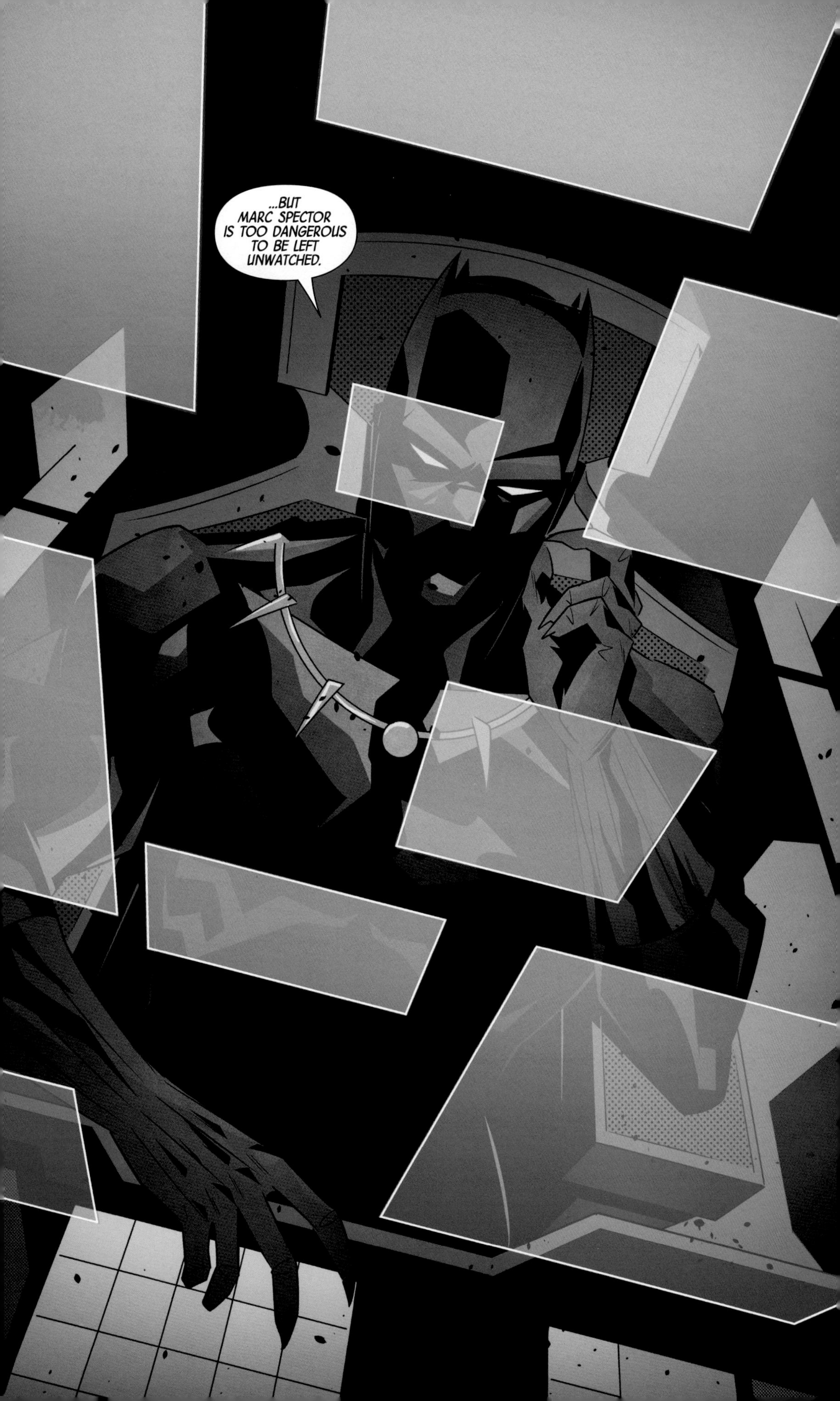
...BUT MARC SPECTOR IS TOO DANGEROUS TO BE LEFT UNWATCHED.

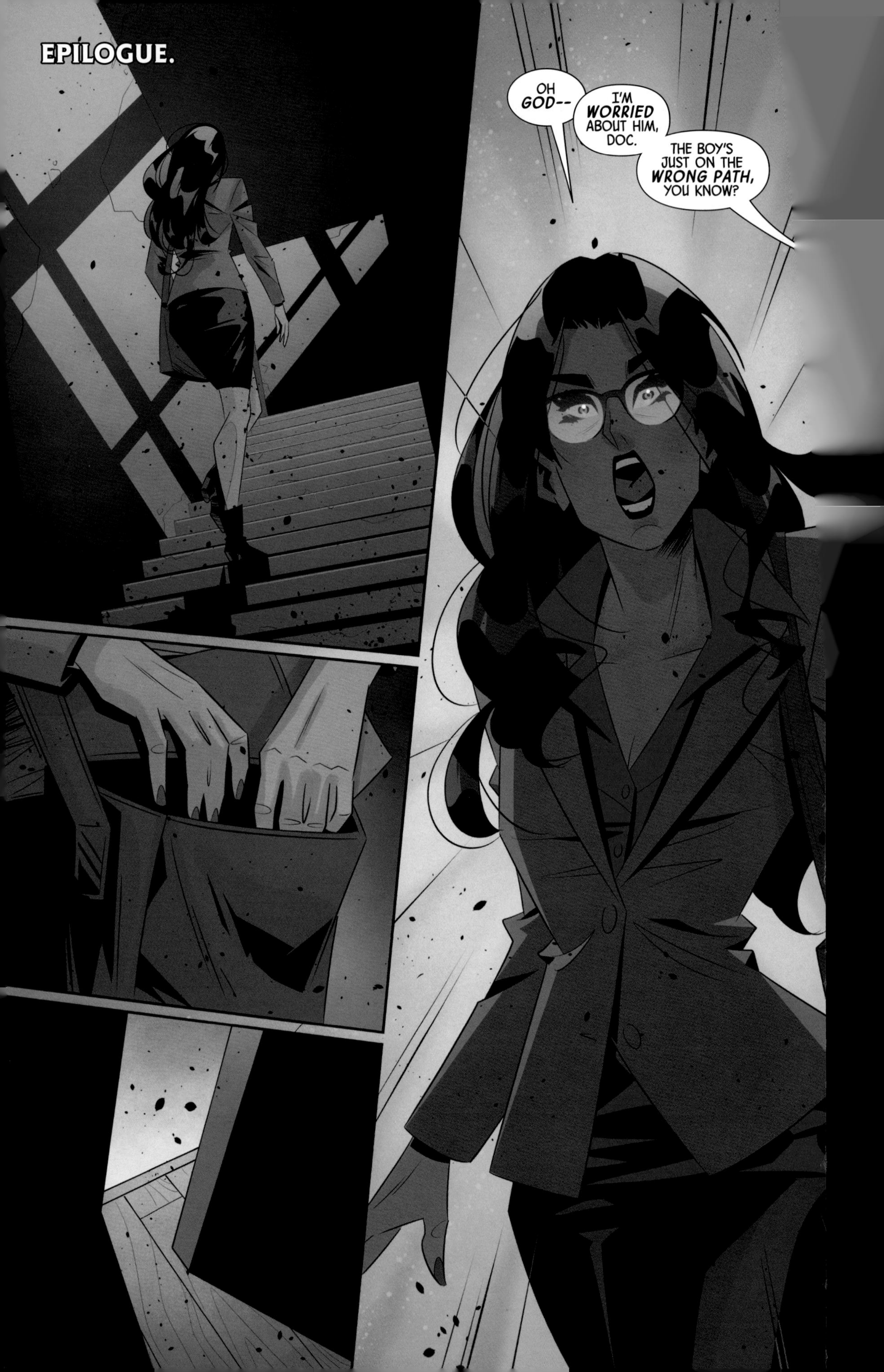
EPILOGUE.
OH GOD--
I'M WORRIED ABOUT HIM, DOC.
THE BOY'S JUST ON THE WRONG PATH, YOU KNOW?

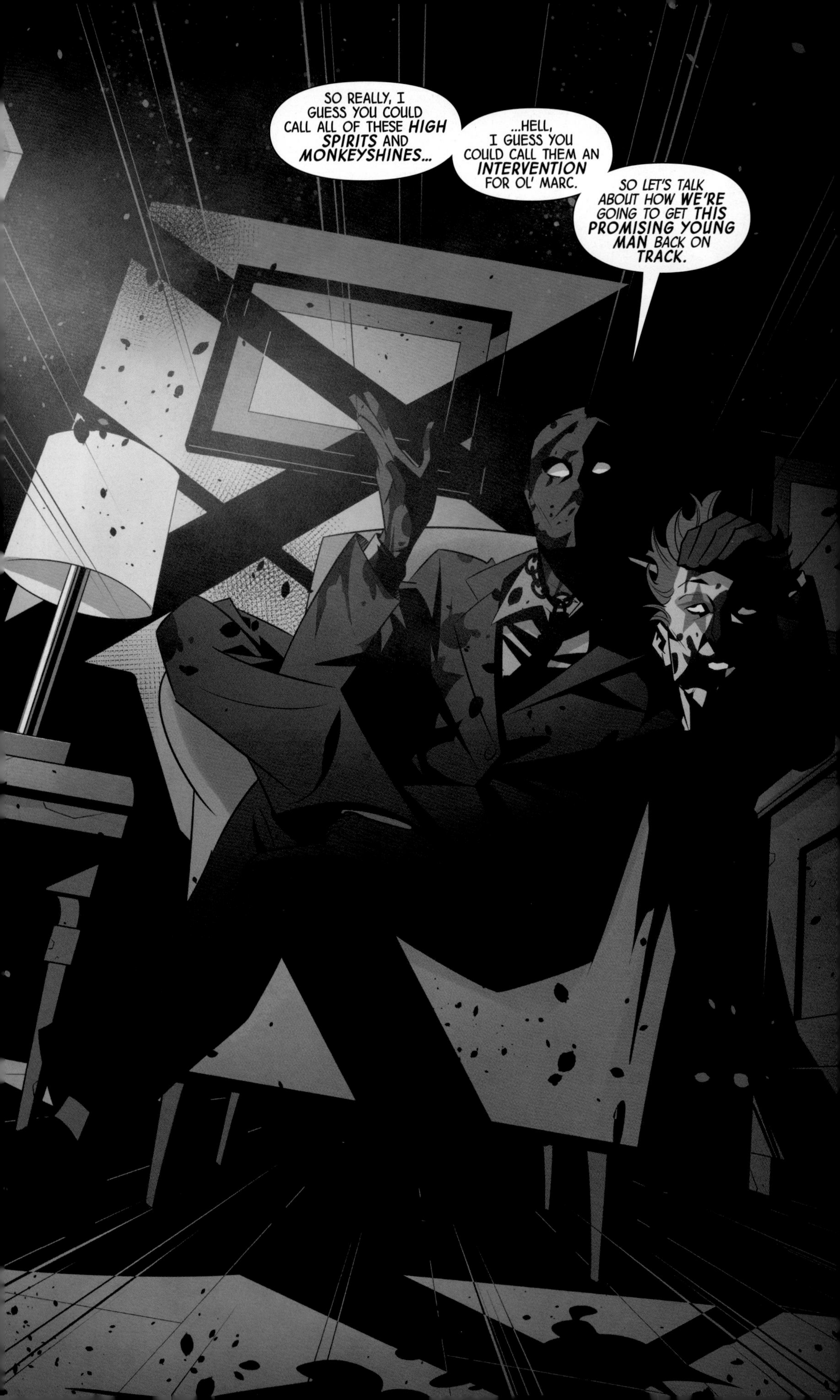

SO REALLY, I GUESS YOU COULD CALL ALL OF THESE **HIGH SPIRITS** AND **MONKEYSHINES...**
...HELL, I GUESS YOU COULD CALL THEM AN **INTERVENTION** FOR OL' MARC.
SO LET'S TALK ABOUT HOW **WE'RE** GOING TO GET **THIS PROMISING YOUNG MAN** BACK ON **TRACK.**

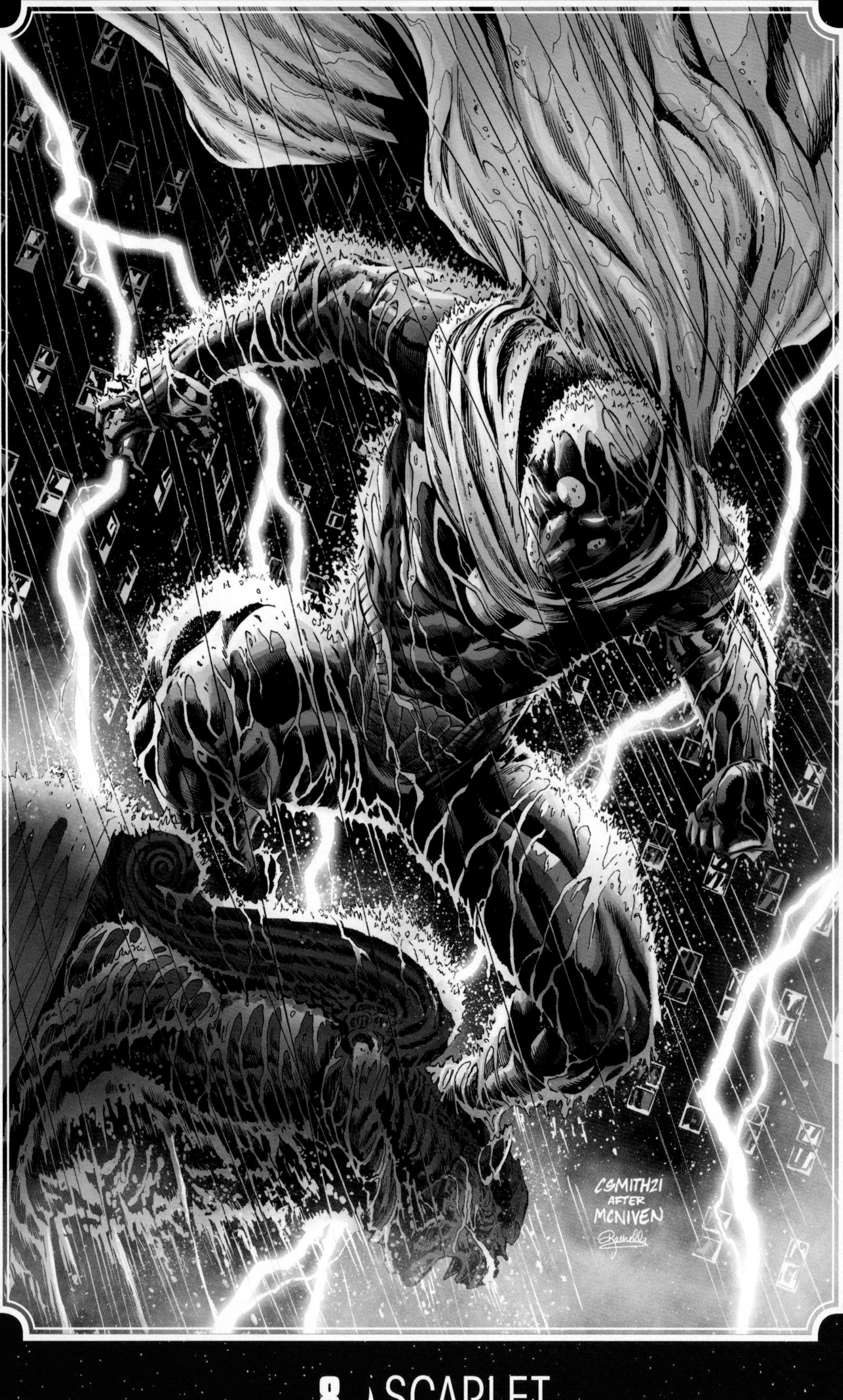
CSMITH21
AFTER
MCNIVEN

8 SCARLET

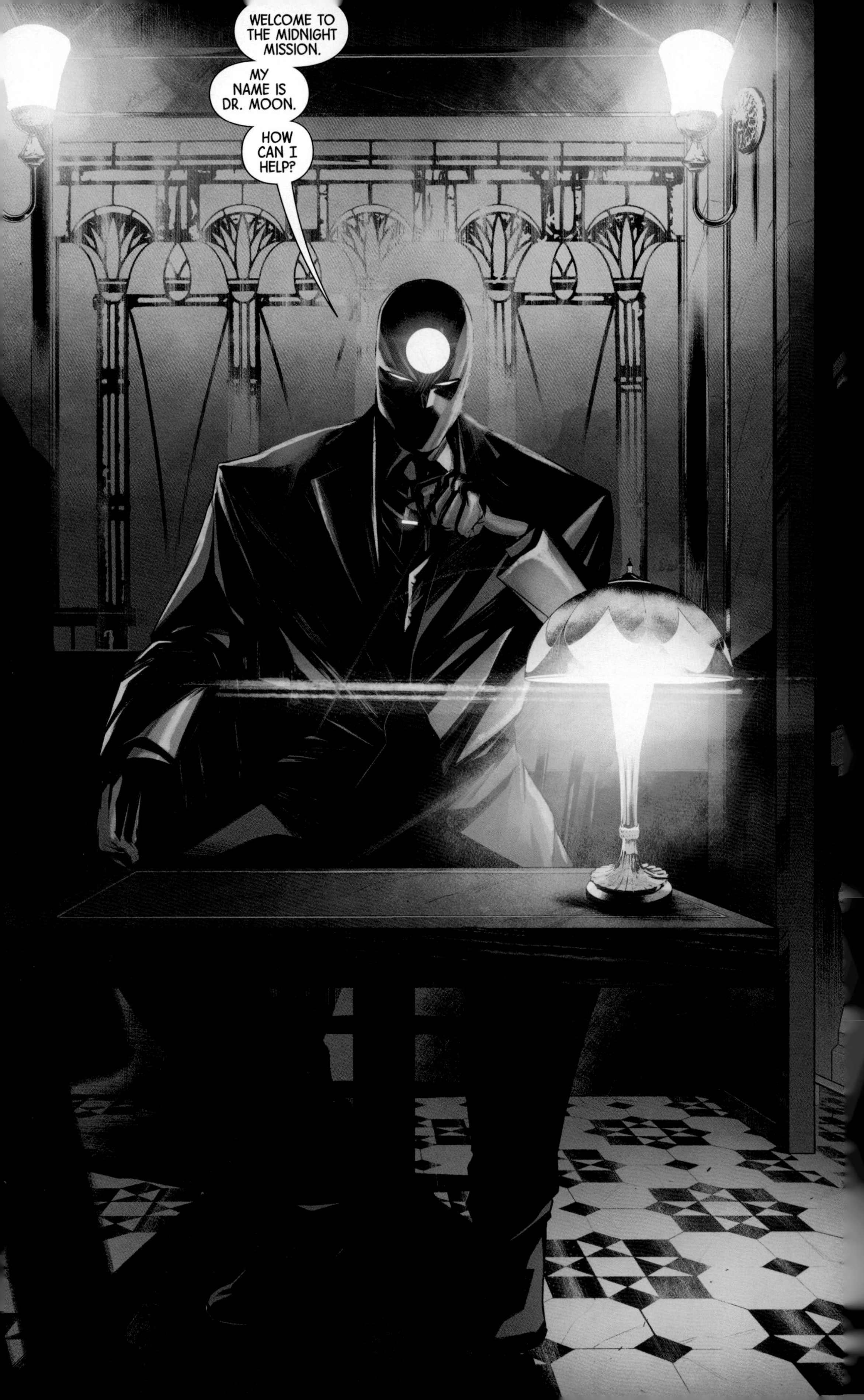
WELCOME TO THE MIDNIGHT MISSION.
MY NAME IS DR. MOON.
HOW CAN I HELP?

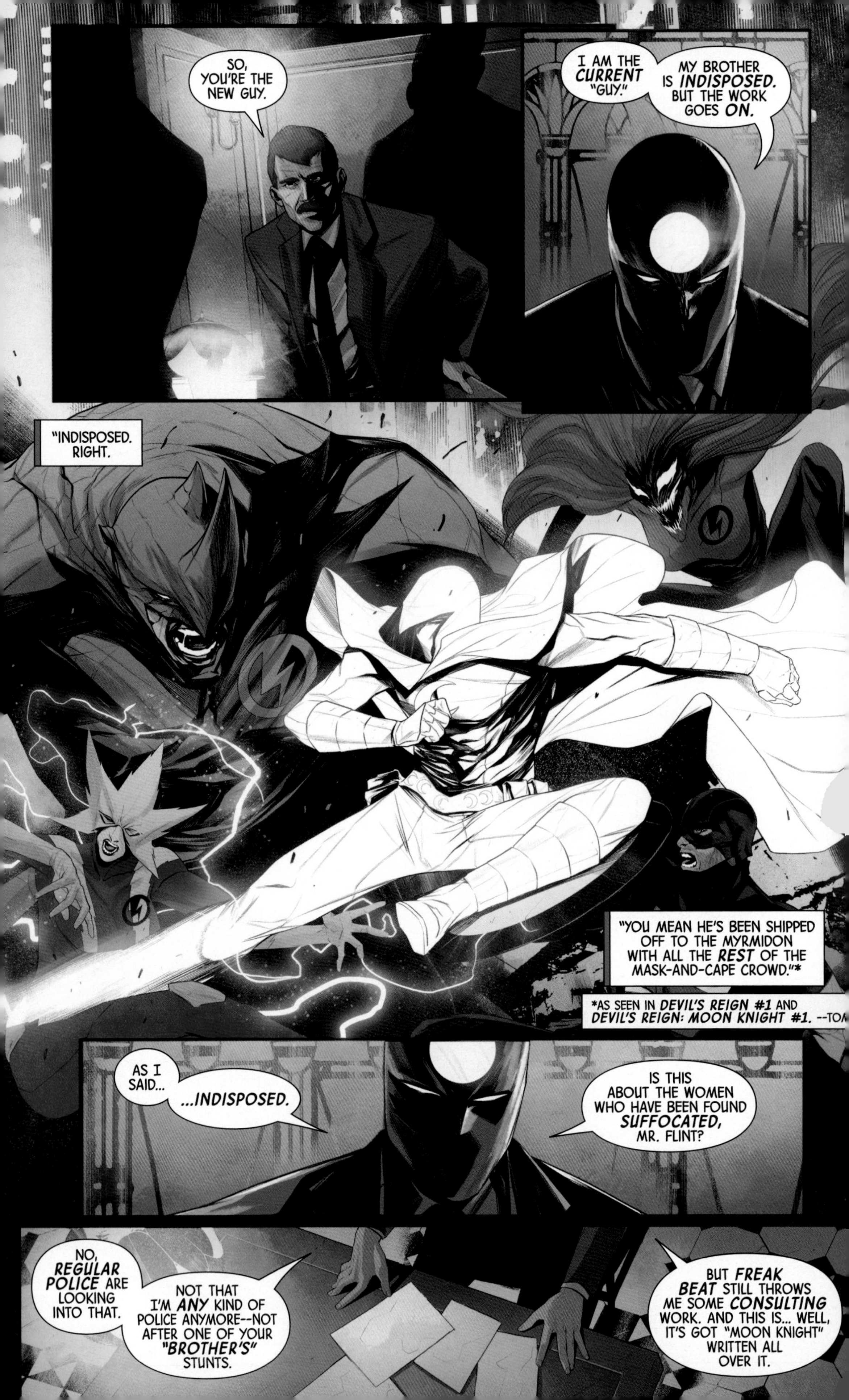
SO, YOU'RE THE NEW GUY.
I AM THE CURRENT "GUY."
MY BROTHER IS INDISPOSED. BUT THE WORK GOES ON.
"INDISPOSED. RIGHT.
"YOU MEAN HE'S BEEN SHIPPED OFF TO THE MYRMIDON WITH ALL THE REST OF THE MASK-AND-CAPE CROWD."*
*AS SEEN IN DEVIL'S REIGN #1 AND DEVIL'S REIGN: MOON KNIGHT #1. --TOM
AS I SAID...
...INDISPOSED.
IS THIS ABOUT THE WOMEN WHO HAVE BEEN FOUND SUFFOCATED, MR. FLINT?
NO, REGULAR POLICE ARE LOOKING INTO THAT.
NOT THAT I'M ANY KIND OF POLICE ANYMORE--NOT AFTER ONE OF YOUR "BROTHER'S" STUNTS.
BUT FREAK BEAT STILL THROWS ME SOME CONSULTING WORK. AND THIS IS... WELL, IT'S GOT "MOON KNIGHT" WRITTEN ALL OVER IT.

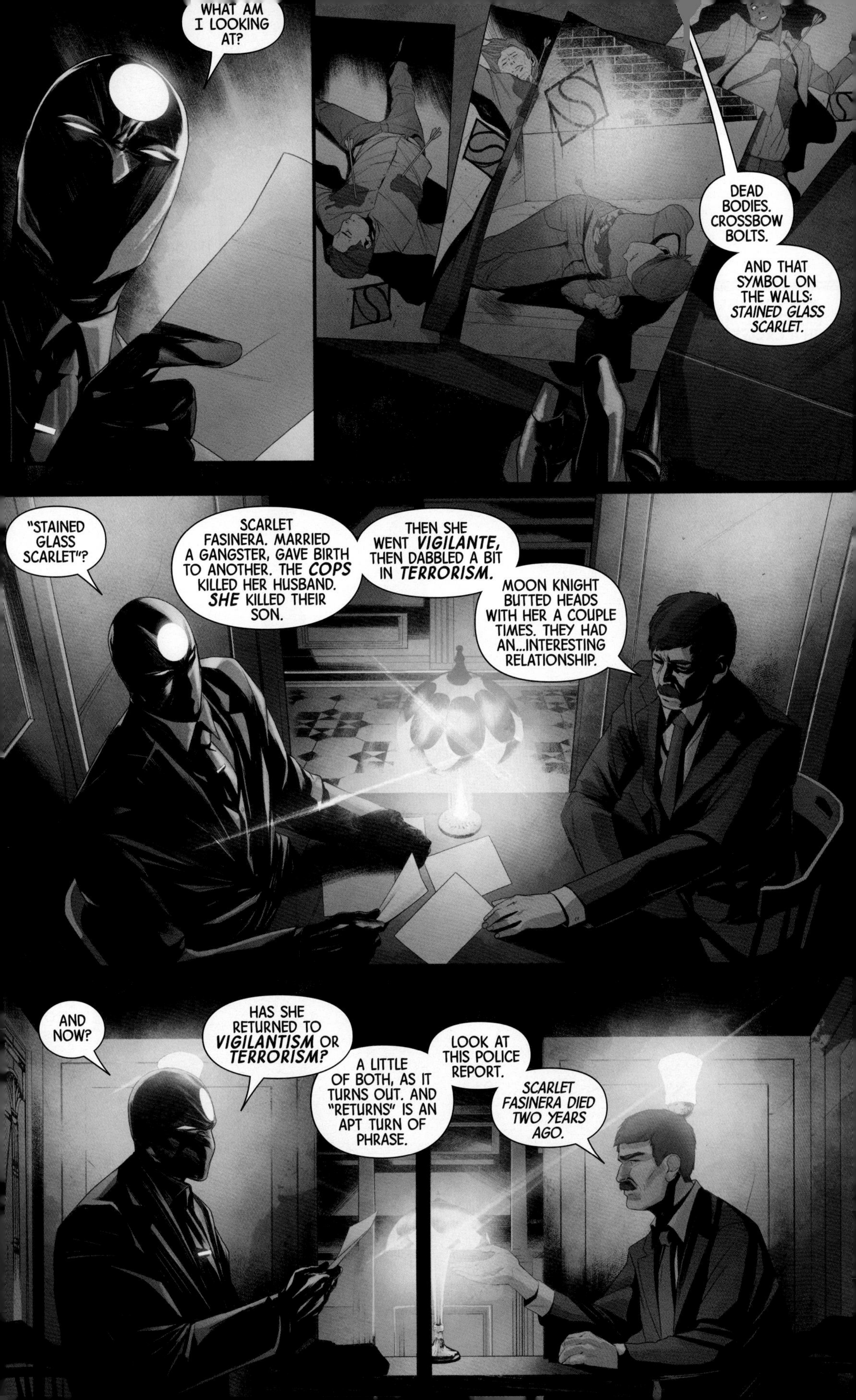
WHAT AM I LOOKING AT?
DEAD BODIES. CROSSBOW BOLTS.
AND THAT SYMBOL ON THE WALLS: STAINED GLASS SCARLET.
"STAINED GLASS SCARLET"?
SCARLET FASINERA. MARRIED A GANGSTER, GAVE BIRTH TO ANOTHER. THE COPS KILLED HER HUSBAND. SHE KILLED THEIR SON.
THEN SHE WENT VIGILANTE, THEN DABBLED A BIT IN TERRORISM.
MOON KNIGHT BUTTED HEADS WITH HER A COUPLE TIMES. THEY HAD AN...INTERESTING RELATIONSHIP.
AND NOW?
HAS SHE RETURNED TO VIGILANTISM OR TERRORISM?
A LITTLE OF BOTH, AS IT TURNS OUT. AND "RETURNS" IS AN APT TURN OF PHRASE.
LOOK AT THIS POLICE REPORT.
SCARLET FASINERA DIED TWO YEARS AGO.

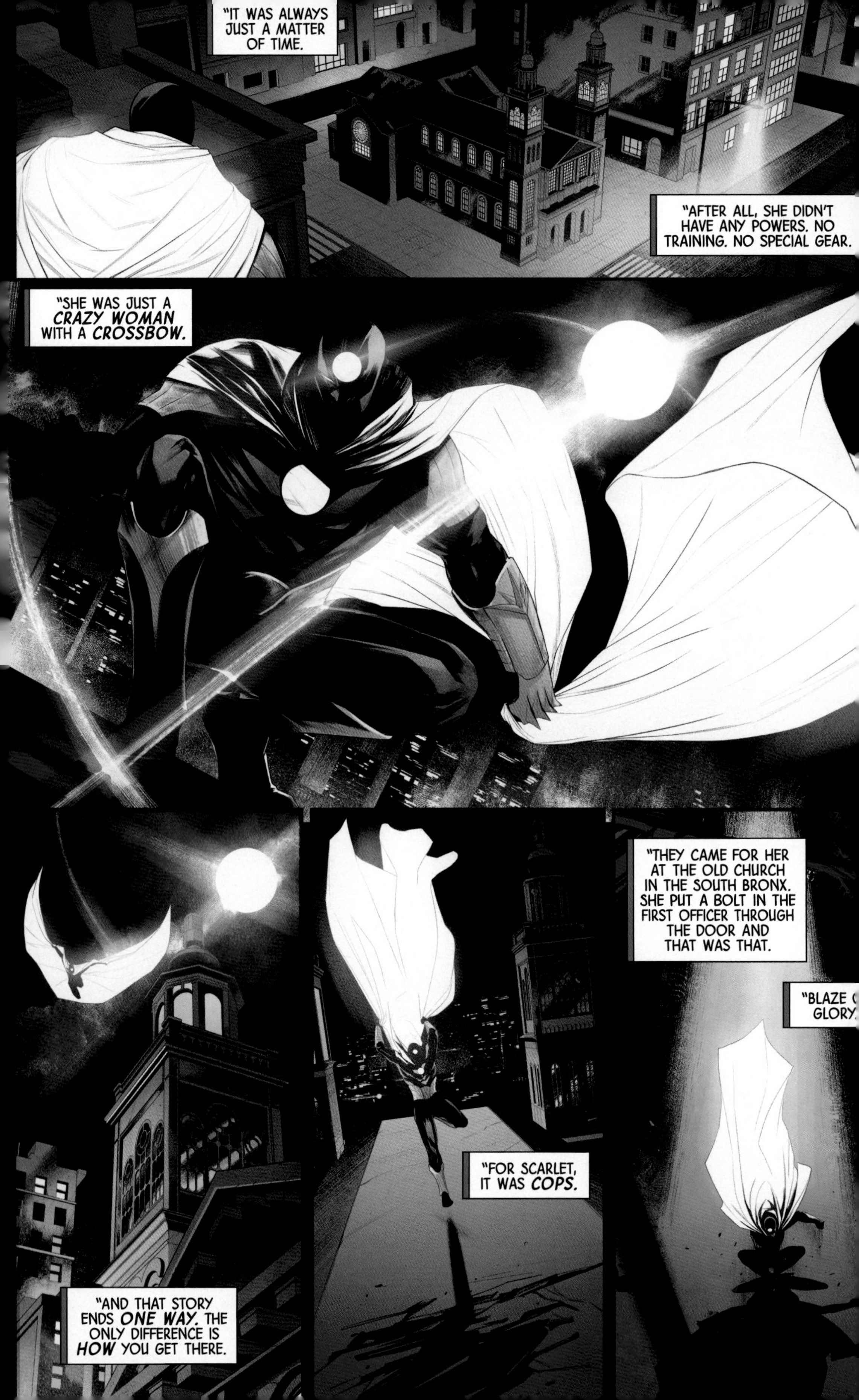
"IT WAS ALWAYS JUST A MATTER OF TIME.
"AFTER ALL, SHE DIDN'T HAVE ANY POWERS. NO TRAINING. NO SPECIAL GEAR.
"SHE WAS JUST A CRAZY WOMAN WITH A CROSSBOW.
"AND THAT STORY ENDS ONE WAY. THE ONLY DIFFERENCE IS HOW YOU GET THERE.
"FOR SCARLET, IT WAS COPS.
"THEY CAME FOR HER AT THE OLD CHURCH IN THE SOUTH BRONX. SHE PUT A BOLT IN THE FIRST OFFICER THROUGH THE DOOR AND THAT WAS THAT.
"BLAZE
GLORY

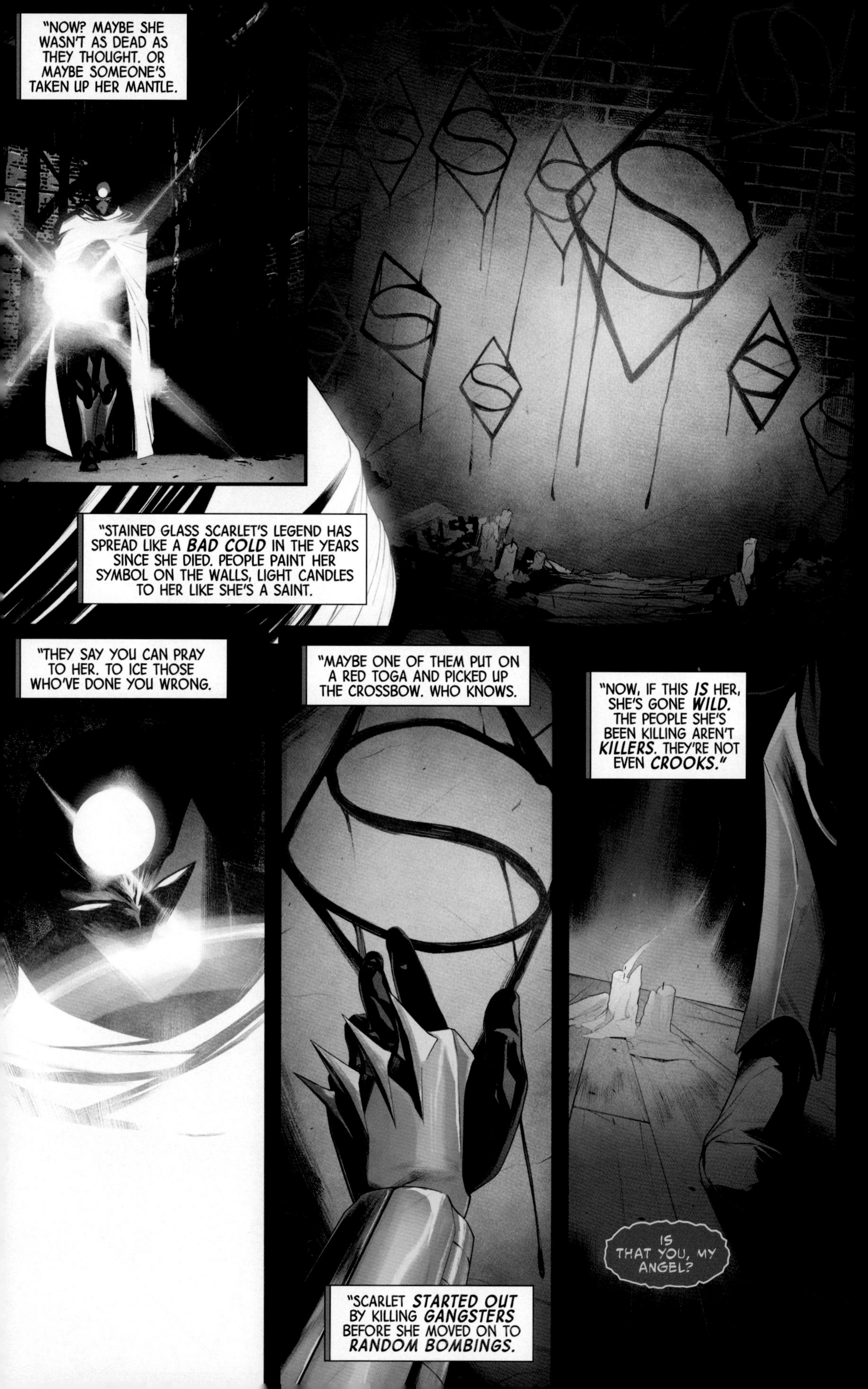
"NOW? MAYBE SHE WASN'T AS DEAD AS THEY THOUGHT. OR MAYBE SOMEONE'S TAKEN UP HER MANTLE.
"STAINED GLASS SCARLET'S LEGEND HAS SPREAD LIKE A BAD COLD IN THE YEARS SINCE SHE DIED. PEOPLE PAINT HER SYMBOL ON THE WALLS, LIGHT CANDLES TO HER LIKE SHE'S A SAINT.
"THEY SAY YOU CAN PRAY TO HER. TO ICE THOSE WHO'VE DONE YOU WRONG.
"MAYBE ONE OF THEM PUT ON A RED TOGA AND PICKED UP THE CROSSBOW. WHO KNOWS.
"SCARLET STARTED OUT BY KILLING GANGSTERS BEFORE SHE MOVED ON TO RANDOM BOMBINGS.
"NOW, IF THIS IS HER, SHE'S GONE WILD. THE PEOPLE SHE'S BEEN KILLING AREN'T KILLERS. THEY'RE NOT EVEN CROOKS."
IS THAT YOU, MY ANGEL?

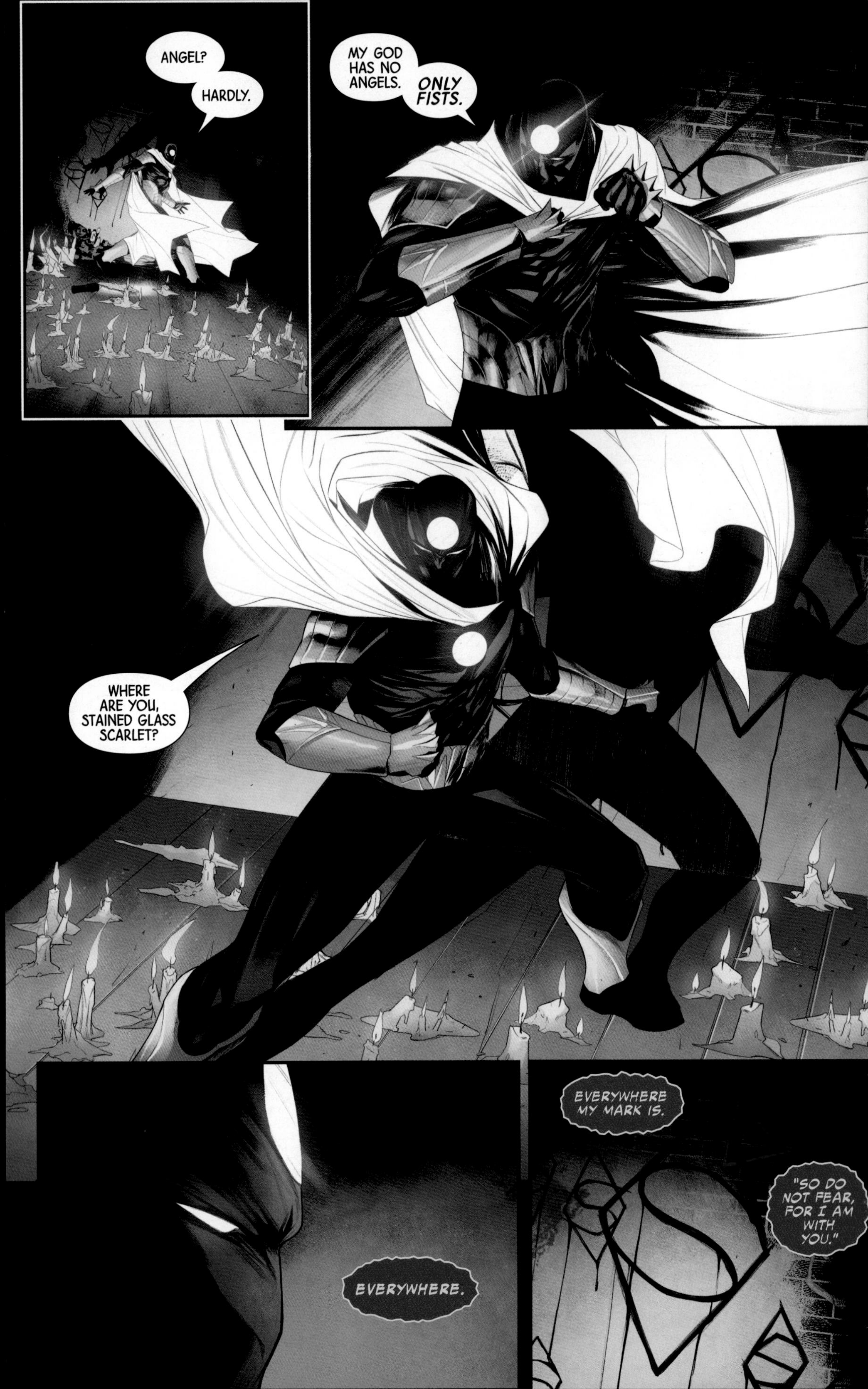
ANGEL?
HARDLY.
MY GOD HAS NO ANGELS.
ONLY FISTS.
WHERE ARE YOU, STAINED GLASS SCARLET?
EVERYWHERE MY MARK IS.
EVERYWHERE.
"SO DO NOT FEAR, FOR I AM WITH YOU."

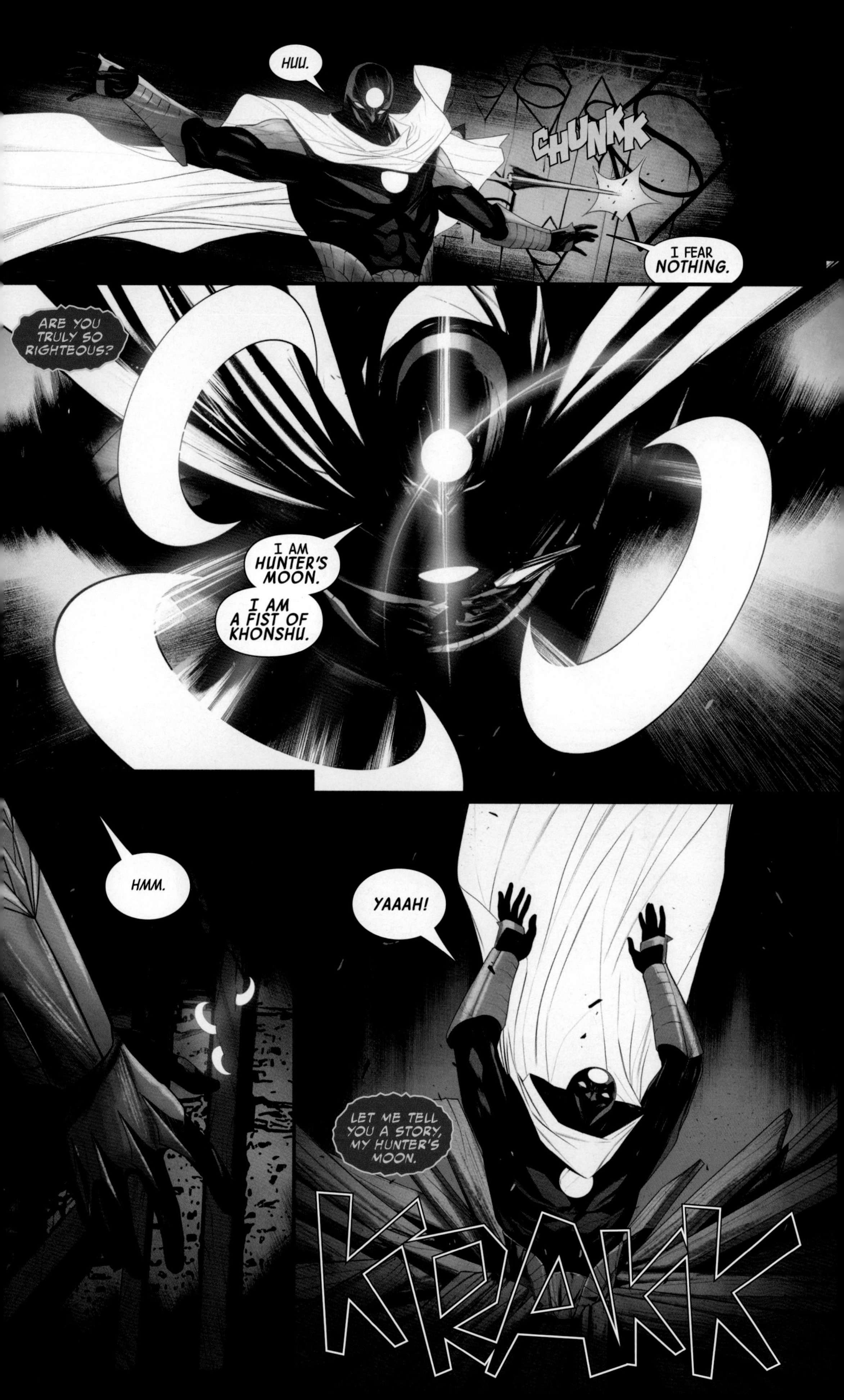
HUU.
CHUNKK
I FEAR NOTHING.
ARE YOU TRULY SO RIGHTEOUS?
I AM HUNTER'S MOON.
I AM A FIST OF KHONSHU.
HMM.
YAAAH!
LET ME TELL YOU A STORY, MY HUNTER'S MOON.
KRAKK

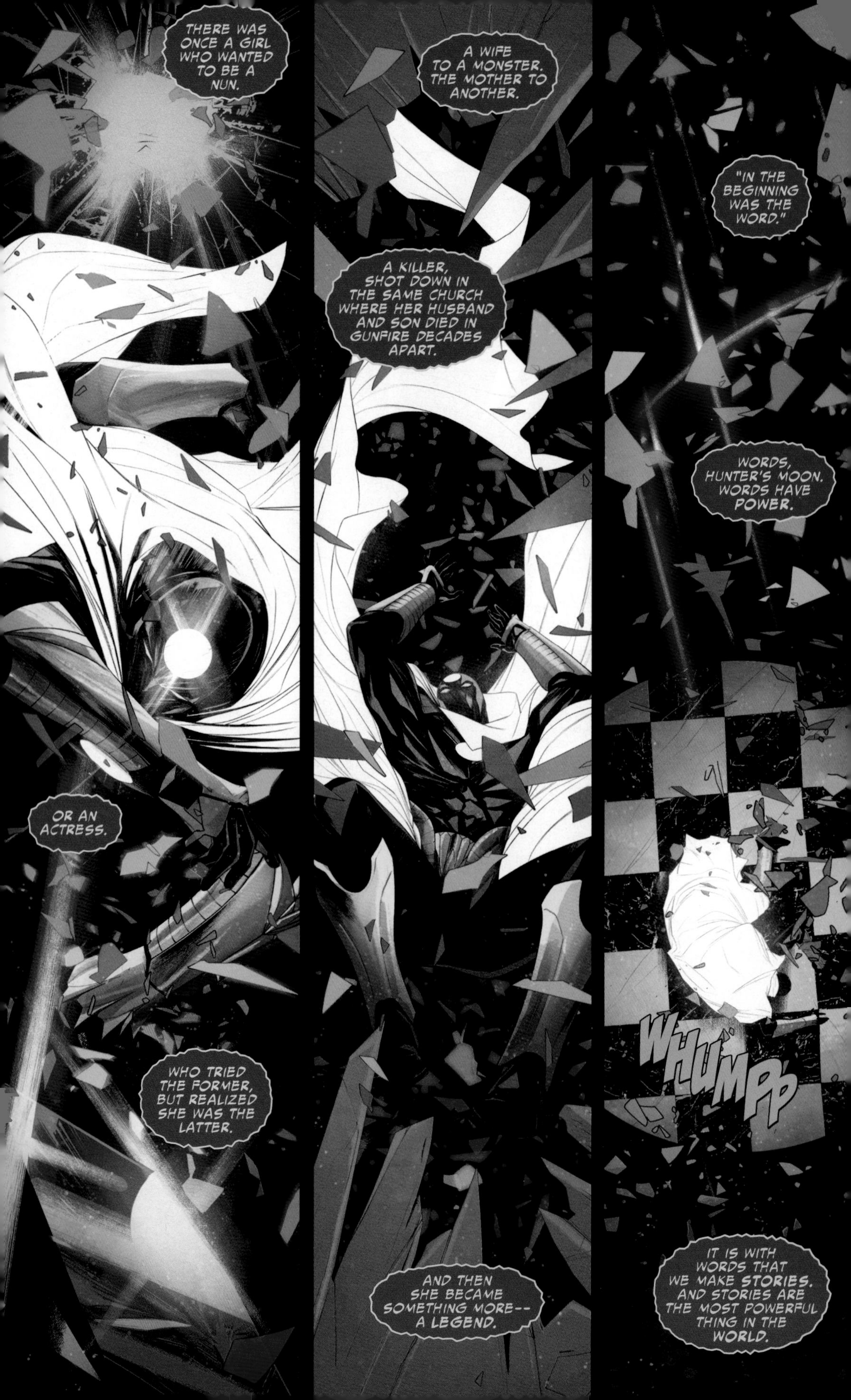
THERE WAS ONCE A GIRL WHO WANTED TO BE A NUN.
OR AN ACTRESS.
WHO TRIED THE FORMER, BUT REALIZED SHE WAS THE LATTER.
A WIFE TO A MONSTER. THE MOTHER TO ANOTHER.
A KILLER, SHOT DOWN IN THE SAME CHURCH WHERE HER HUSBAND AND SON DIED IN GUNFIRE DECADES APART.
AND THEN SHE BECAME SOMETHING MORE-- A LEGEND.
"IN THE BEGINNING WAS THE WORD."
WORDS, HUNTER'S MOON. WORDS HAVE POWER.
WHUMPP
IT IS WITH WORDS THAT WE MAKE STORIES. AND STORIES ARE THE MOST POWERFUL THING IN THE WORLD.

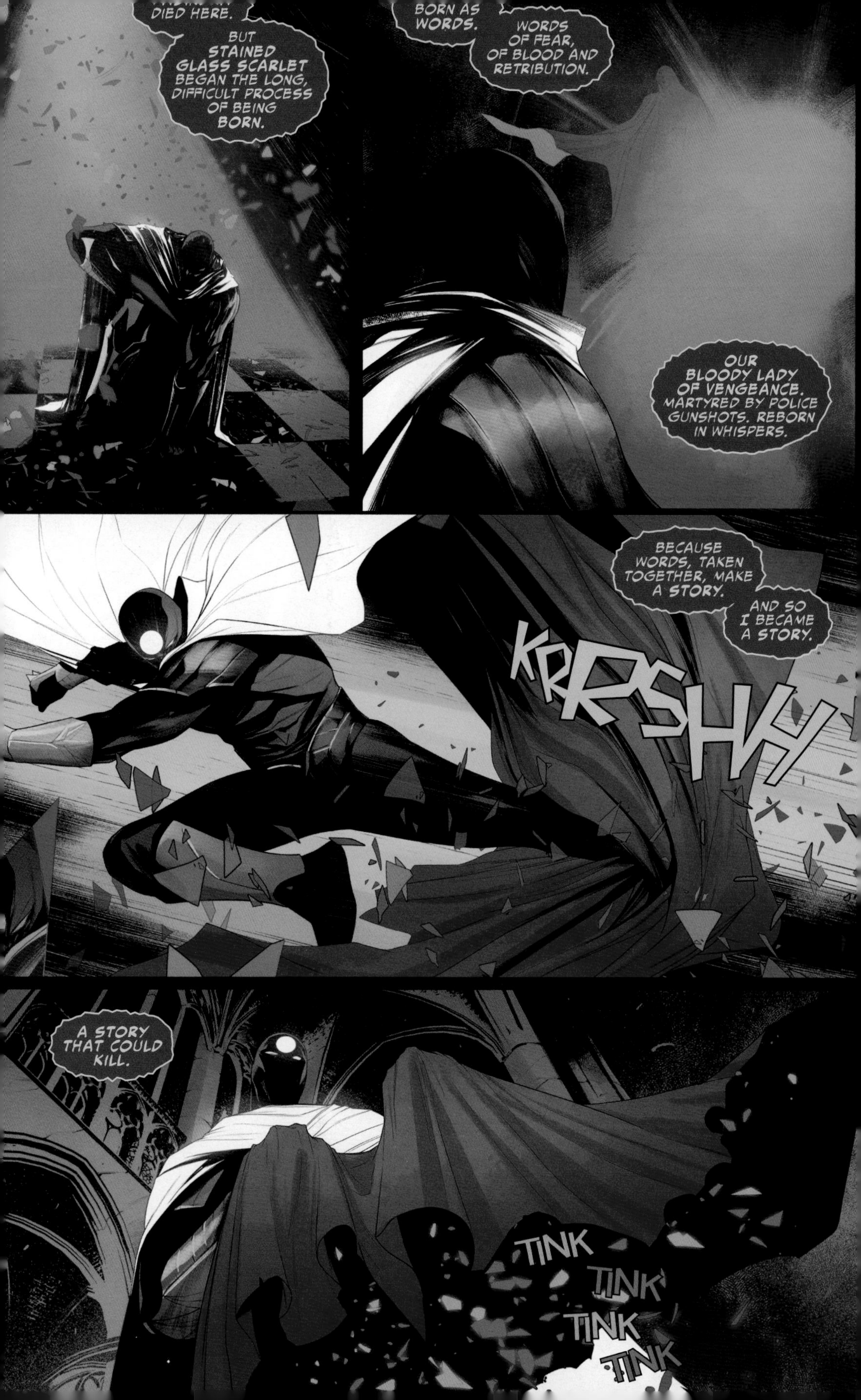

DIED HERE.
BUT STAINED GLASS SCARLET BEGAN THE LONG, DIFFICULT PROCESS OF BEING BORN.
BORN AS WORDS.
WORDS OF FEAR, OF BLOOD AND RETRIBUTION.
OUR BLOODY LADY OF VENGEANCE. MARTYRED BY POLICE GUNSHOTS. REBORN IN WHISPERS.
BECAUSE WORDS, TAKEN TOGETHER, MAKE A STORY.
AND SO I BECAME A STORY.
KRRSHH
A STORY THAT COULD KILL.
TINK
TINK
TINK
TINK

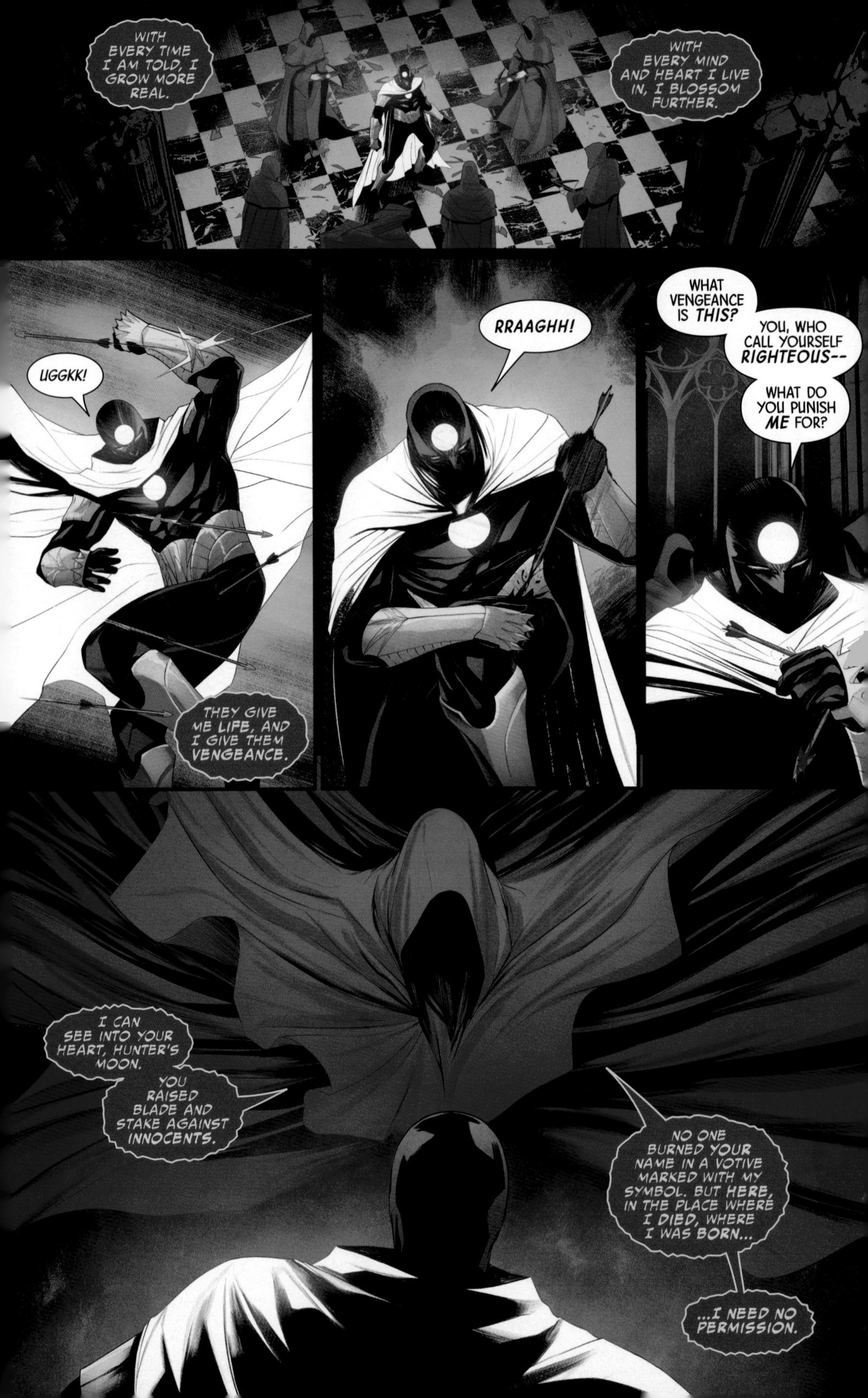
WITH EVERY TIME I AM TOLD, I GROW MORE REAL.
WITH EVERY MIND AND HEART I LIVE IN, I BLOSSOM FURTHER.
UGGKK!
THEY GIVE ME LIFE, AND I GIVE THEM VENGEANCE.
RRAAGHH!
WHAT VENGEANCE IS THIS?
YOU, WHO CALL YOURSELF RIGHTEOUS--
WHAT DO YOU PUNISH ME FOR?
I CAN SEE INTO YOUR HEART, HUNTER'S MOON.
YOU RAISED BLADE AND STAKE AGAINST INNOCENTS.
NO ONE BURNED YOUR NAME IN A VOTIVE MARKED WITH MY SYMBOL. BUT HERE, IN THE PLACE WHERE I DIED, WHERE I WAS BORN...
...I NEED NO PERMISSION.

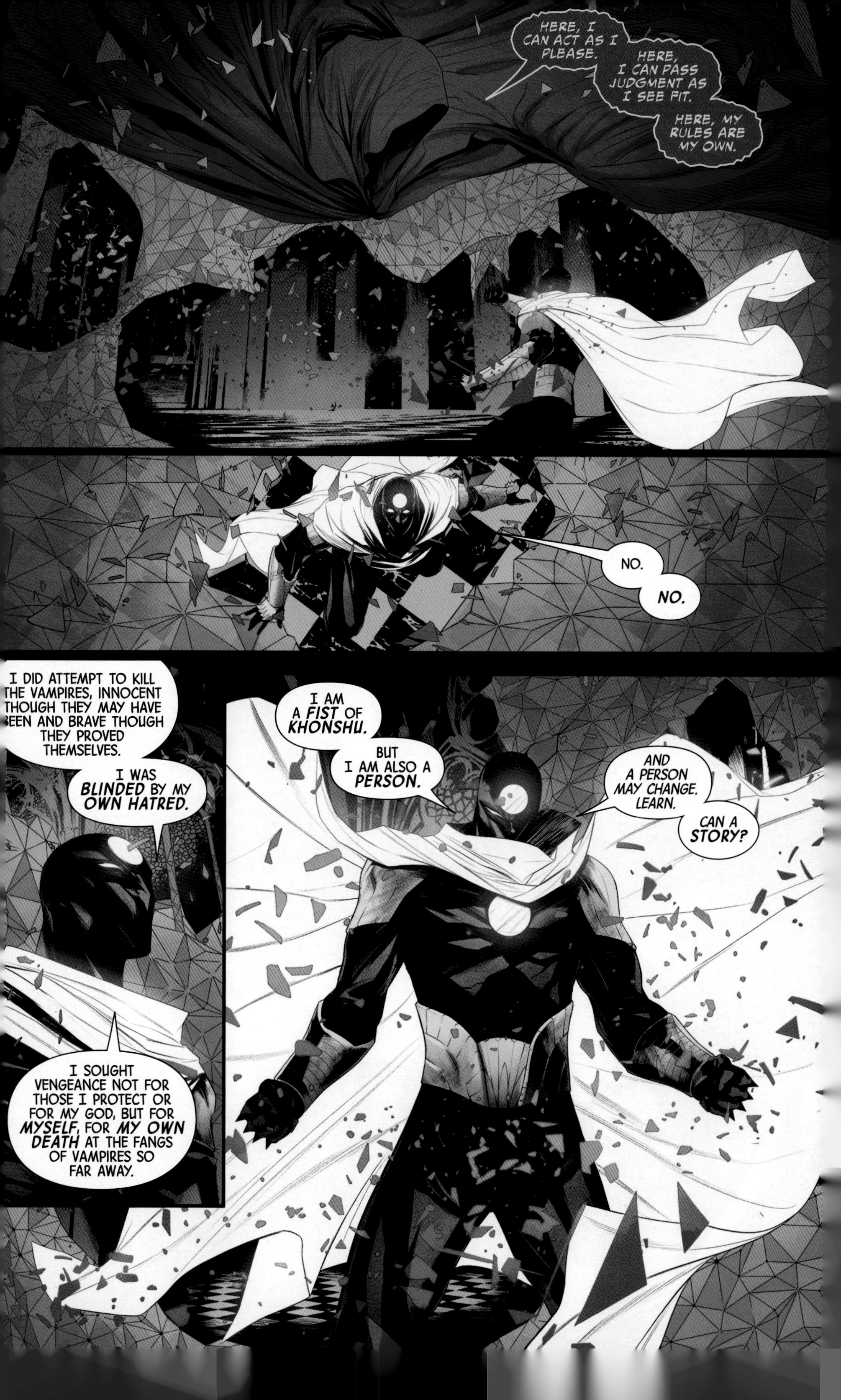
HERE, I CAN ACT AS I PLEASE.
HERE, I CAN PASS JUDGMENT AS I SEE FIT.
HERE, MY RULES ARE MY OWN.
NO.
NO.
I DID ATTEMPT TO KILL THE VAMPIRES, INNOCENT THOUGH THEY MAY HAVE BEEN AND BRAVE THOUGH THEY PROVED THEMSELVES.
I WAS BLINDED BY MY OWN HATRED.
I SOUGHT VENGEANCE NOT FOR THOSE I PROTECT OR FOR MY GOD, BUT FOR MYSELF, FOR MY OWN DEATH AT THE FANGS OF VAMPIRES SO FAR AWAY.
I AM A FIST OF KHONSHU.
BUT I AM ALSO A PERSON.
AND A PERSON MAY CHANGE. LEARN.
CAN A STORY?

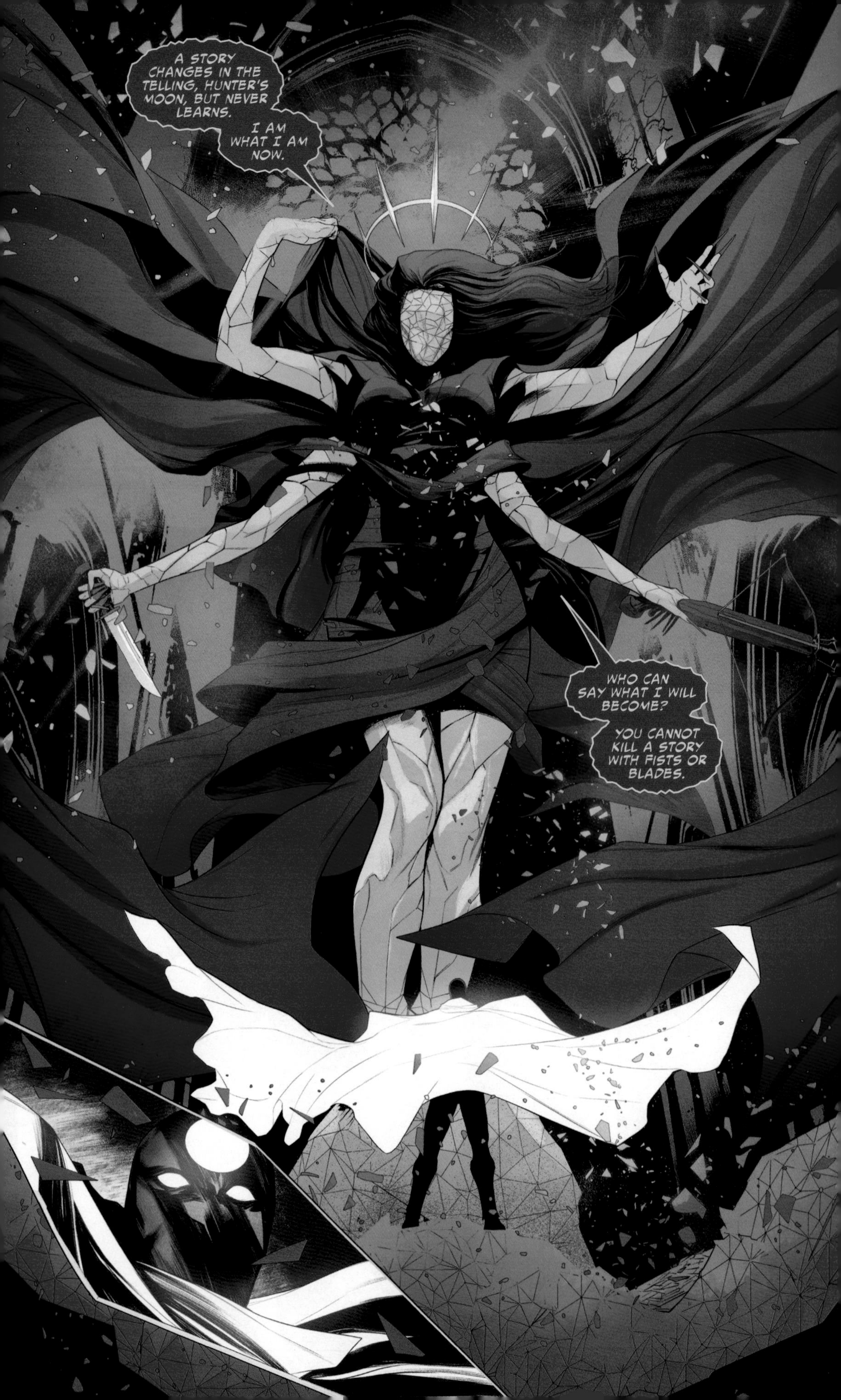
A STORY CHANGES IN THE TELLING, HUNTER'S MOON, BUT NEVER LEARNS.
I AM WHAT I AM NOW.
WHO CAN SAY WHAT I WILL BECOME?
YOU CANNOT KILL A STORY WITH FISTS OR BLADES.

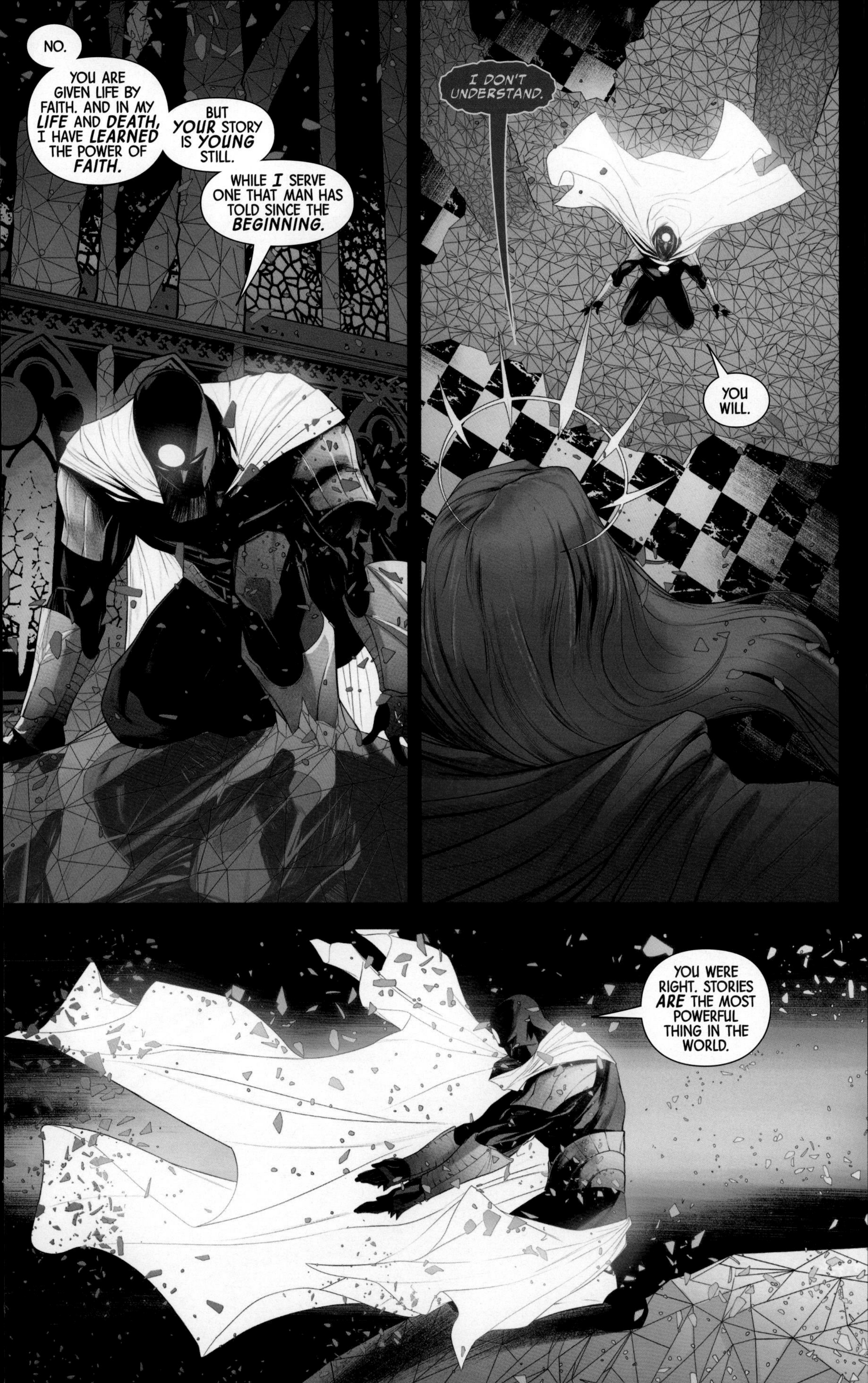
NO.
YOU ARE GIVEN LIFE BY FAITH. AND IN MY LIFE AND DEATH, I HAVE LEARNED THE POWER OF FAITH.
BUT YOUR STORY IS YOUNG STILL.
WHILE I SERVE ONE THAT MAN HAS TOLD SINCE THE BEGINNING.
I DON'T UNDERSTAND.
YOU WILL.
YOU WERE RIGHT. STORIES ARE THE MOST POWERFUL THING IN THE WORLD.

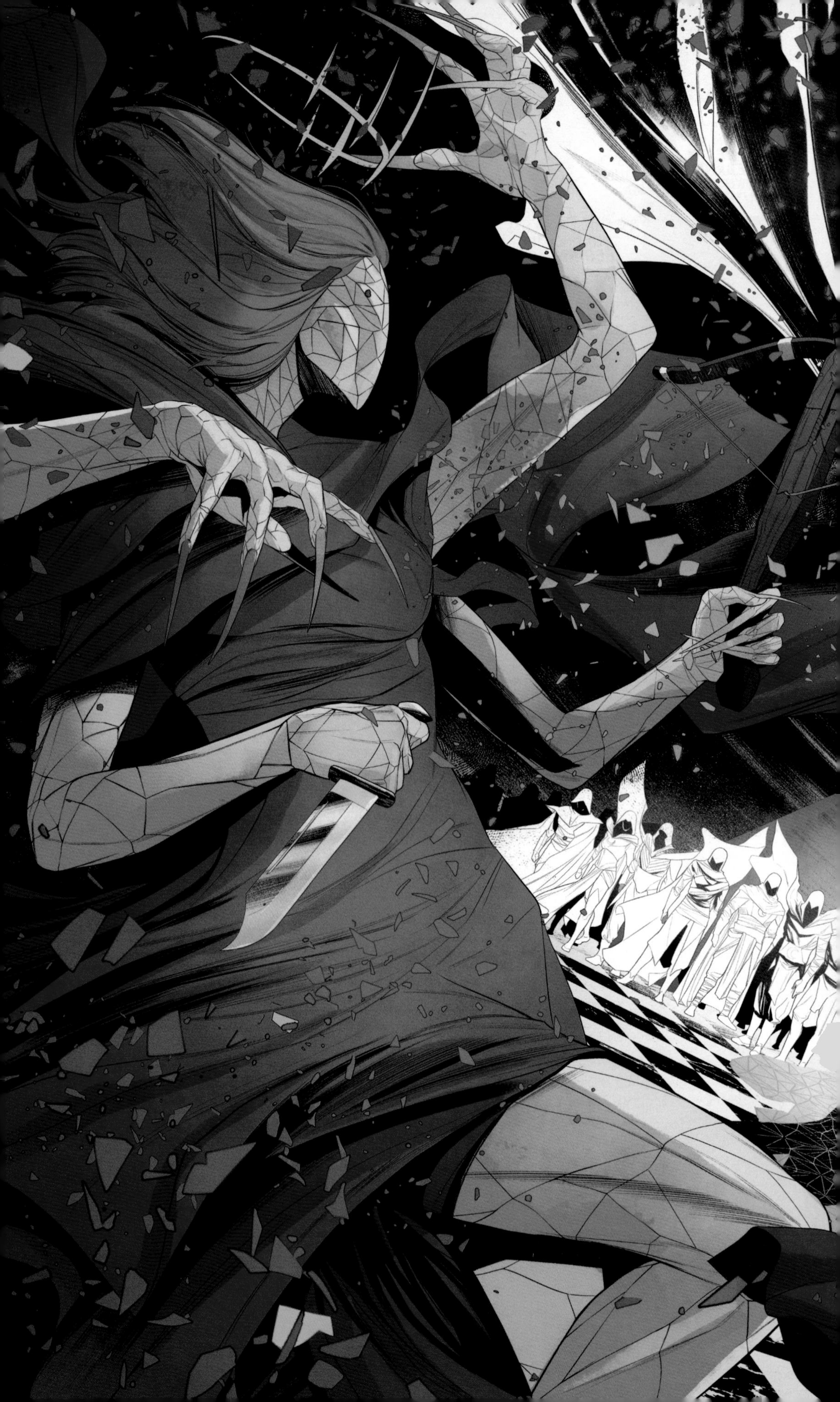

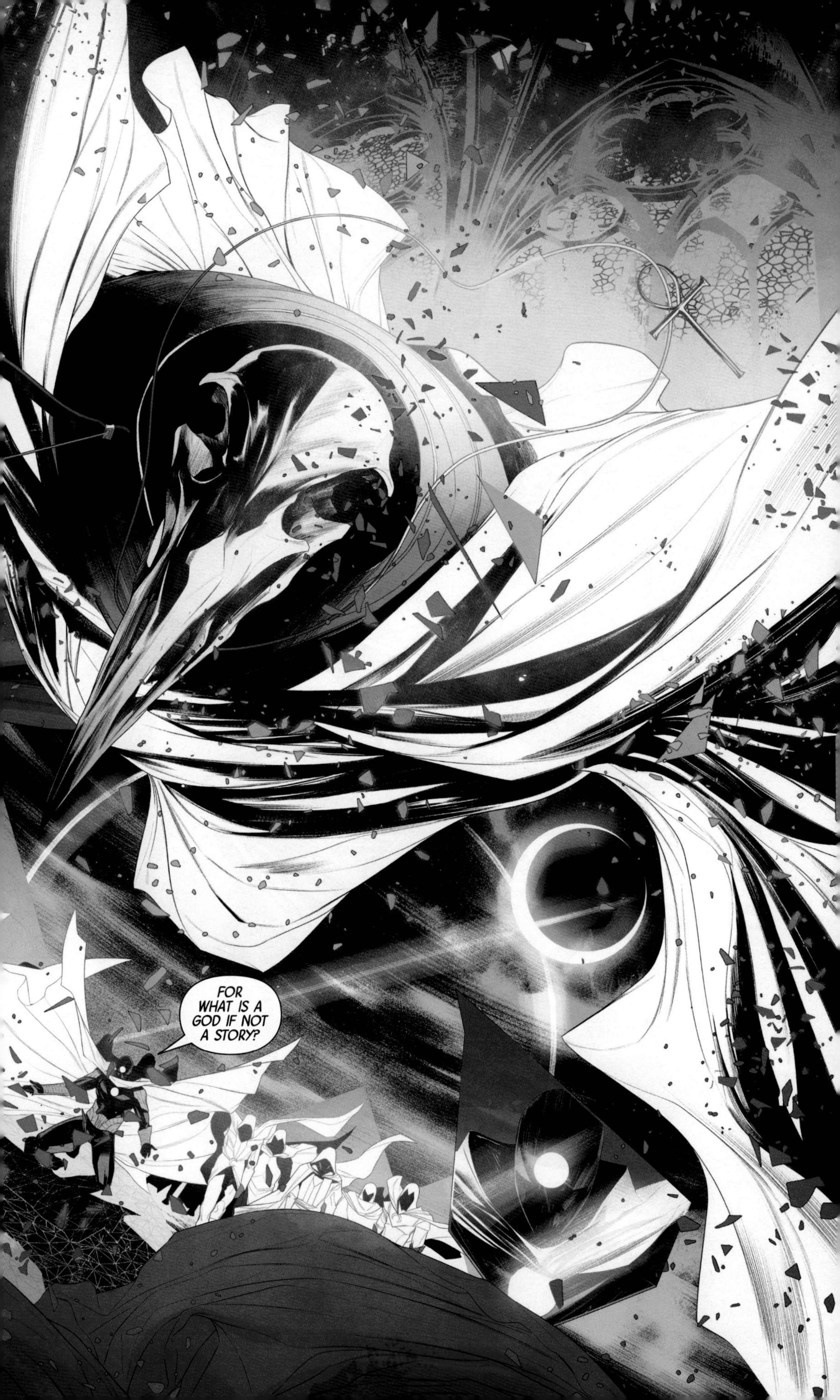
FOR WHAT IS A GOD IF NOT A STORY?

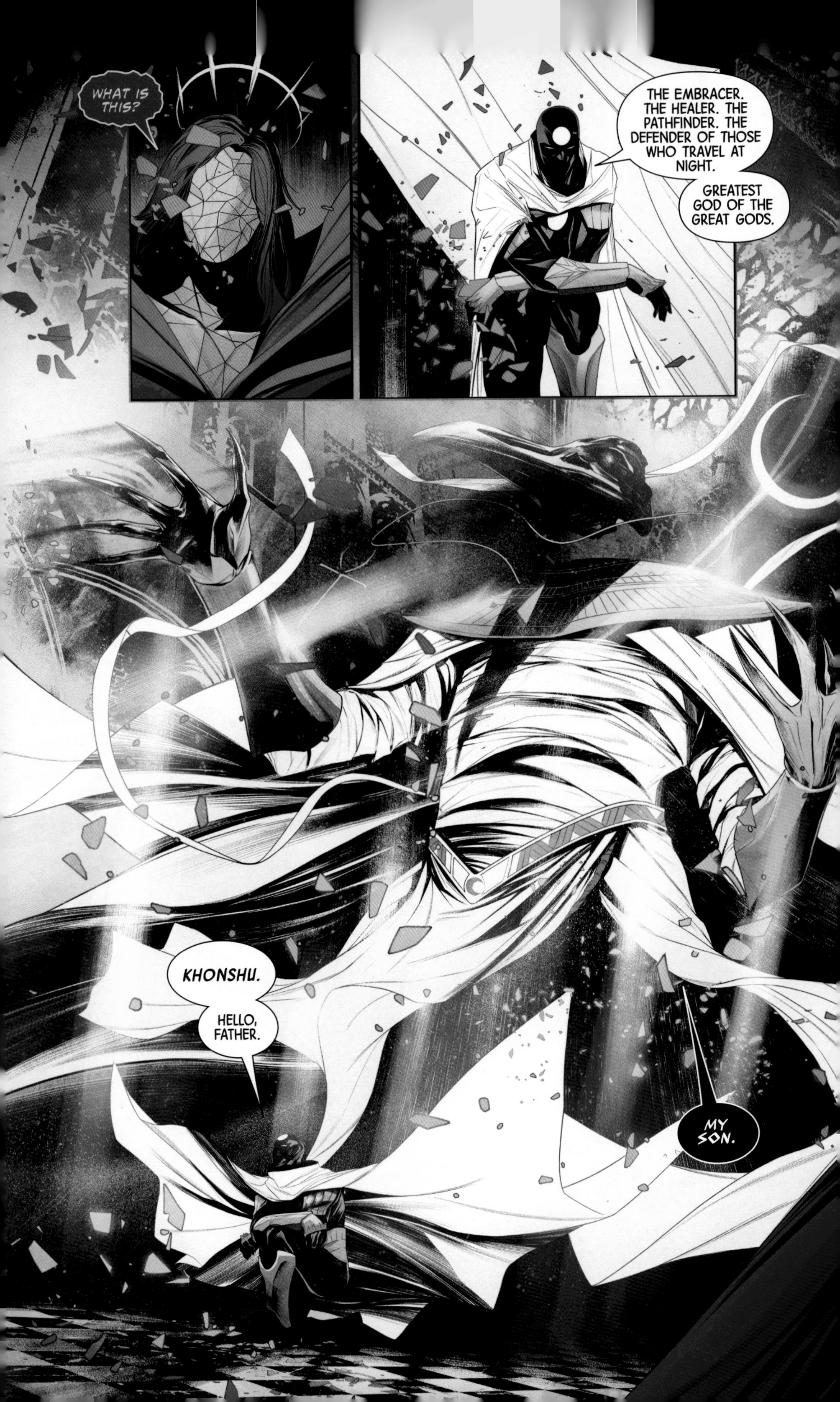
WHAT IS THIS?
THE EMBRACER. THE HEALER. THE PATHFINDER. THE DEFENDER OF THOSE WHO TRAVEL AT NIGHT.
GREATEST GOD OF THE GREAT GODS.
KHONSHU.
HELLO, FATHER.
MY SON.

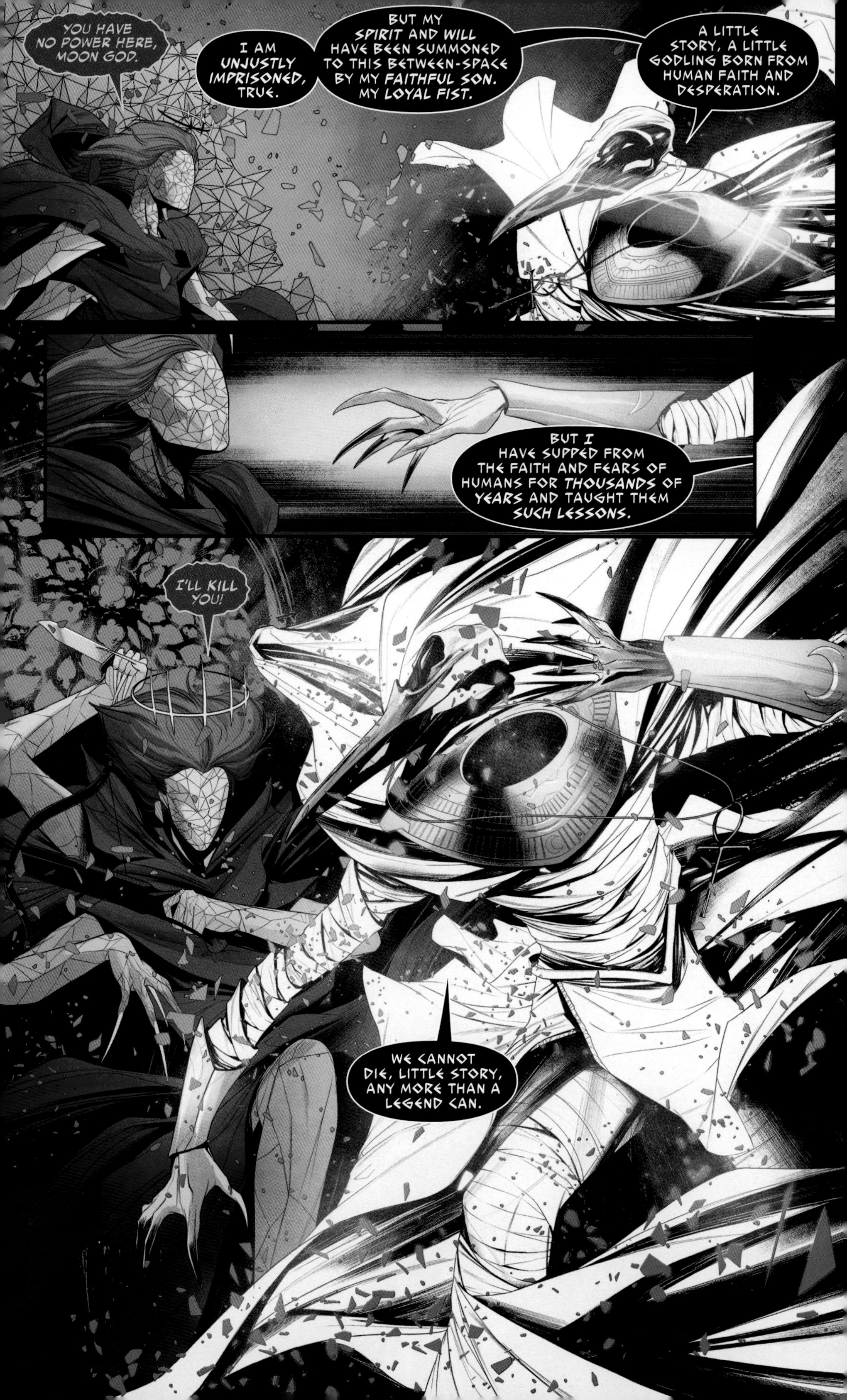
YOU HAVE NO POWER HERE, MOON GOD.
I AM UNJUSTLY IMPRISONED, TRUE.
BUT MY SPIRIT AND WILL HAVE BEEN SUMMONED TO THIS BETWEEN-SPACE BY MY FAITHFUL SON. MY LOYAL FIST.
A LITTLE STORY, A LITTLE GODLING BORN FROM HUMAN FAITH AND DESPERATION.
BUT I HAVE SUPPED FROM THE FAITH AND FEARS OF HUMANS FOR THOUSANDS OF YEARS AND TAUGHT THEM SUCH LESSONS.
I'LL KILL YOU!
WE CANNOT DIE, LITTLE STORY, ANY MORE THAN A LEGEND CAN.

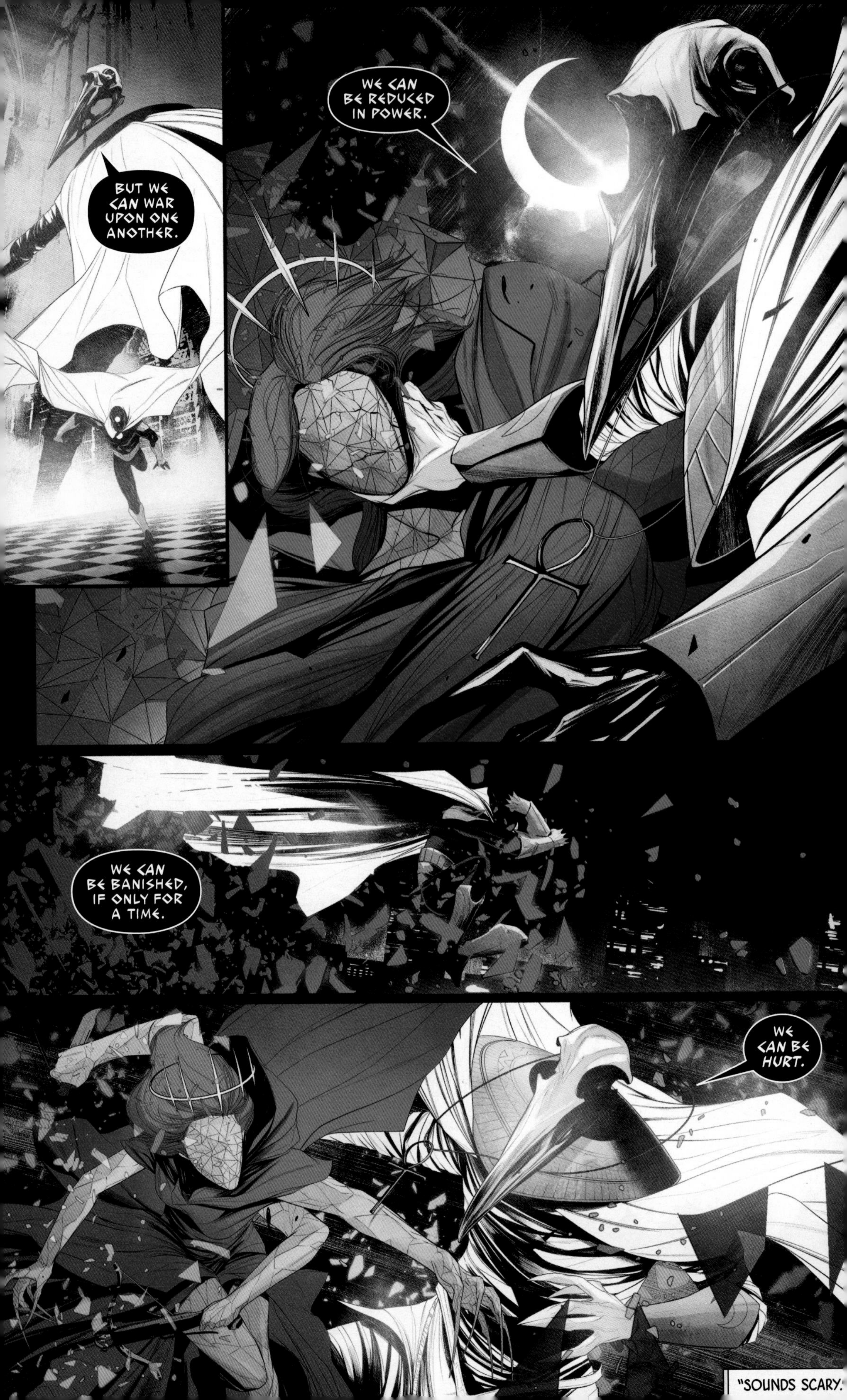
BUT WE CAN WAR UPON ONE ANOTHER.
WE CAN BE REDUCED IN POWER.
WE CAN BE BANISHED, IF ONLY FOR A TIME.
WE CAN BE HURT.
"SOUNDS SCARY.

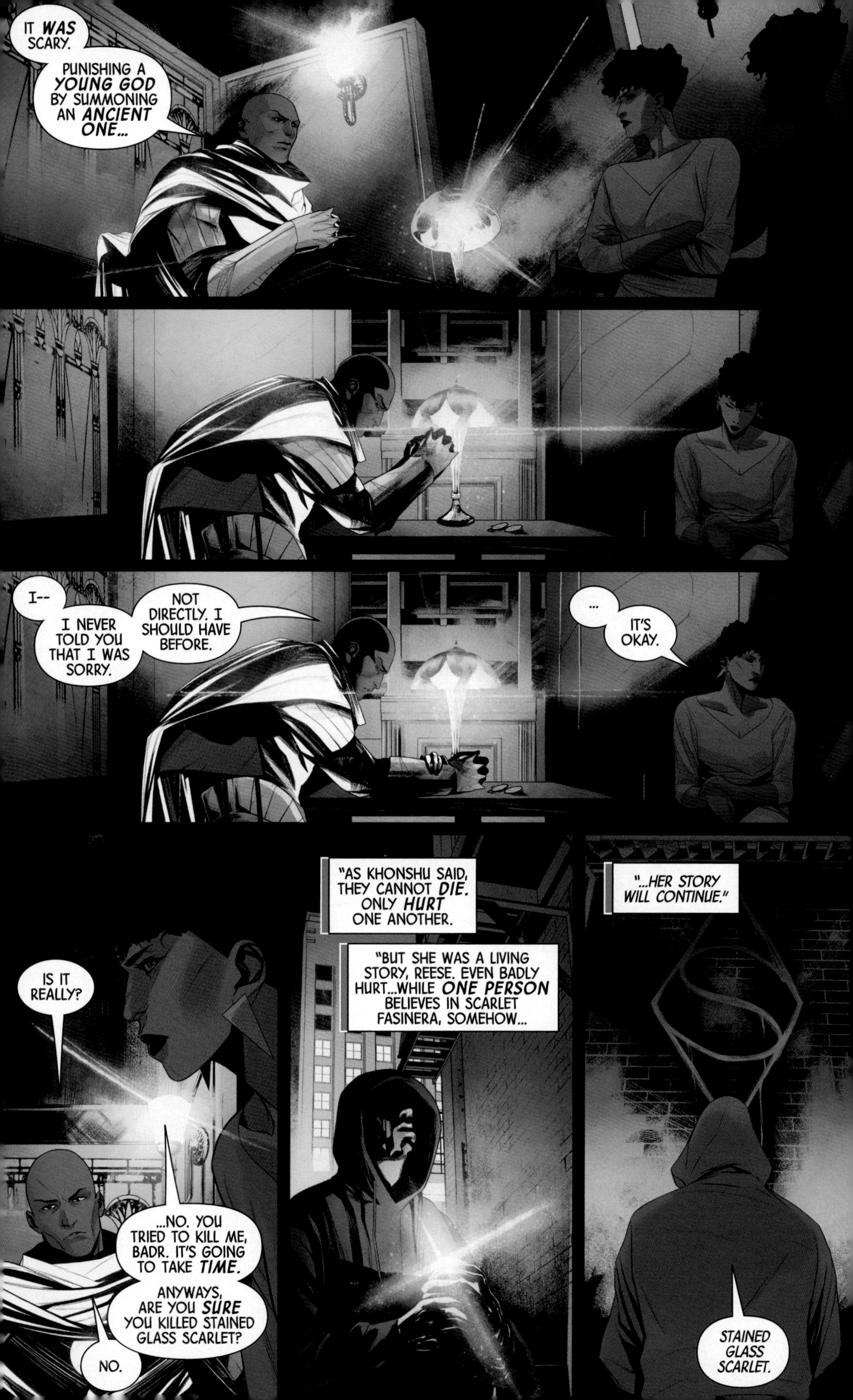
IT WAS SCARY.
PUNISHING A YOUNG GOD BY SUMMONING AN ANCIENT ONE...
I--
NOT DIRECTLY. I SHOULD HAVE BEFORE.
I NEVER TOLD YOU THAT I WAS SORRY.
...
IT'S OKAY.
IS IT REALLY?
...NO. YOU TRIED TO KILL ME, BADR. IT'S GOING TO TAKE TIME.
ANYWAYS, ARE YOU SURE YOU KILLED STAINED GLASS SCARLET?
NO.
"AS KHONSHU SAID, THEY CANNOT DIE. ONLY HURT ONE ANOTHER.
"BUT SHE WAS A LIVING STORY, REESE. EVEN BADLY HURT...WHILE ONE PERSON BELIEVES IN SCARLET FASINERA, SOMEHOW...
"...HER STORY WILL CONTINUE."
STAINED GLASS SCARLET.

EPILOGUE.

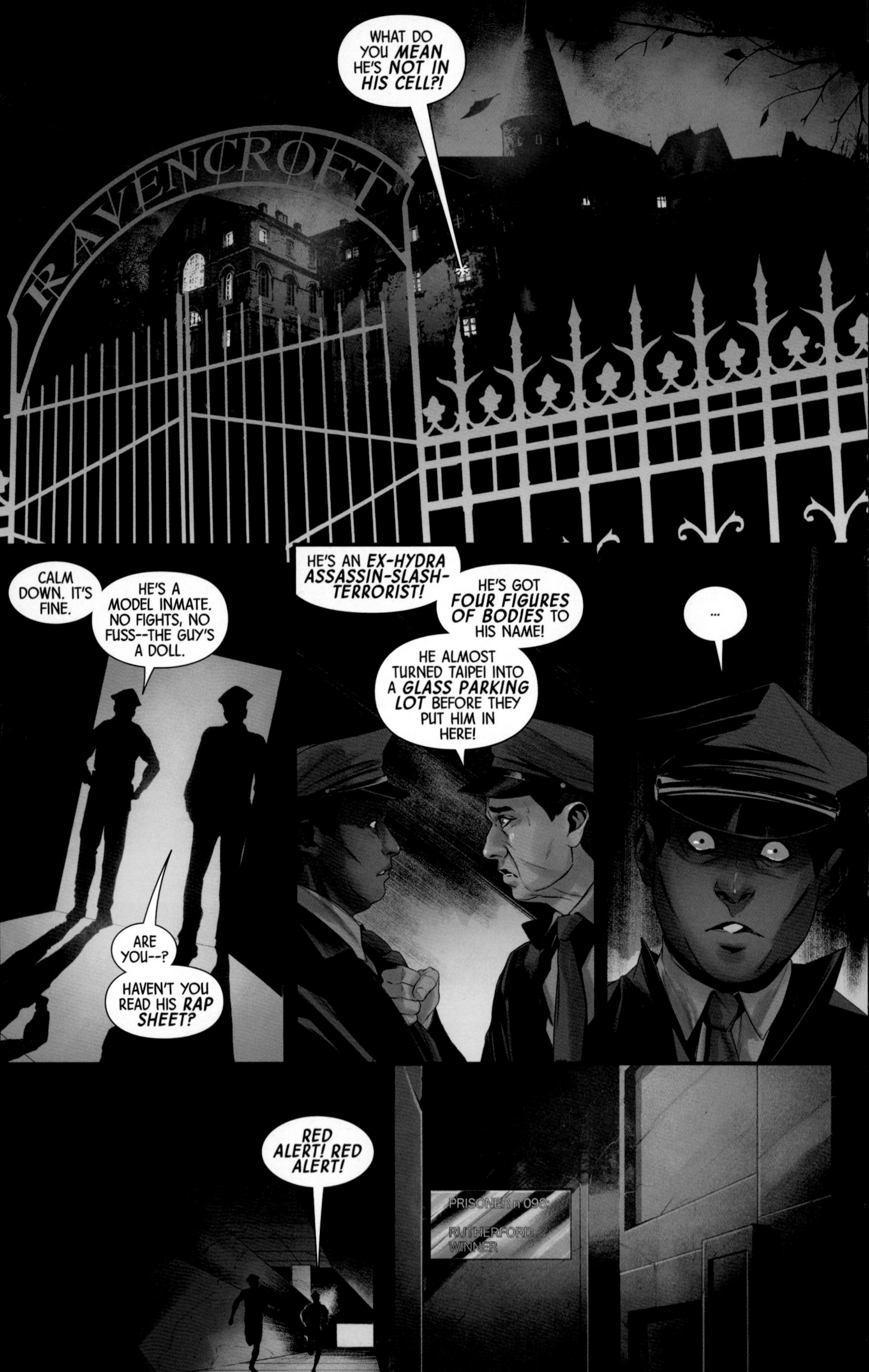
RAVENCROFT
WHAT DO YOU MEAN HE'S NOT IN HIS CELL?!
CALM DOWN. IT'S FINE.
HE'S A MODEL INMATE. NO FIGHTS, NO FUSS--THE GUY'S A DOLL.
ARE YOU--?
HAVEN'T YOU READ HIS RAP SHEET?
HE'S AN EX-HYDRA ASSASSIN-SLASH-TERRORIST!
HE'S GOT FOUR FIGURES OF BODIES TO HIS NAME!
HE ALMOST TURNED TAIPEI INTO A GLASS PARKING LOT BEFORE THEY PUT HIM IN HERE!
...
RED ALERT! RED ALERT!
PRISONER n 098:
RUTHERFORD WINNER

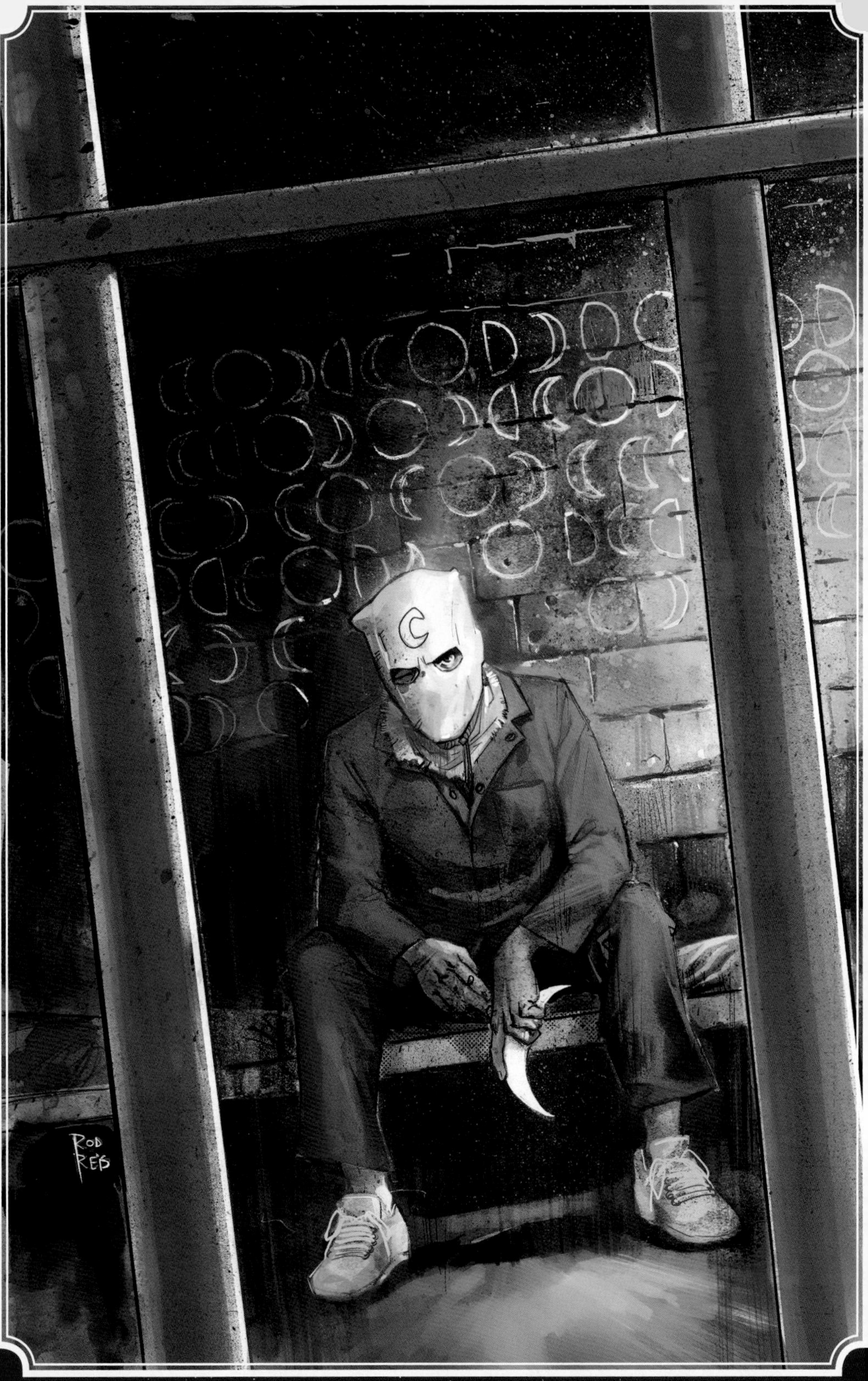
ROD REIS

DEVIL'S REIGN: MOON KNIGHT

NO OUTLAW HAS EVADED JUSTICE MORE THAN WILSON FISK, FORMERLY THE RINGPIN OF A VAST CRIMINAL EMPIRE THAT TOUCHED EVERY CORNER OF NEW YORK CITY (AND BEYOND). NOW THE DULY ELECTED MAYOR OF NEW YORK, FISK HAS FAILED TO WASH HIS HANDS OF HIS OLD LIFE--AND THE BLOODSHED IT BORE. AFTER WEDDING TYPHOID MARY AND RETREATING TO UPSTATE NEW YORK FOR THEIR HONEYMOON, FISK HAS DISCOVERED A SECRET THAT HAS MADE HIS BLOOD BOIL AND SET HIS IRE UPON THE CITY AND EVERY COSTUMED VIGILANTE IN IT.

MOON KNIGHT

DEVIL'S REIGN

Mercenary Marc Spector died and was reborn in the shadow of Khonshu, the Egyptian god of the moon. Spector became Moon Knight, the Fist of Khonshu, to fight evil. Through his Midnight Mission, he is the defender of all those who travel at night. Moon Knight was recently arrested during Mayor Fisk's crackdown on New York City vigilantes and was imprisoned in the Myrmidon.

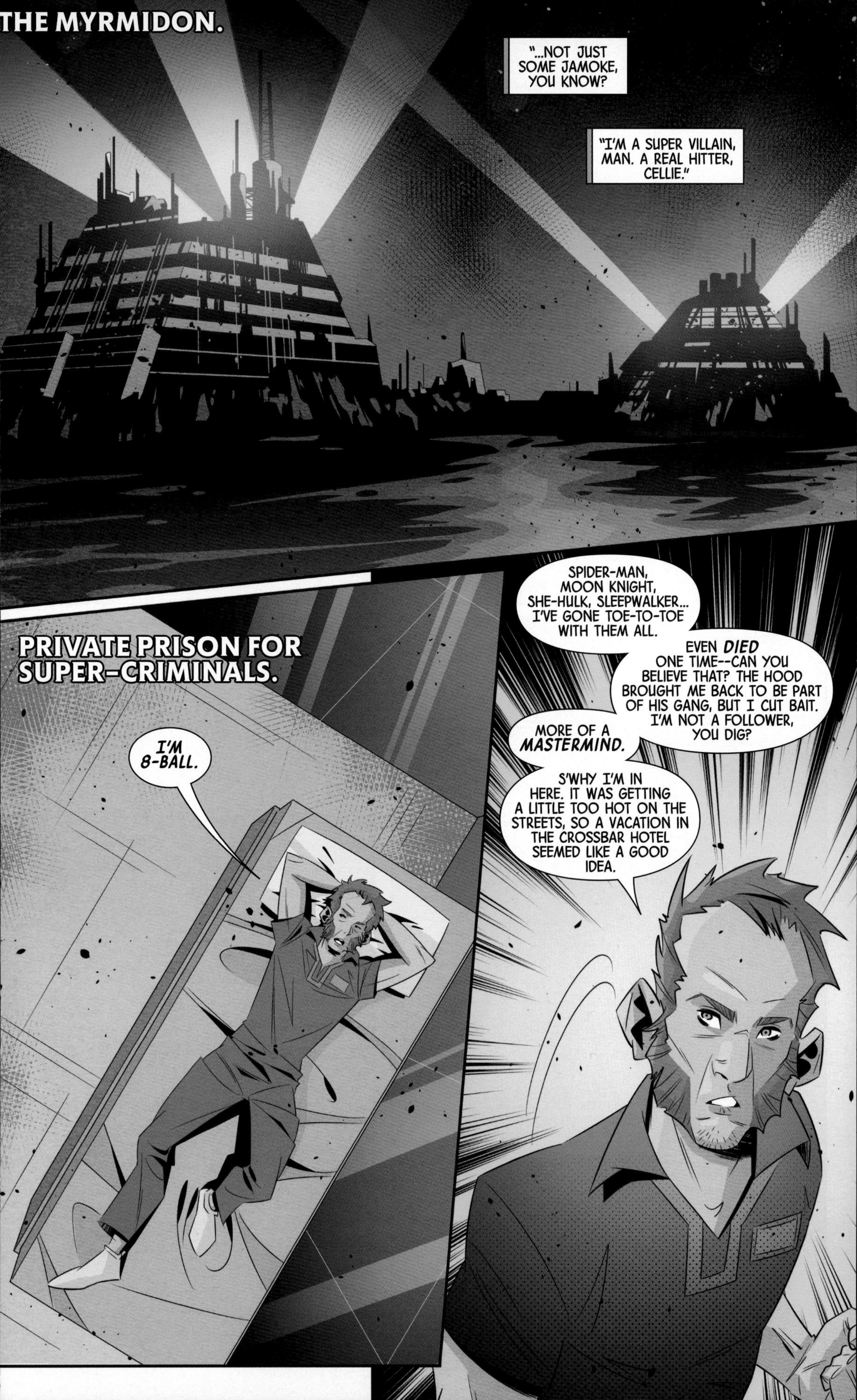
THE MYRMIDON.
"...NOT JUST SOME JAMOKE, YOU KNOW?
"I'M A SUPER VILLAIN, MAN. A REAL HITTER, CELLIE."
PRIVATE PRISON FOR SUPER-CRIMINALS.
I'M 8-BALL.
SPIDER-MAN, MOON KNIGHT, SHE-HULK, SLEEPWALKER... I'VE GONE TOE-TO-TOE WITH THEM ALL.
EVEN DIED ONE TIME--CAN YOU BELIEVE THAT? THE HOOD BROUGHT ME BACK TO BE PART OF HIS GANG, BUT I CUT BAIT. I'M NOT A FOLLOWER, YOU DIG?
MORE OF A MASTERMIND.
S'WHY I'M IN HERE. IT WAS GETTING A LITTLE TOO HOT ON THE STREETS, SO A VACATION IN THE CROSSBAR HOTEL SEEMED LIKE A GOOD IDEA.

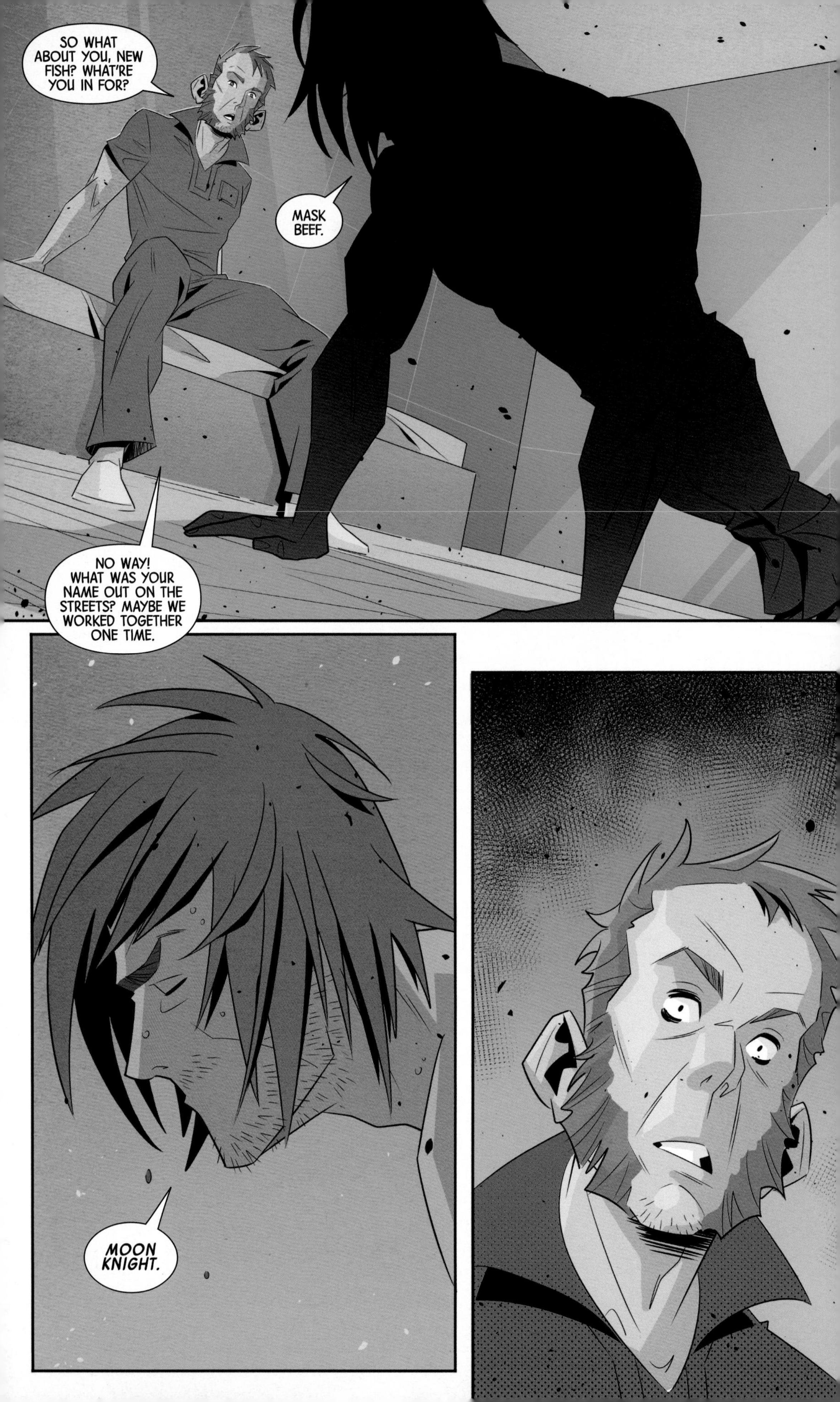
SO WHAT ABOUT YOU, NEW FISH? WHAT'RE YOU IN FOR?
MASK BEEF.
NO WAY! WHAT WAS YOUR NAME OUT ON THE STREETS? MAYBE WE WORKED TOGETHER ONE TIME.
MOON KNIGHT.

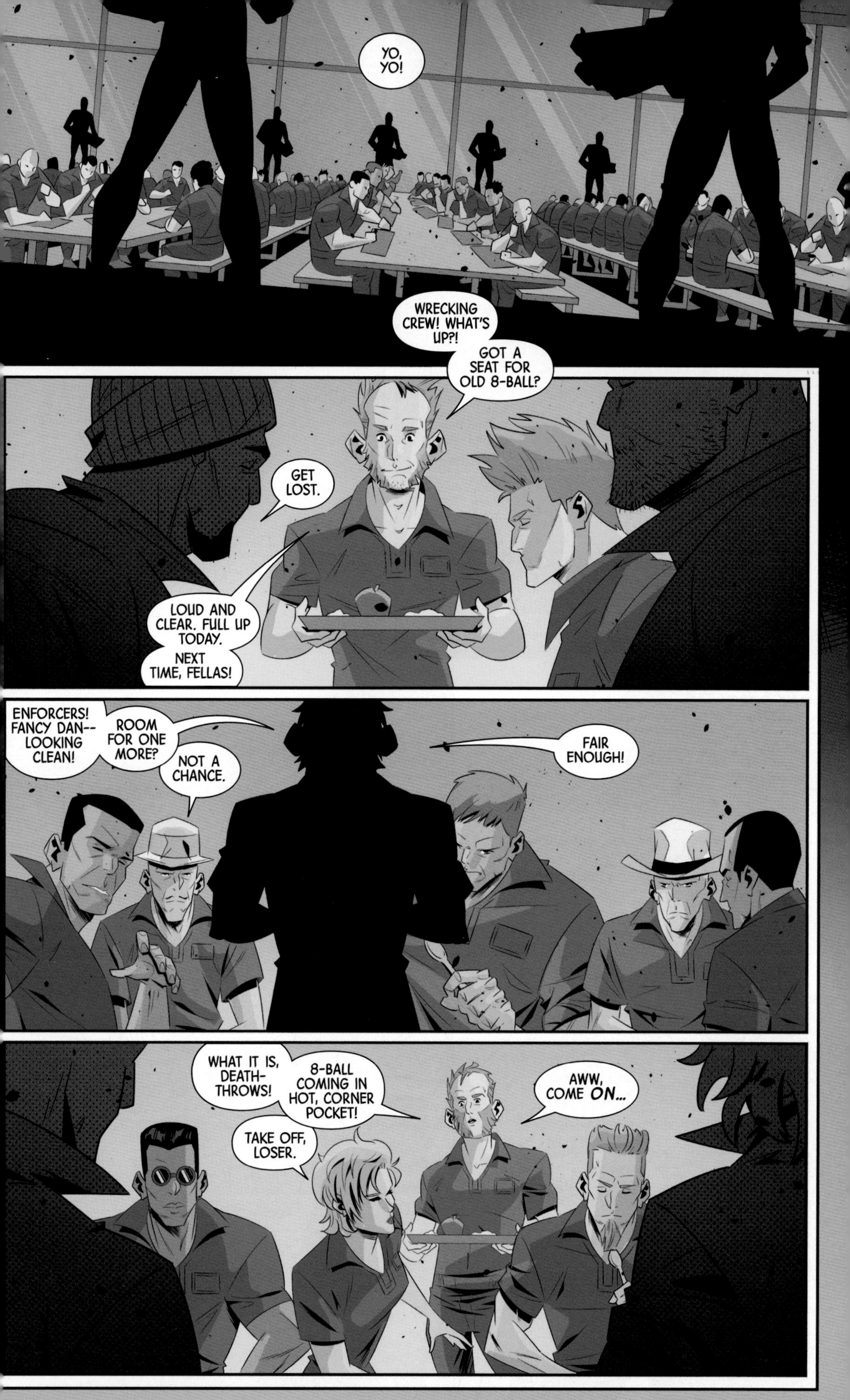
YO, YO!
WRECKING CREW! WHAT'S UP?!
GOT A SEAT FOR OLD 8-BALL?
GET LOST.
LOUD AND CLEAR. FULL UP TODAY.
NEXT TIME, FELLAS!
ENFORCERS! FANCY DAN-- LOOKING CLEAN!
ROOM FOR ONE MORE?
NOT A CHANCE.
FAIR ENOUGH!
WHAT IT IS, DEATH-THROWS!
8-BALL COMING IN HOT, CORNER POCKET!
TAKE OFF, LOSER.
AWW, COME ON...

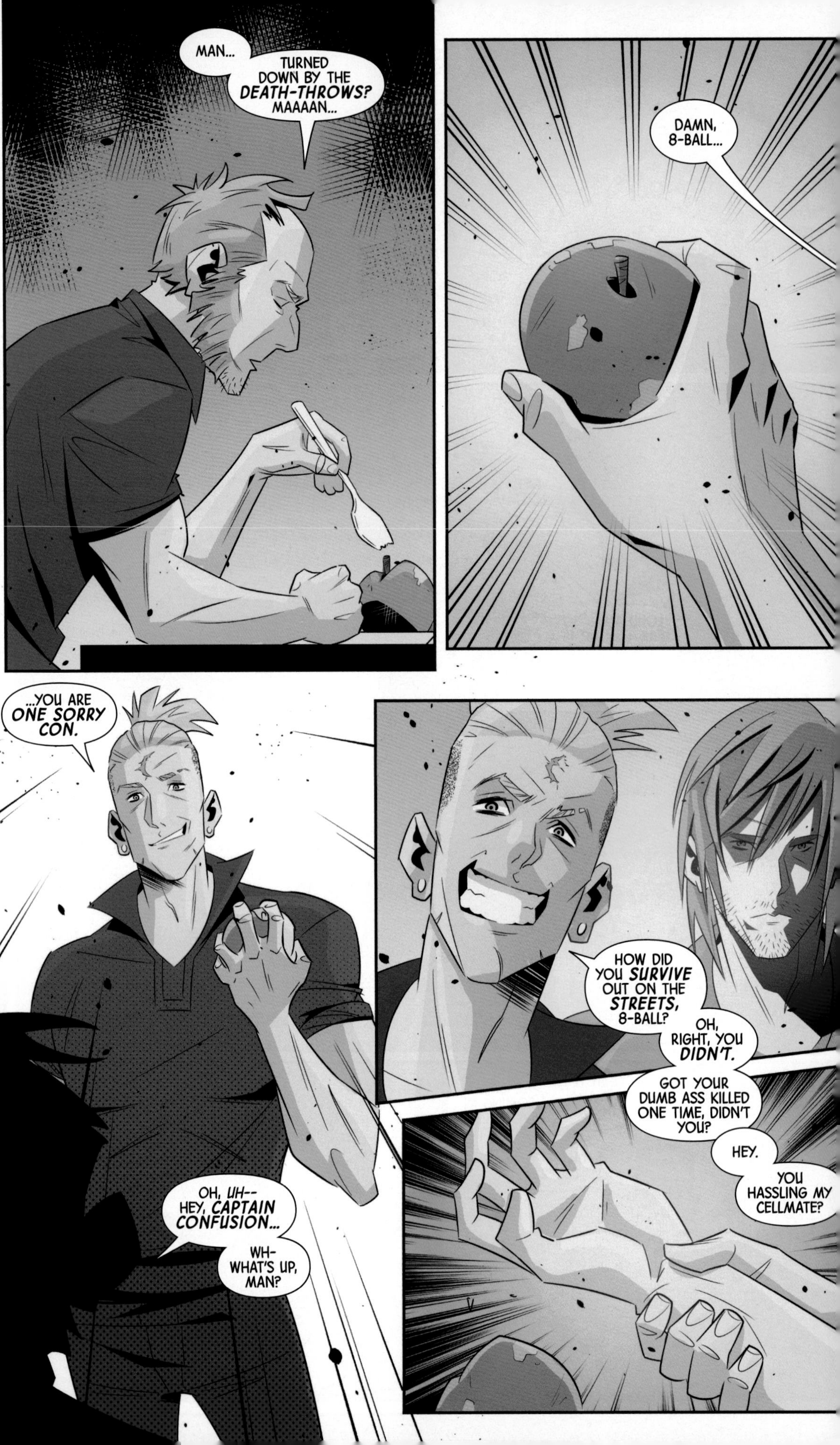
MAN...
TURNED DOWN BY THE DEATH-THROWS? MAAAAN...
DAMN, 8-BALL...
...YOU ARE ONE SORRY CON.
HOW DID YOU SURVIVE OUT ON THE STREETS, 8-BALL?
OH, RIGHT, YOU DIDN'T.
GOT YOUR DUMB ASS KILLED ONE TIME, DIDN'T YOU?
HEY.
YOU HASSLING MY CELLMATE?
OH, UH-- HEY, CAPTAIN CONFUSION...
WH- WHAT'S UP, MAN?

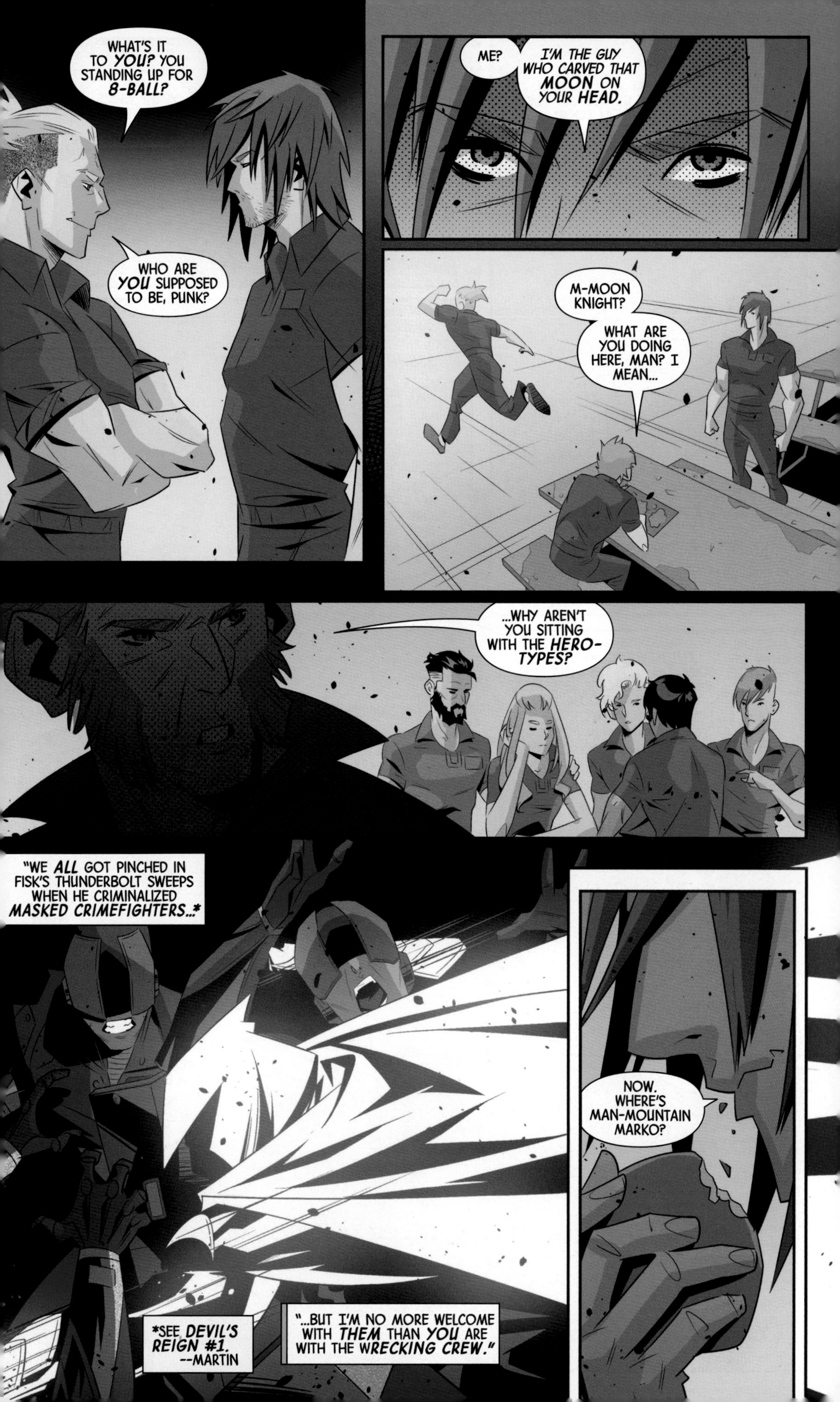

WHAT'S IT TO YOU? YOU STANDING UP FOR 8-BALL?
WHO ARE YOU SUPPOSED TO BE, PUNK?
ME?
I'M THE GUY WHO CARVED THAT MOON ON YOUR HEAD.
M-MOON KNIGHT?
WHAT ARE YOU DOING HERE, MAN? I MEAN...
...WHY AREN'T YOU SITTING WITH THE HERO-TYPES?
"WE ALL GOT PINCHED IN FISK'S THUNDERBOLT SWEEPS WHEN HE CRIMINALIZED MASKED CRIMEFIGHTERS...*
*SEE DEVIL'S REIGN #1. --MARTIN
"...BUT I'M NO MORE WELCOME WITH THEM THAN YOU ARE WITH THE WRECKING CREW."
NOW. WHERE'S MAN-MOUNTAIN MARKO?

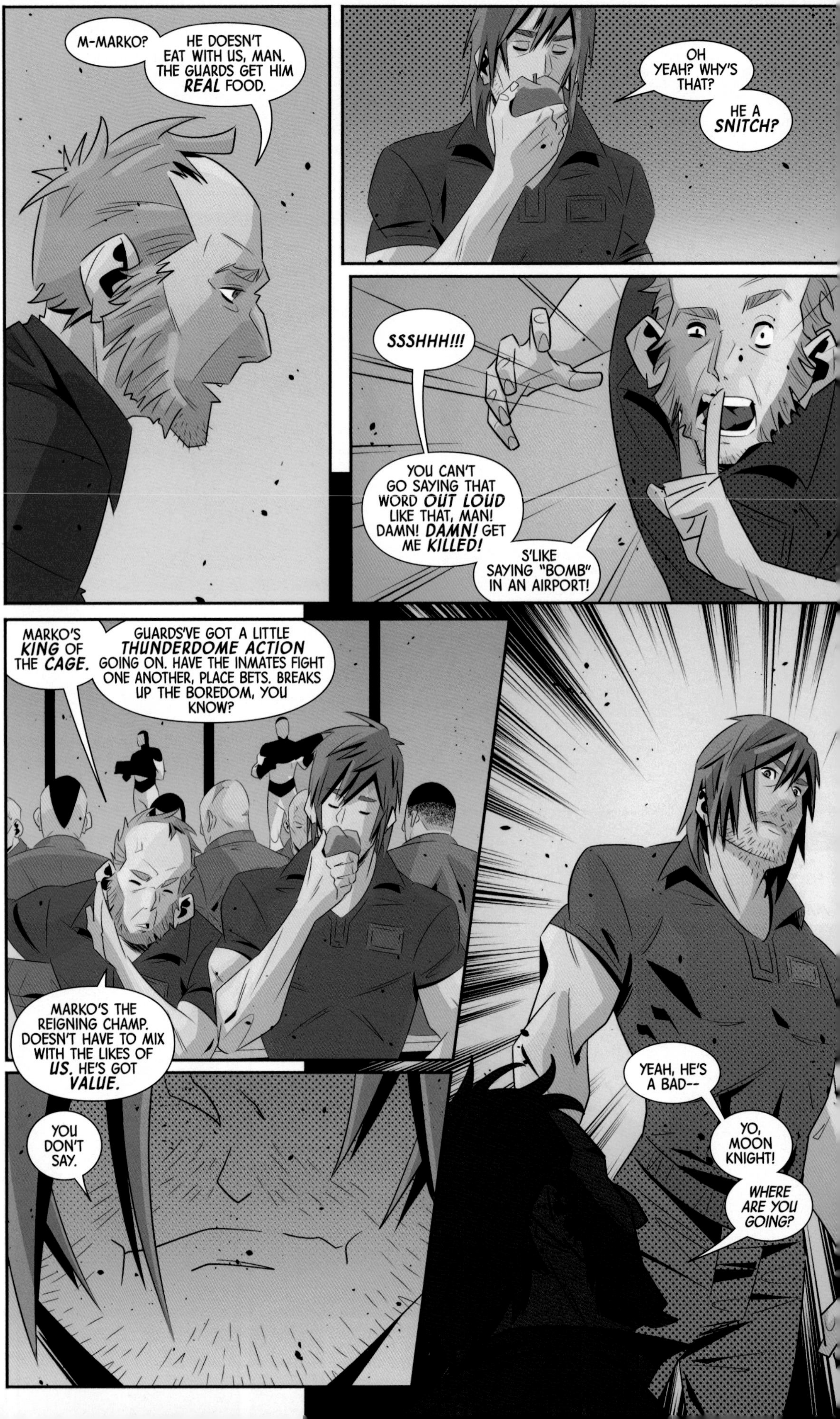

M-MARKO?
HE DOESN'T EAT WITH US, MAN. THE GUARDS GET HIM REAL FOOD.
OH YEAH? WHY'S THAT?
HE A SNITCH?
SSSHHH!!!
YOU CAN'T GO SAYING THAT WORD OUT LOUD LIKE THAT, MAN! DAMN! DAMN! GET ME KILLED!
S'LIKE SAYING "BOMB" IN AN AIRPORT!
MARKO'S KING OF THE CAGE.
GUARDS'VE GOT A LITTLE THUNDERDOME ACTION GOING ON. HAVE THE INMATES FIGHT ONE ANOTHER, PLACE BETS. BREAKS UP THE BOREDOM, YOU KNOW?
MARKO'S THE REIGNING CHAMP. DOESN'T HAVE TO MIX WITH THE LIKES OF US. HE'S GOT VALUE.
YOU DON'T SAY.
YEAH, HE'S A BAD--
YO, MOON KNIGHT!
WHERE ARE YOU GOING?

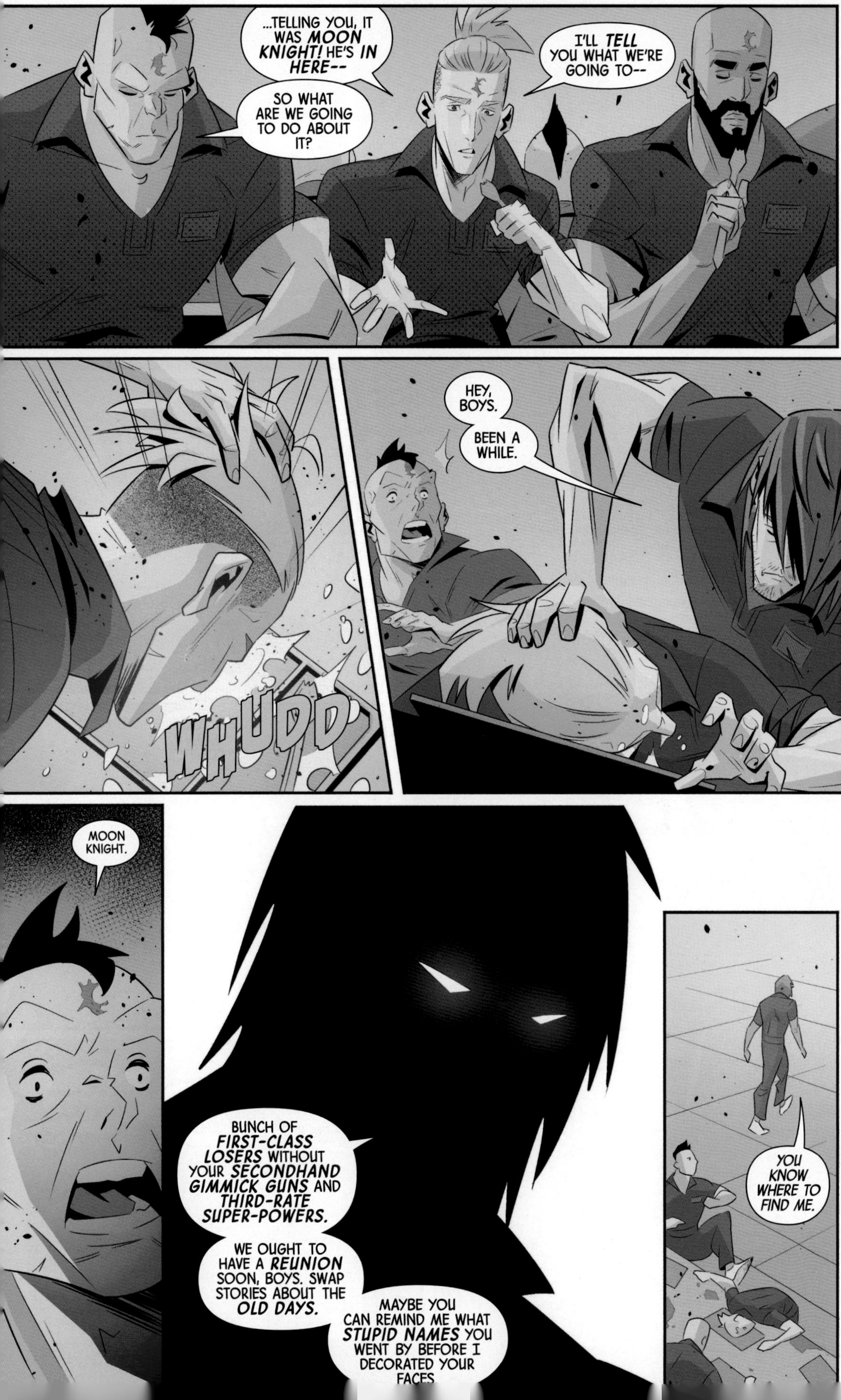
...TELLING YOU, IT WAS MOON KNIGHT! HE'S IN HERE--
SO WHAT ARE WE GOING TO DO ABOUT IT?
I'LL TELL YOU WHAT WE'RE GOING TO--
WHUDD
HEY, BOYS.
BEEN A WHILE.
MOON KNIGHT.
BUNCH OF FIRST-CLASS LOSERS WITHOUT YOUR SECONDHAND GIMMICK GUNS AND THIRD-RATE SUPER-POWERS.
WE OUGHT TO HAVE A REUNION SOON, BOYS. SWAP STORIES ABOUT THE OLD DAYS.
MAYBE YOU CAN REMIND ME WHAT STUPID NAMES YOU WENT BY BEFORE I DECORATED YOUR FACES.
YOU KNOW WHERE TO FIND ME.

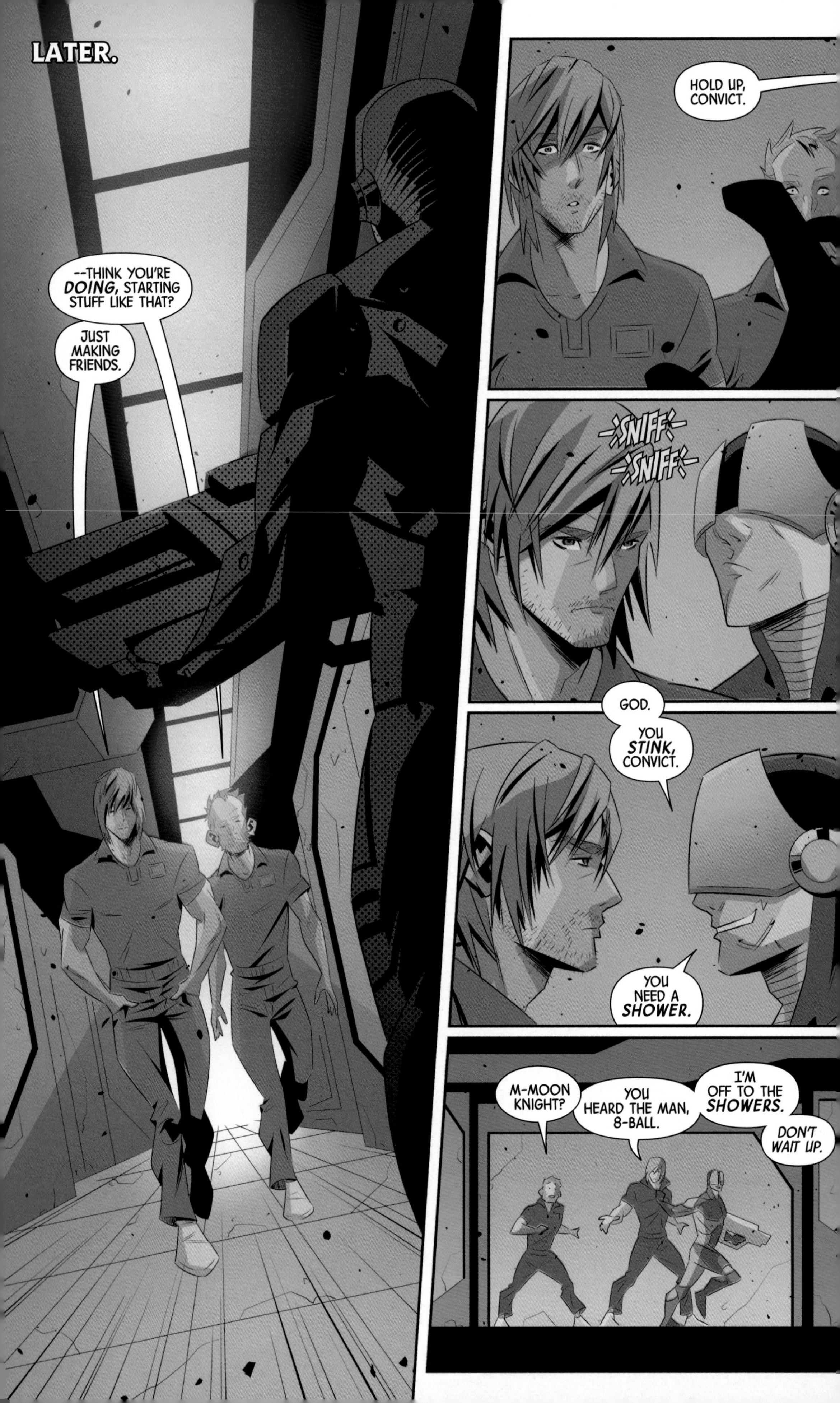
LATER.
--THINK YOU'RE DOING, STARTING STUFF LIKE THAT?
JUST MAKING FRIENDS.
HOLD UP, CONVICT.
-SNIFF-
-SNIFF-
GOD.
YOU STINK, CONVICT.
YOU NEED A SHOWER.
M-MOON KNIGHT?
YOU HEARD THE MAN, 8-BALL.
I'M OFF TO THE SHOWERS.
DON'T WAIT UP.

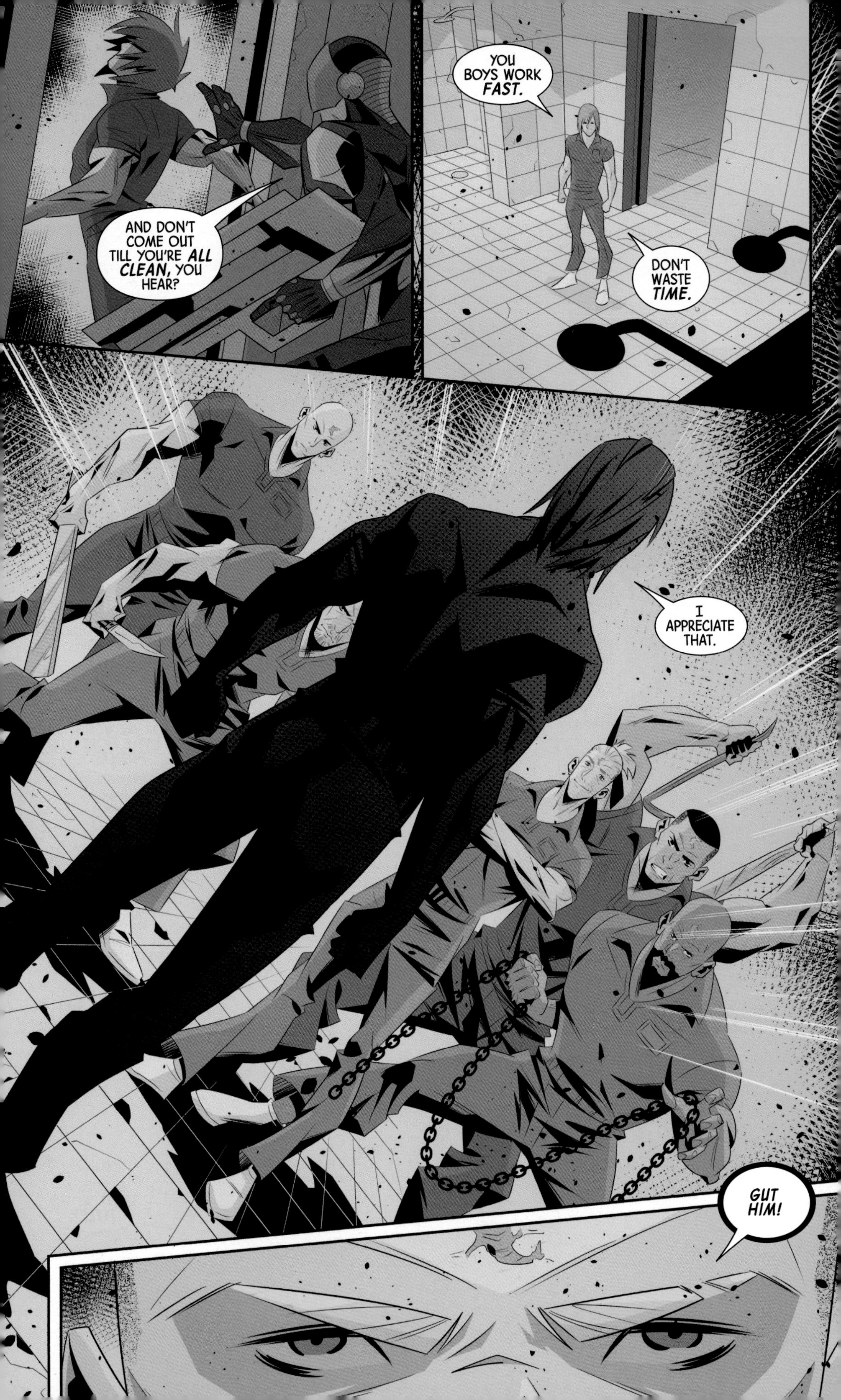
AND DON'T COME OUT TILL YOU'RE ALL CLEAN, YOU HEAR?
YOU BOYS WORK FAST.
DON'T WASTE TIME.
I APPRECIATE THAT.
GUT HIM!

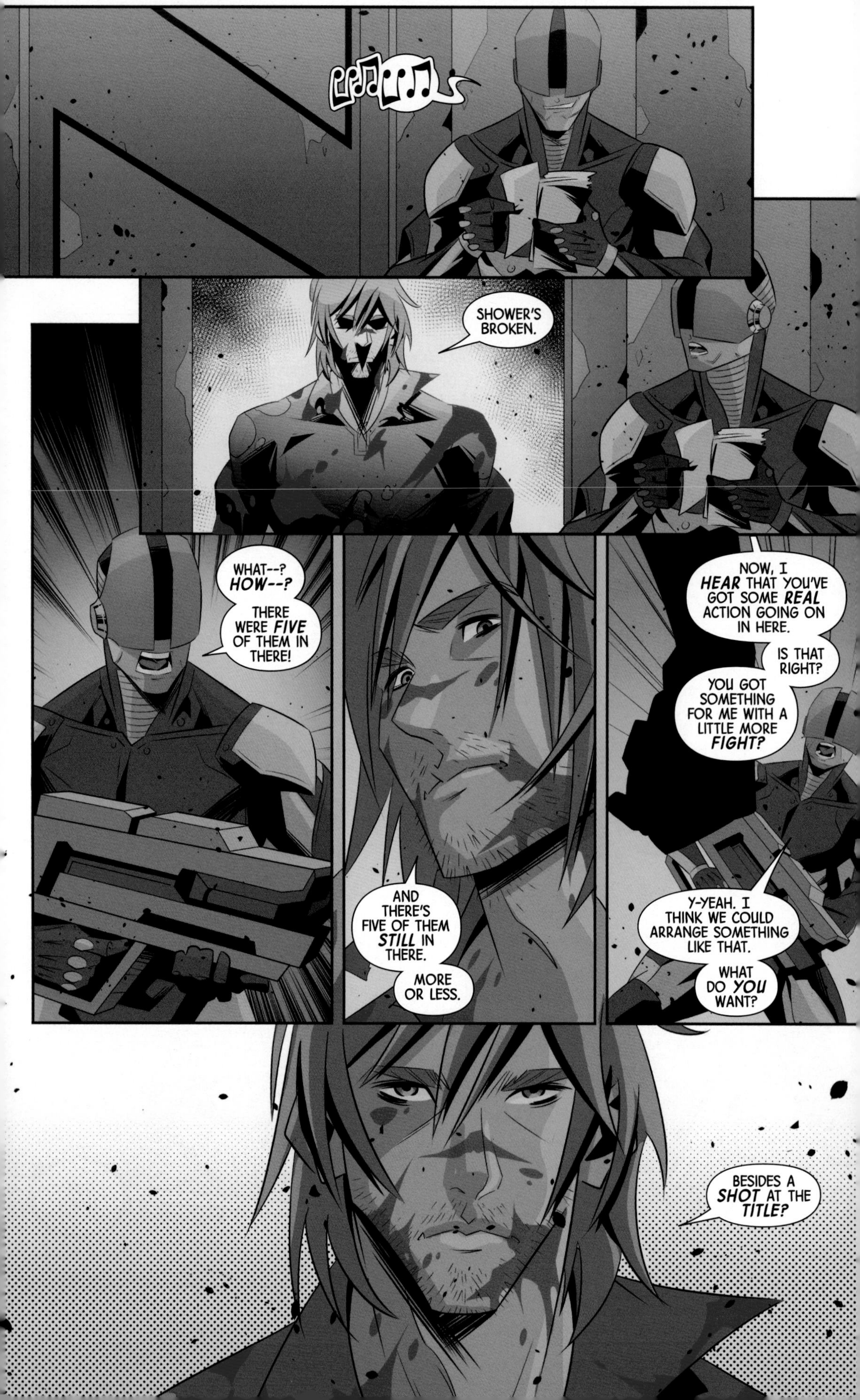
SHOWER'S BROKEN.
WHAT--? HOW--?
THERE WERE FIVE OF THEM IN THERE!
AND THERE'S FIVE OF THEM STILL IN THERE.
MORE OR LESS.
NOW, I HEAR THAT YOU'VE GOT SOME REAL ACTION GOING ON IN HERE.
IS THAT RIGHT?
YOU GOT SOMETHING FOR ME WITH A LITTLE MORE FIGHT?
Y-YEAH. I THINK WE COULD ARRANGE SOMETHING LIKE THAT.
WHAT DO YOU WANT?
BESIDES A SHOT AT THE TITLE?

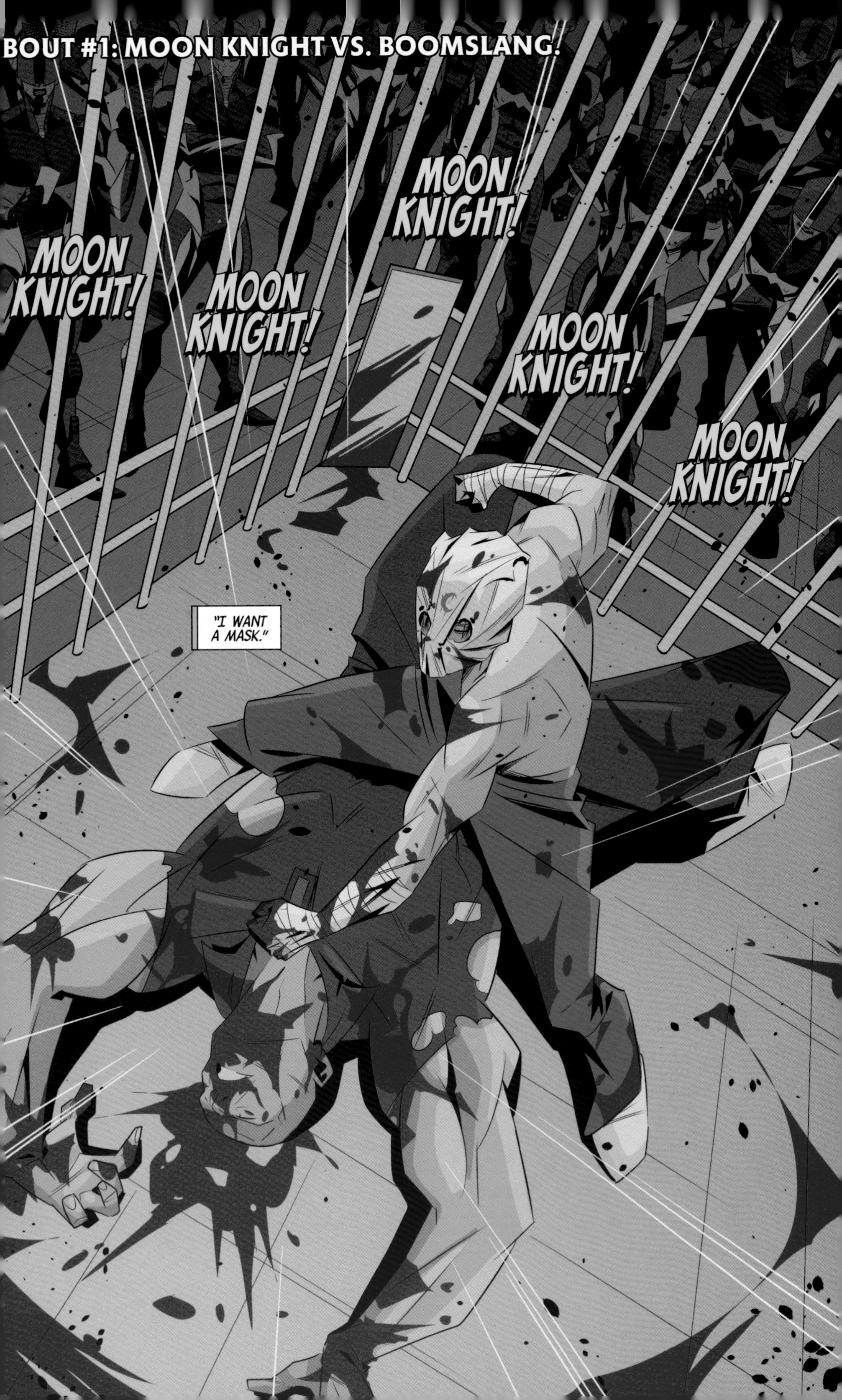
BOUT #1: MOON KNIGHT VS. BOOMSLANG.
MOON KNIGHT!
MOON KNIGHT!
MOON KNIGHT!
MOON KNIGHT!
MOON KNIGHT!
"I WANT A MASK."

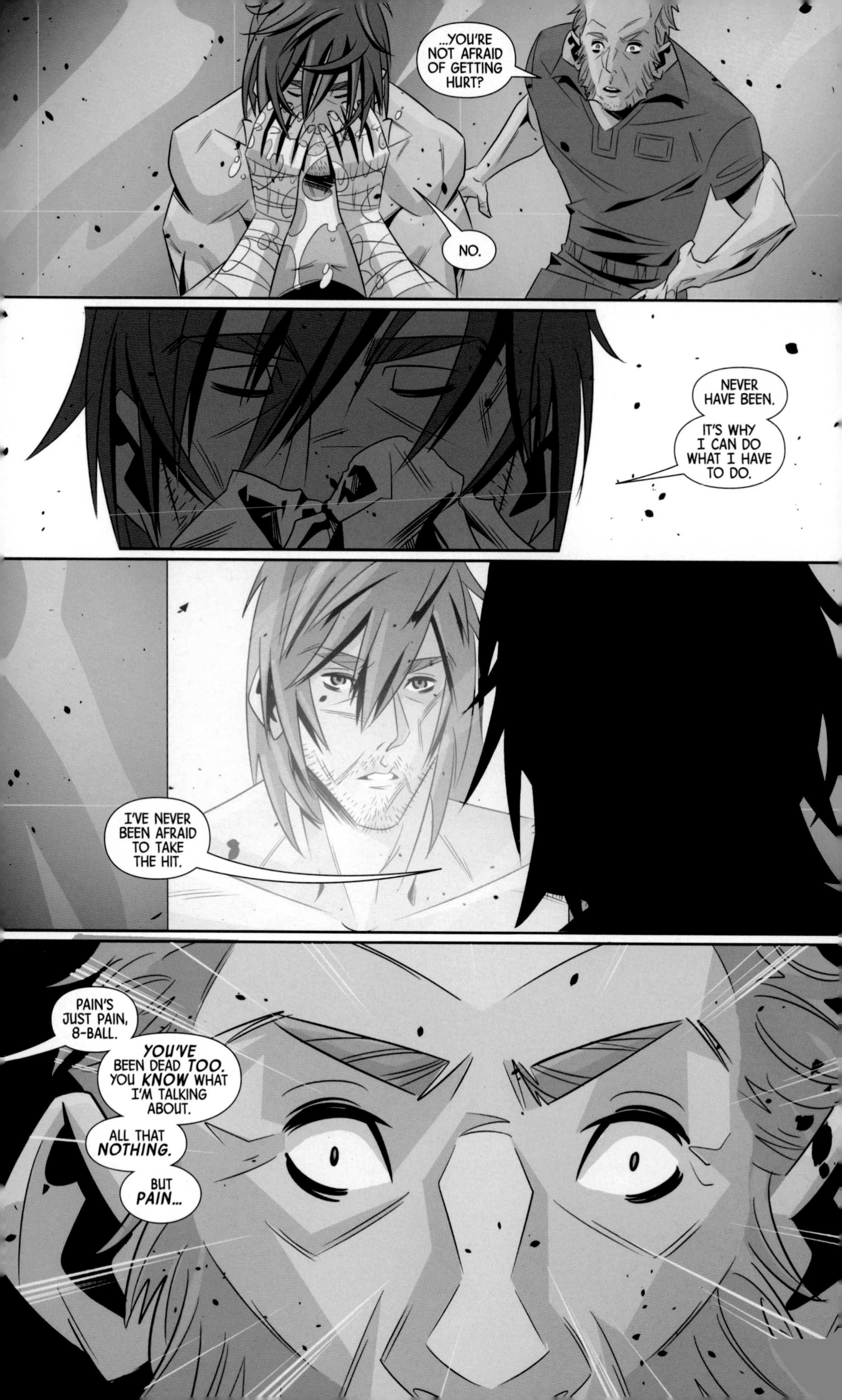
...YOU'RE NOT AFRAID OF GETTING HURT?
NO.
NEVER HAVE BEEN.
IT'S WHY I CAN DO WHAT I HAVE TO DO.
I'VE NEVER BEEN AFRAID TO TAKE THE HIT.
PAIN'S JUST PAIN, 8-BALL.
YOU'VE BEEN DEAD TOO. YOU KNOW WHAT I'M TALKING ABOUT.
ALL THAT NOTHING.
BUT PAIN...

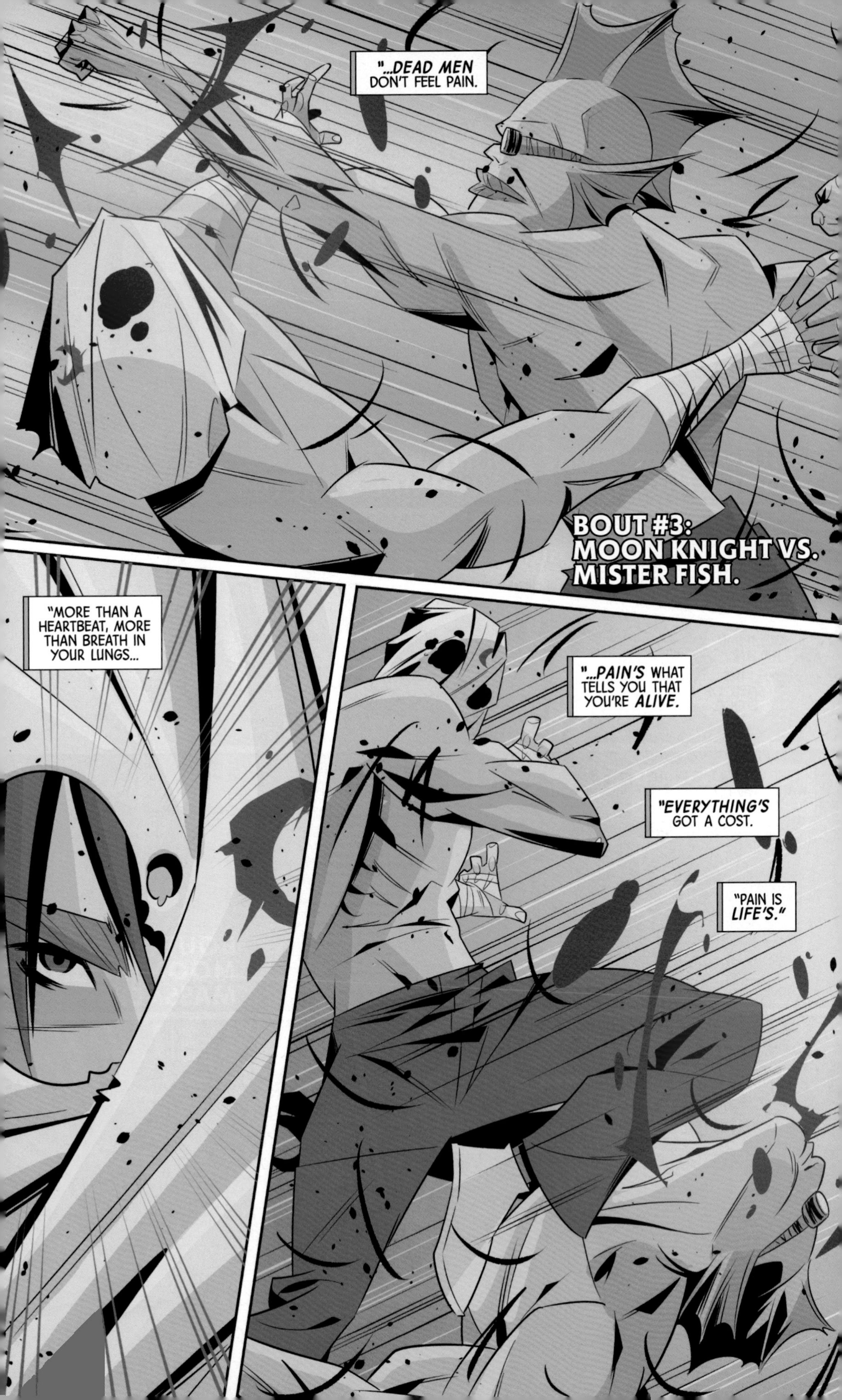
"...DEAD MEN DON'T FEEL PAIN.
BOUT #3: MOON KNIGHT VS. MISTER FISH.
"MORE THAN A HEARTBEAT, MORE THAN BREATH IN YOUR LUNGS...
"...PAIN'S WHAT TELLS YOU THAT YOU'RE ALIVE.
"EVERYTHING'S GOT A COST.
"PAIN IS LIFE'S."

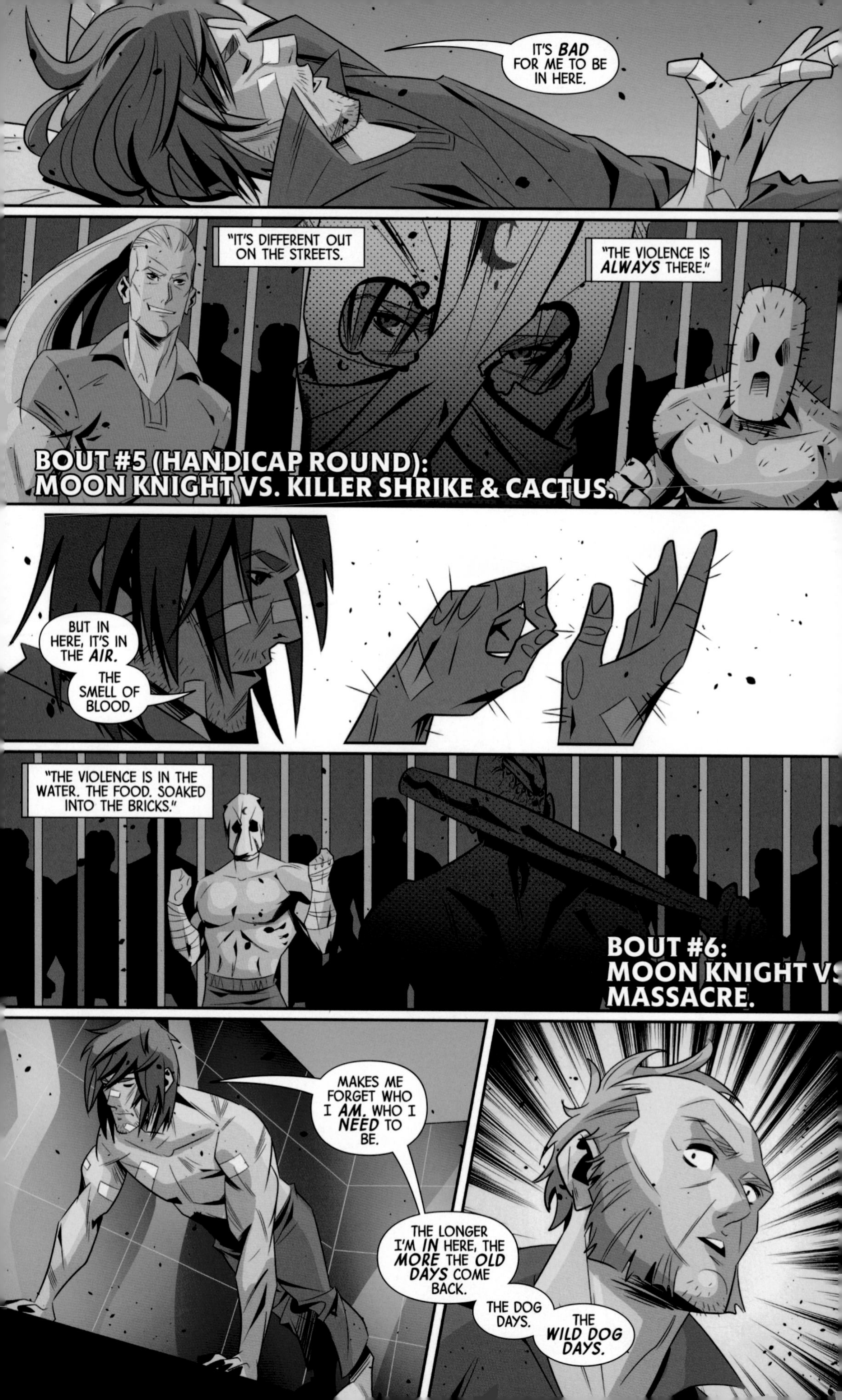
IT'S BAD FOR ME TO BE IN HERE.
"IT'S DIFFERENT OUT ON THE STREETS.
"THE VIOLENCE IS ALWAYS THERE."
BOUT #5 (HANDICAP ROUND): MOON KNIGHT VS. KILLER SHRIKE & CACTUS.
BUT IN HERE, IT'S IN THE AIR.
THE SMELL OF BLOOD.
"THE VIOLENCE IS IN THE WATER. THE FOOD. SOAKED INTO THE BRICKS."
BOUT #6: MOON KNIGHT VS MASSACRE.
MAKES ME FORGET WHO I AM. WHO I NEED TO BE.
THE LONGER I'M IN HERE, THE MORE THE OLD DAYS COME BACK.
THE DOG DAYS.
THE WILD DOG DAYS.

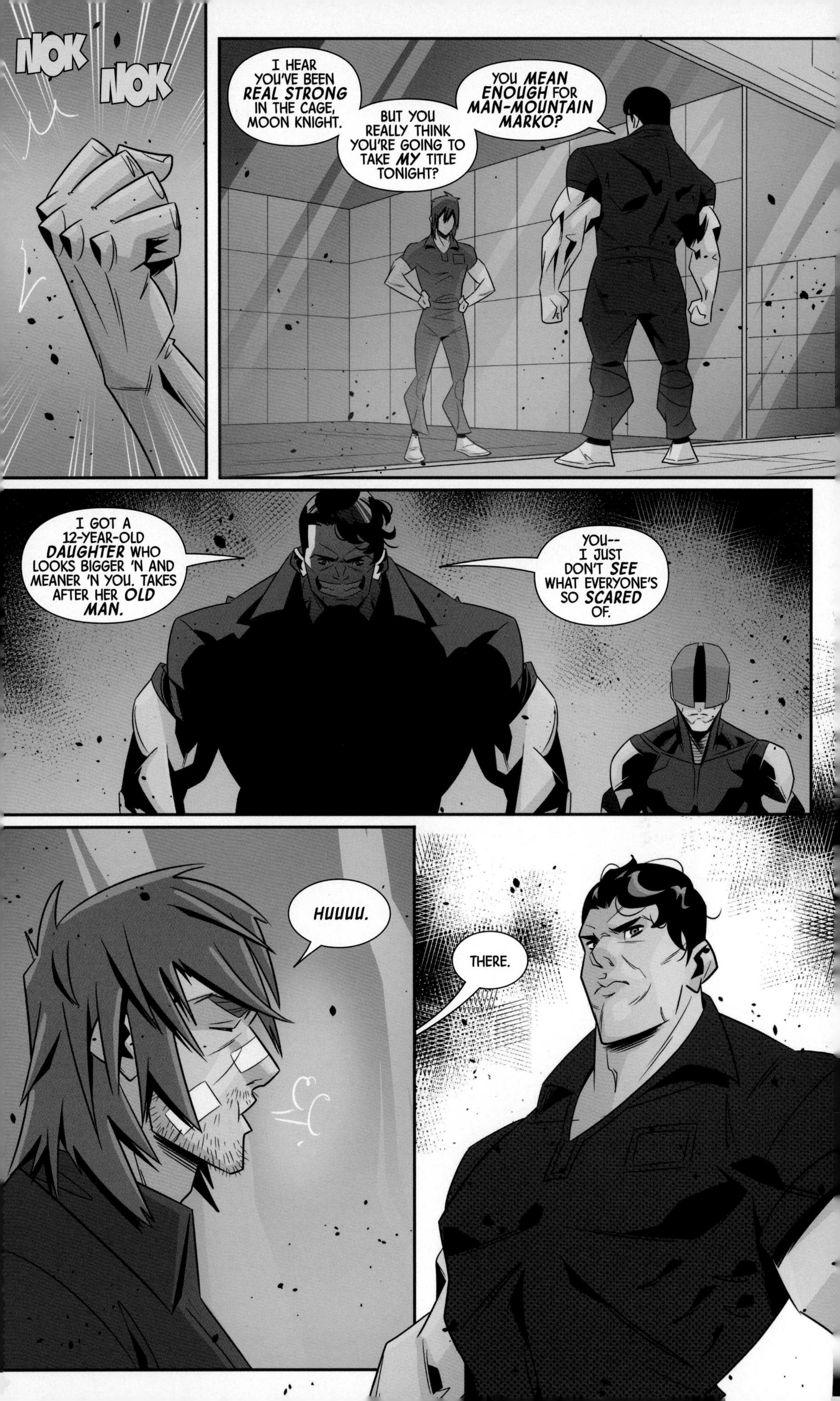
NOK NOK
I HEAR YOU'VE BEEN REAL STRONG IN THE CAGE, MOON KNIGHT.
BUT YOU REALLY THINK YOU'RE GOING TO TAKE MY TITLE TONIGHT?
YOU MEAN ENOUGH FOR MAN-MOUNTAIN MARKO?
I GOT A 12-YEAR-OLD DAUGHTER WHO LOOKS BIGGER 'N AND MEANER 'N YOU. TAKES AFTER HER OLD MAN.
YOU-- I JUST DON'T SEE WHAT EVERYONE'S SO SCARED OF.
HUUUU.
THERE.

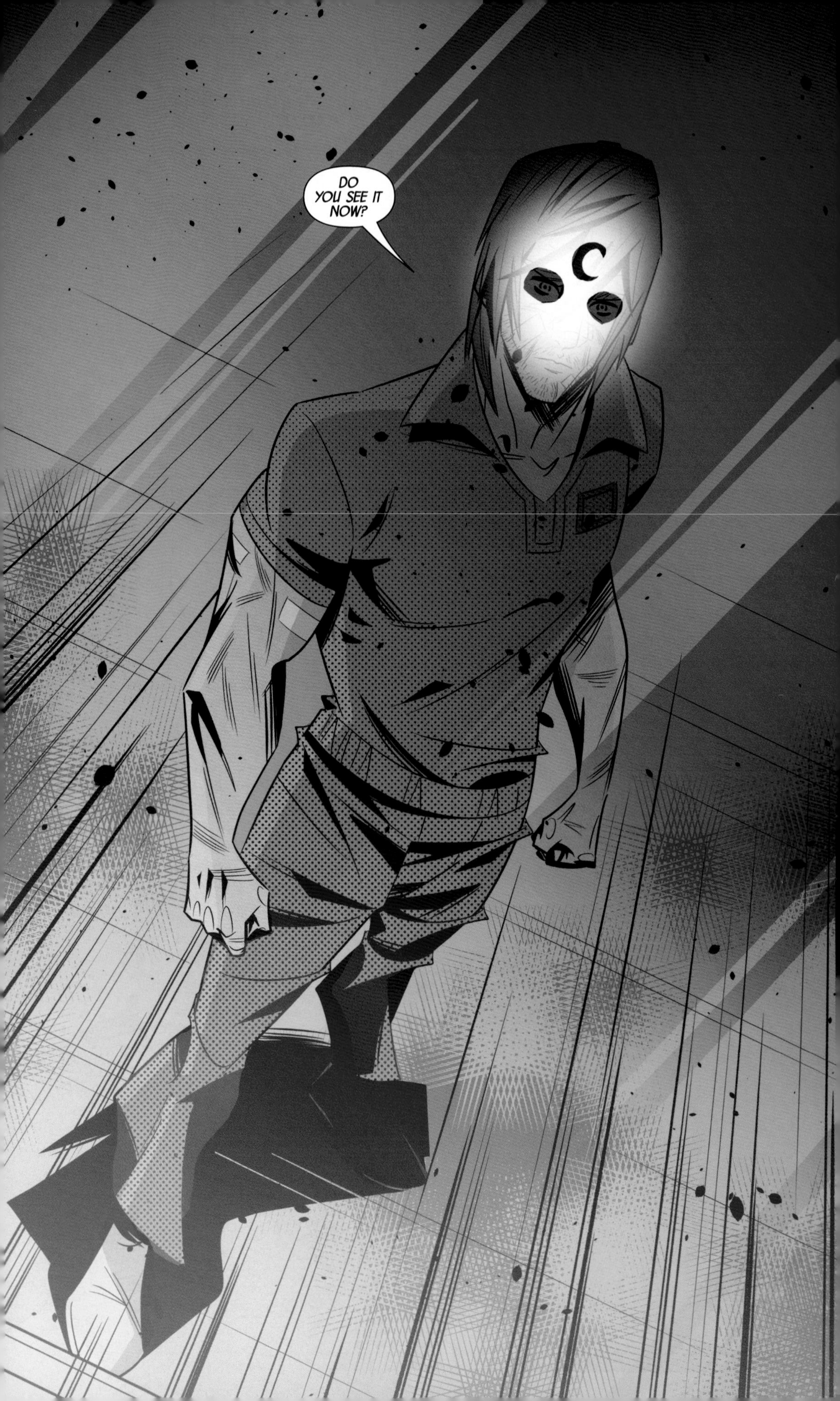
DO YOU SEE IT NOW?

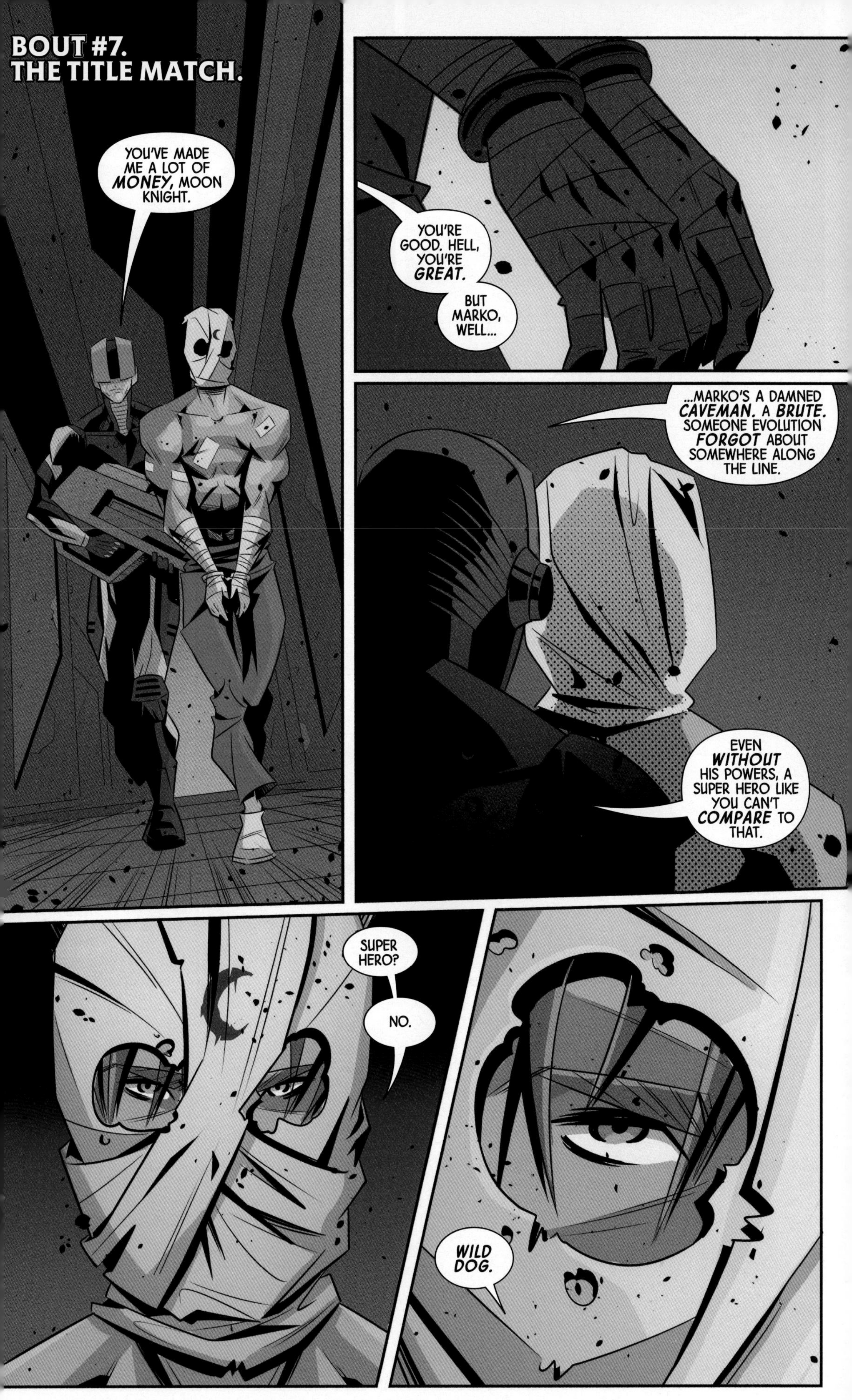
BOUT #7.
THE TITLE MATCH.
YOU'VE MADE ME A LOT OF MONEY, MOON KNIGHT.
YOU'RE GOOD. HELL, YOU'RE GREAT.
BUT MARKO, WELL...
...MARKO'S A DAMNED CAVEMAN. A BRUTE. SOMEONE EVOLUTION FORGOT ABOUT SOMEWHERE ALONG THE LINE.
EVEN WITHOUT HIS POWERS, A SUPER HERO LIKE YOU CAN'T COMPARE TO THAT.
SUPER HERO?
NO.
WILD DOG.

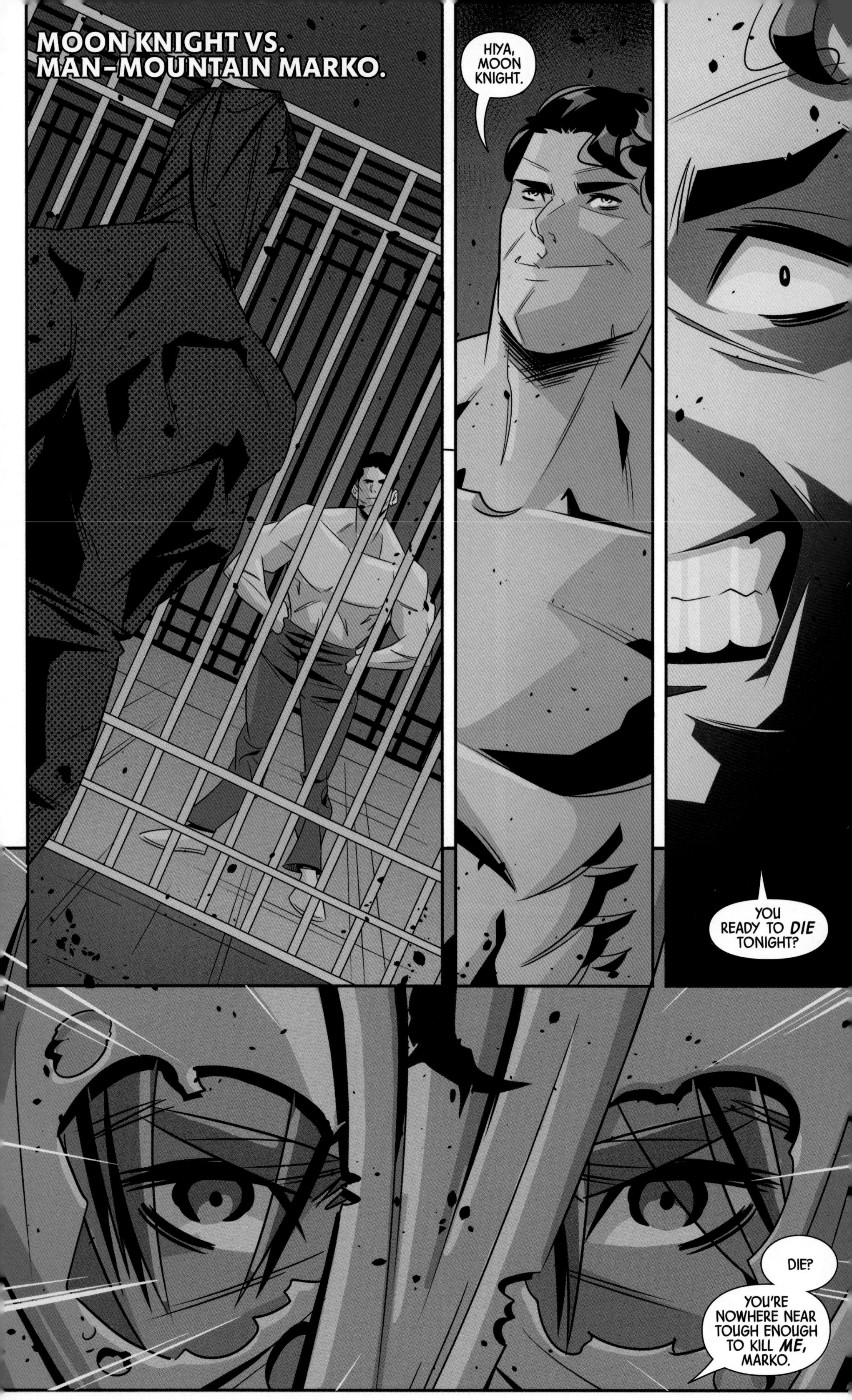
MOON KNIGHT VS.
MAN-MOUNTAIN MARKO.
HIYA, MOON KNIGHT.
YOU READY TO *DIE* TONIGHT?
DIE?
YOU'RE NOWHERE NEAR TOUGH ENOUGH TO KILL *ME,* MARKO.

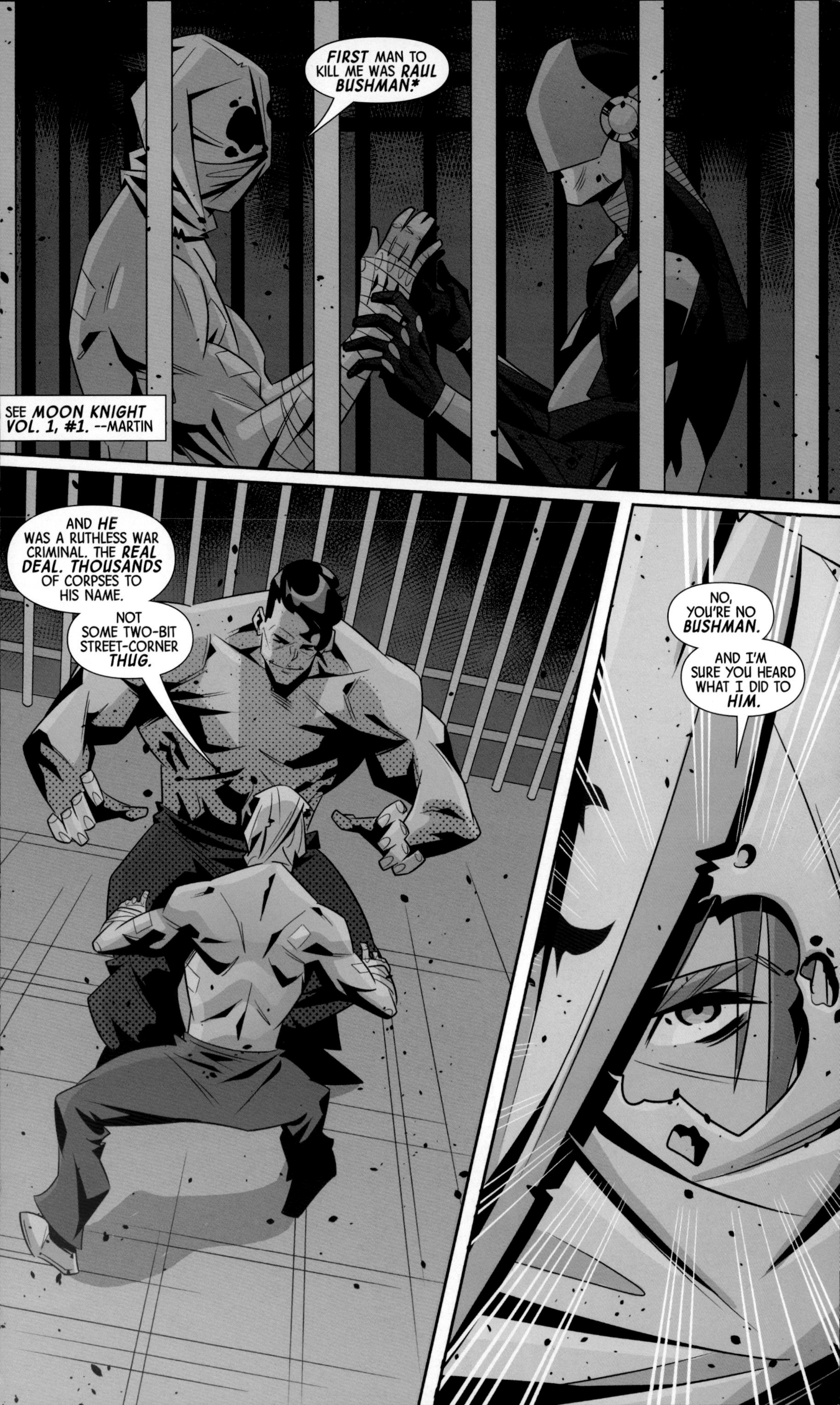
FIRST MAN TO KILL ME WAS RAUL BUSHMAN.*
SEE MOON KNIGHT VOL. 1, #1. --MARTIN
AND HE WAS A RUTHLESS WAR CRIMINAL. THE REAL DEAL. THOUSANDS OF CORPSES TO HIS NAME.
NOT SOME TWO-BIT STREET-CORNER THUG.
NO, YOU'RE NO BUSHMAN.
AND I'M SURE YOU HEARD WHAT I DID TO HIM.

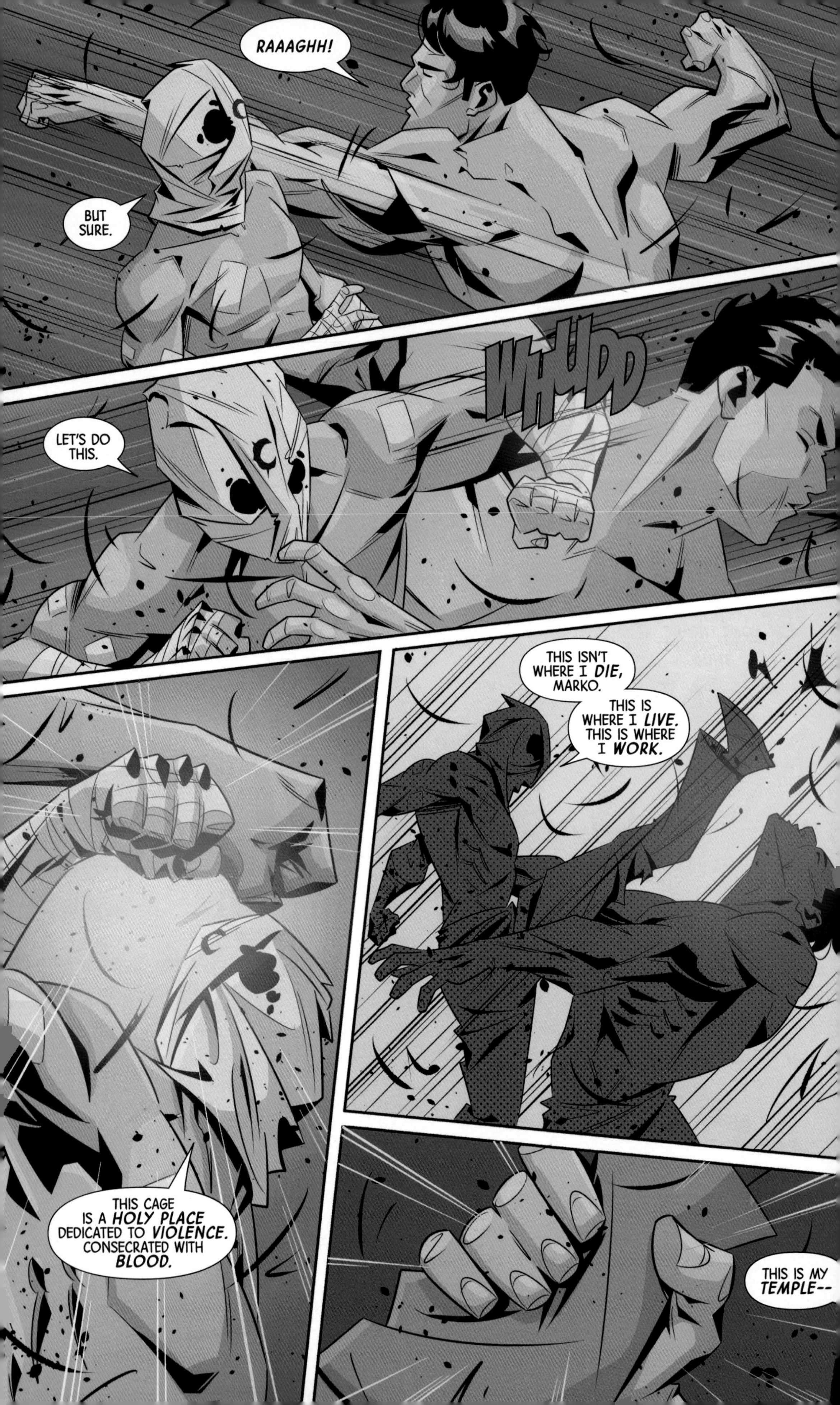
RAAAGHH!
BUT SURE.
WHUDD
LET'S DO THIS.
THIS ISN'T WHERE I *DIE*, MARKO.
THIS IS WHERE I *LIVE.* THIS IS WHERE I *WORK.*
THIS CAGE IS A *HOLY PLACE* DEDICATED TO *VIOLENCE.* CONSECRATED WITH *BLOOD.*
THIS IS MY *TEMPLE--*

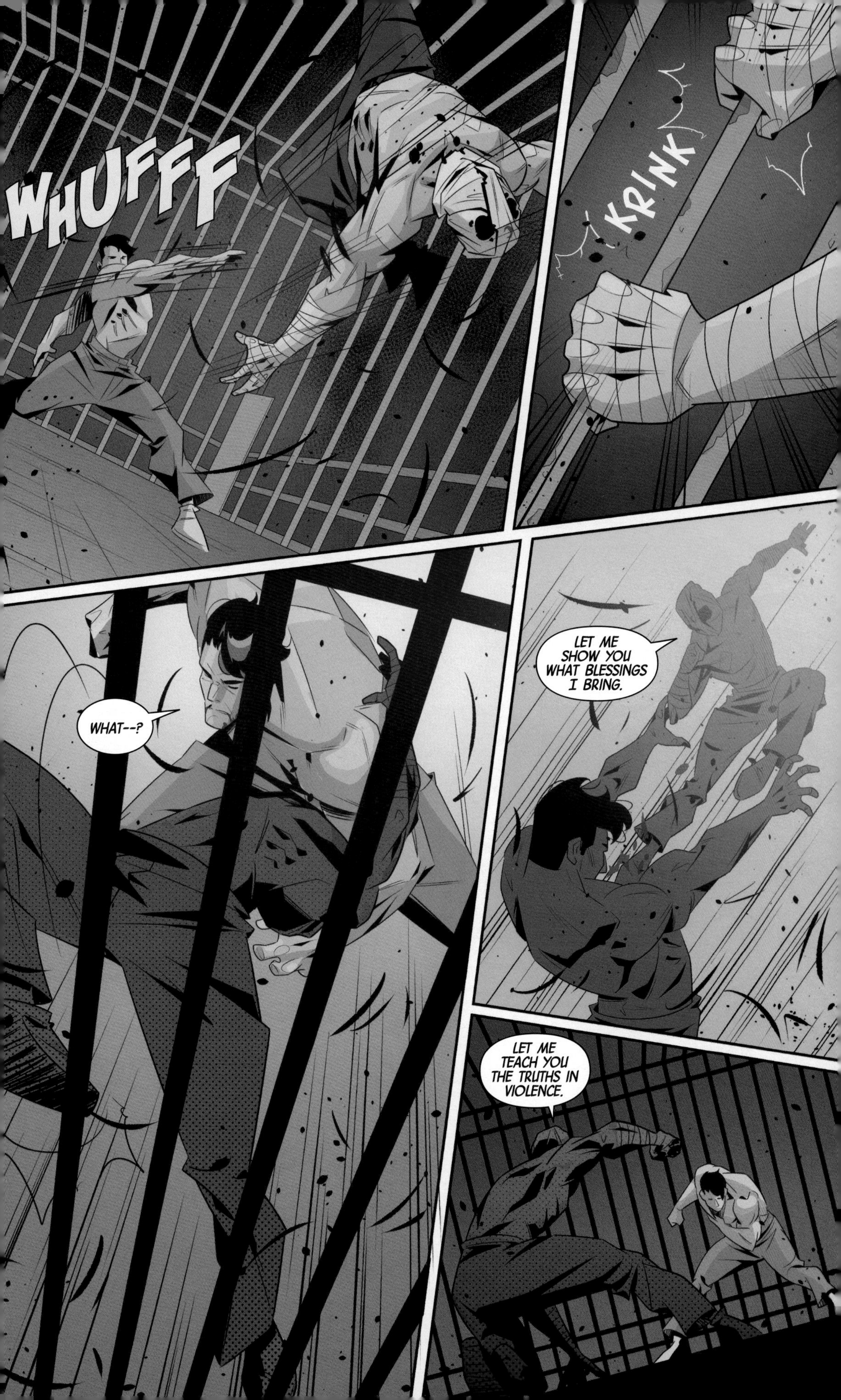
WHUFFF
KRINK
WHAT--?
LET ME SHOW YOU WHAT BLESSINGS I BRING.
LET ME TEACH YOU THE TRUTHS IN VIOLENCE.

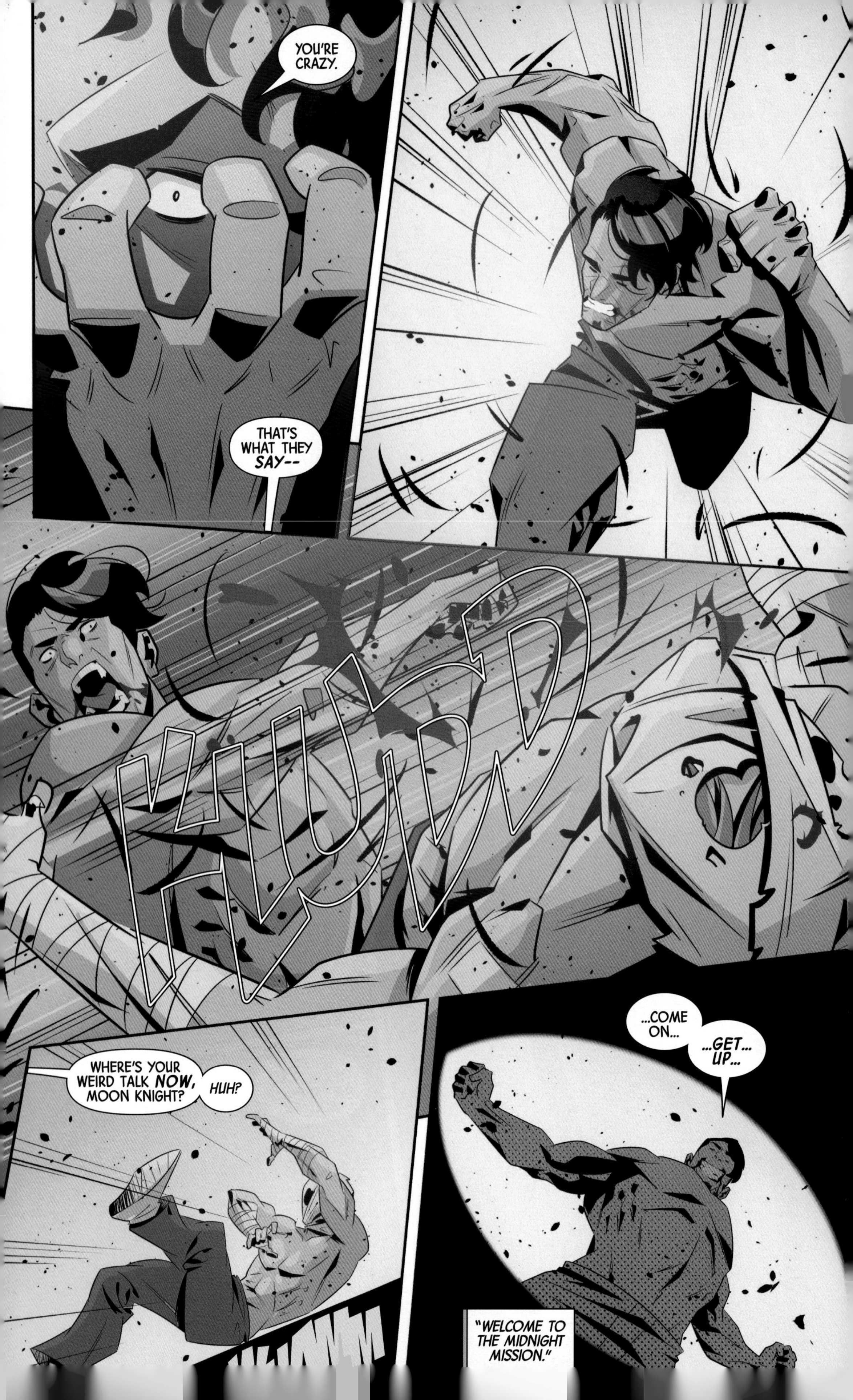
YOU'RE CRAZY.
THAT'S WHAT THEY *SAY*--
WHERE'S YOUR WEIRD TALK *NOW*, MOON KNIGHT?
HUH?
...COME ON...
...GET... UP...
"WELCOME TO THE MIDNIGHT MISSION."

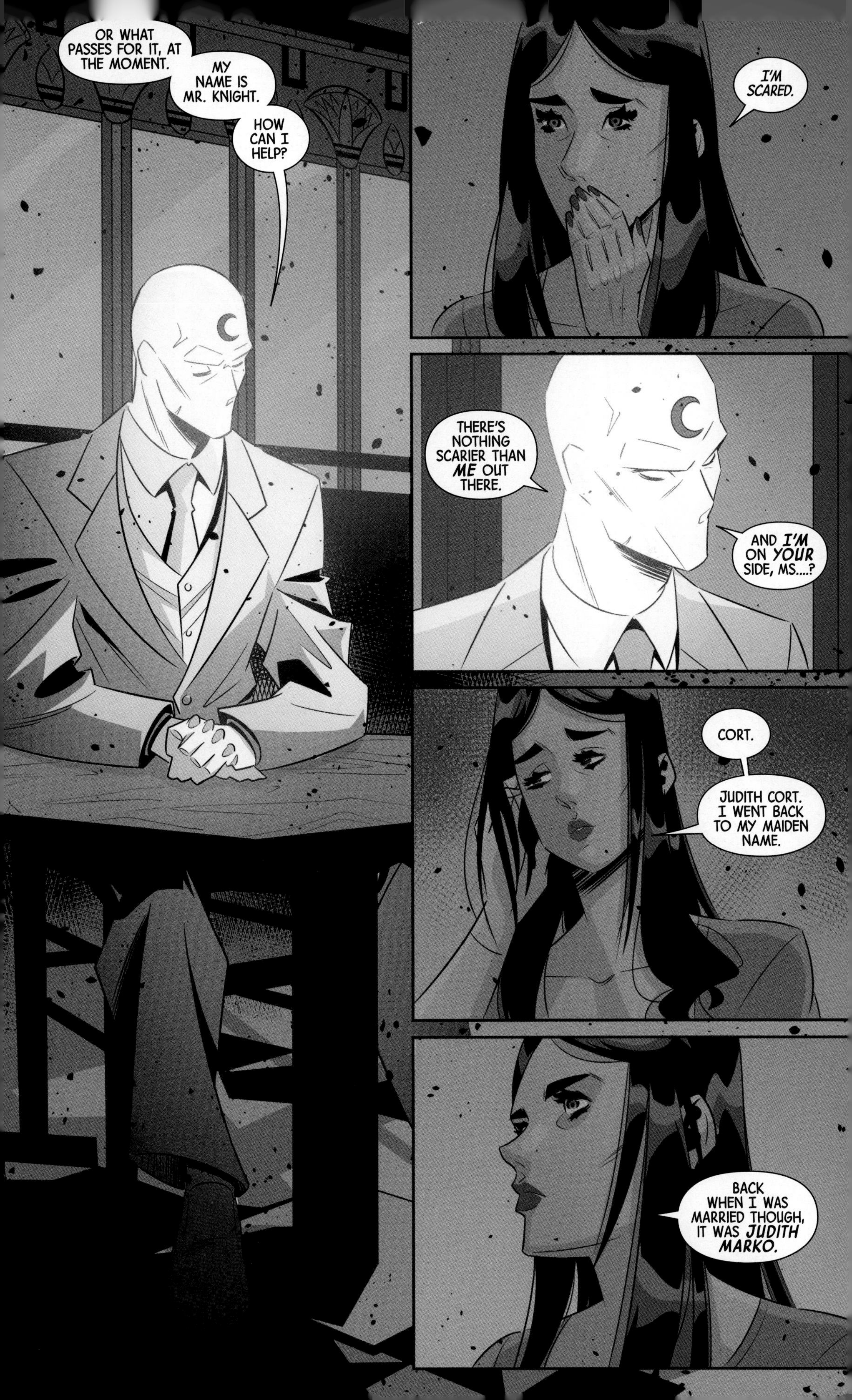

OR WHAT PASSES FOR IT, AT THE MOMENT.
MY NAME IS MR. KNIGHT.
HOW CAN I HELP?
I'M SCARED.
THERE'S NOTHING SCARIER THAN *ME* OUT THERE.
AND *I'M* ON *YOUR* SIDE, MS....?
CORT.
JUDITH CORT. I WENT BACK TO MY MAIDEN NAME.
BACK WHEN I WAS MARRIED THOUGH, IT WAS *JUDITH MARKO.*

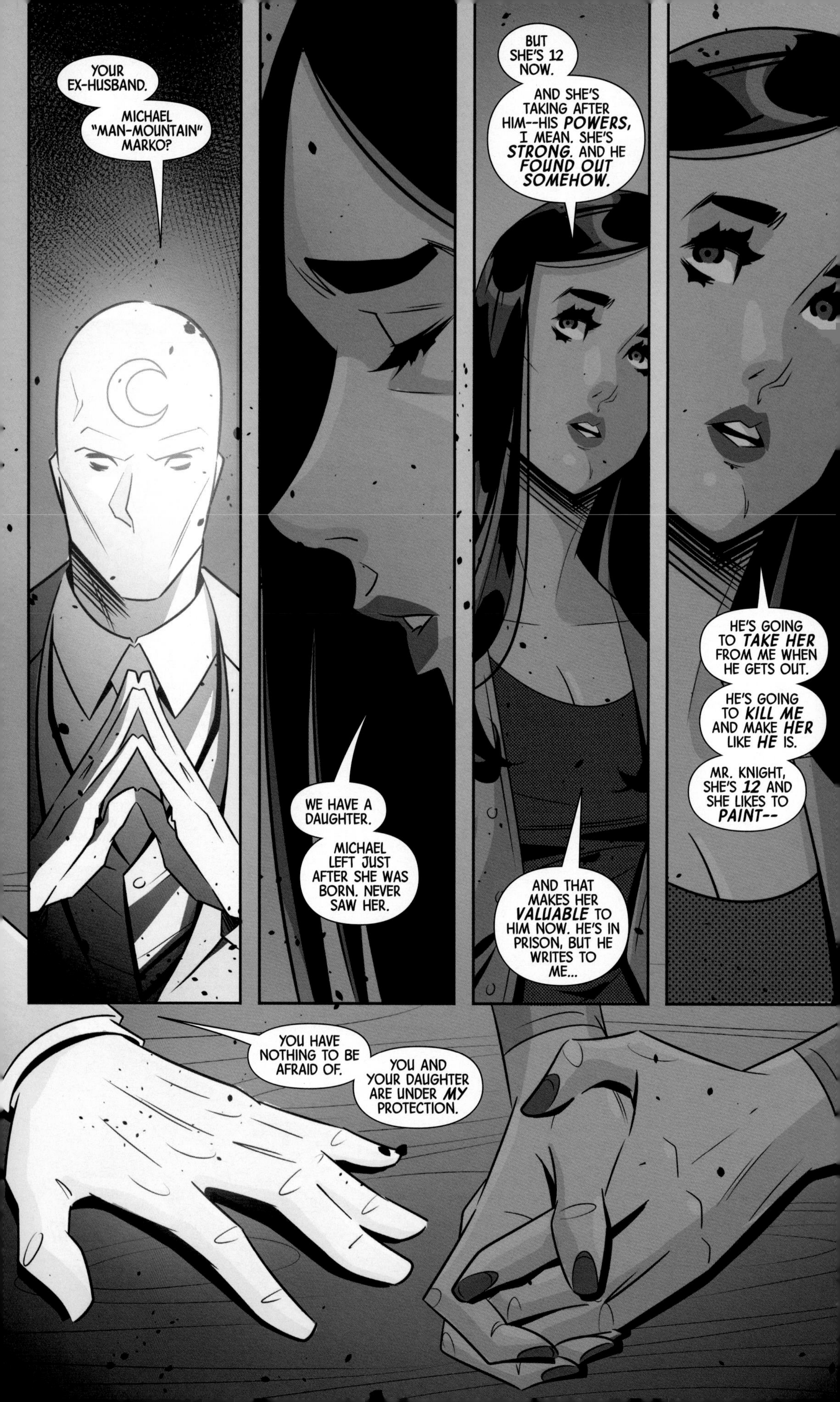
YOUR EX-HUSBAND.
MICHAEL "MAN-MOUNTAIN" MARKO?
WE HAVE A DAUGHTER.
MICHAEL LEFT JUST AFTER SHE WAS BORN. NEVER SAW HER.
BUT SHE'S 12 NOW.
AND SHE'S TAKING AFTER HIM--HIS POWERS, I MEAN. SHE'S STRONG. AND HE FOUND OUT SOMEHOW.
AND THAT MAKES HER VALUABLE TO HIM NOW. HE'S IN PRISON, BUT HE WRITES TO ME...
HE'S GOING TO TAKE HER FROM ME WHEN HE GETS OUT.
HE'S GOING TO KILL ME AND MAKE HER LIKE HE IS.
MR. KNIGHT, SHE'S 12 AND SHE LIKES TO PAINT--
YOU HAVE NOTHING TO BE AFRAID OF.
YOU AND YOUR DAUGHTER ARE UNDER MY PROTECTION.

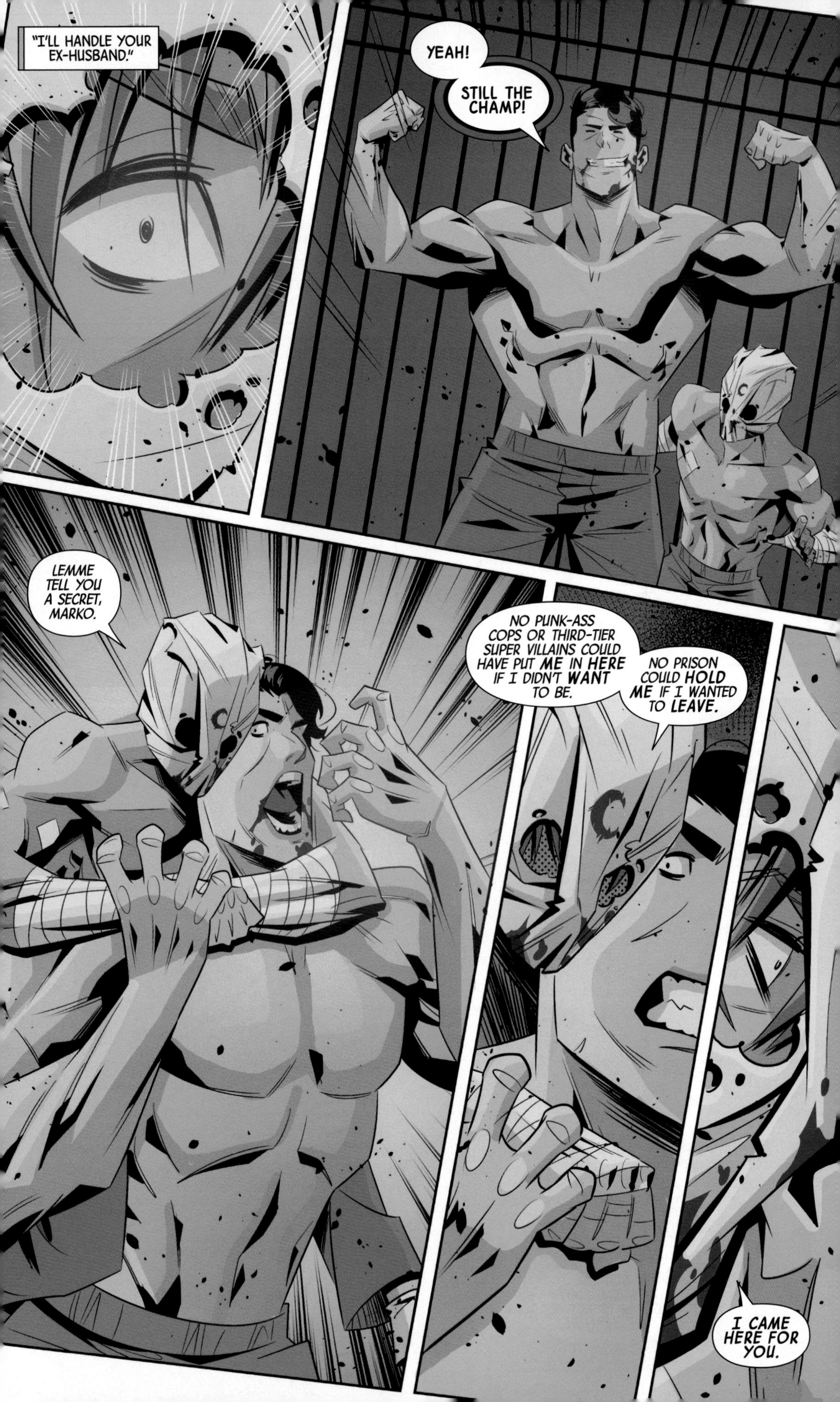
"I'LL HANDLE YOUR EX-HUSBAND."
YEAH!
STILL THE CHAMP!
LEMME TELL YOU A SECRET, MARKO.
NO PUNK-ASS COPS OR THIRD-TIER SUPER VILLAINS COULD HAVE PUT ME IN HERE IF I DIDN'T WANT TO BE.
NO PRISON COULD HOLD ME IF I WANTED TO LEAVE.
I CAME HERE FOR YOU.

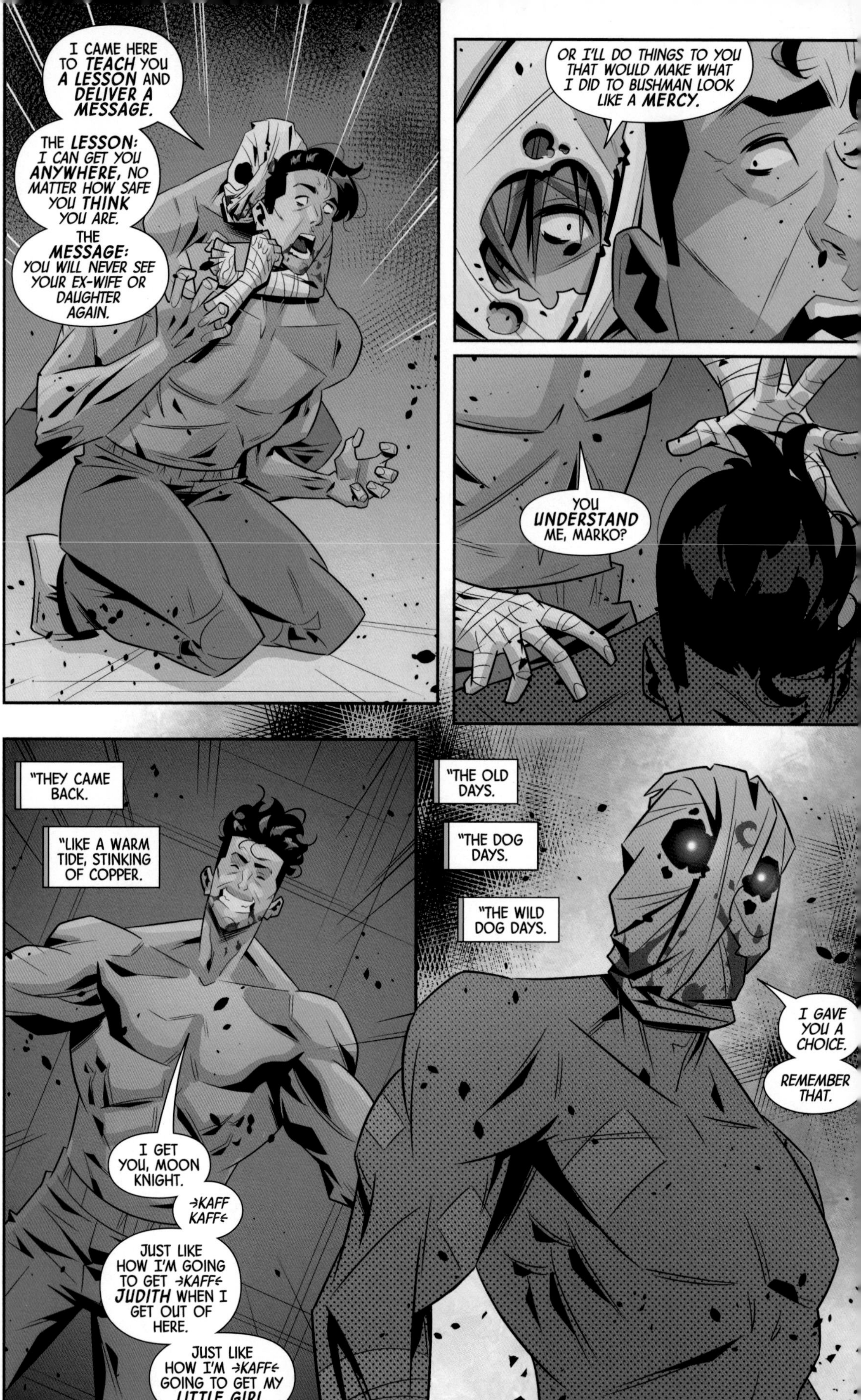

I CAME HERE TO TEACH YOU A LESSON AND DELIVER A MESSAGE.
THE LESSON: I CAN GET YOU ANYWHERE, NO MATTER HOW SAFE YOU THINK YOU ARE.
THE MESSAGE: YOU WILL NEVER SEE YOUR EX-WIFE OR DAUGHTER AGAIN.
OR I'LL DO THINGS TO YOU THAT WOULD MAKE WHAT I DID TO BUSHMAN LOOK LIKE A MERCY.
YOU UNDERSTAND ME, MARKO?
"THEY CAME BACK.
"LIKE A WARM TIDE, STINKING OF COPPER.
I GET YOU, MOON KNIGHT.
→KAFF KAFF←
JUST LIKE HOW I'M GOING TO GET →KAFF← JUDITH WHEN I GET OUT OF HERE.
JUST LIKE HOW I'M →KAFF← GOING TO GET MY LITTLE GIRL.
"THE OLD DAYS.
"THE DOG DAYS.
"THE WILD DOG DAYS.
I GAVE YOU A CHOICE.
REMEMBER THAT.

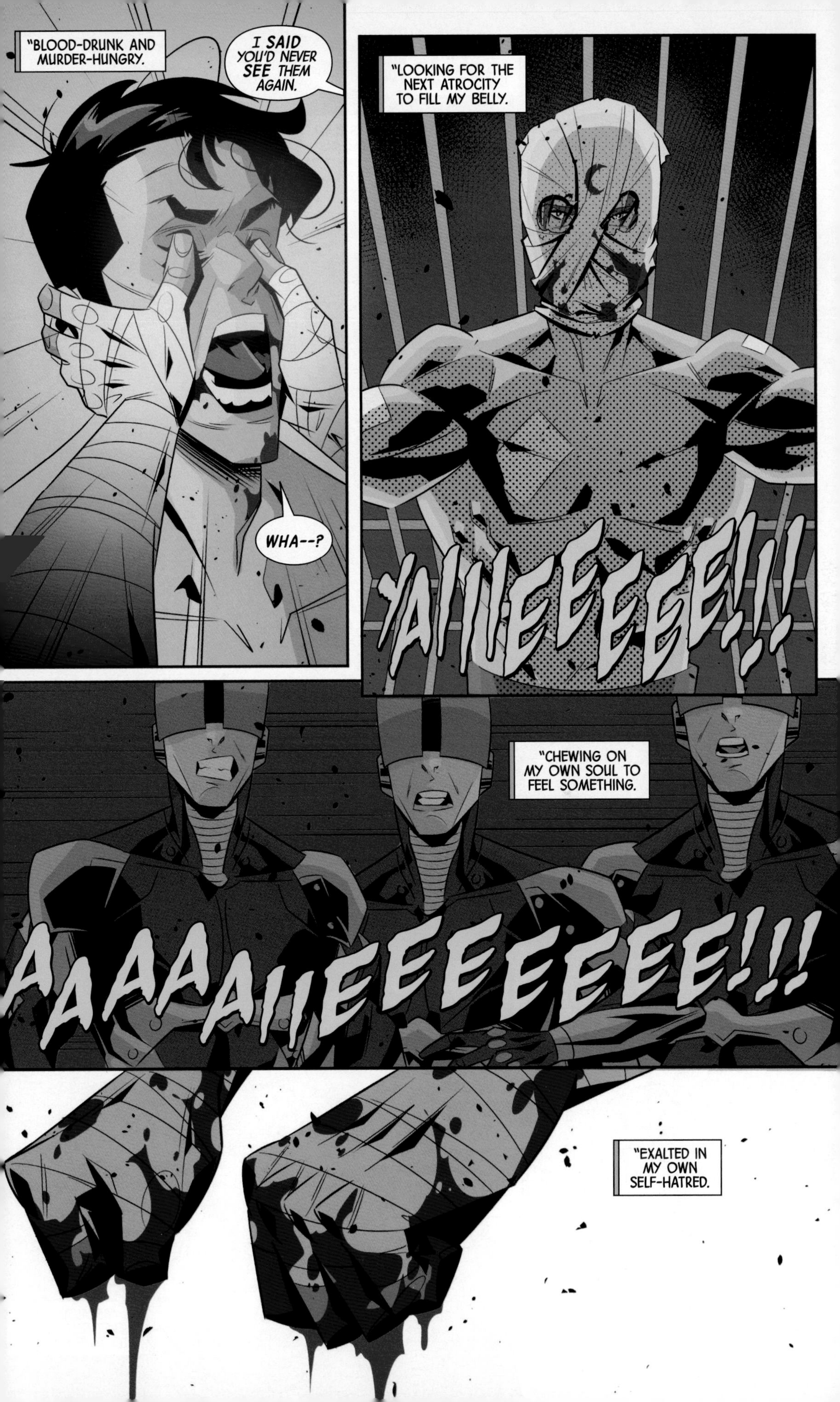
"BLOOD-DRUNK AND MURDER-HUNGRY.
I SAID YOU'D NEVER SEE THEM AGAIN.
WHA--?
"LOOKING FOR THE NEXT ATROCITY TO FILL MY BELLY.
YAIIEEEEEE!!!
"CHEWING ON MY OWN SOUL TO FEEL SOMETHING.
AAAAIIEEEEEEEE!!!
"EXALTED IN MY OWN SELF-HATRED.

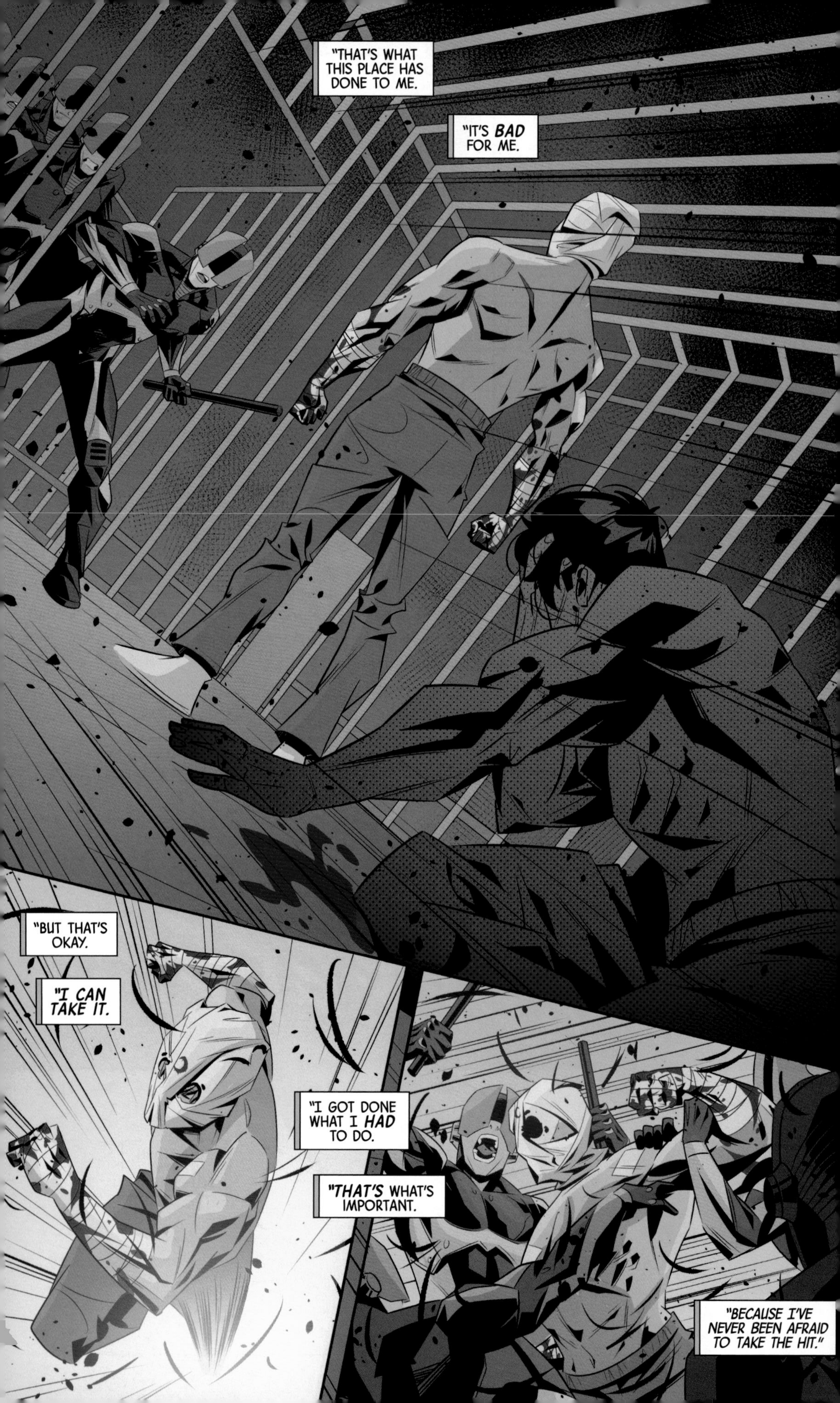

"THAT'S WHAT THIS PLACE HAS DONE TO ME.
"IT'S *BAD* FOR ME.
"BUT THAT'S OKAY.
"I CAN TAKE IT.
"I GOT DONE WHAT I *HAD* TO DO.
"THAT'S WHAT'S IMPORTANT.
"BECAUSE I'VE NEVER BEEN AFRAID TO TAKE THE HIT."

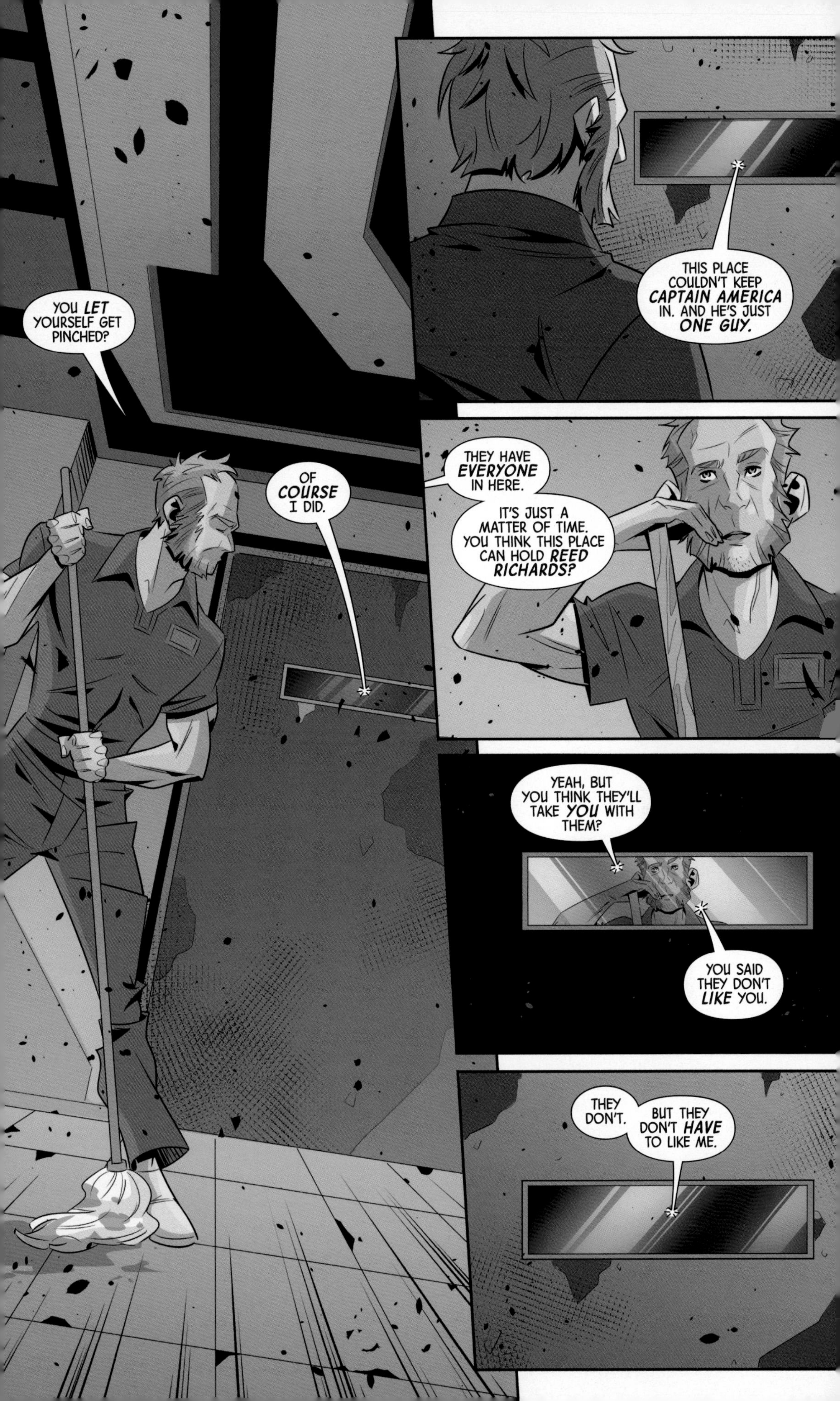
YOU LET YOURSELF GET PINCHED?
THIS PLACE COULDN'T KEEP CAPTAIN AMERICA IN. AND HE'S JUST ONE GUY.
OF COURSE I DID.
THEY HAVE EVERYONE IN HERE.
IT'S JUST A MATTER OF TIME. YOU THINK THIS PLACE CAN HOLD REED RICHARDS?
YEAH, BUT YOU THINK THEY'LL TAKE YOU WITH THEM?
YOU SAID THEY DON'T LIKE YOU.
THEY DON'T.
BUT THEY DON'T HAVE TO LIKE ME.

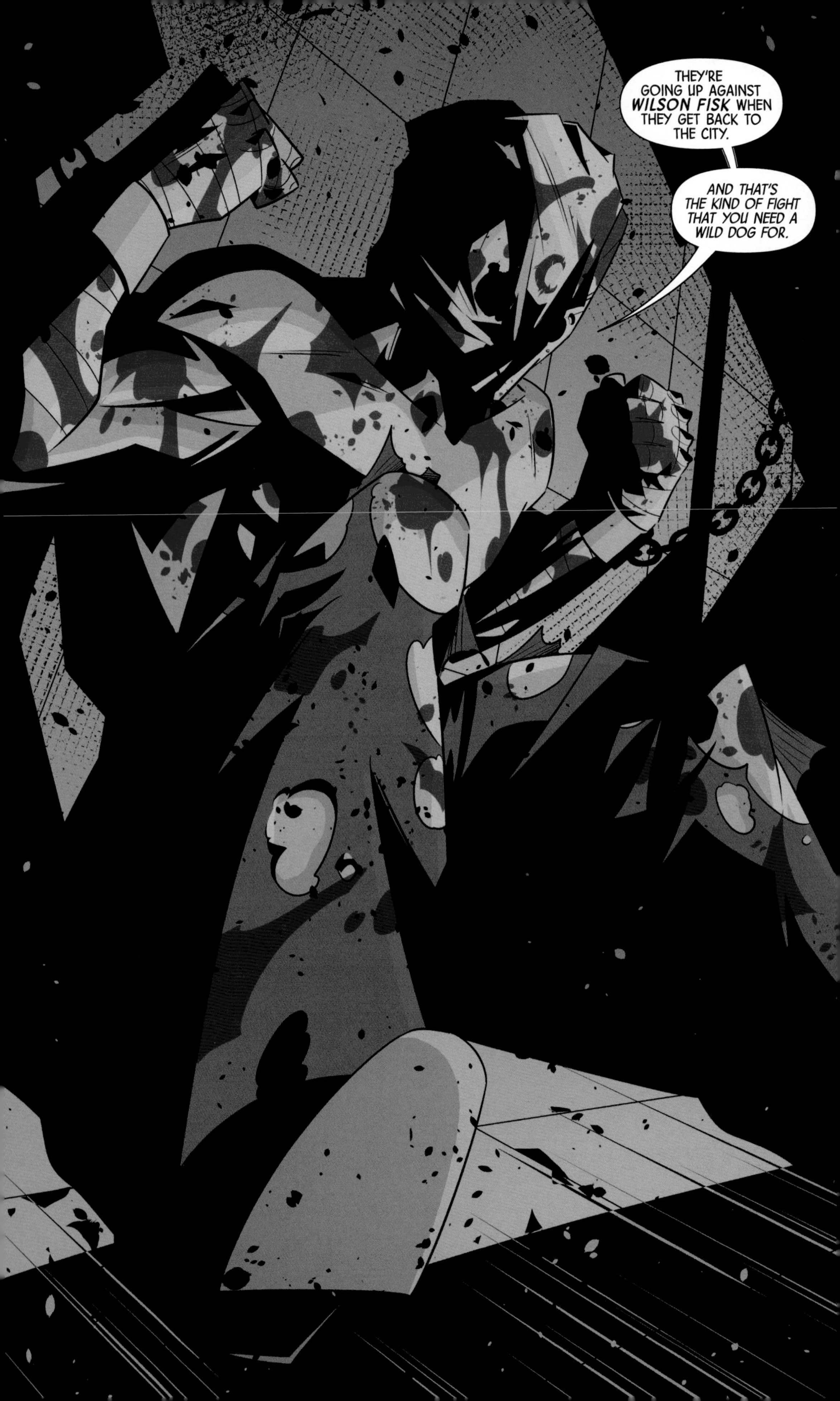
THEY'RE GOING UP AGAINST WILSON FISK WHEN THEY GET BACK TO THE CITY.
AND THAT'S THE KIND OF FIGHT THAT YOU NEED A WILD DOG FOR.

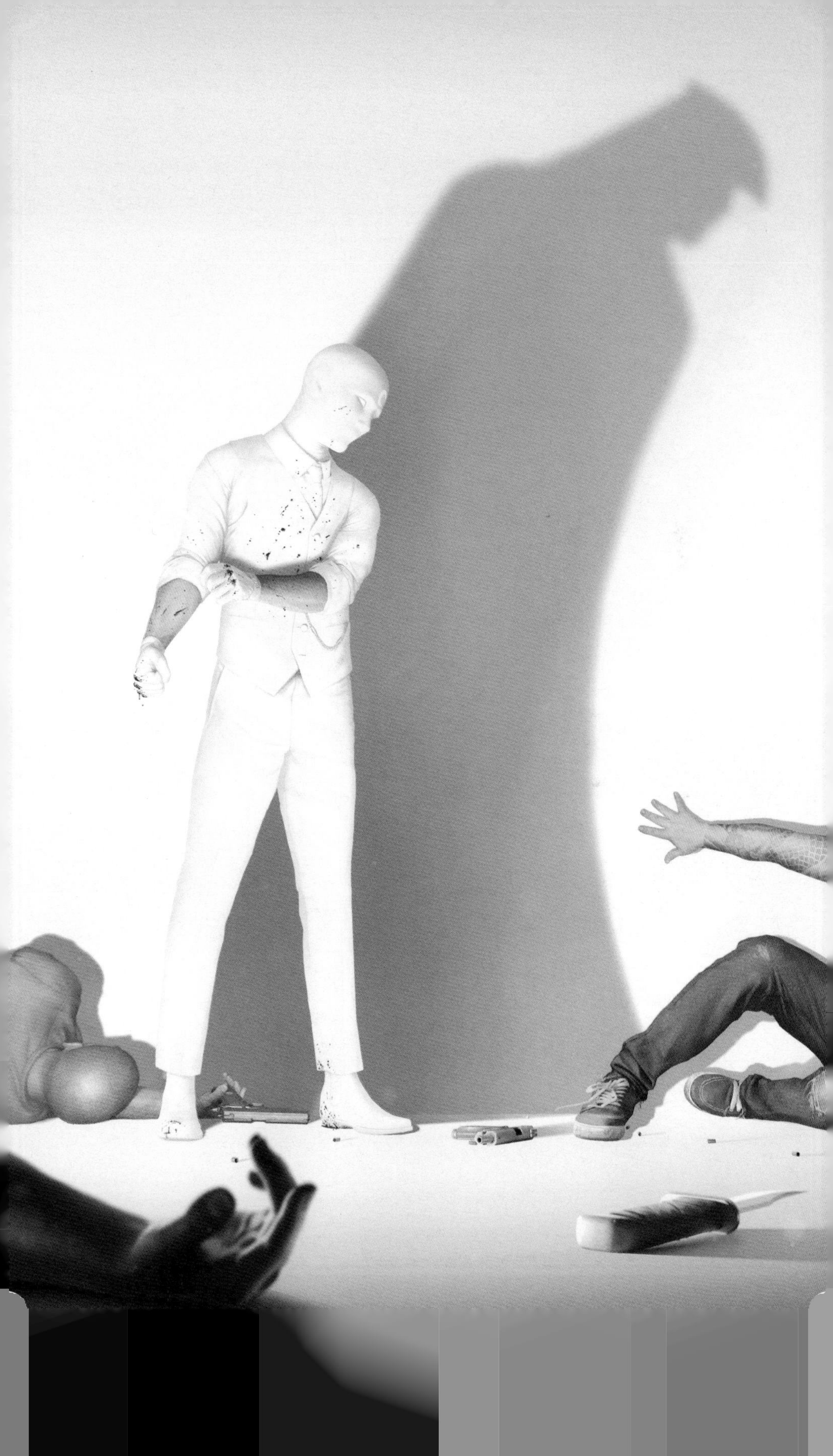

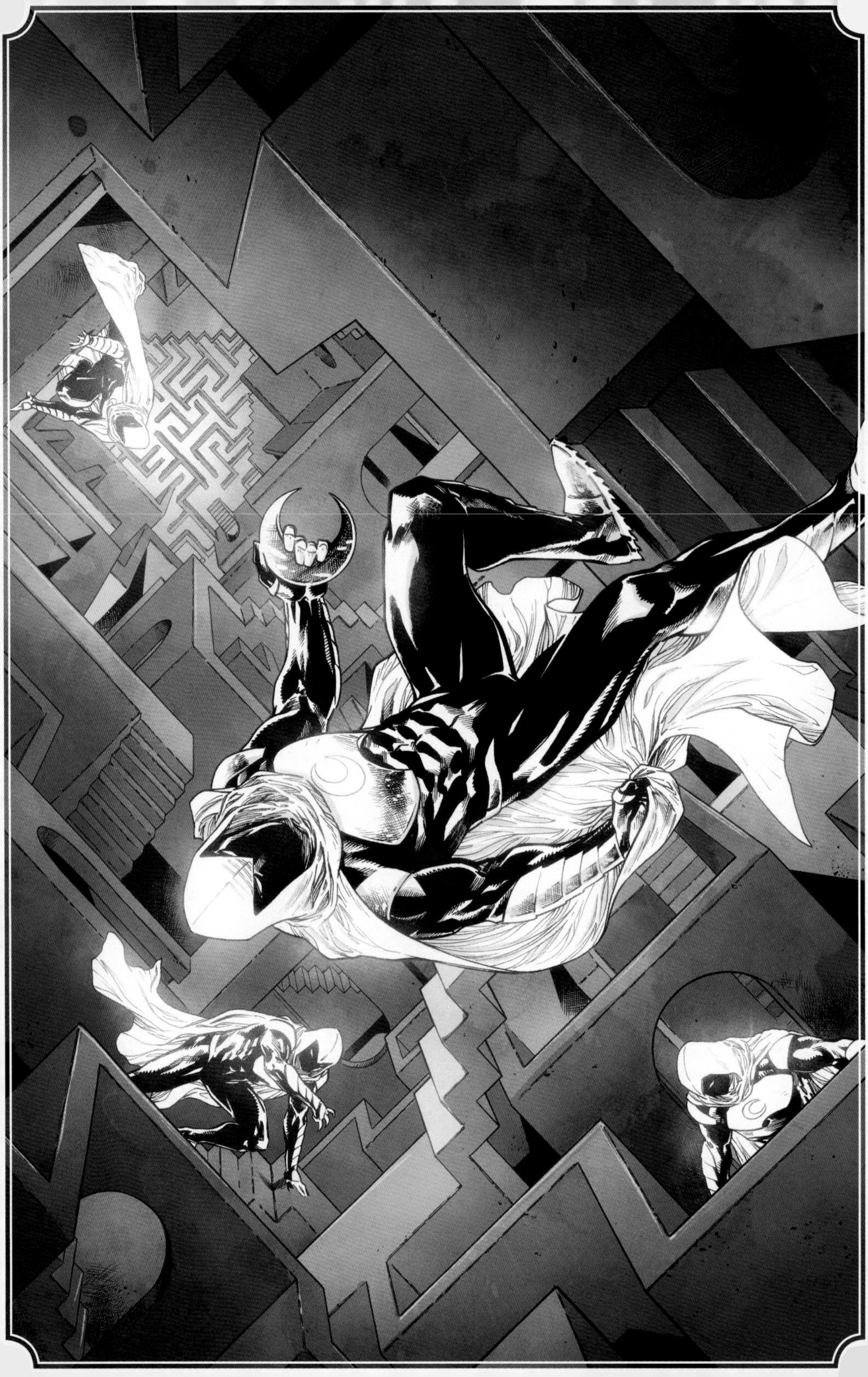

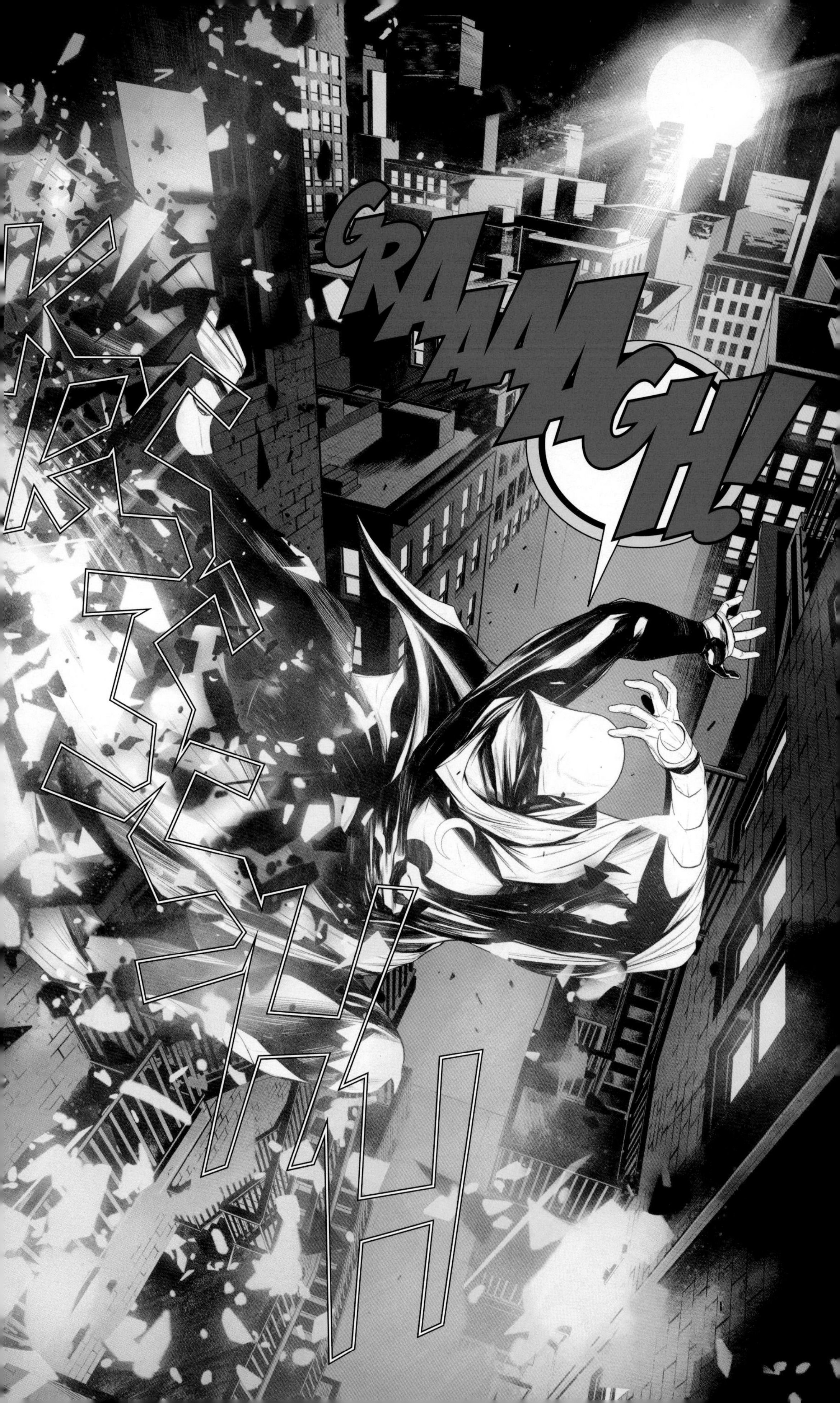
GRAAAAGH!

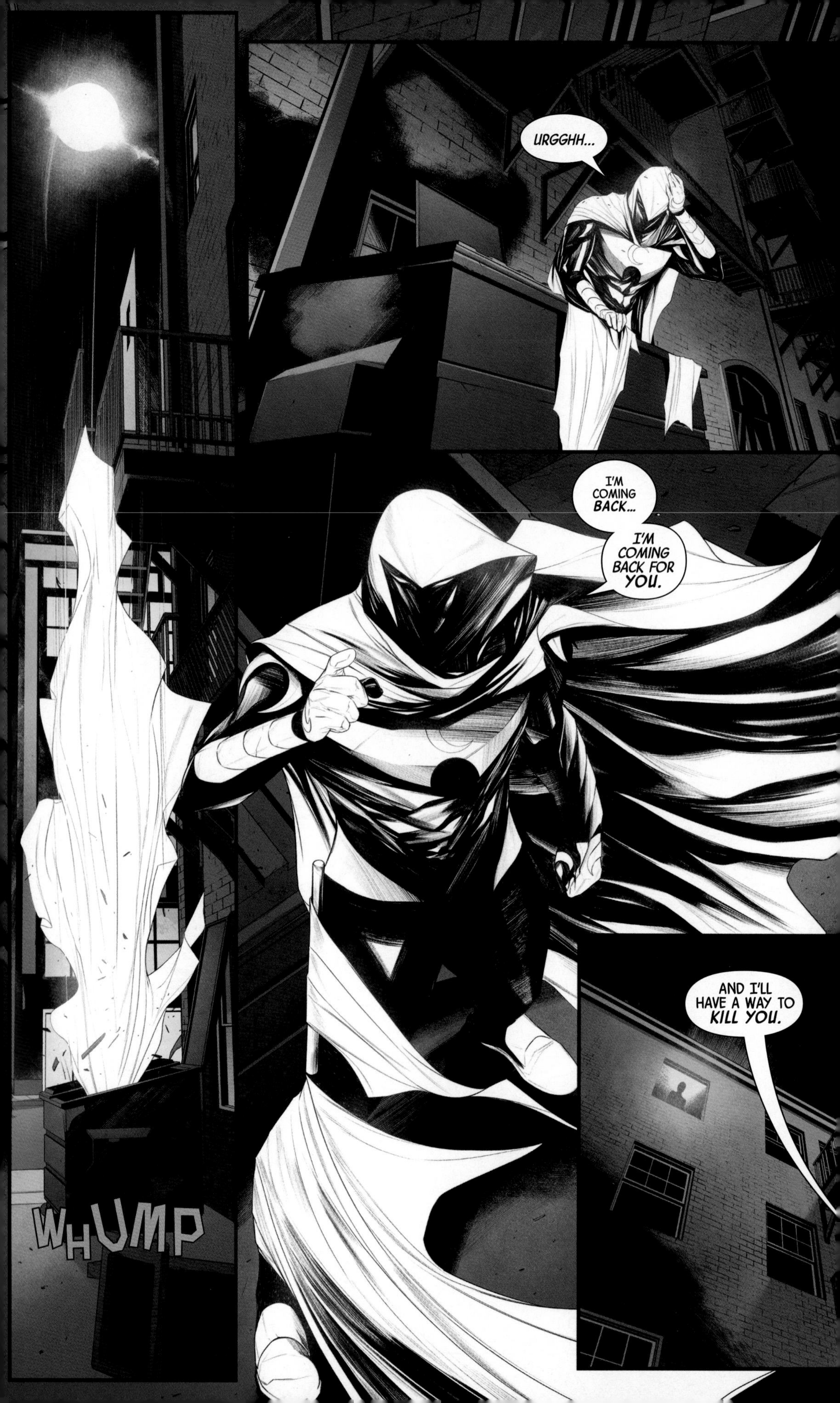
URGGHH...
I'M COMING BACK...
I'M COMING BACK FOR YOU.
WHUMP
AND I'LL HAVE A WAY TO KILL YOU.

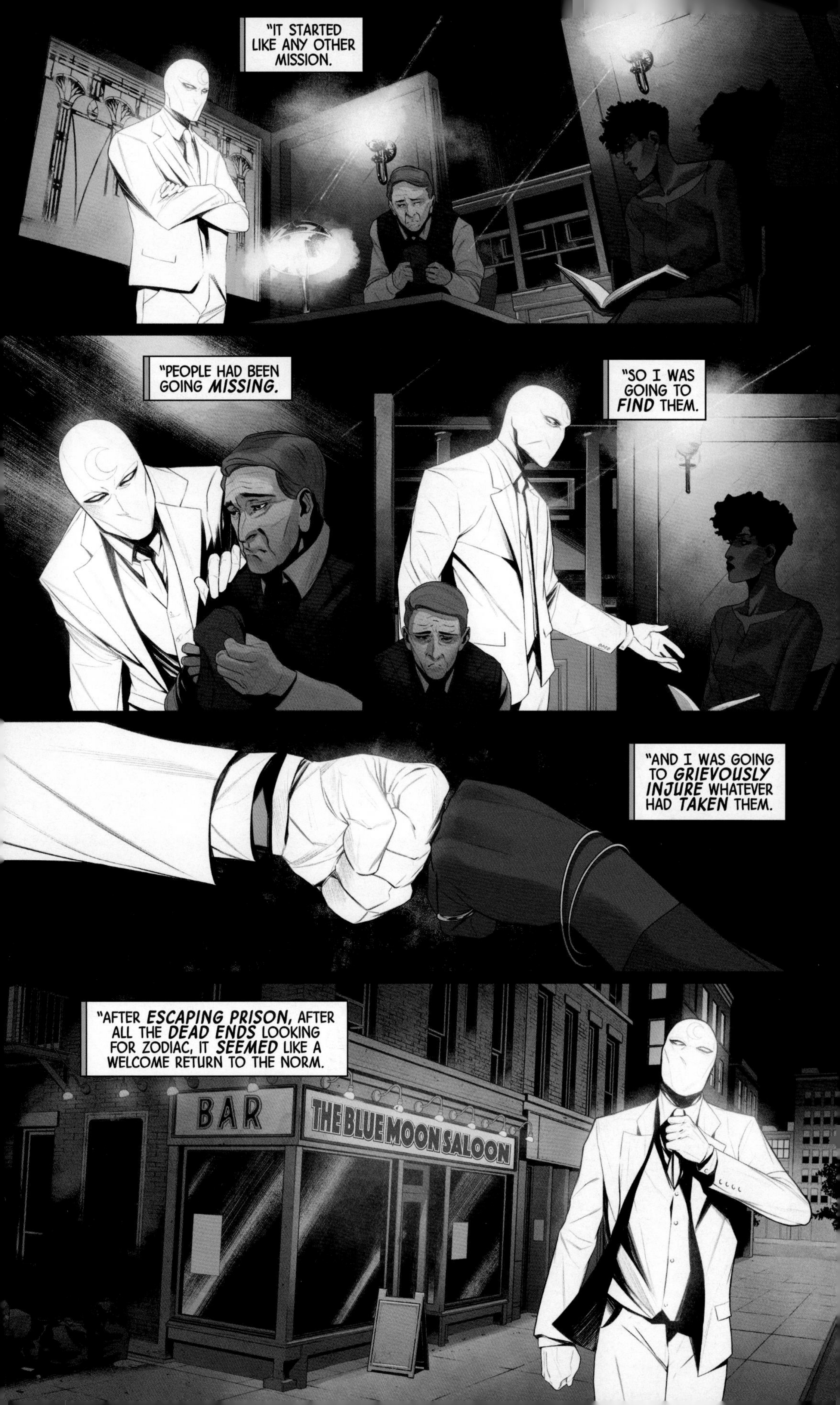
"IT STARTED LIKE ANY OTHER MISSION.
"PEOPLE HAD BEEN GOING MISSING.
"SO I WAS GOING TO FIND THEM.
"AND I WAS GOING TO GRIEVOUSLY INJURE WHATEVER HAD TAKEN THEM.
"AFTER ESCAPING PRISON, AFTER ALL THE DEAD ENDS LOOKING FOR ZODIAC, IT SEEMED LIKE A WELCOME RETURN TO THE NORM.
BAR
THE BLUE MOON SALOON

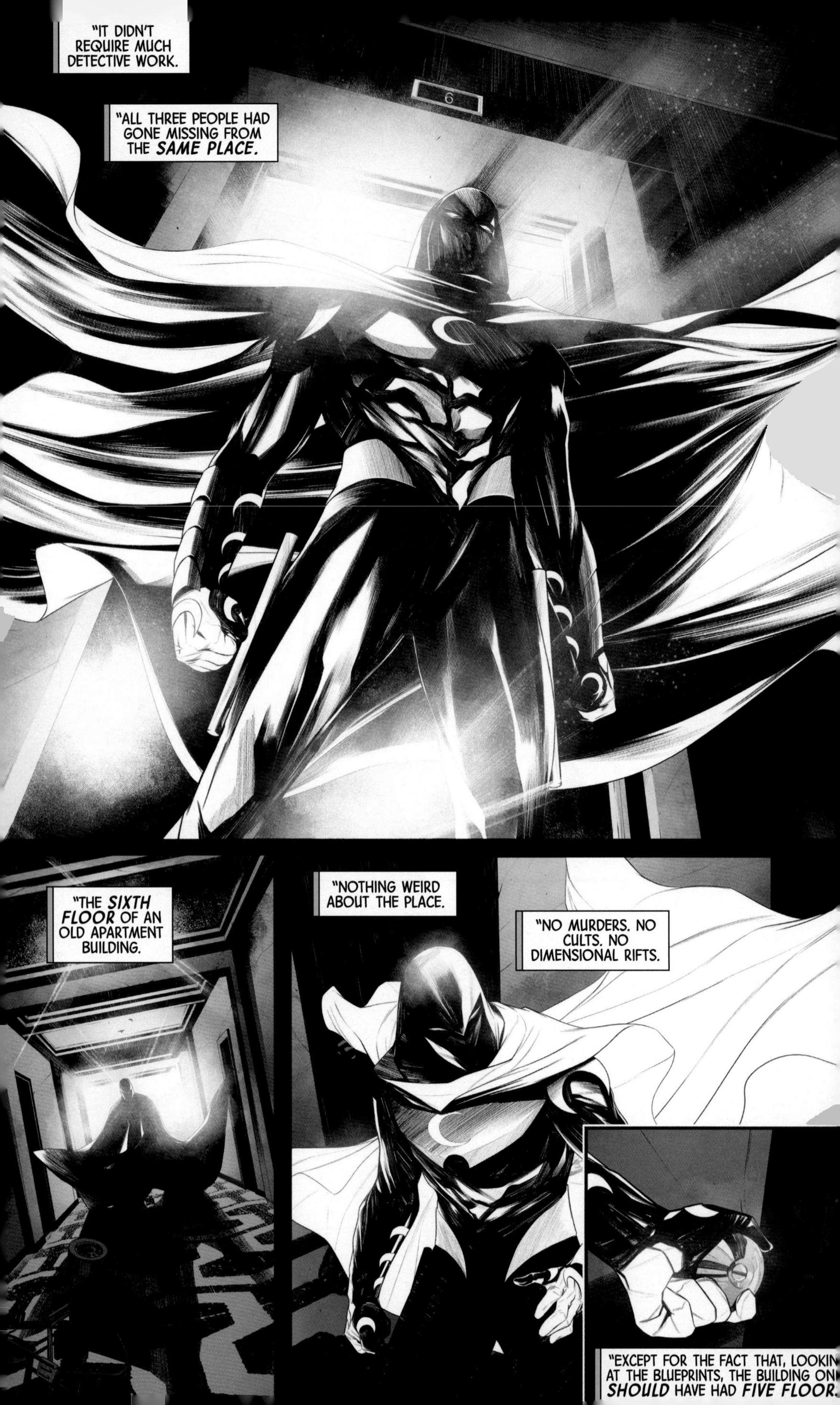
"IT DIDN'T REQUIRE MUCH DETECTIVE WORK.
6
"ALL THREE PEOPLE HAD GONE MISSING FROM THE SAME PLACE.
"THE SIXTH FLOOR OF AN OLD APARTMENT BUILDING.
"NOTHING WEIRD ABOUT THE PLACE.
"NO MURDERS. NO CULTS. NO DIMENSIONAL RIFTS.
"EXCEPT FOR THE FACT THAT, LOOKIN AT THE BLUEPRINTS, THE BUILDING ON SHOULD HAVE HAD FIVE FLOOR.

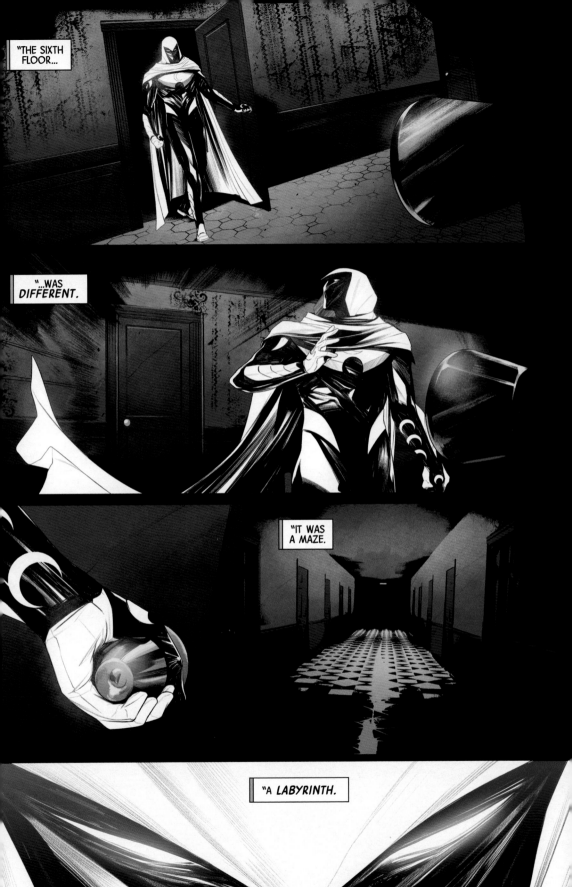

"THE SIXTH FLOOR...

"...WAS DIFFERENT.

"IT WAS A MAZE.

"A LABYRINTH.

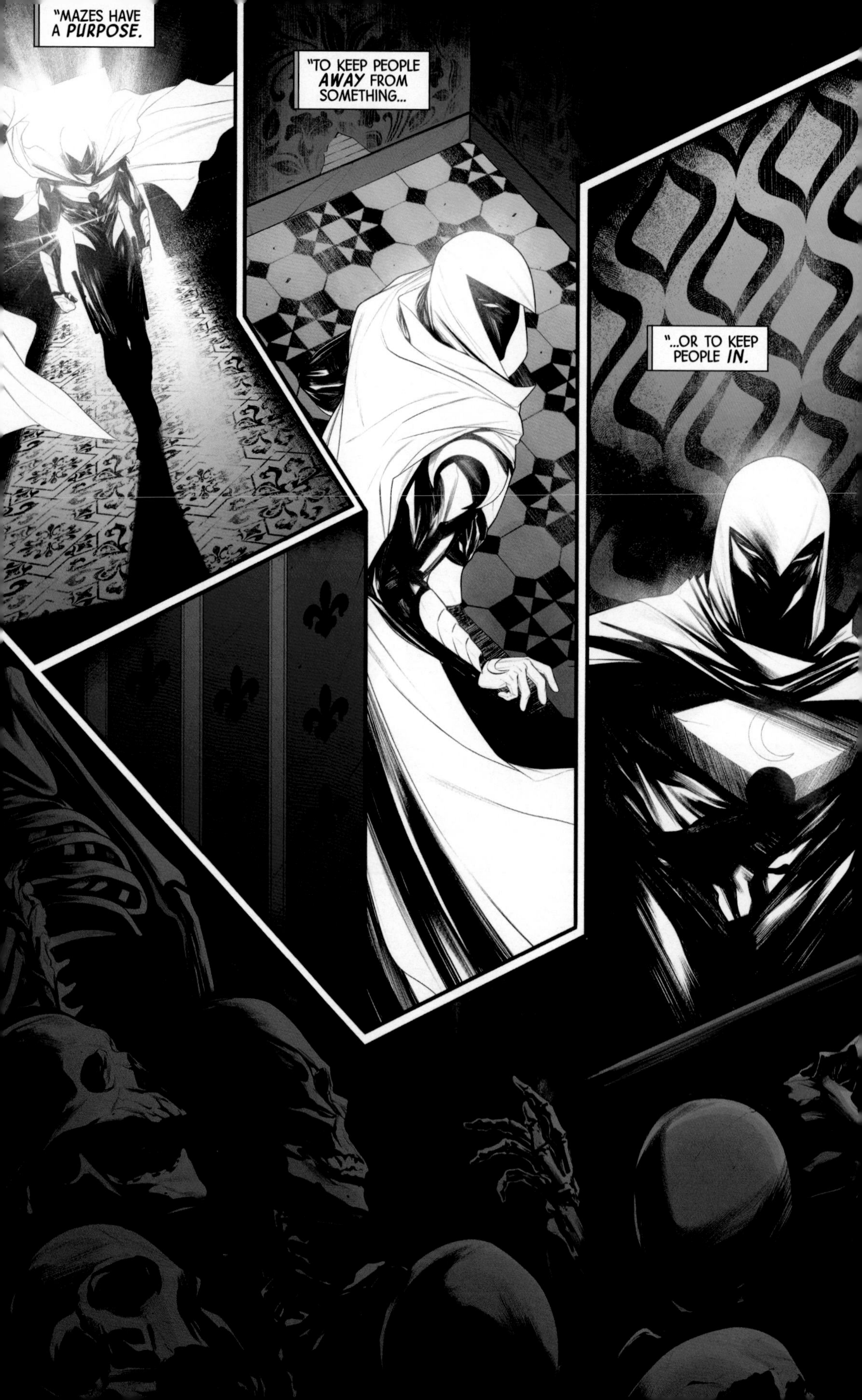
"MAZES HAVE A PURPOSE.
"TO KEEP PEOPLE AWAY FROM SOMETHING...
"...OR TO KEEP PEOPLE IN.

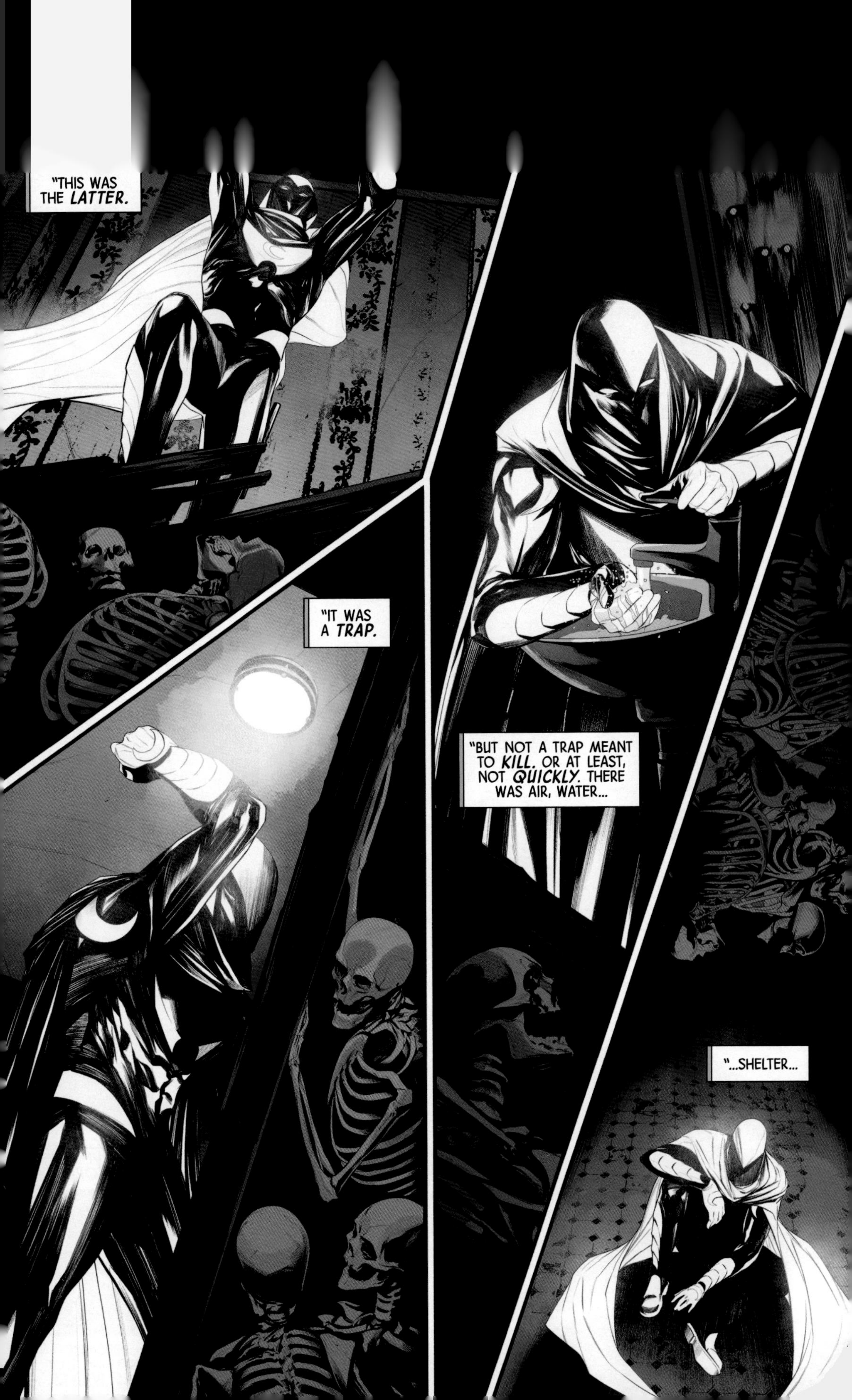
"THIS WAS THE LATTER.
"IT WAS A TRAP.
"BUT NOT A TRAP MEANT TO KILL. OR AT LEAST, NOT QUICKLY. THERE WAS AIR, WATER...
"...SHELTER...

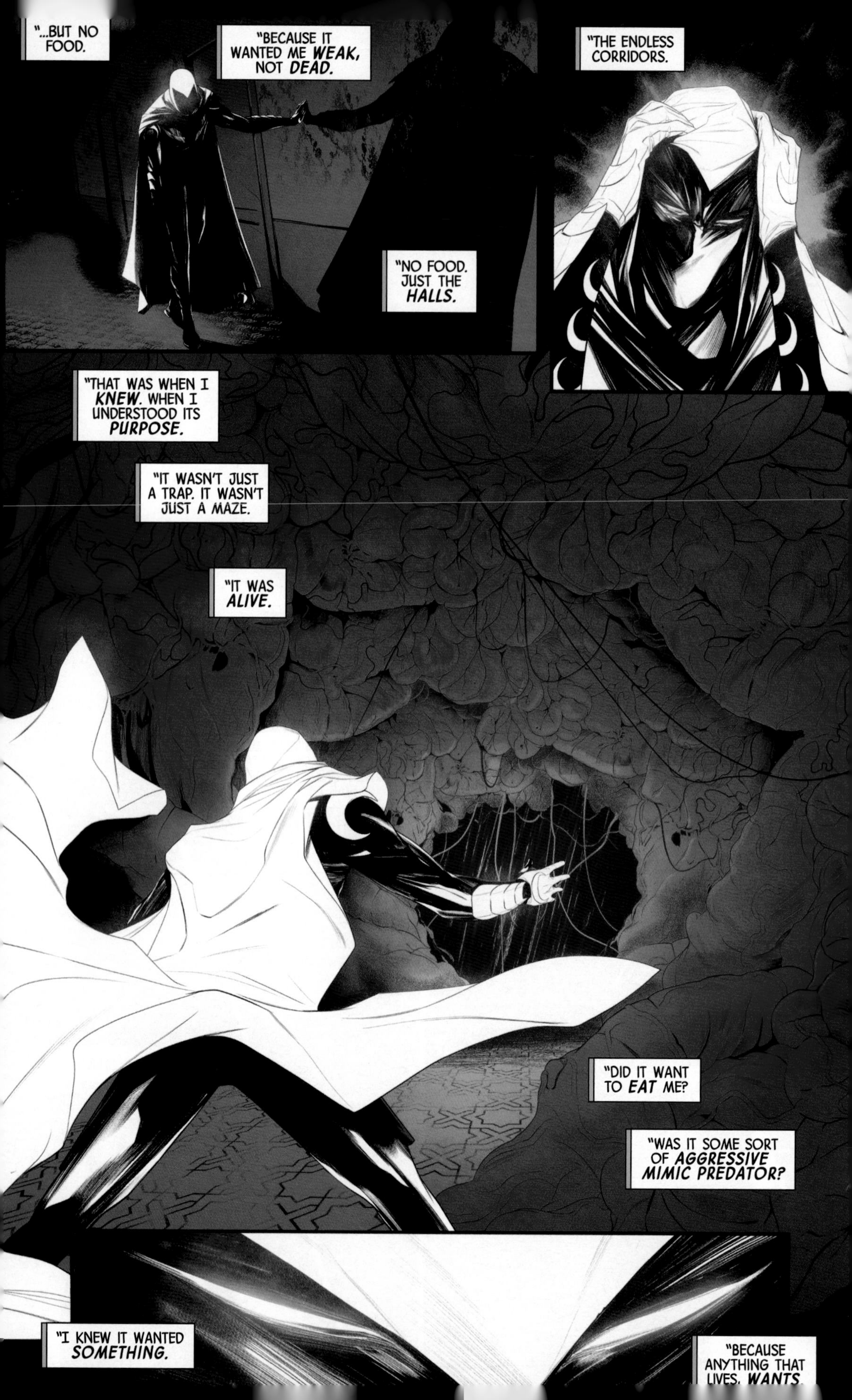
"...BUT NO FOOD.
"BECAUSE IT WANTED ME WEAK, NOT DEAD.
"NO FOOD. JUST THE HALLS.
"THE ENDLESS CORRIDORS.
"THAT WAS WHEN I KNEW. WHEN I UNDERSTOOD ITS PURPOSE.
"IT WASN'T JUST A TRAP. IT WASN'T JUST A MAZE.
"IT WAS ALIVE.
"DID IT WANT TO EAT ME?
"WAS IT SOME SORT OF AGGRESSIVE MIMIC PREDATOR?
"I KNEW IT WANTED SOMETHING.
"BECAUSE ANYTHING THAT LIVES, WANTS.

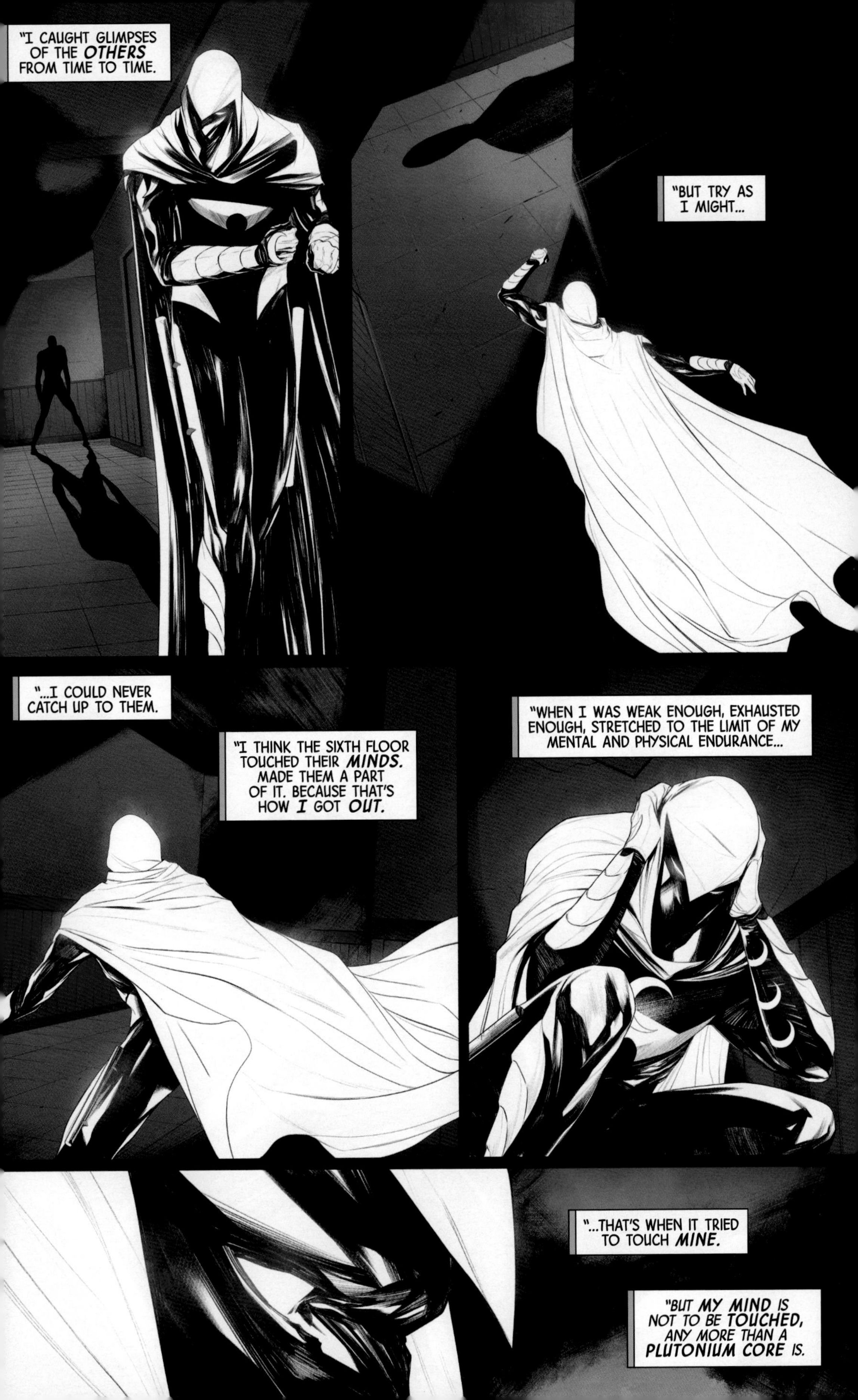
"I CAUGHT GLIMPSES OF THE OTHERS FROM TIME TO TIME.
"BUT TRY AS I MIGHT...
"...I COULD NEVER CATCH UP TO THEM.
"I THINK THE SIXTH FLOOR TOUCHED THEIR MINDS. MADE THEM A PART OF IT. BECAUSE THAT'S HOW I GOT OUT.
"WHEN I WAS WEAK ENOUGH, EXHAUSTED ENOUGH, STRETCHED TO THE LIMIT OF MY MENTAL AND PHYSICAL ENDURANCE...
"...THAT'S WHEN IT TRIED TO TOUCH MINE.
"BUT MY MIND IS NOT TO BE TOUCHED, ANY MORE THAN A PLUTONIUM CORE IS.

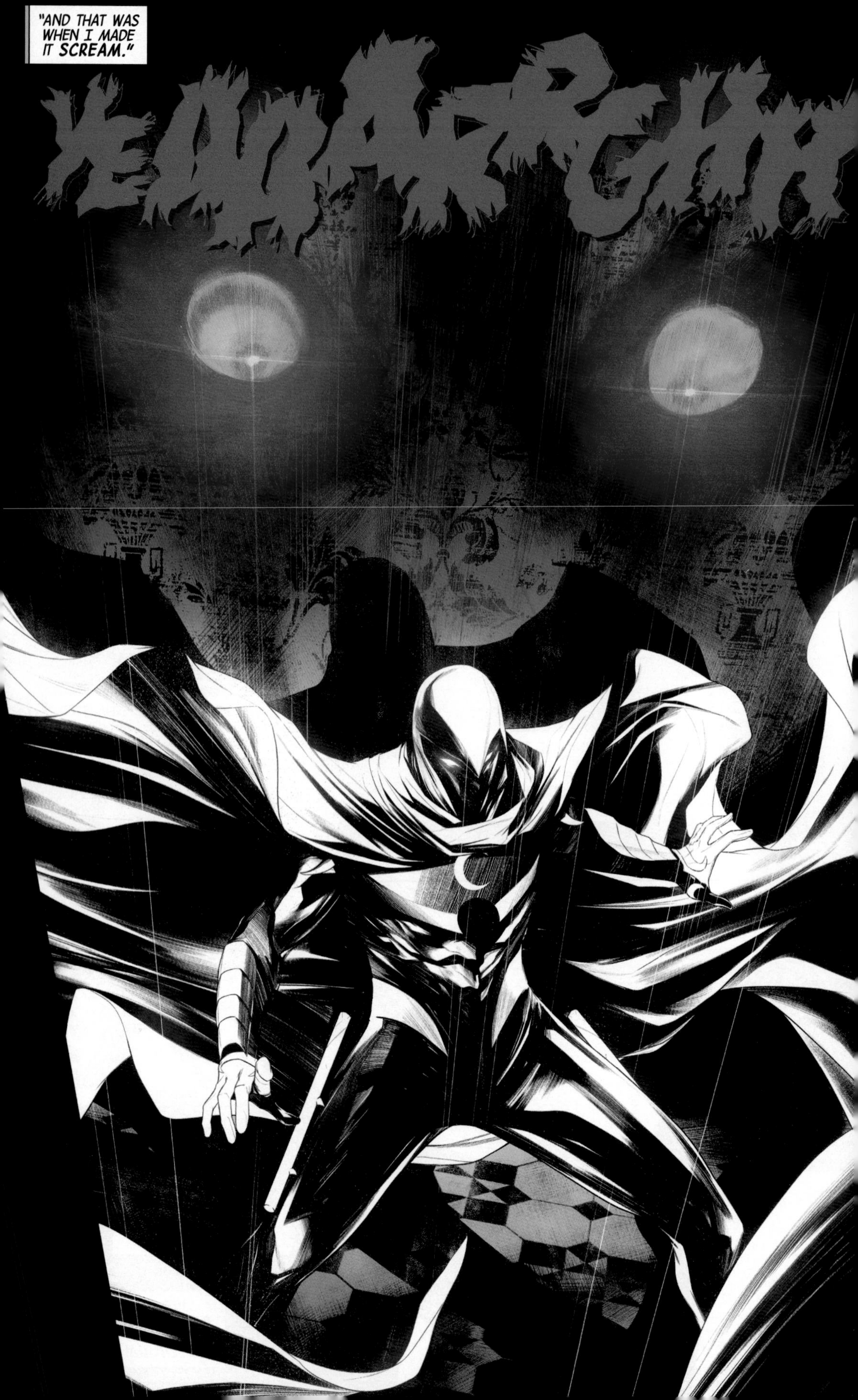
"AND THAT WAS WHEN I MADE IT SCREAM."

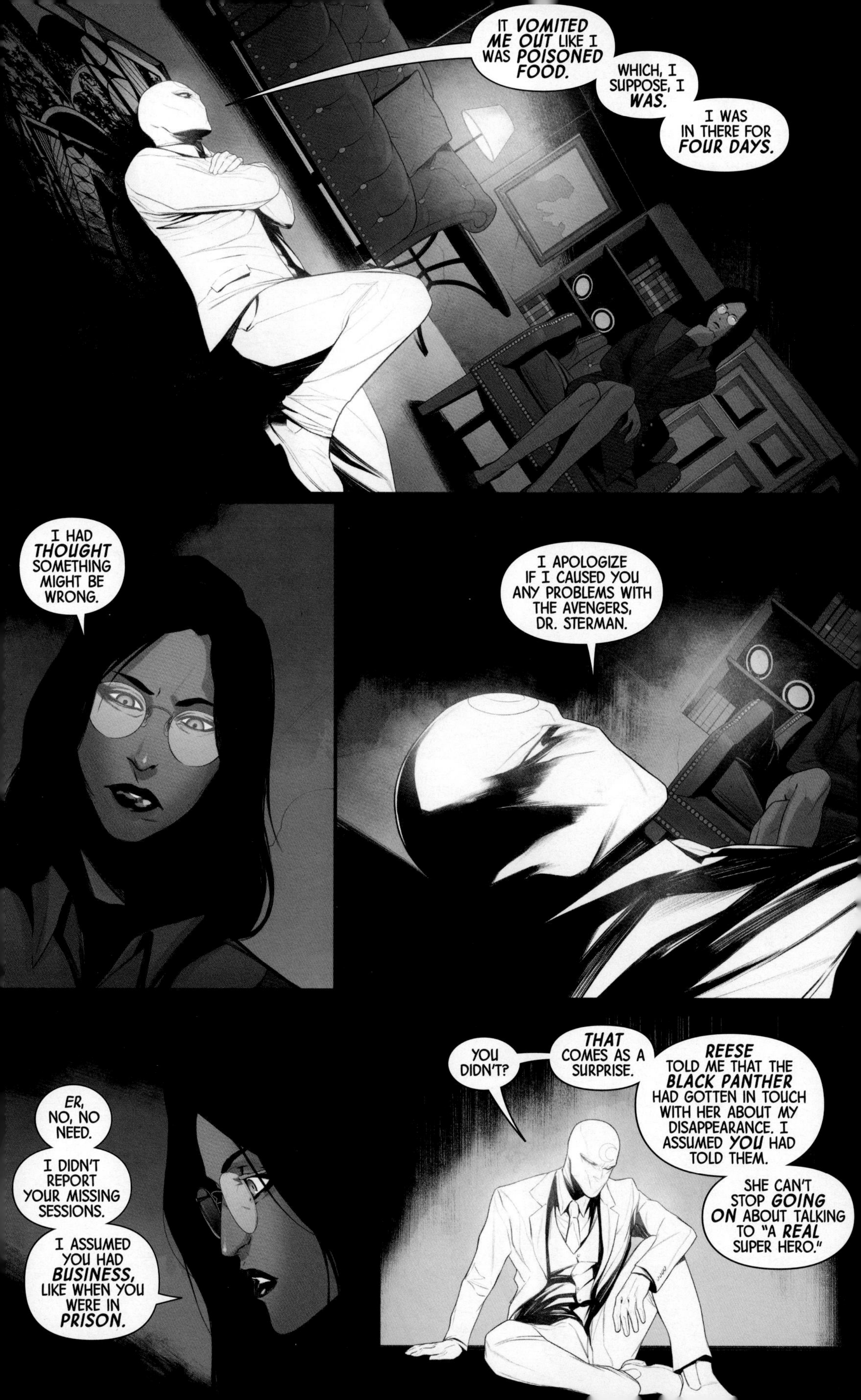

IT VOMITED ME OUT LIKE I WAS POISONED FOOD.
WHICH, I SUPPOSE, I WAS.
I WAS IN THERE FOR FOUR DAYS.
I HAD THOUGHT SOMETHING MIGHT BE WRONG.
I APOLOGIZE IF I CAUSED YOU ANY PROBLEMS WITH THE AVENGERS, DR. STERMAN.
ER, NO, NO NEED.
I DIDN'T REPORT YOUR MISSING SESSIONS.
I ASSUMED YOU HAD BUSINESS, LIKE WHEN YOU WERE IN PRISON.
YOU DIDN'T?
THAT COMES AS A SURPRISE.
REESE TOLD ME THAT THE BLACK PANTHER HAD GOTTEN IN TOUCH WITH HER ABOUT MY DISAPPEARANCE. I ASSUMED YOU HAD TOLD THEM.
SHE CAN'T STOP GOING ON ABOUT TALKING TO "A REAL SUPER HERO."

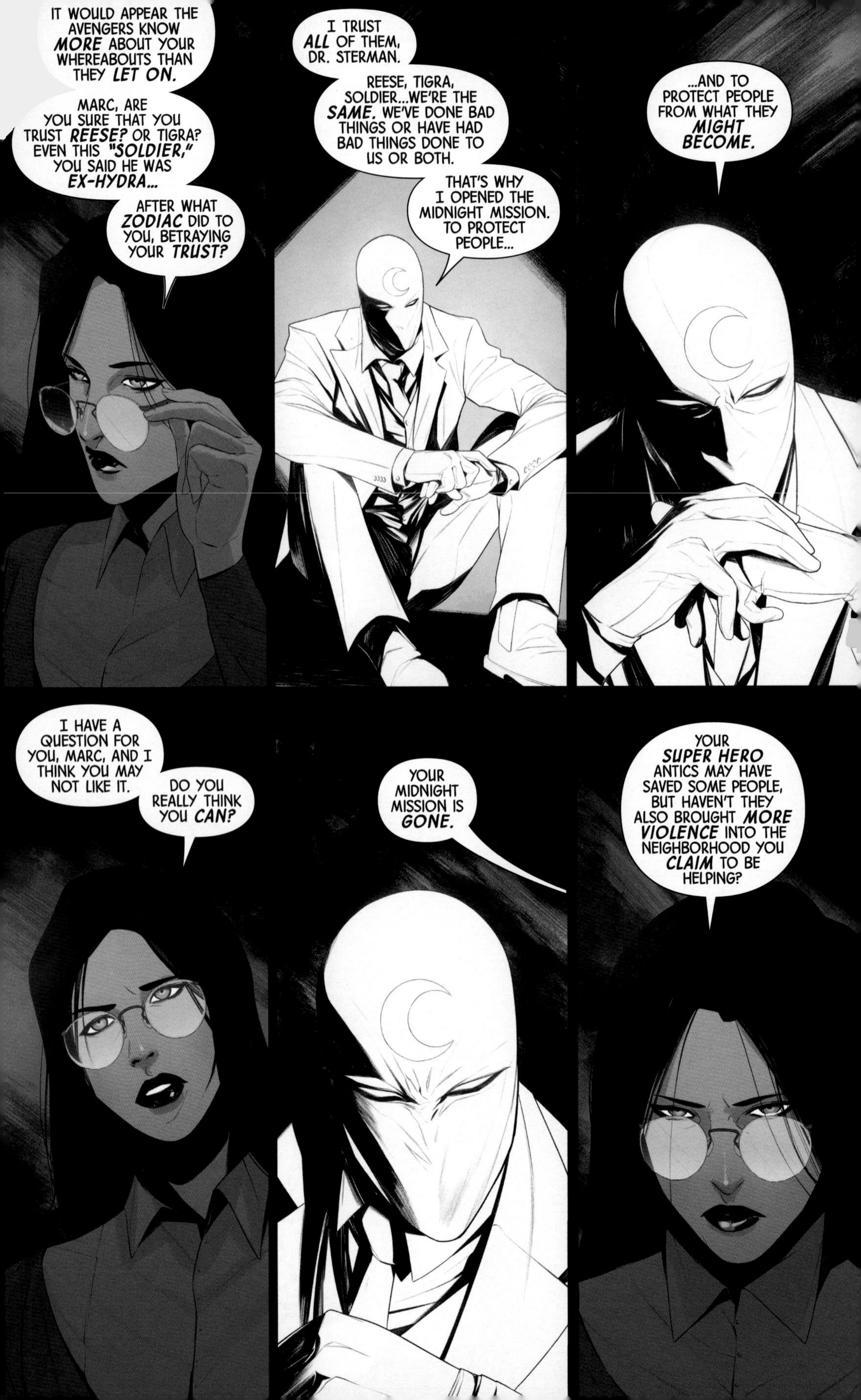
IT WOULD APPEAR THE AVENGERS KNOW MORE ABOUT YOUR WHEREABOUTS THAN THEY LET ON.
MARC, ARE YOU SURE THAT YOU TRUST REESE? OR TIGRA? EVEN THIS "SOLDIER," YOU SAID HE WAS EX-HYDRA...
AFTER WHAT ZODIAC DID TO YOU, BETRAYING YOUR TRUST?
I TRUST ALL OF THEM, DR. STERMAN.
REESE, TIGRA, SOLDIER...WE'RE THE SAME. WE'VE DONE BAD THINGS OR HAVE HAD BAD THINGS DONE TO US OR BOTH.
THAT'S WHY I OPENED THE MIDNIGHT MISSION. TO PROTECT PEOPLE...
...AND TO PROTECT PEOPLE FROM WHAT THEY MIGHT BECOME.
I HAVE A QUESTION FOR YOU, MARC, AND I THINK YOU MAY NOT LIKE IT.
DO YOU REALLY THINK YOU CAN?
YOUR MIDNIGHT MISSION IS GONE.
YOUR SUPER HERO ANTICS MAY HAVE SAVED SOME PEOPLE, BUT HAVEN'T THEY ALSO BROUGHT MORE VIOLENCE INTO THE NEIGHBORHOOD YOU CLAIM TO BE HELPING?

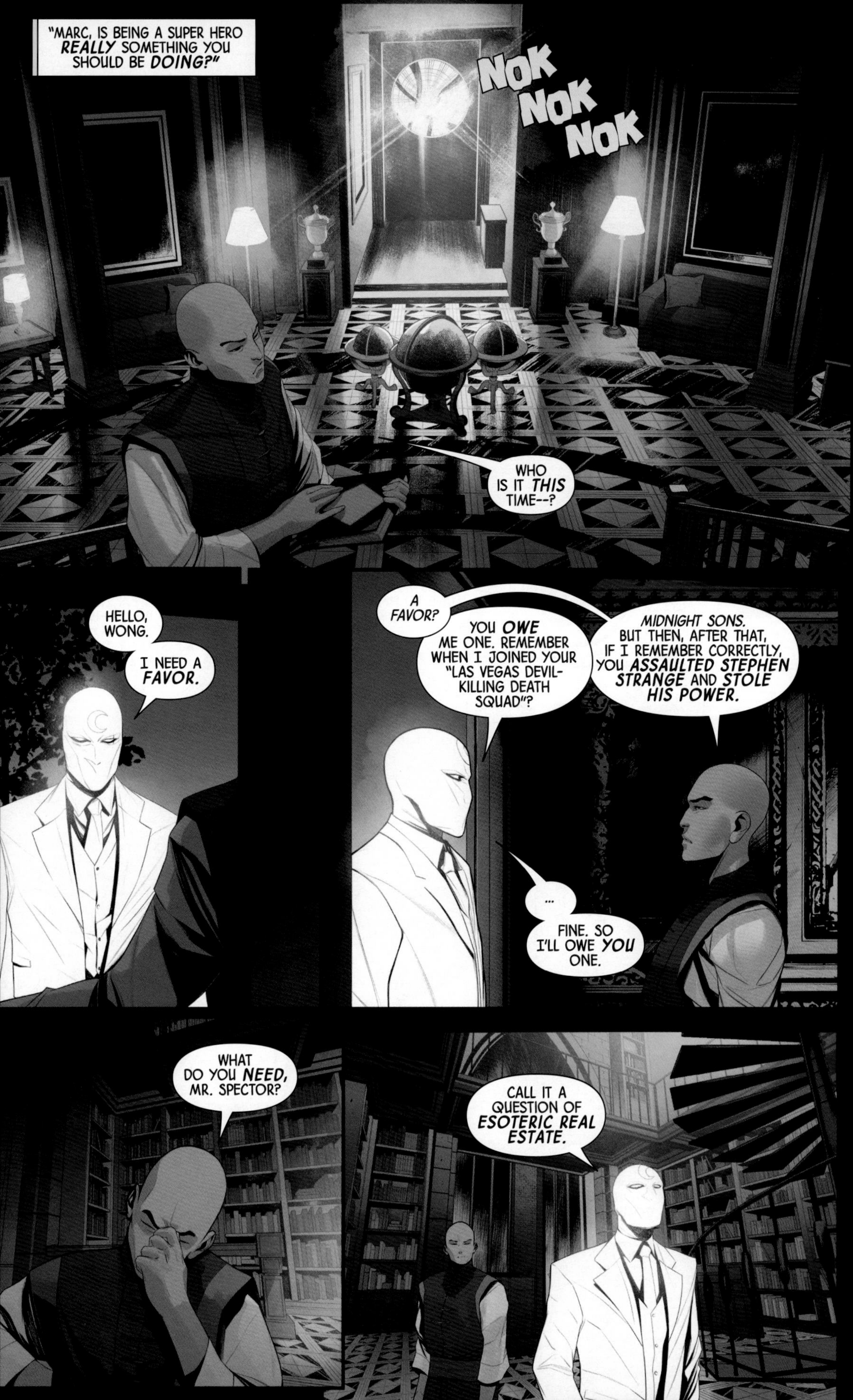
"MARC, IS BEING A SUPER HERO *REALLY* SOMETHING YOU SHOULD BE *DOING?*"
NOK NOK NOK
WHO IS IT *THIS* TIME--?
HELLO, WONG.
I NEED A *FAVOR.*
A FAVOR?
YOU *OWE* ME ONE. REMEMBER WHEN I JOINED YOUR "LAS VEGAS DEVIL-KILLING DEATH SQUAD"?
MIDNIGHT SONS. BUT THEN, AFTER THAT, IF I REMEMBER CORRECTLY, YOU *ASSAULTED STEPHEN STRANGE* AND *STOLE HIS POWER.*
...
FINE. SO I'LL OWE *YOU* ONE.
WHAT DO YOU *NEED,* MR. SPECTOR?
CALL IT A QUESTION OF *ESOTERIC REAL ESTATE.*

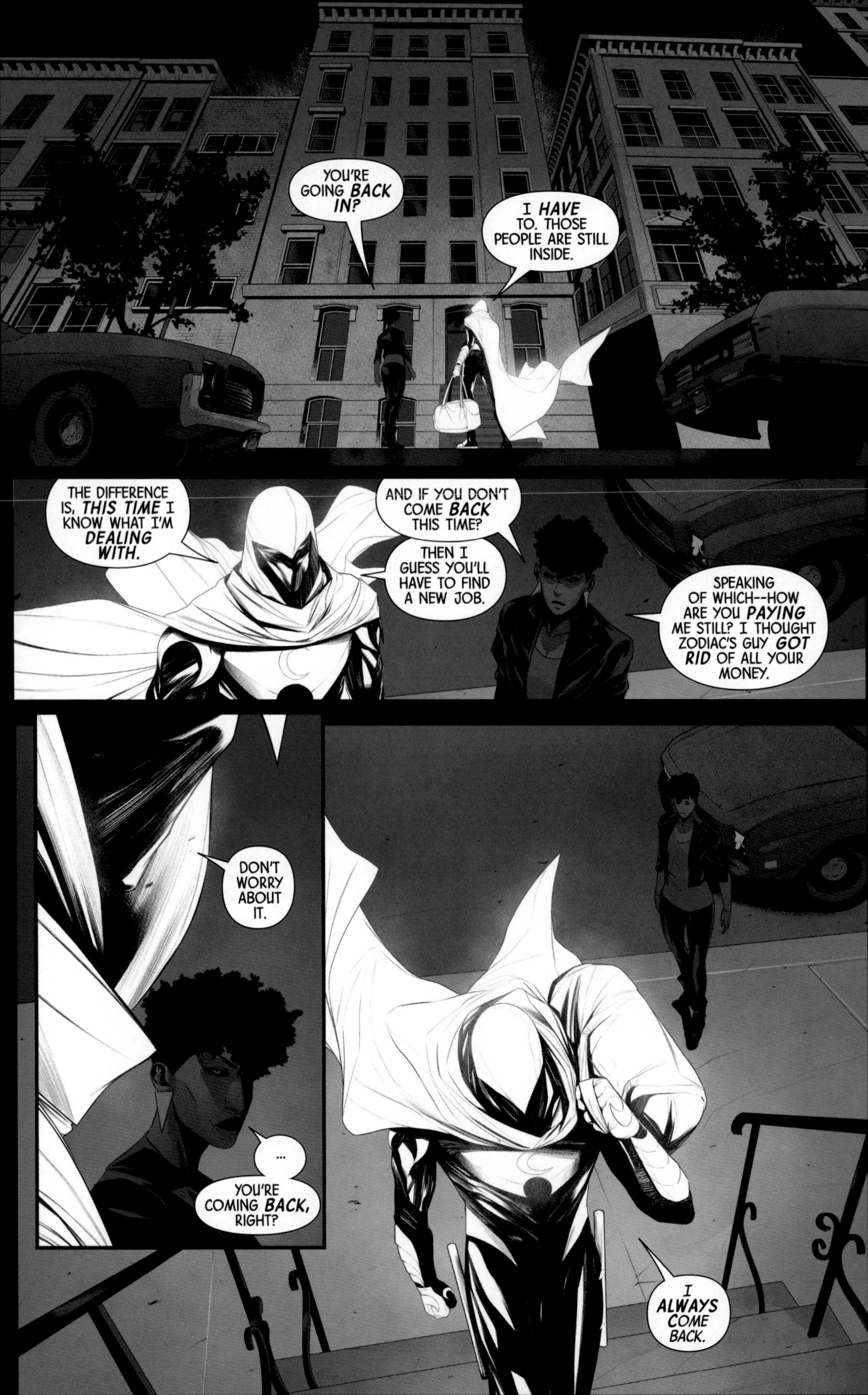
YOU'RE GOING BACK IN?
I HAVE TO. THOSE PEOPLE ARE STILL INSIDE.
THE DIFFERENCE IS, THIS TIME I KNOW WHAT I'M DEALING WITH.
AND IF YOU DON'T COME BACK THIS TIME?
THEN I GUESS YOU'LL HAVE TO FIND A NEW JOB.
SPEAKING OF WHICH--HOW ARE YOU PAYING ME STILL? I THOUGHT ZODIAC'S GUY GOT RID OF ALL YOUR MONEY.
DON'T WORRY ABOUT IT.
...
YOU'RE COMING BACK, RIGHT?
I ALWAYS COME BACK.

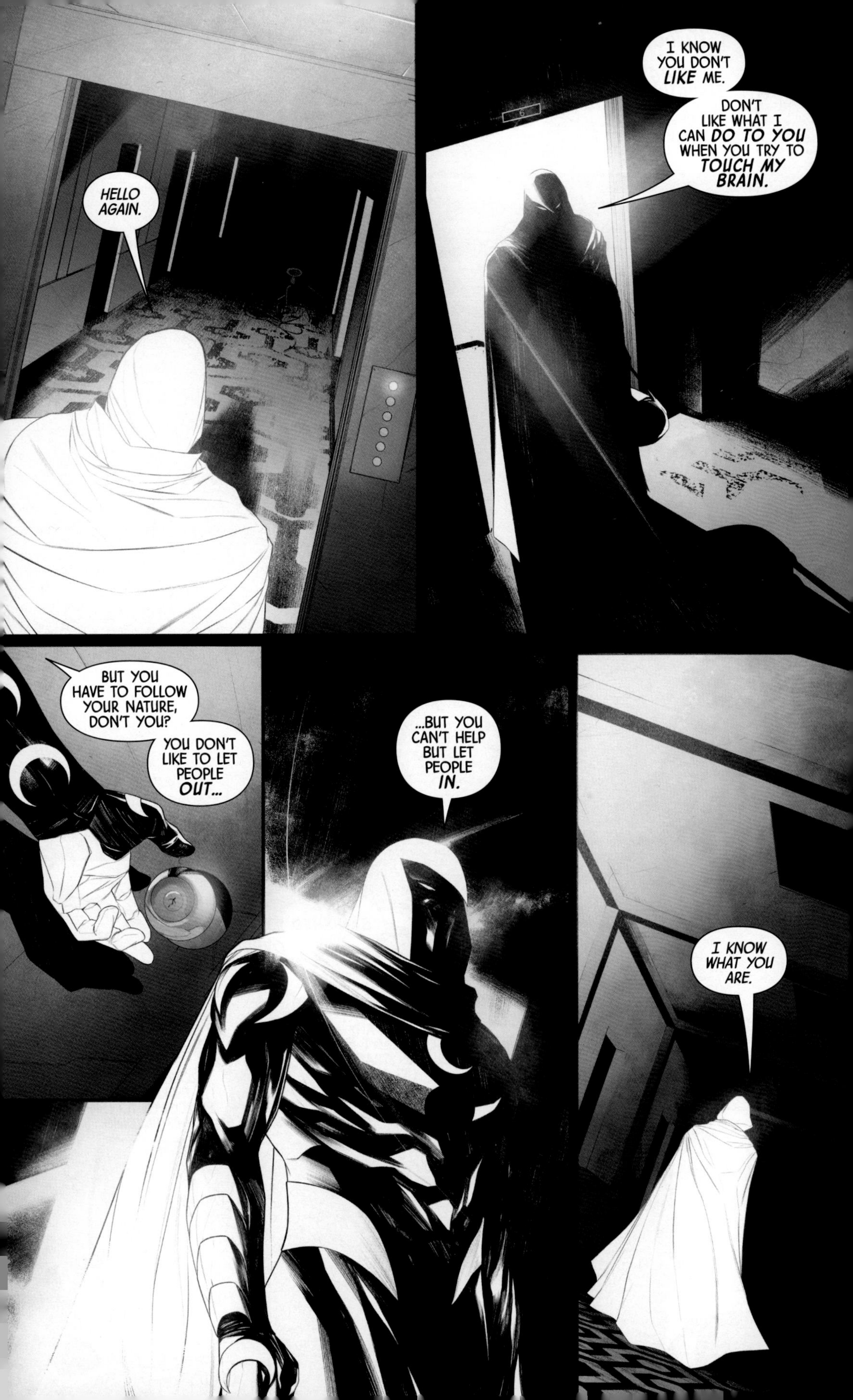
HELLO AGAIN.
I KNOW YOU DON'T LIKE ME.
DON'T LIKE WHAT I CAN DO TO YOU WHEN YOU TRY TO TOUCH MY BRAIN.
BUT YOU HAVE TO FOLLOW YOUR NATURE, DON'T YOU?
YOU DON'T LIKE TO LET PEOPLE OUT...
...BUT YOU CAN'T HELP BUT LET PEOPLE IN.
I KNOW WHAT YOU ARE.

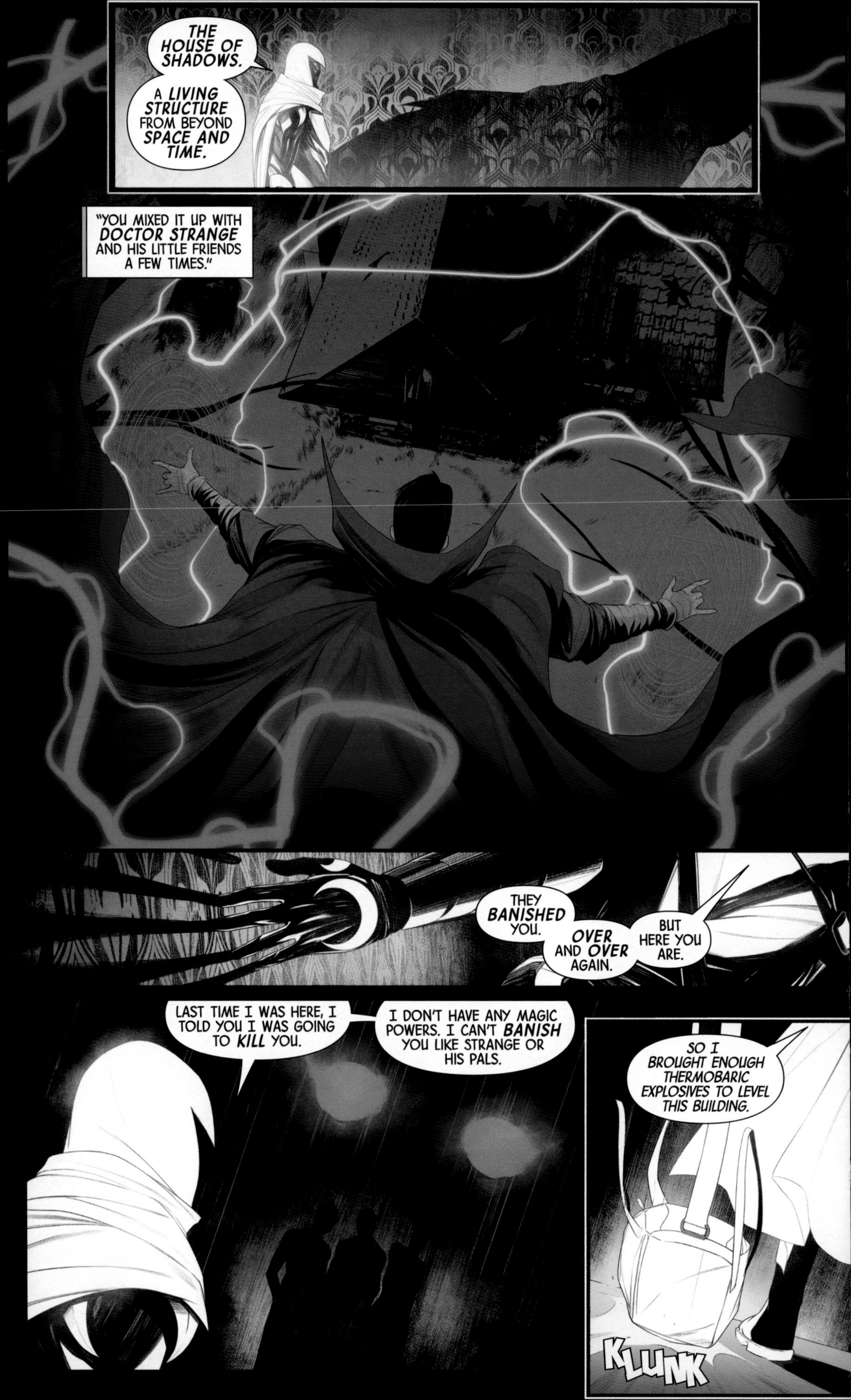
THE HOUSE OF SHADOWS.
A LIVING STRUCTURE FROM BEYOND SPACE AND TIME.
"YOU MIXED IT UP WITH DOCTOR STRANGE AND HIS LITTLE FRIENDS A FEW TIMES."
THEY BANISHED YOU.
OVER AND OVER AGAIN.
BUT HERE YOU ARE.
LAST TIME I WAS HERE, I TOLD YOU I WAS GOING TO KILL YOU.
I DON'T HAVE ANY MAGIC POWERS. I CAN'T BANISH YOU LIKE STRANGE OR HIS PALS.
SO I BROUGHT ENOUGH THERMOBARIC EXPLOSIVES TO LEVEL THIS BUILDING.
KLUNK

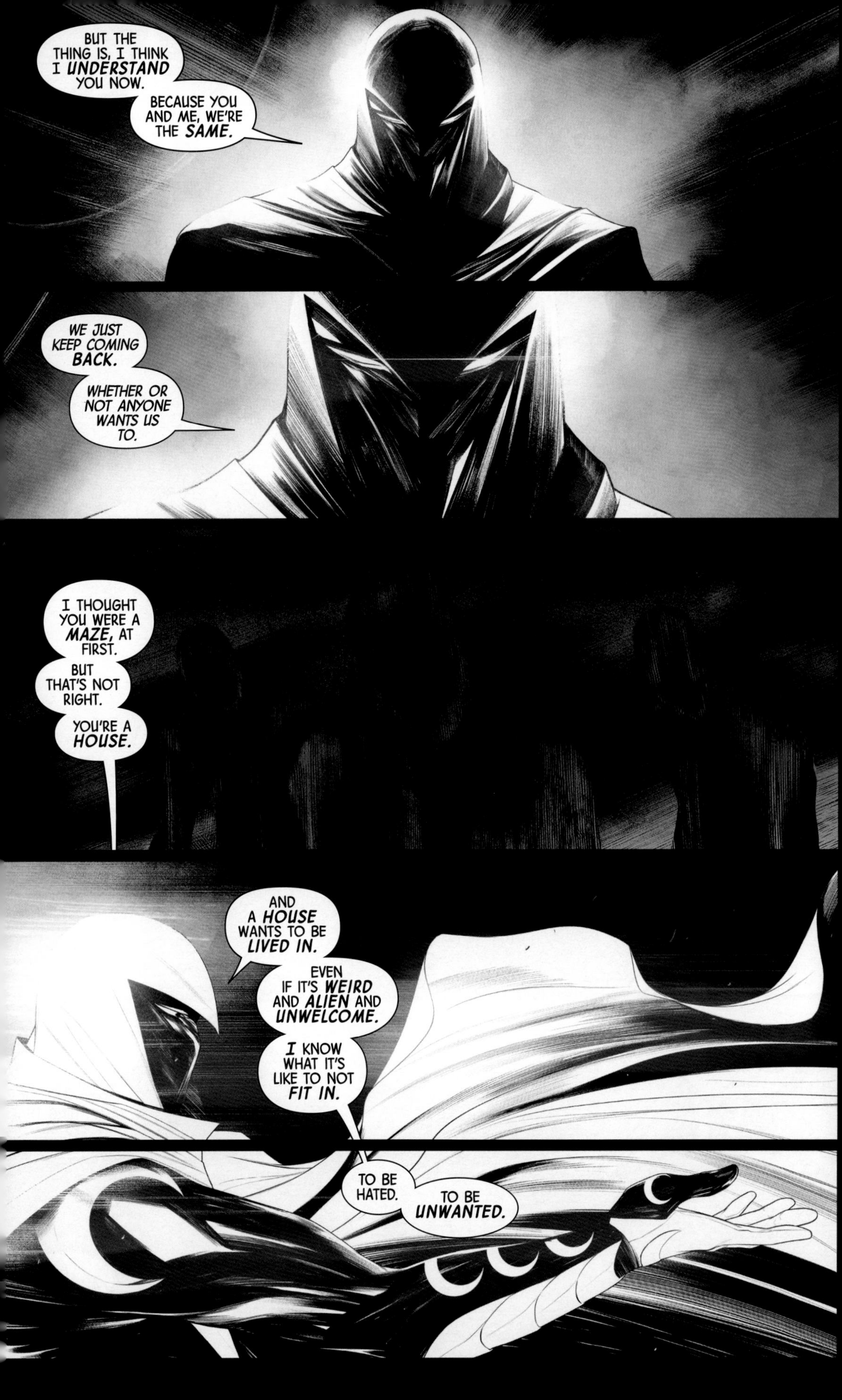
BUT THE THING IS, I THINK I UNDERSTAND YOU NOW.
BECAUSE YOU AND ME, WE'RE THE SAME.
WE JUST KEEP COMING BACK.
WHETHER OR NOT ANYONE WANTS US TO.
I THOUGHT YOU WERE A MAZE, AT FIRST.
BUT THAT'S NOT RIGHT.
YOU'RE A HOUSE.
AND A HOUSE WANTS TO BE LIVED IN.
EVEN IF IT'S WEIRD AND ALIEN AND UNWELCOME.
I KNOW WHAT IT'S LIKE TO NOT FIT IN.
TO BE HATED.
TO BE UNWANTED.

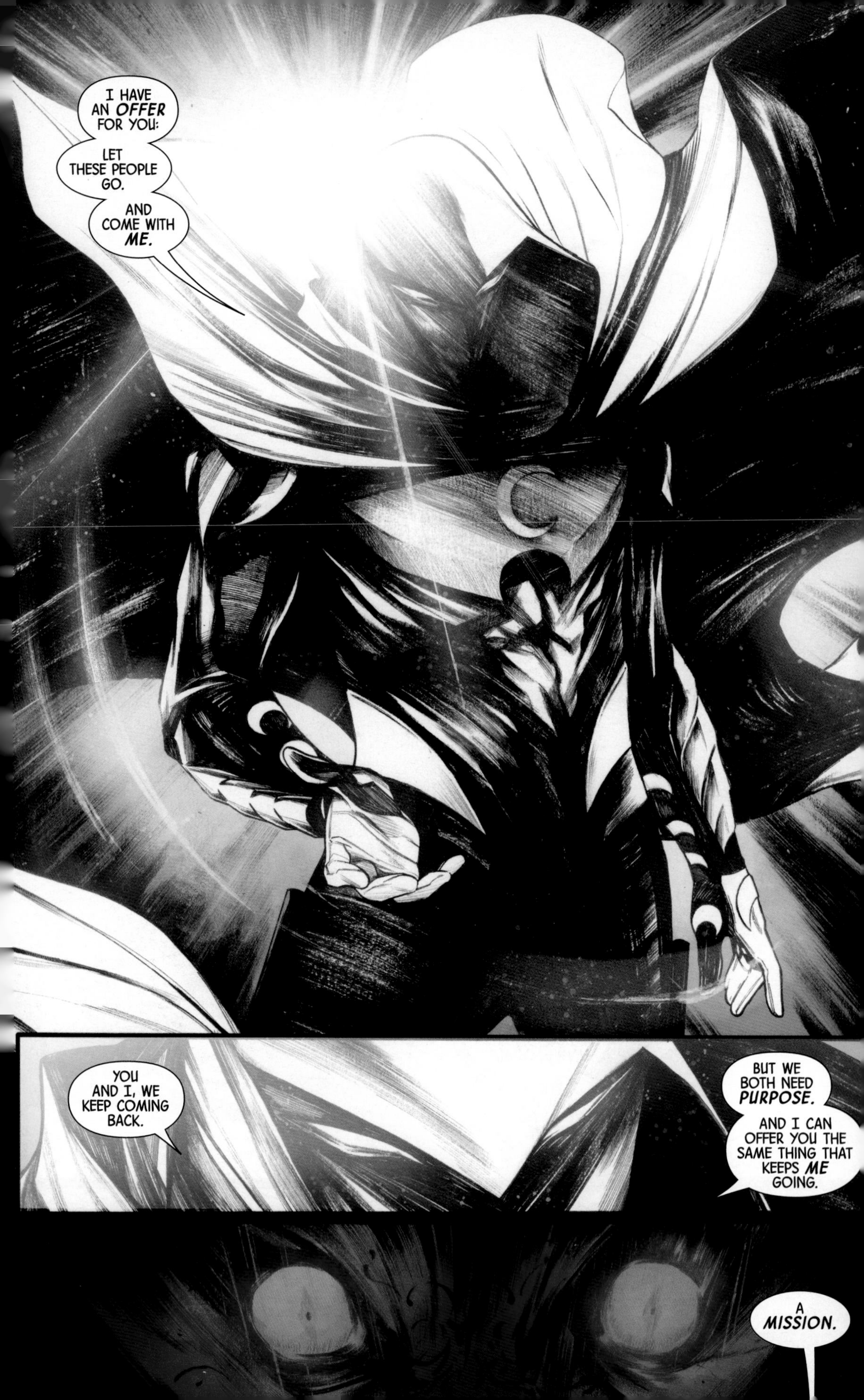
I HAVE AN OFFER FOR YOU:
LET THESE PEOPLE GO.
AND COME WITH ME.
YOU AND I, WE KEEP COMING BACK.
BUT WE BOTH NEED PURPOSE.
AND I CAN OFFER YOU THE SAME THING THAT KEEPS ME GOING.
A MISSION.

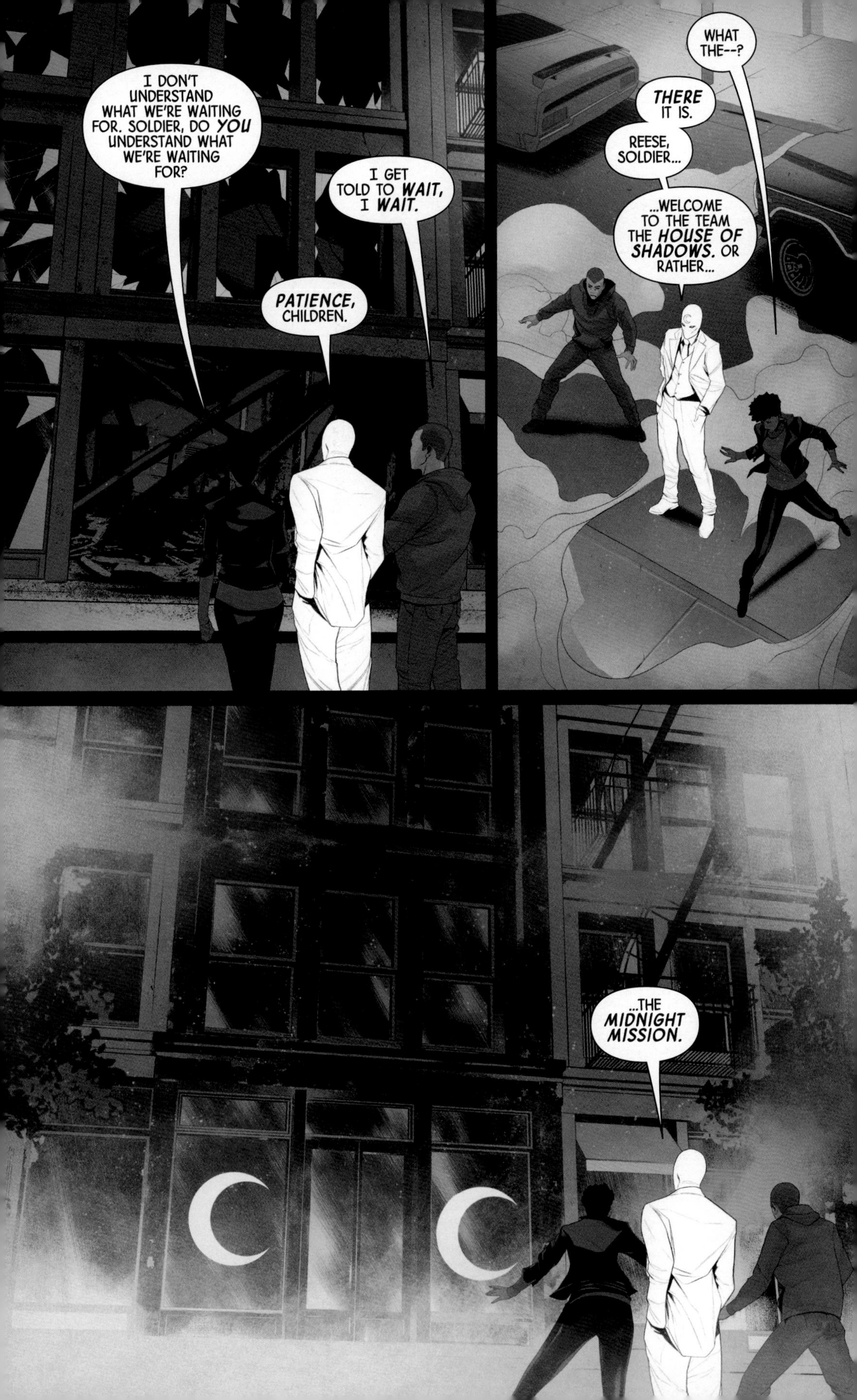
I DON'T UNDERSTAND WHAT WE'RE WAITING FOR. SOLDIER, DO YOU UNDERSTAND WHAT WE'RE WAITING FOR?
I GET TOLD TO WAIT, I WAIT.
PATIENCE, CHILDREN.
WHAT THE--?
THERE IT IS.
REESE, SOLDIER...
...WELCOME TO THE TEAM THE HOUSE OF SHADOWS. OR RATHER...
...THE MIDNIGHT MISSION.

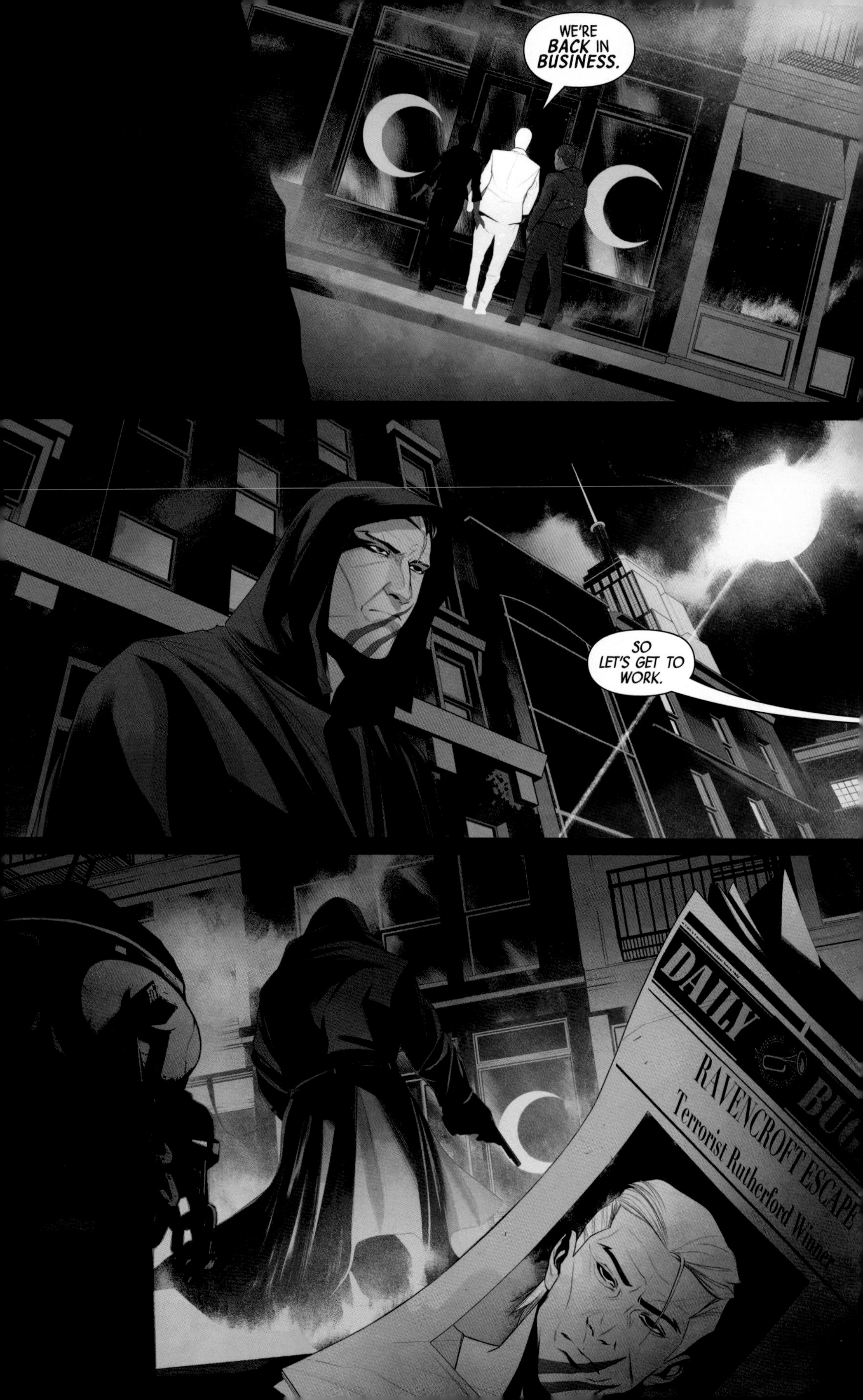
WE'RE BACK IN BUSINESS.
SO LET'S GET TO WORK.
DAILY BUGLE
RAVENCROFT ESCAPE
Terrorist Rutherford Winner

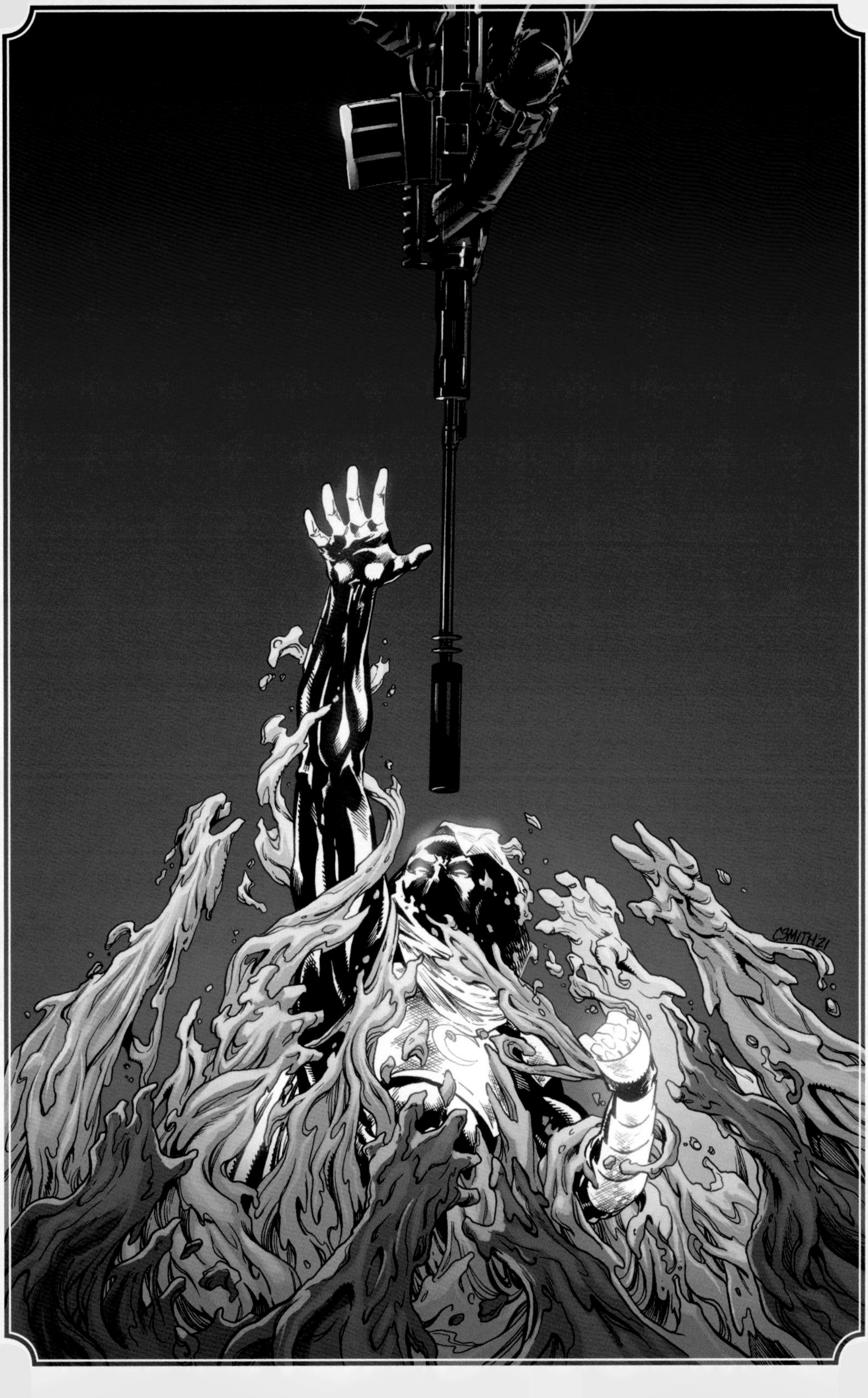
CSMITH'21

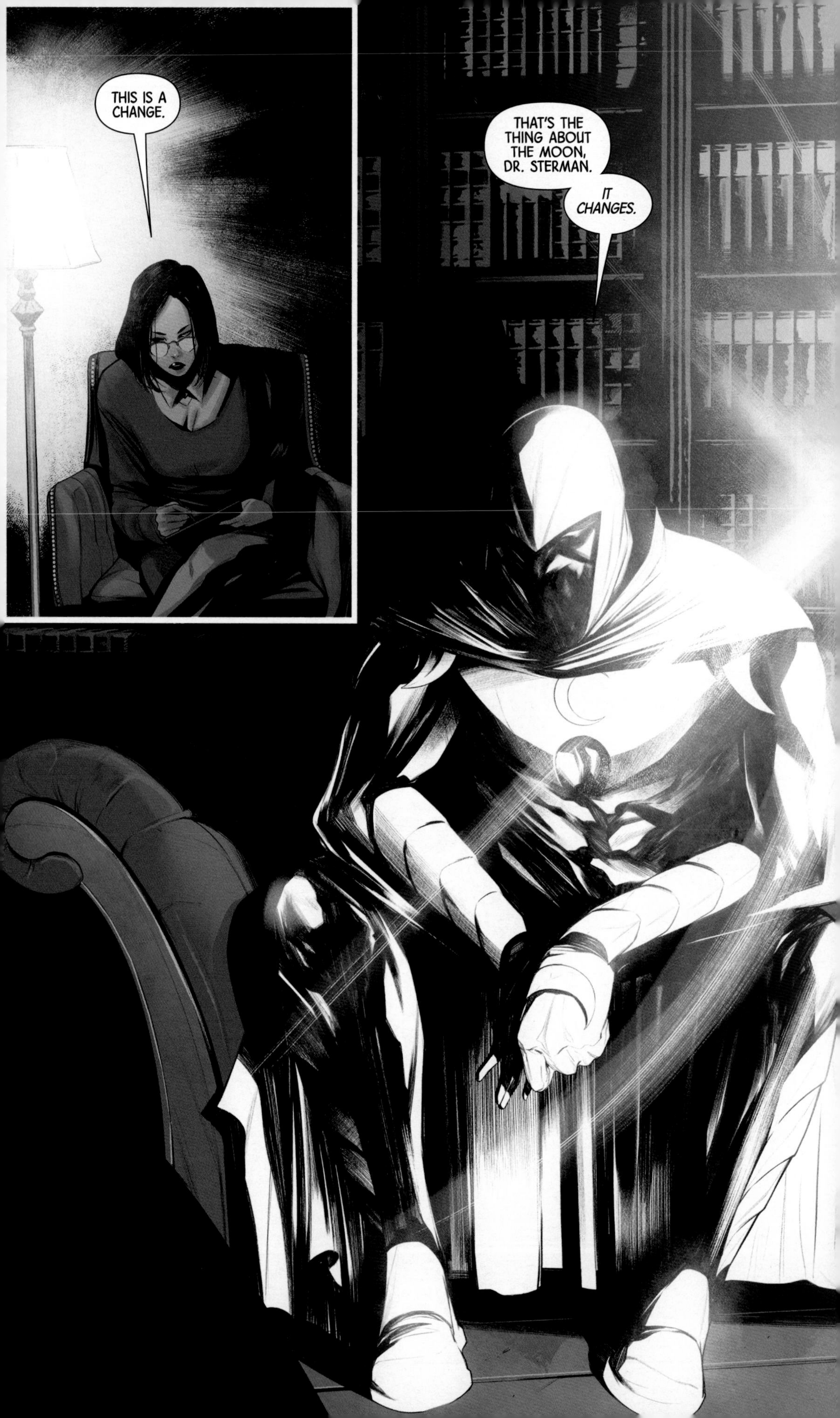
THIS IS A CHANGE.
THAT'S THE THING ABOUT THE MOON, DR. STERMAN.
IT CHANGES.

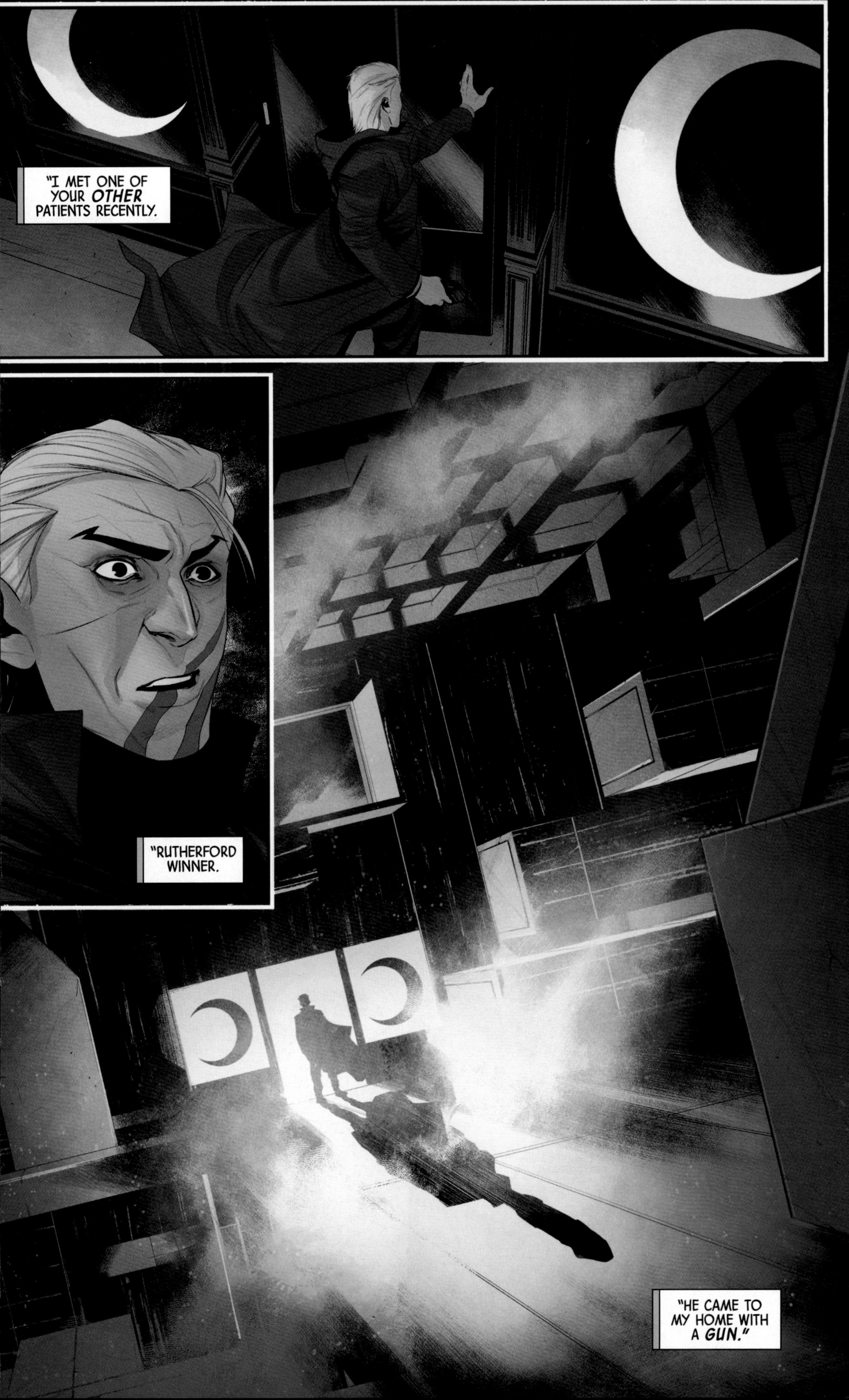
"I MET ONE OF YOUR *OTHER* PATIENTS RECENTLY.
"RUTHERFORD WINNER.
"HE CAME TO MY HOME WITH A *GUN*."

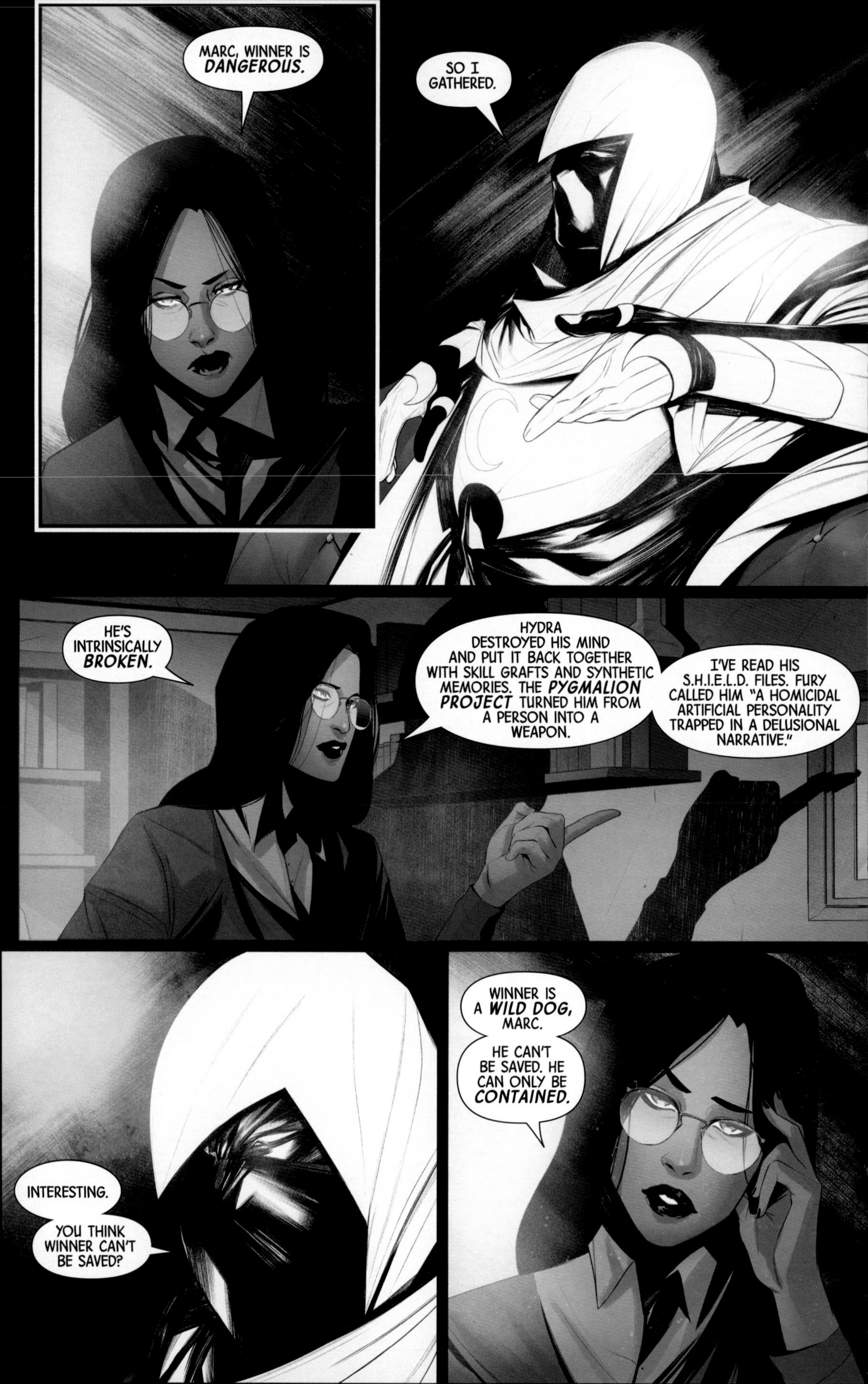

MARC, WINNER IS DANGEROUS.
SO I GATHERED.
HE'S INTRINSICALLY BROKEN.
HYDRA DESTROYED HIS MIND AND PUT IT BACK TOGETHER WITH SKILL GRAFTS AND SYNTHETIC MEMORIES. THE PYGMALION PROJECT TURNED HIM FROM A PERSON INTO A WEAPON.
I'VE READ HIS S.H.I.E.L.D. FILES. FURY CALLED HIM "A HOMICIDAL ARTIFICIAL PERSONALITY TRAPPED IN A DELUSIONAL NARRATIVE."
WINNER IS A WILD DOG, MARC.
HE CAN'T BE SAVED. HE CAN ONLY BE CONTAINED.
INTERESTING.
YOU THINK WINNER CAN'T BE SAVED?

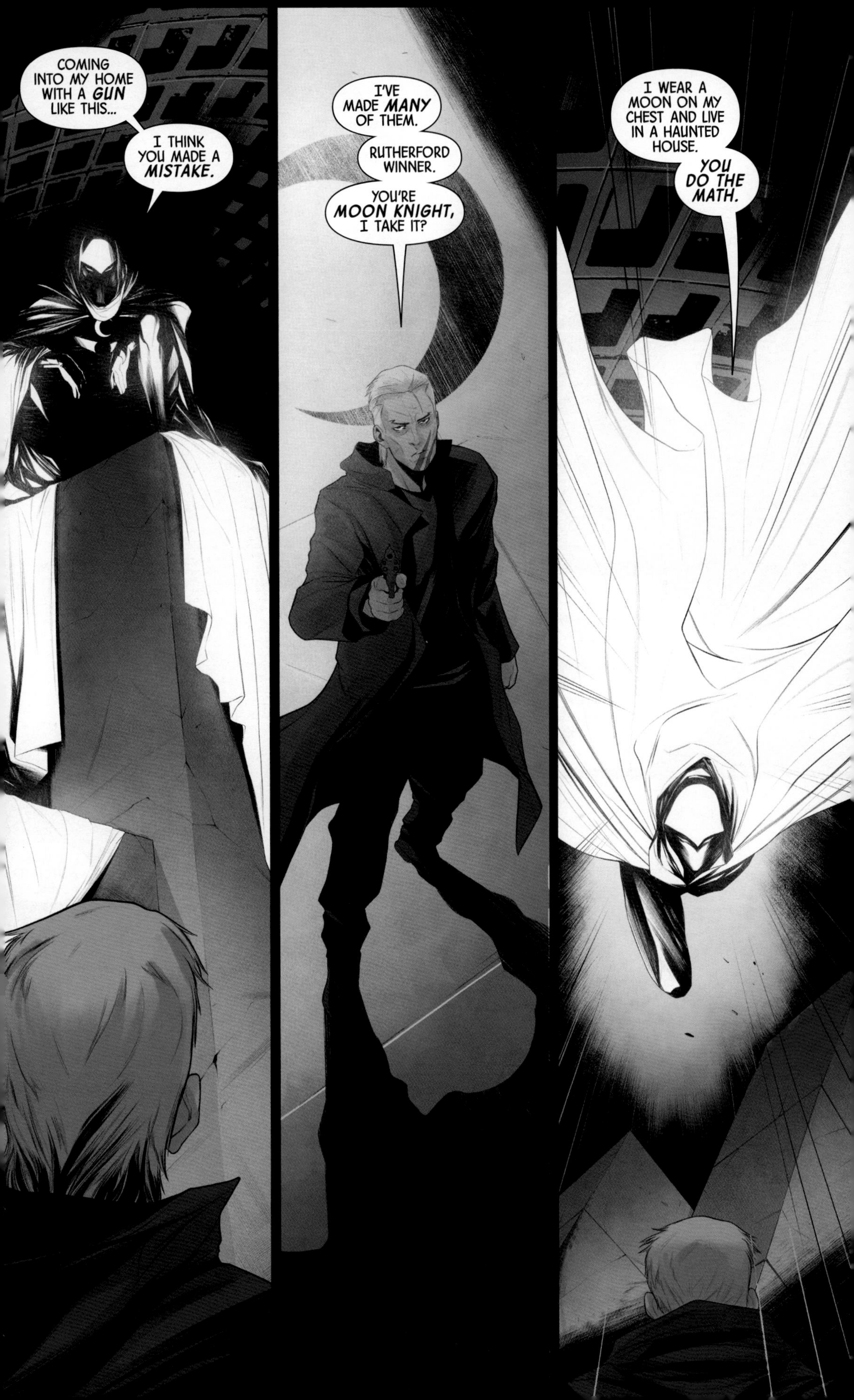

COMING INTO MY HOME WITH A GUN LIKE THIS...
I THINK YOU MADE A MISTAKE.
I'VE MADE MANY OF THEM.
RUTHERFORD WINNER.
YOU'RE MOON KNIGHT, I TAKE IT?
I WEAR A MOON ON MY CHEST AND LIVE IN A HAUNTED HOUSE.
YOU DO THE MATH.

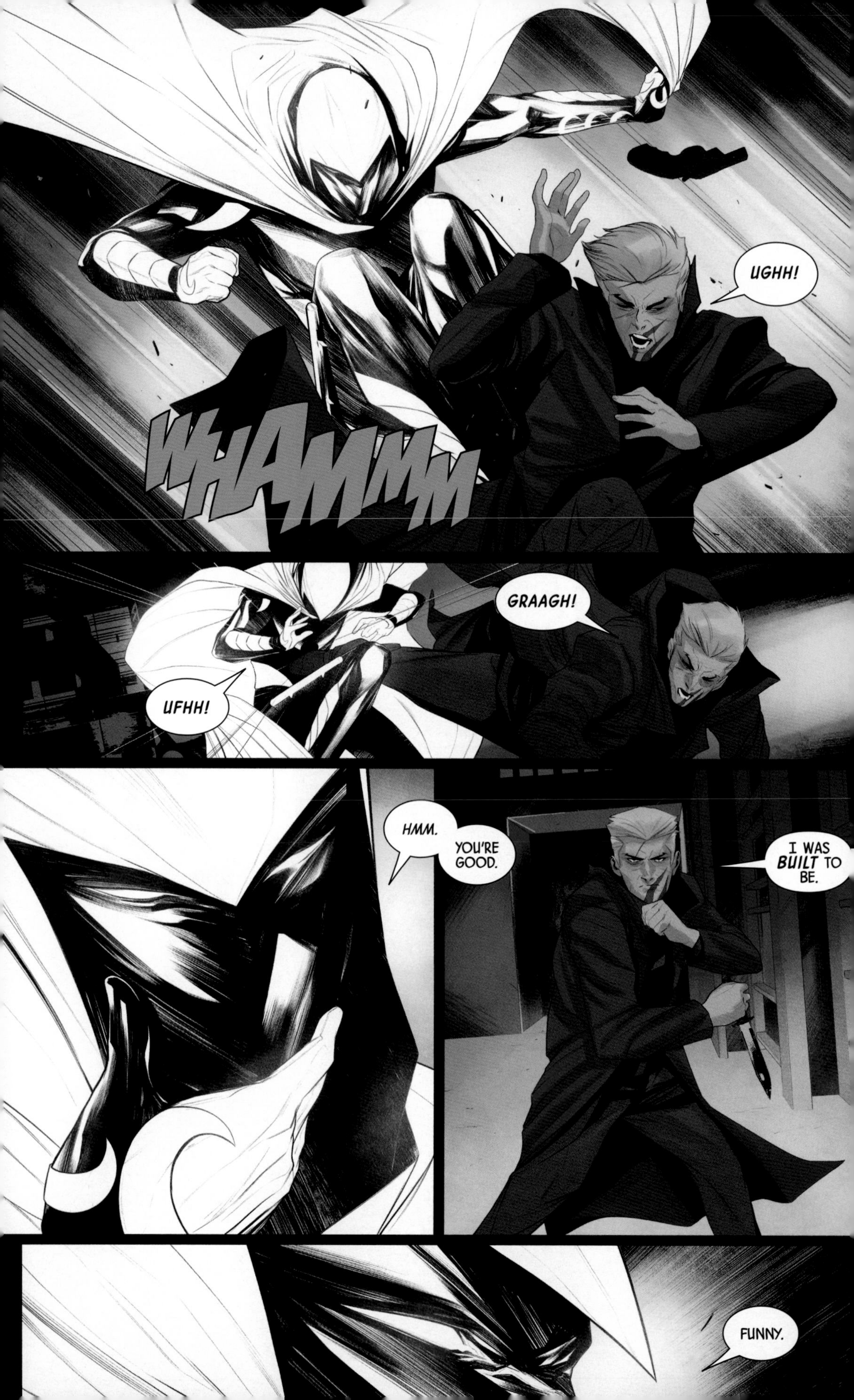
UGHH!
WHAMMM
GRAAGH!
UFHH!
HMM.
YOU'RE GOOD.
I WAS BUILT TO BE.
FUNNY.

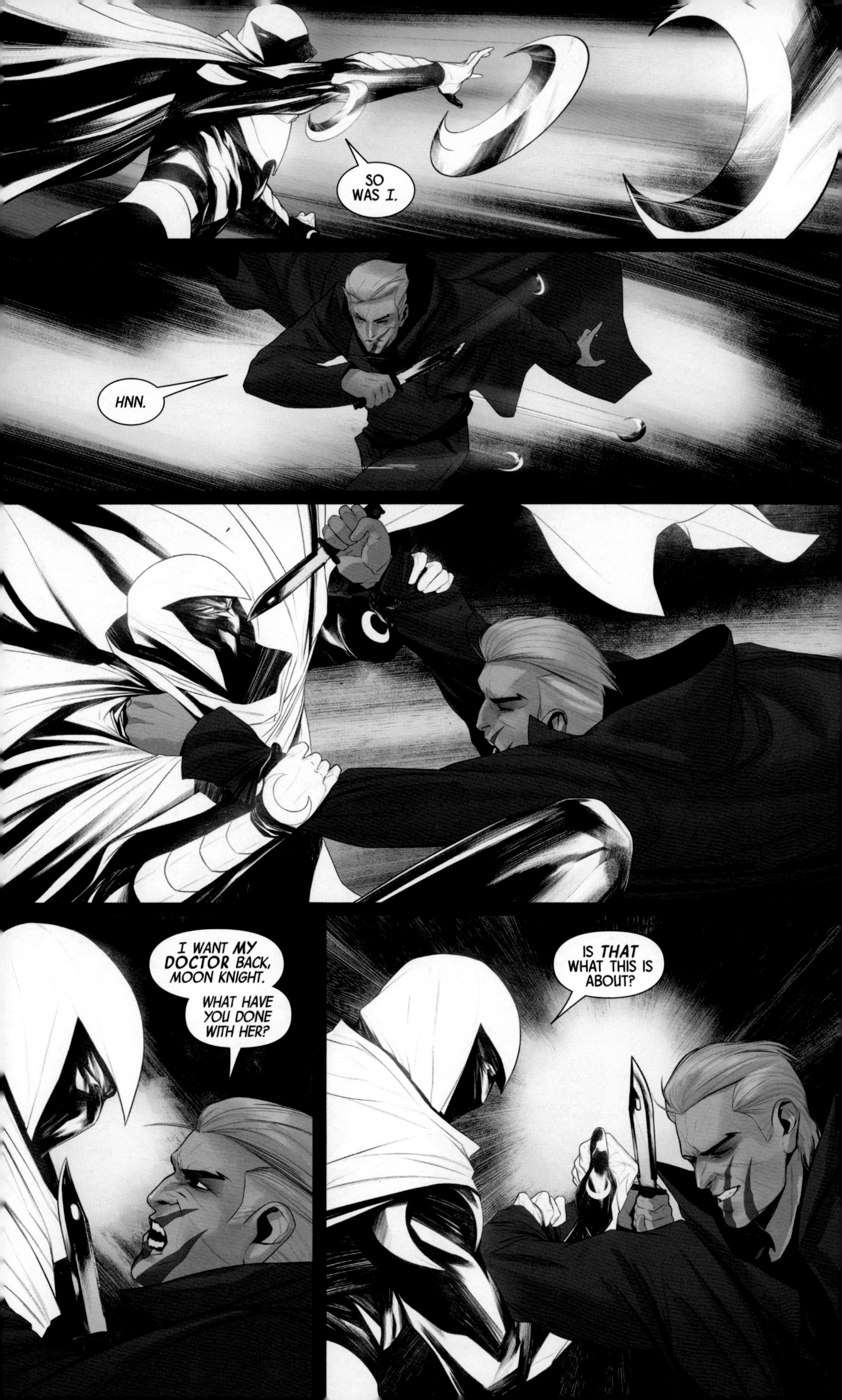

SO WAS I.
HNN.
I WANT MY DOCTOR BACK, MOON KNIGHT.
WHAT HAVE YOU DONE WITH HER?
IS THAT WHAT THIS IS ABOUT?

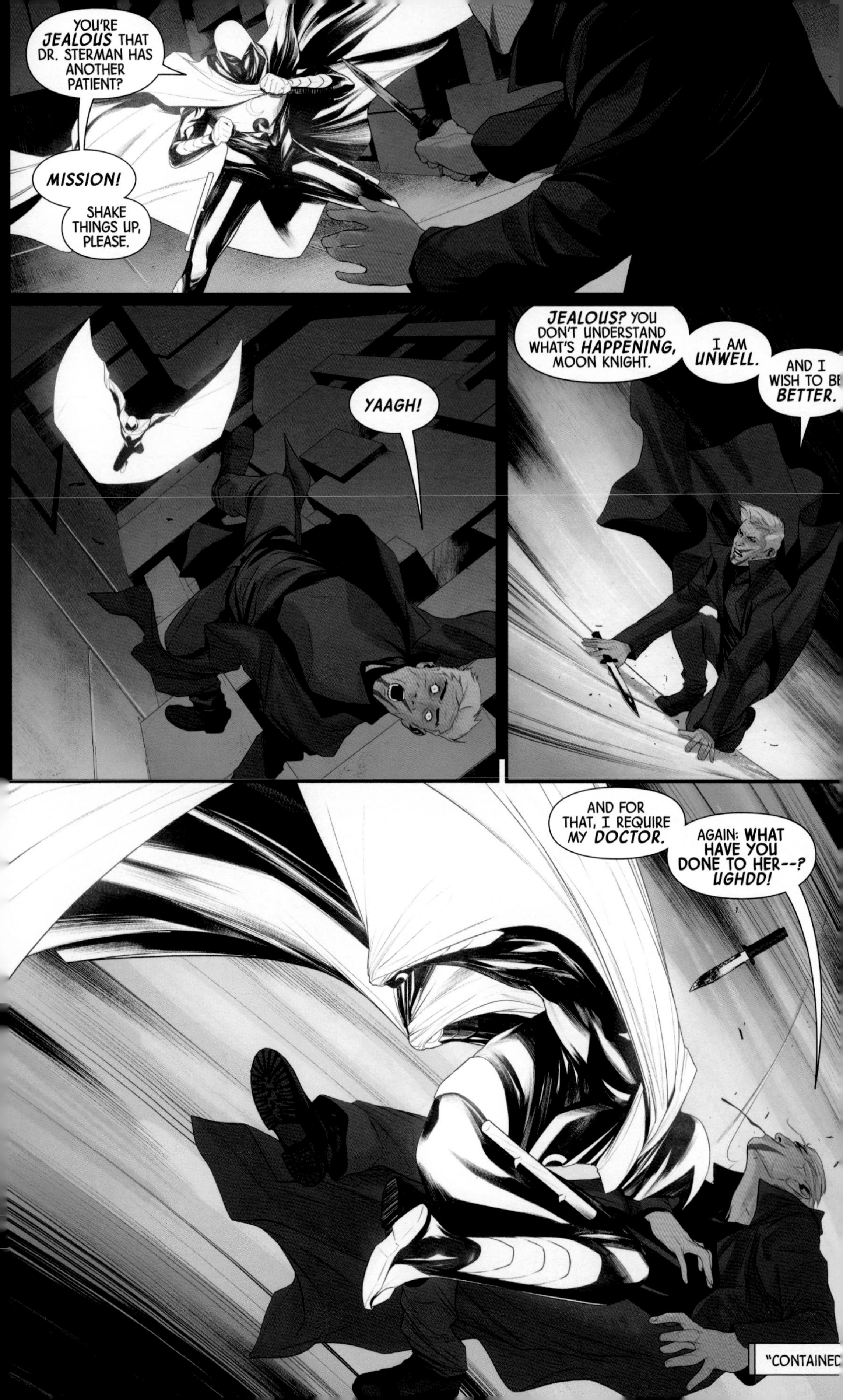
YOU'RE JEALOUS THAT DR. STERMAN HAS ANOTHER PATIENT?
MISSION!
SHAKE THINGS UP, PLEASE.
YAAGH!
JEALOUS? YOU DON'T UNDERSTAND WHAT'S HAPPENING, MOON KNIGHT.
I AM UNWELL.
AND I WISH TO BE BETTER.
AND FOR THAT, I REQUIRE MY DOCTOR.
AGAIN: WHAT HAVE YOU DONE TO HER--? UGHDD!
"CONTAINED

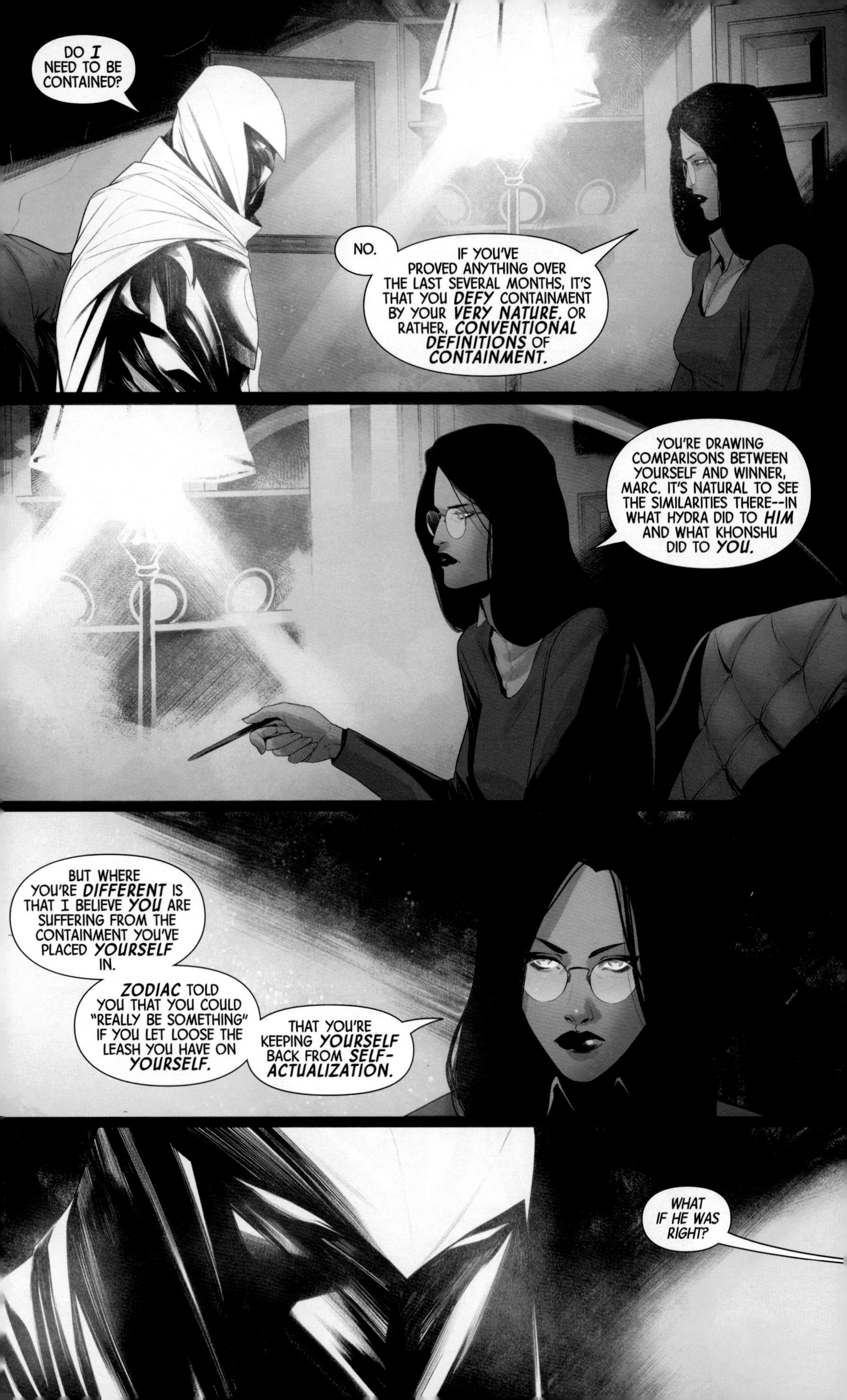
DO I NEED TO BE CONTAINED?
NO.
IF YOU'VE PROVED ANYTHING OVER THE LAST SEVERAL MONTHS, IT'S THAT YOU DEFY CONTAINMENT BY YOUR VERY NATURE. OR RATHER, CONVENTIONAL DEFINITIONS OF CONTAINMENT.
YOU'RE DRAWING COMPARISONS BETWEEN YOURSELF AND WINNER, MARC. IT'S NATURAL TO SEE THE SIMILARITIES THERE--IN WHAT HYDRA DID TO HIM AND WHAT KHONSHU DID TO YOU.
BUT WHERE YOU'RE DIFFERENT IS THAT I BELIEVE YOU ARE SUFFERING FROM THE CONTAINMENT YOU'VE PLACED YOURSELF IN.
ZODIAC TOLD YOU THAT YOU COULD "REALLY BE SOMETHING" IF YOU LET LOOSE THE LEASH YOU HAVE ON YOURSELF.
THAT YOU'RE KEEPING YOURSELF BACK FROM SELF-ACTUALIZATION.
WHAT IF HE WAS RIGHT?

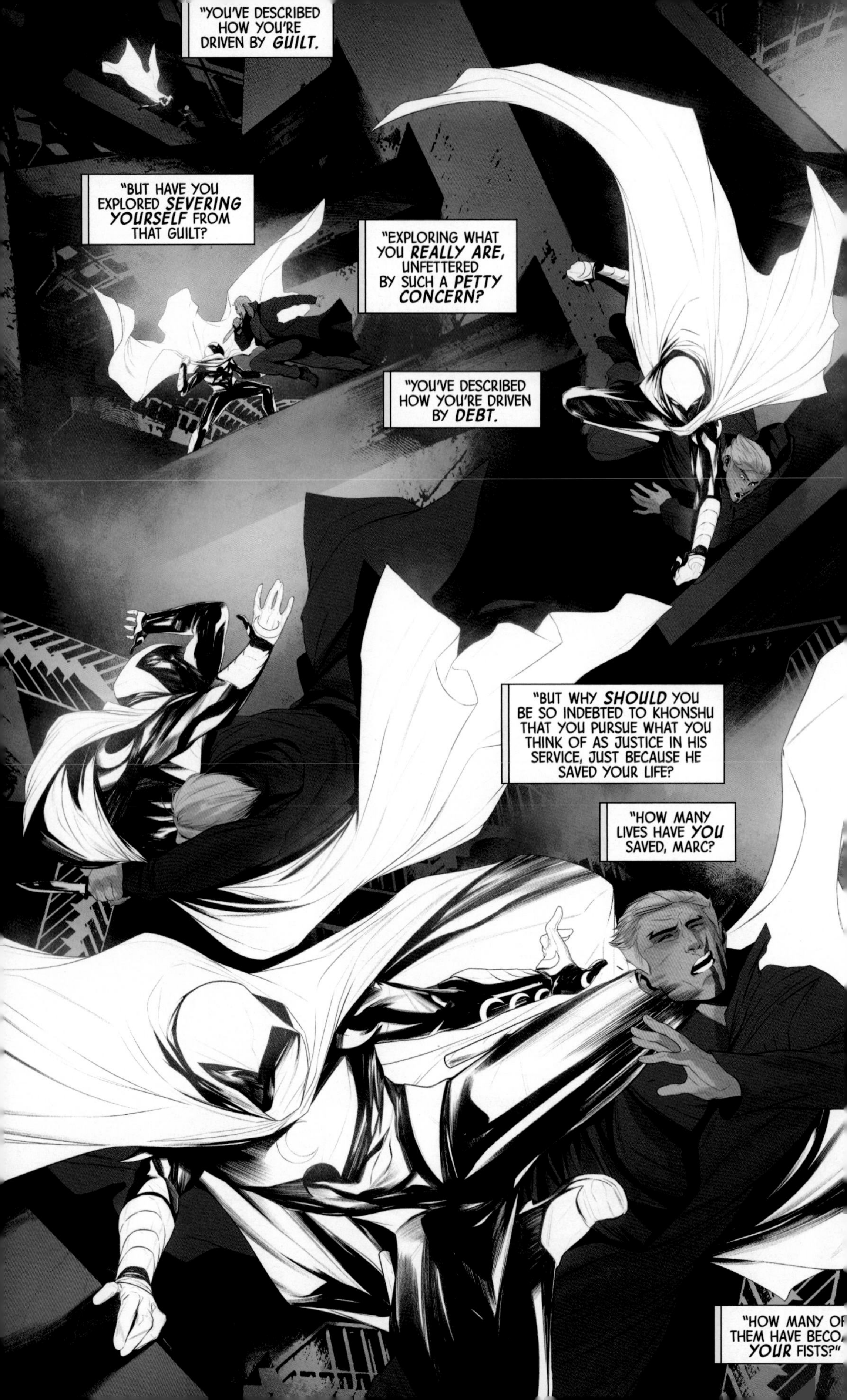
"YOU'VE DESCRIBED HOW YOU'RE DRIVEN BY GUILT.
"BUT HAVE YOU EXPLORED SEVERING YOURSELF FROM THAT GUILT?
"EXPLORING WHAT YOU REALLY ARE, UNFETTERED BY SUCH A PETTY CONCERN?
"YOU'VE DESCRIBED HOW YOU'RE DRIVEN BY DEBT.
"BUT WHY SHOULD YOU BE SO INDEBTED TO KHONSHU THAT YOU PURSUE WHAT YOU THINK OF AS JUSTICE IN HIS SERVICE, JUST BECAUSE HE SAVED YOUR LIFE?
"HOW MANY LIVES HAVE YOU SAVED, MARC?
"HOW MANY OF THEM HAVE BECO YOUR FISTS?"

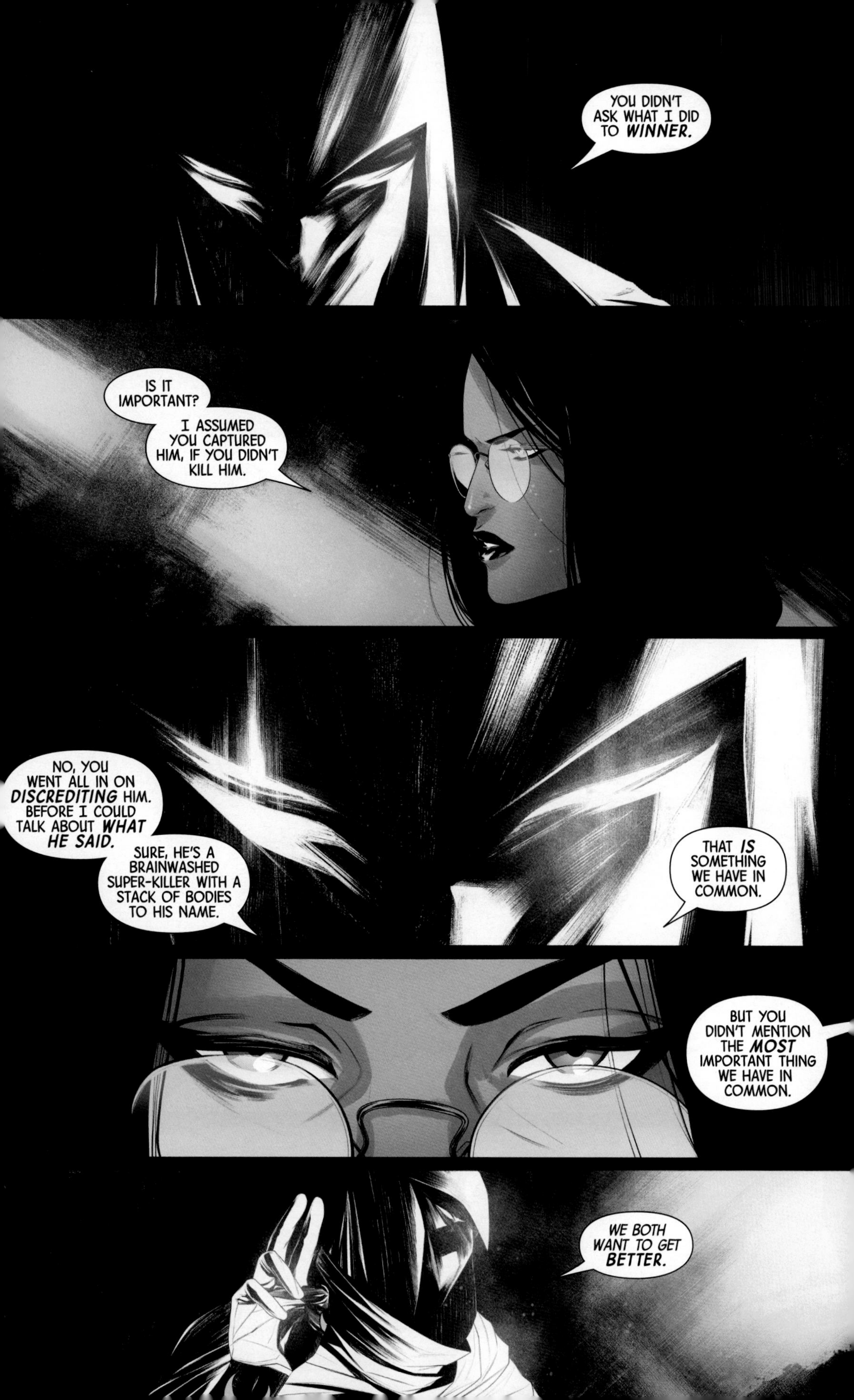
YOU DIDN'T ASK WHAT I DID TO WINNER.
IS IT IMPORTANT?
I ASSUMED YOU CAPTURED HIM, IF YOU DIDN'T KILL HIM.
NO, YOU WENT ALL IN ON DISCREDITING HIM. BEFORE I COULD TALK ABOUT WHAT HE SAID.
SURE, HE'S A BRAINWASHED SUPER-KILLER WITH A STACK OF BODIES TO HIS NAME.
THAT IS SOMETHING WE HAVE IN COMMON.
BUT YOU DIDN'T MENTION THE MOST IMPORTANT THING WE HAVE IN COMMON.
WE BOTH WANT TO GET BETTER.

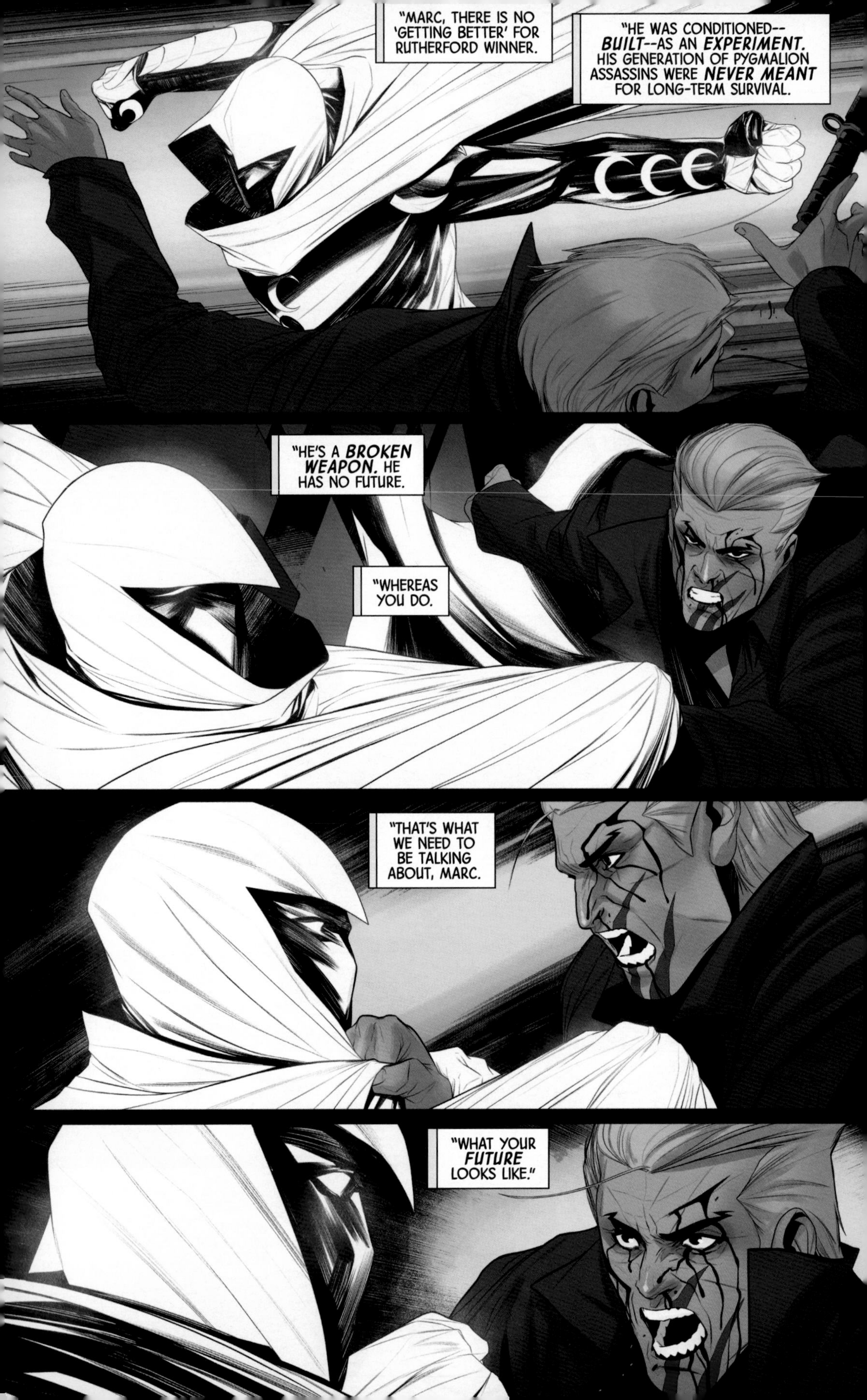
"MARC, THERE IS NO 'GETTING BETTER' FOR RUTHERFORD WINNER.
"HE WAS CONDITIONED-- BUILT--AS AN EXPERIMENT. HIS GENERATION OF PYGMALION ASSASSINS WERE NEVER MEANT FOR LONG-TERM SURVIVAL.
"HE'S A BROKEN WEAPON. HE HAS NO FUTURE.
"WHEREAS YOU DO.
"THAT'S WHAT WE NEED TO BE TALKING ABOUT, MARC.
"WHAT YOUR FUTURE LOOKS LIKE."

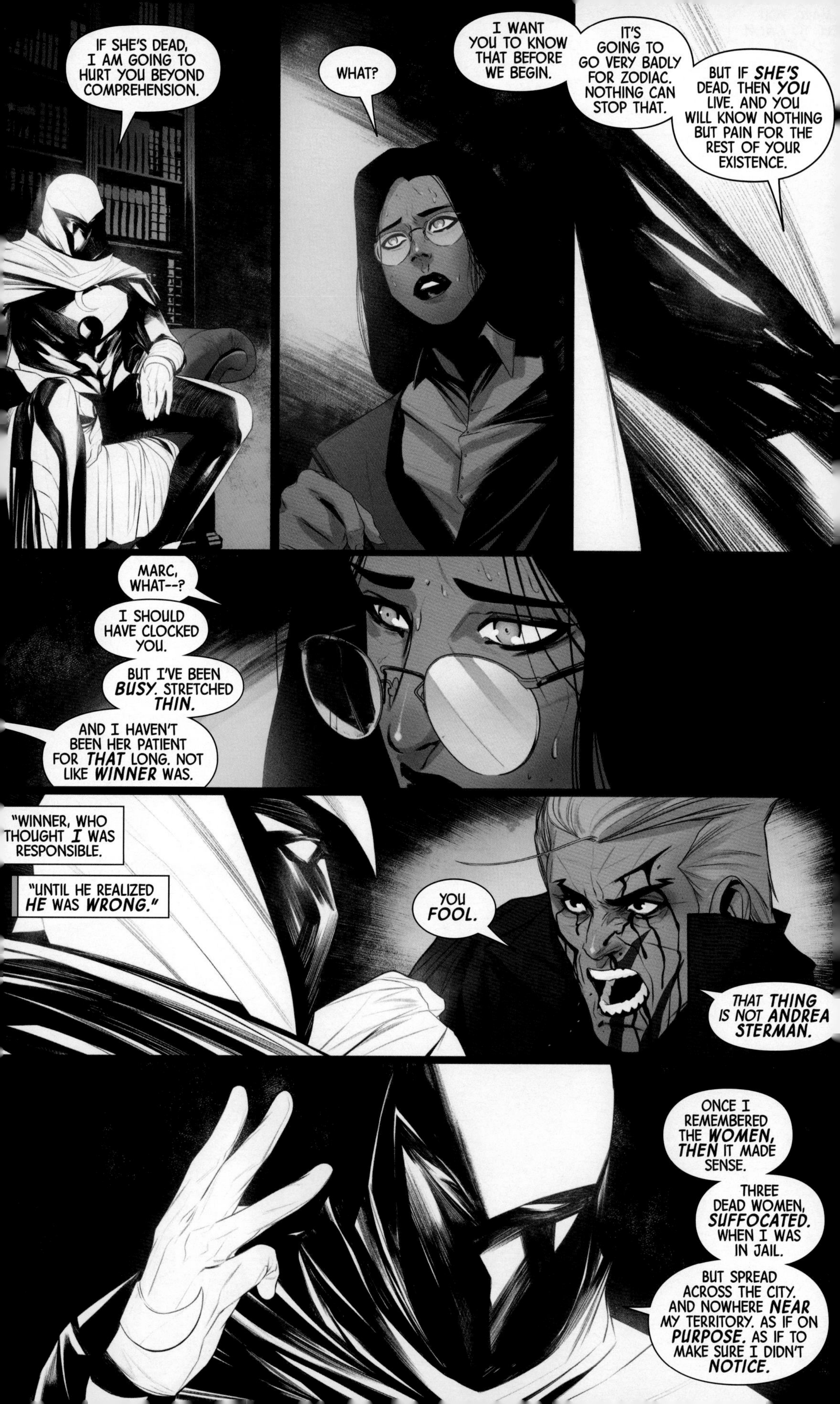
IF SHE'S DEAD, I AM GOING TO HURT YOU BEYOND COMPREHENSION.
WHAT?
I WANT YOU TO KNOW THAT BEFORE WE BEGIN.
IT'S GOING TO GO VERY BADLY FOR ZODIAC. NOTHING CAN STOP THAT.
BUT IF *SHE'S* DEAD, THEN *YOU* LIVE. AND YOU WILL KNOW NOTHING BUT PAIN FOR THE REST OF YOUR EXISTENCE.
MARC, WHAT--?
I SHOULD HAVE CLOCKED YOU.
BUT I'VE BEEN *BUSY*. STRETCHED *THIN.*
AND I HAVEN'T BEEN HER PATIENT FOR *THAT* LONG. NOT LIKE *WINNER* WAS.
"WINNER, WHO THOUGHT *I* WAS RESPONSIBLE.
"UNTIL HE REALIZED *HE* WAS *WRONG."*
YOU *FOOL.*
THAT THING IS NOT ANDREA STERMAN.
ONCE I REMEMBERED THE *WOMEN, THEN* IT MADE SENSE.
THREE DEAD WOMEN, *SUFFOCATED.* WHEN I WAS IN JAIL.
BUT SPREAD ACROSS THE CITY. AND NOWHERE *NEAR* MY TERRITORY. AS IF ON *PURPOSE.* AS IF TO MAKE SURE I DIDN'T *NOTICE.*

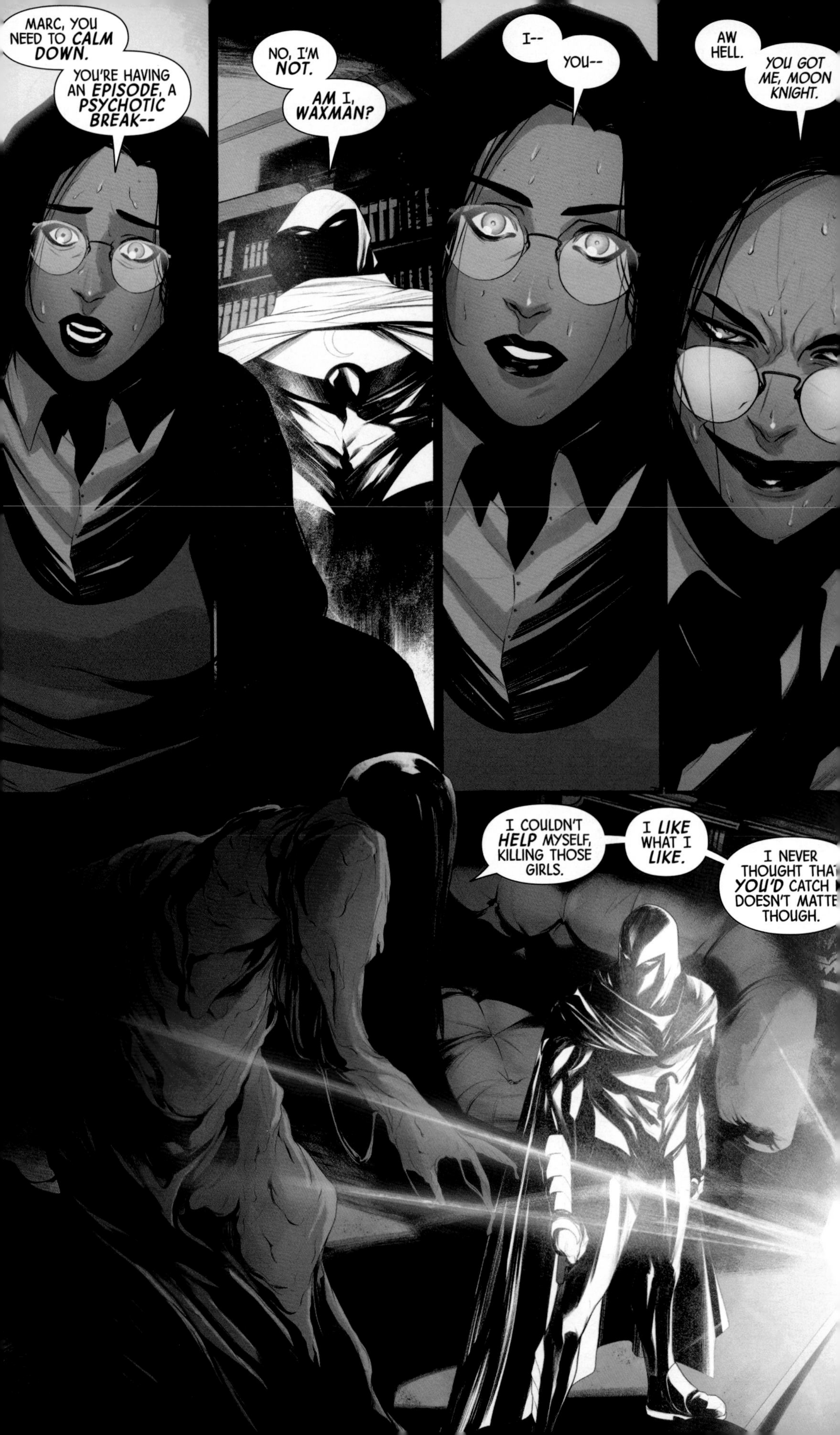

MARC, YOU NEED TO CALM DOWN.
YOU'RE HAVING AN EPISODE, A PSYCHOTIC BREAK--
NO, I'M NOT.
AM I, WAXMAN?
I--
YOU--
AW HELL.
YOU GOT ME, MOON KNIGHT.
I COULDN'T HELP MYSELF, KILLING THOSE GIRLS.
I LIKE WHAT I LIKE.

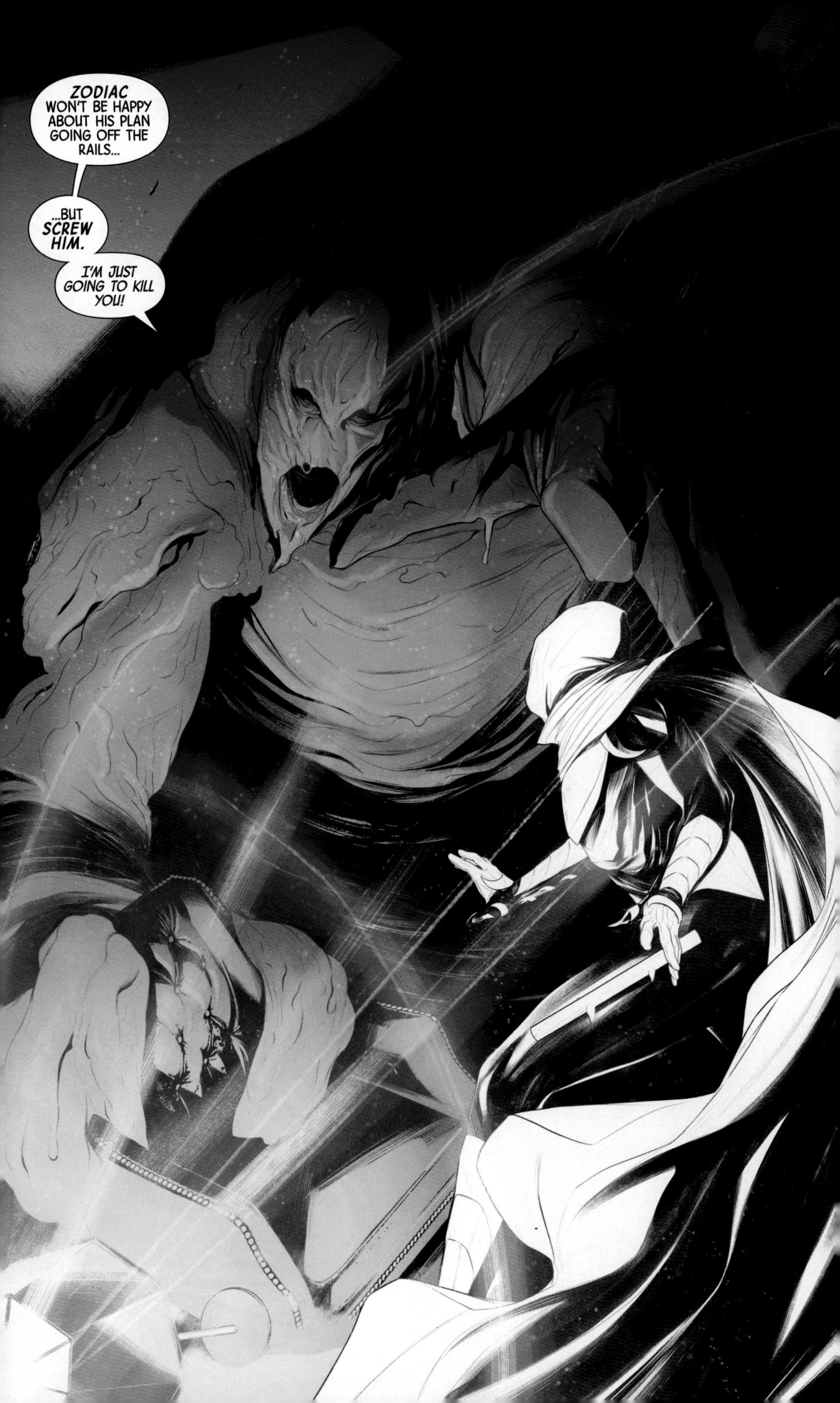
ZODIAC WON'T BE HAPPY ABOUT HIS PLAN GOING OFF THE RAILS...
...BUT SCREW HIM.
I'M JUST GOING TO KILL YOU!

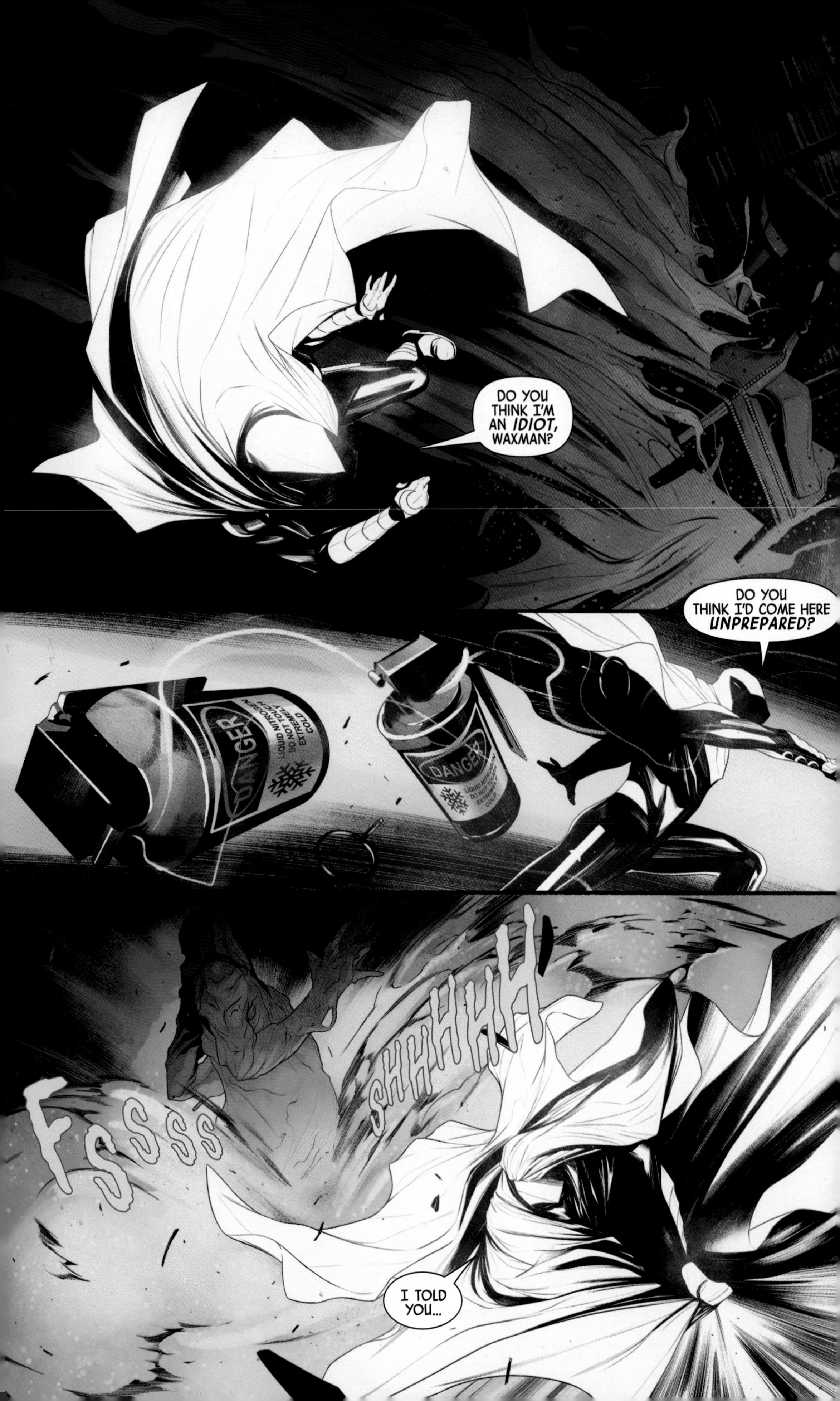
DO YOU THINK I'M AN *IDIOT,* WAXMAN?
DO YOU THINK I'D COME HERE ***UNPREPARED?***
DANGER
DANGER
FSSSS
SHHHHH
I TOLD YOU...

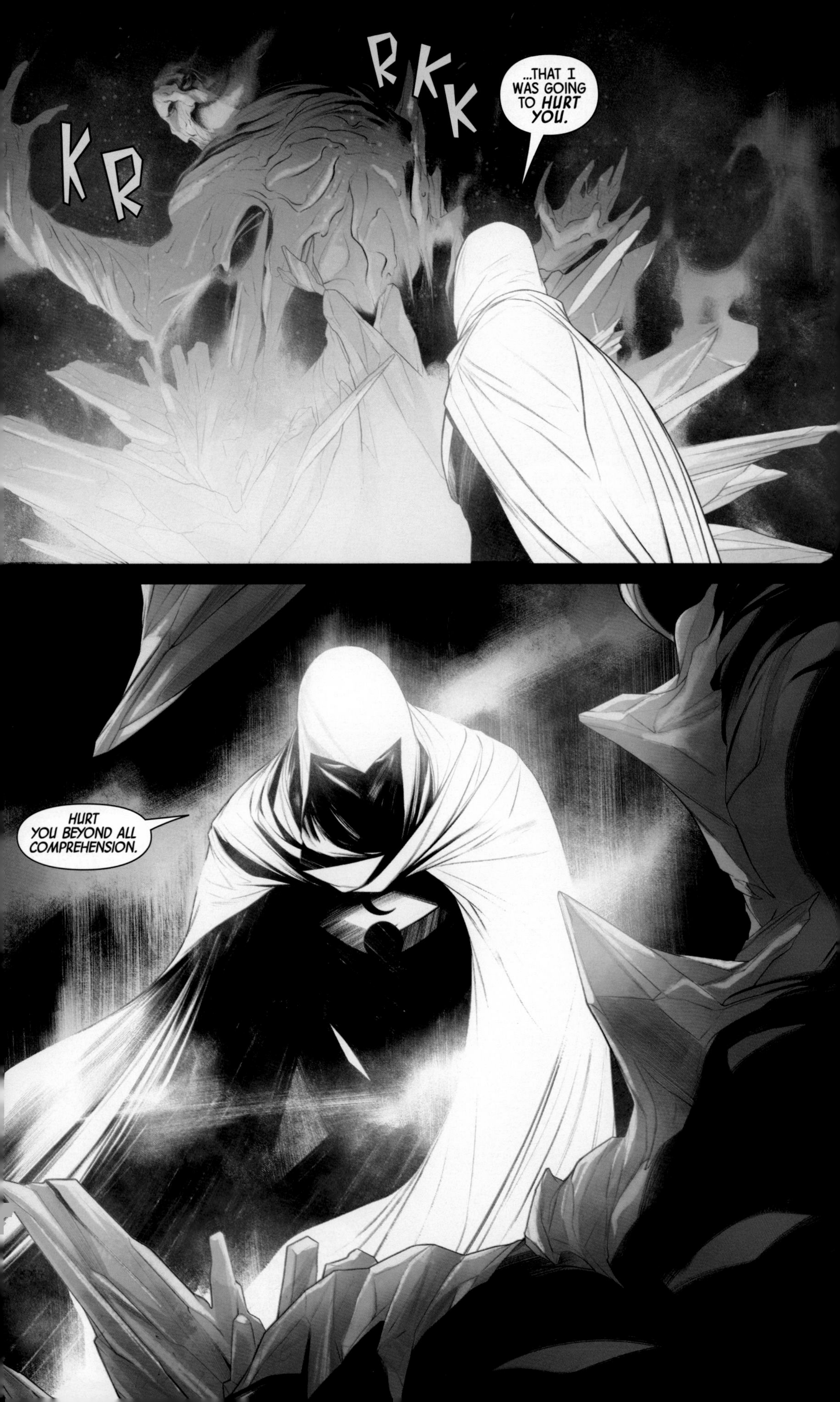
KR
RKK
...THAT I WAS GOING TO HURT YOU.
HURT YOU BEYOND ALL COMPREHENSION.

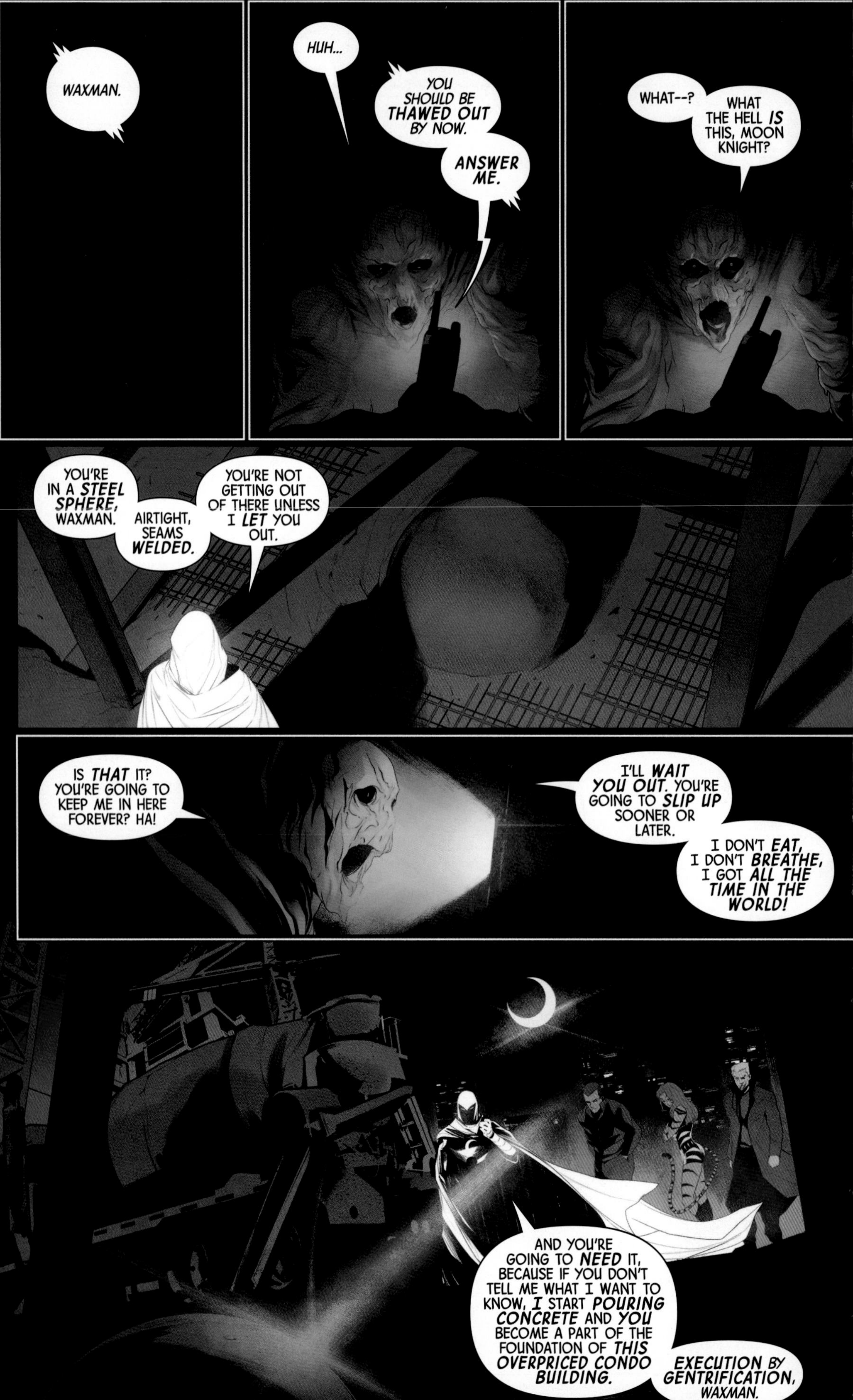

WAXMAN.
HUH...
YOU SHOULD BE THAWED OUT BY NOW.
ANSWER ME.
WHAT--?
WHAT THE HELL IS THIS, MOON KNIGHT?
YOU'RE IN A STEEL SPHERE, WAXMAN.
AIRTIGHT, SEAMS WELDED.
YOU'RE NOT GETTING OUT OF THERE UNLESS I LET YOU OUT.
IS THAT IT? YOU'RE GOING TO KEEP ME IN HERE FOREVER? HA!
I'LL WAIT YOU OUT. YOU'RE GOING TO SLIP UP SOONER OR LATER.
I DON'T EAT, I DON'T BREATHE, I GOT ALL THE TIME IN THE WORLD!
AND YOU'RE GOING TO NEED IT, BECAUSE IF YOU DON'T TELL ME WHAT I WANT TO KNOW, I START POURING CONCRETE AND YOU BECOME A PART OF THE FOUNDATION OF THIS OVERPRICED CONDO BUILDING.
EXECUTION BY GENTRIFICATION, WAXMAN.

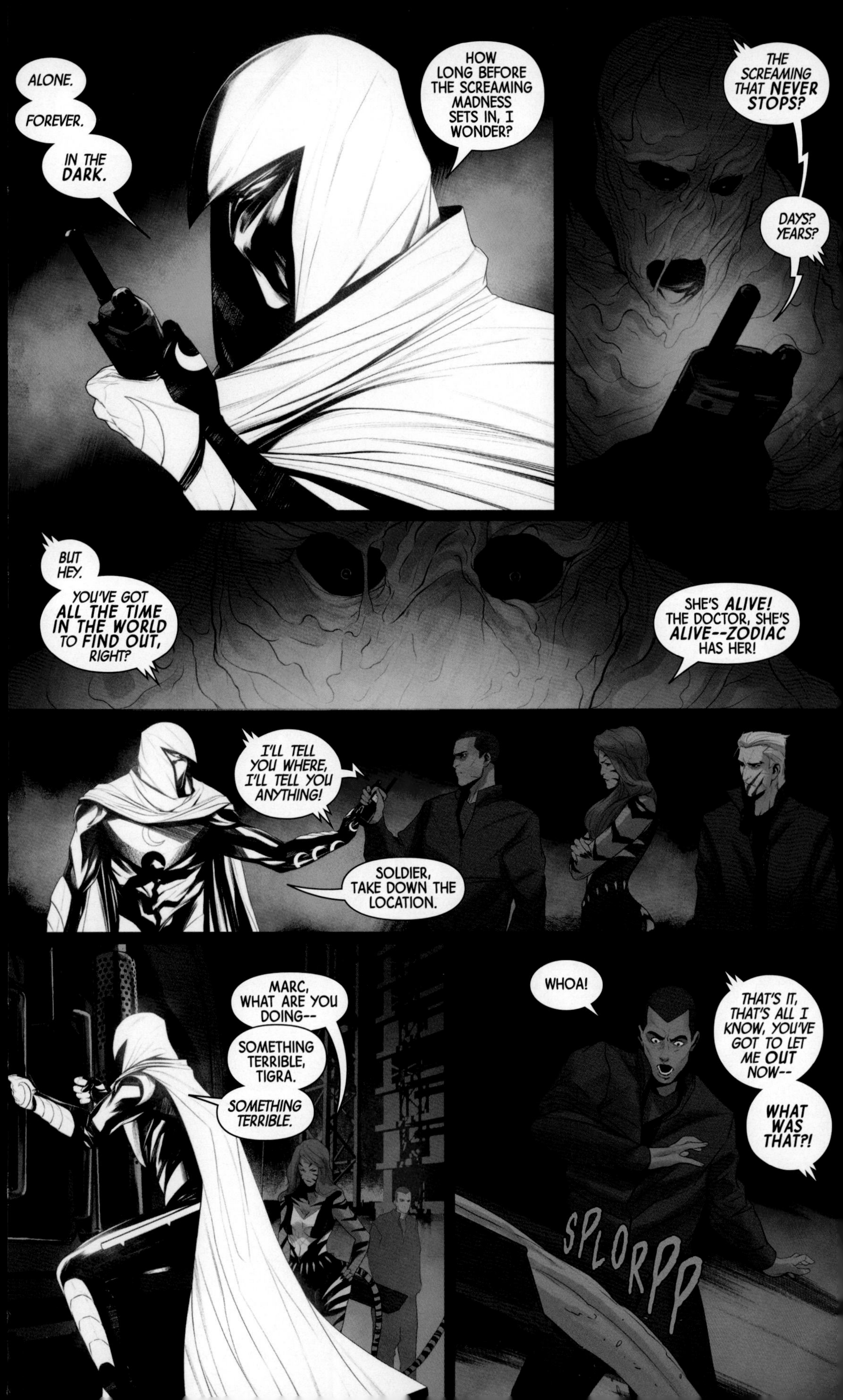

ALONE.
FOREVER.
IN THE DARK.
HOW LONG BEFORE THE SCREAMING MADNESS SETS IN, I WONDER?
THE SCREAMING THAT NEVER STOPS?
DAYS? YEARS?
BUT HEY.
YOU'VE GOT ALL THE TIME IN THE WORLD TO FIND OUT, RIGHT?
SHE'S ALIVE! THE DOCTOR, SHE'S ALIVE--ZODIAC HAS HER!
I'LL TELL YOU WHERE, I'LL TELL YOU ANYTHING!
SOLDIER, TAKE DOWN THE LOCATION.
MARC, WHAT ARE YOU DOING--
SOMETHING TERRIBLE, TIGRA.
SOMETHING TERRIBLE.
WHOA!
THAT'S IT, THAT'S ALL I KNOW, YOU'VE GOT TO LET ME OUT NOW--
WHAT WAS THAT?!
SPLORPP

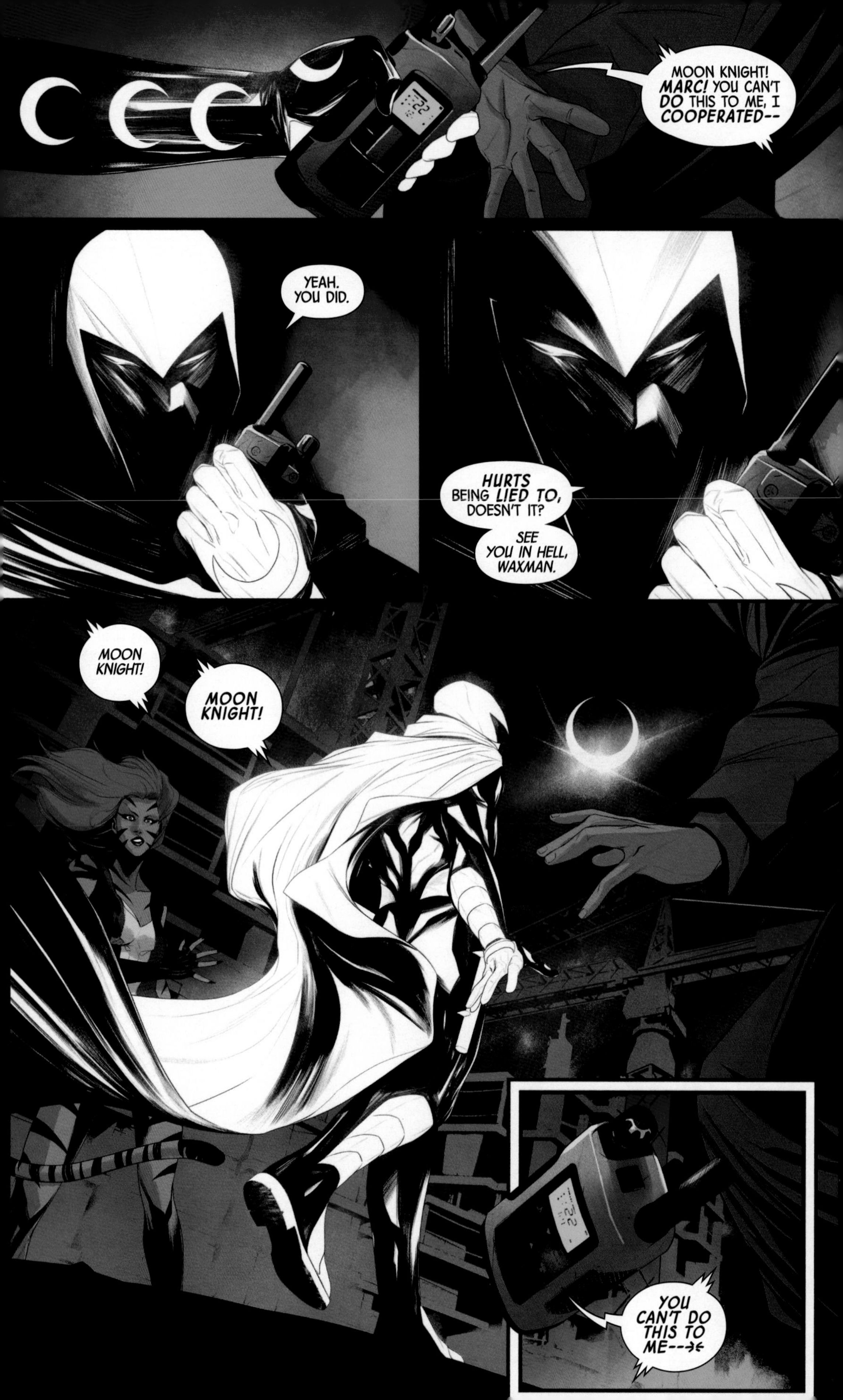

MOON KNIGHT! MARC! YOU CAN'T DO THIS TO ME, I COOPERATED--
YEAH. YOU DID.
HURTS BEING LIED TO, DOESN'T IT?
SEE YOU IN HELL, WAXMAN.
MOON KNIGHT!
MOON KNIGHT!
YOU CAN'T DO THIS TO ME--

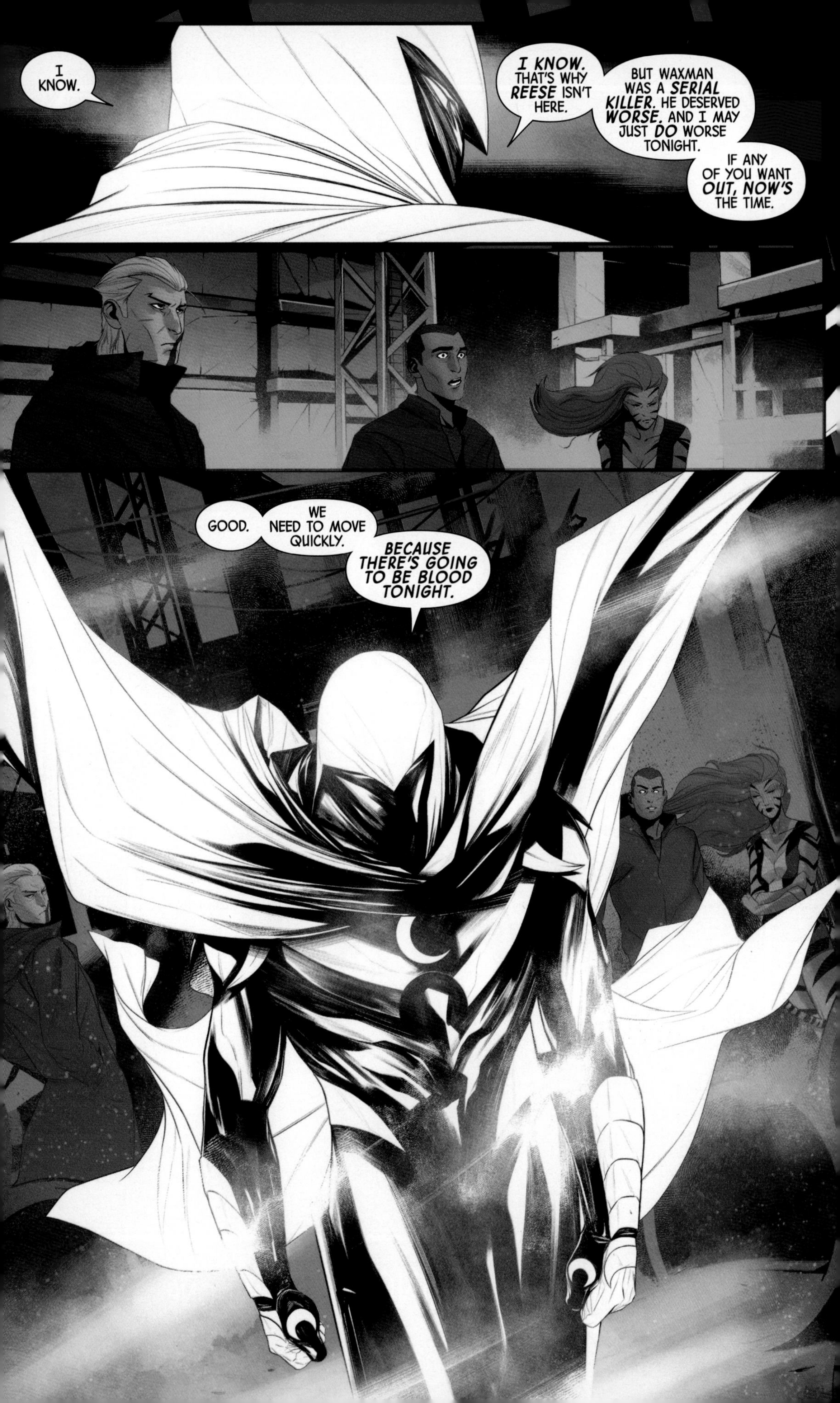
I KNOW.
I KNOW. THAT'S WHY REESE ISN'T HERE.
BUT WAXMAN WAS A SERIAL KILLER. HE DESERVED WORSE. AND I MAY JUST DO WORSE TONIGHT.
IF ANY OF YOU WANT OUT, NOW'S THE TIME.
GOOD.
WE NEED TO MOVE QUICKLY.
BECAUSE THERE'S GOING TO BE BLOOD TONIGHT.

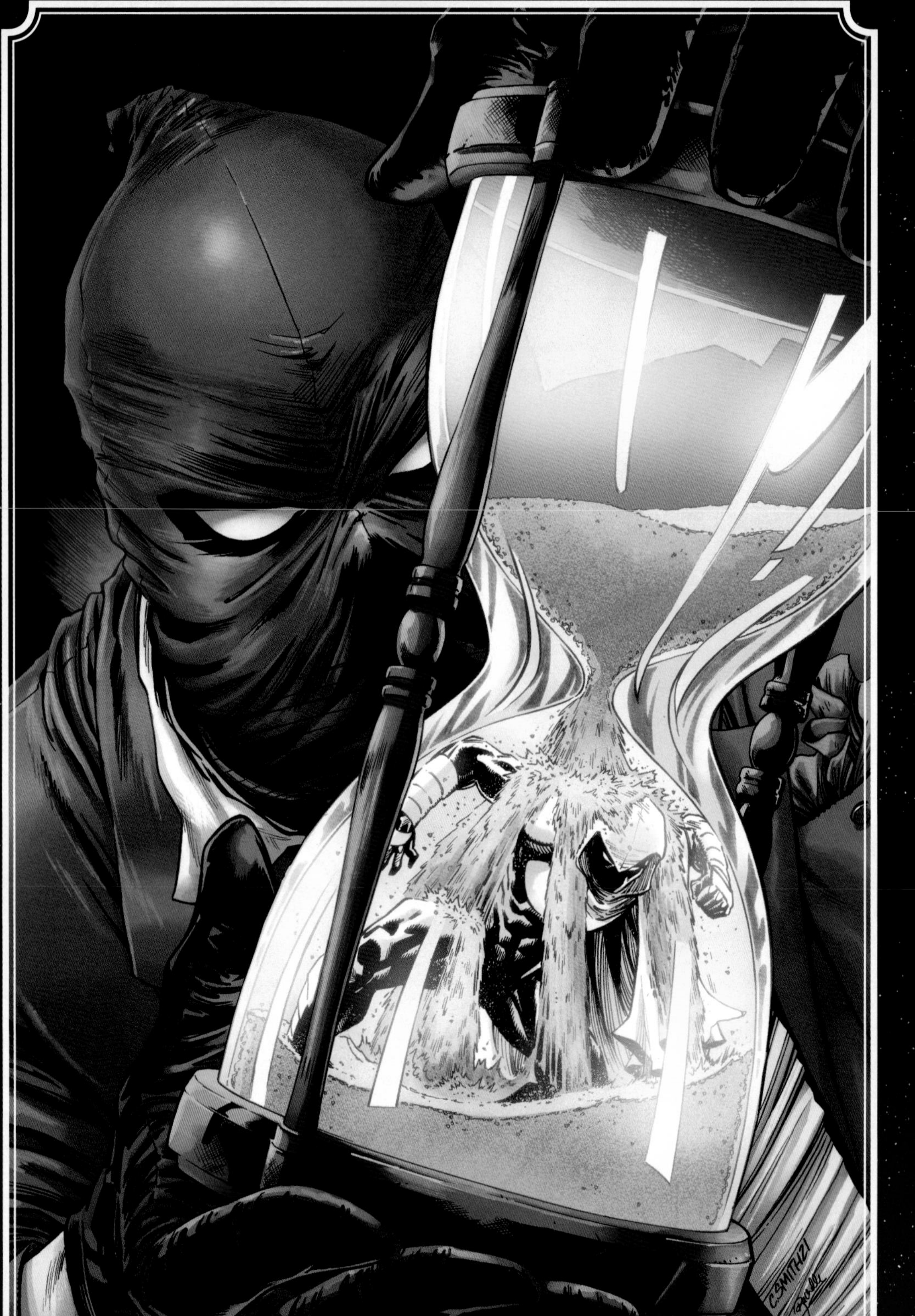
C.SMITH21

11 THE KILLING TIME PART ONE

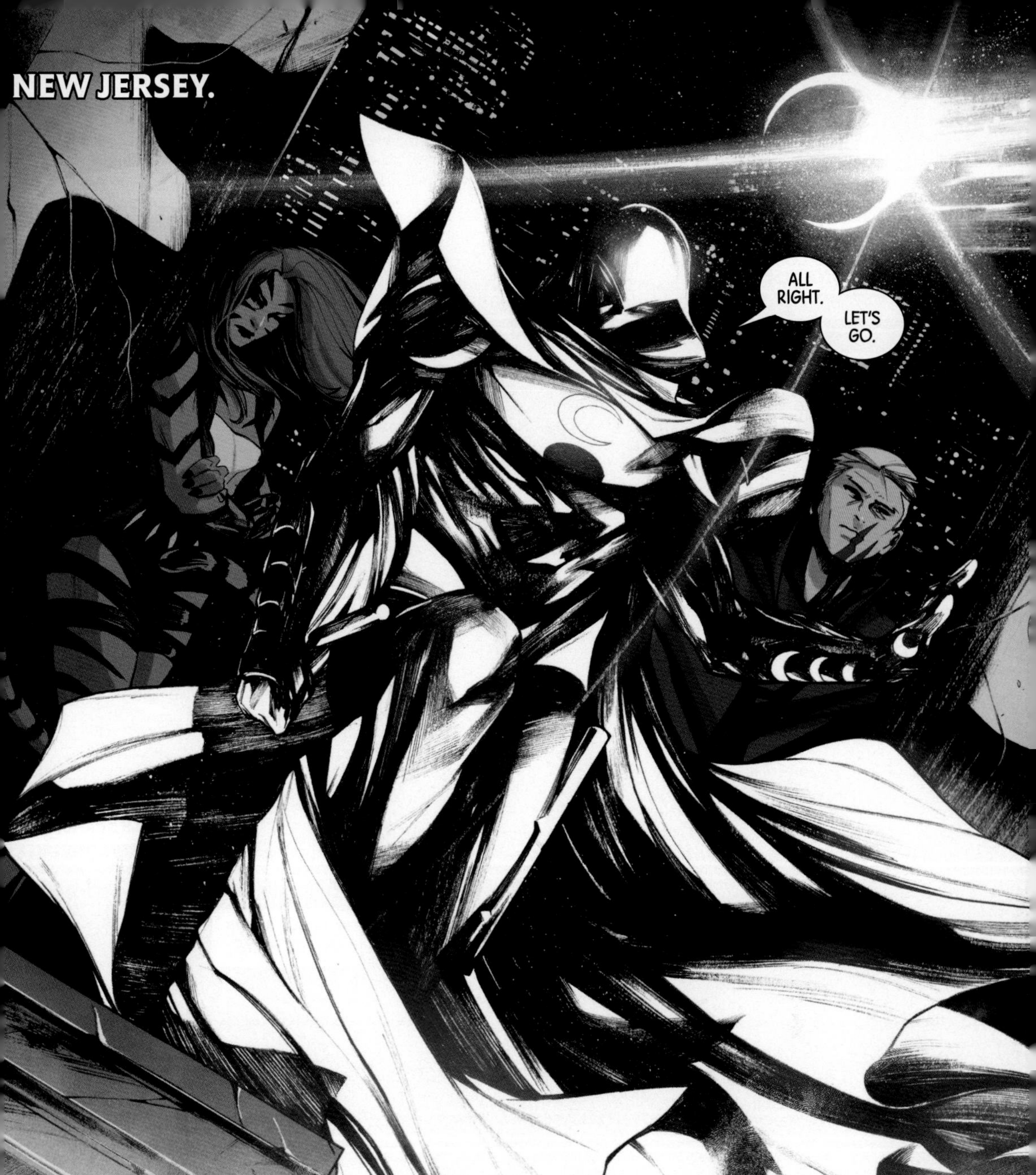
NEW JERSEY.
ALL RIGHT.
LET'S GO.

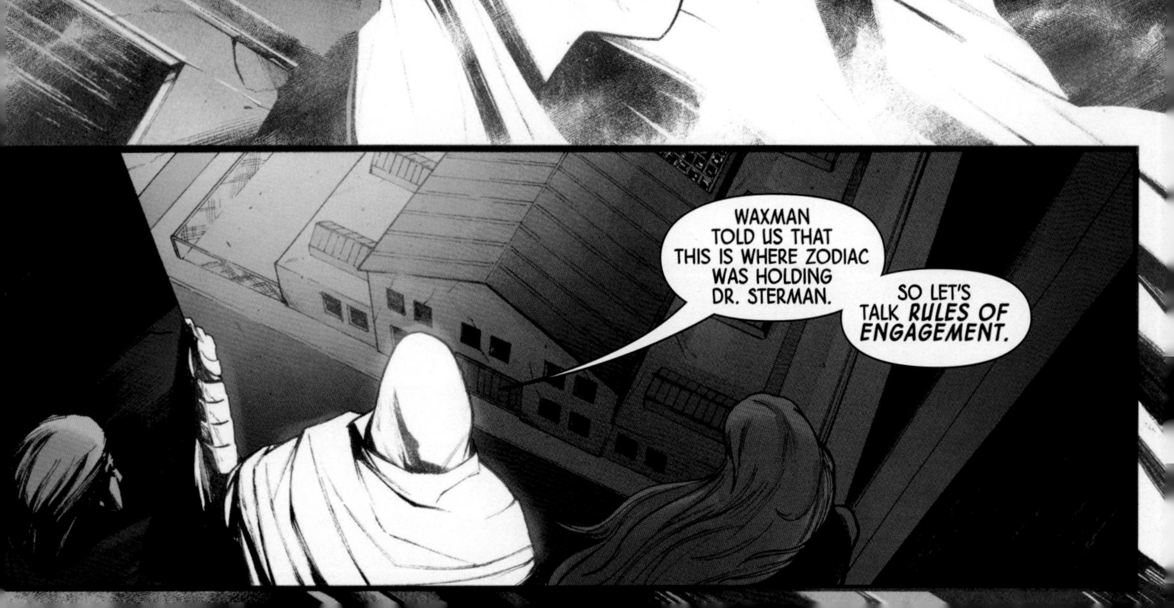
WAXMAN TOLD US THAT THIS IS WHERE ZODIAC WAS HOLDING DR. STERMAN.
SO LET'S TALK *RULES OF ENGAGEMENT.*

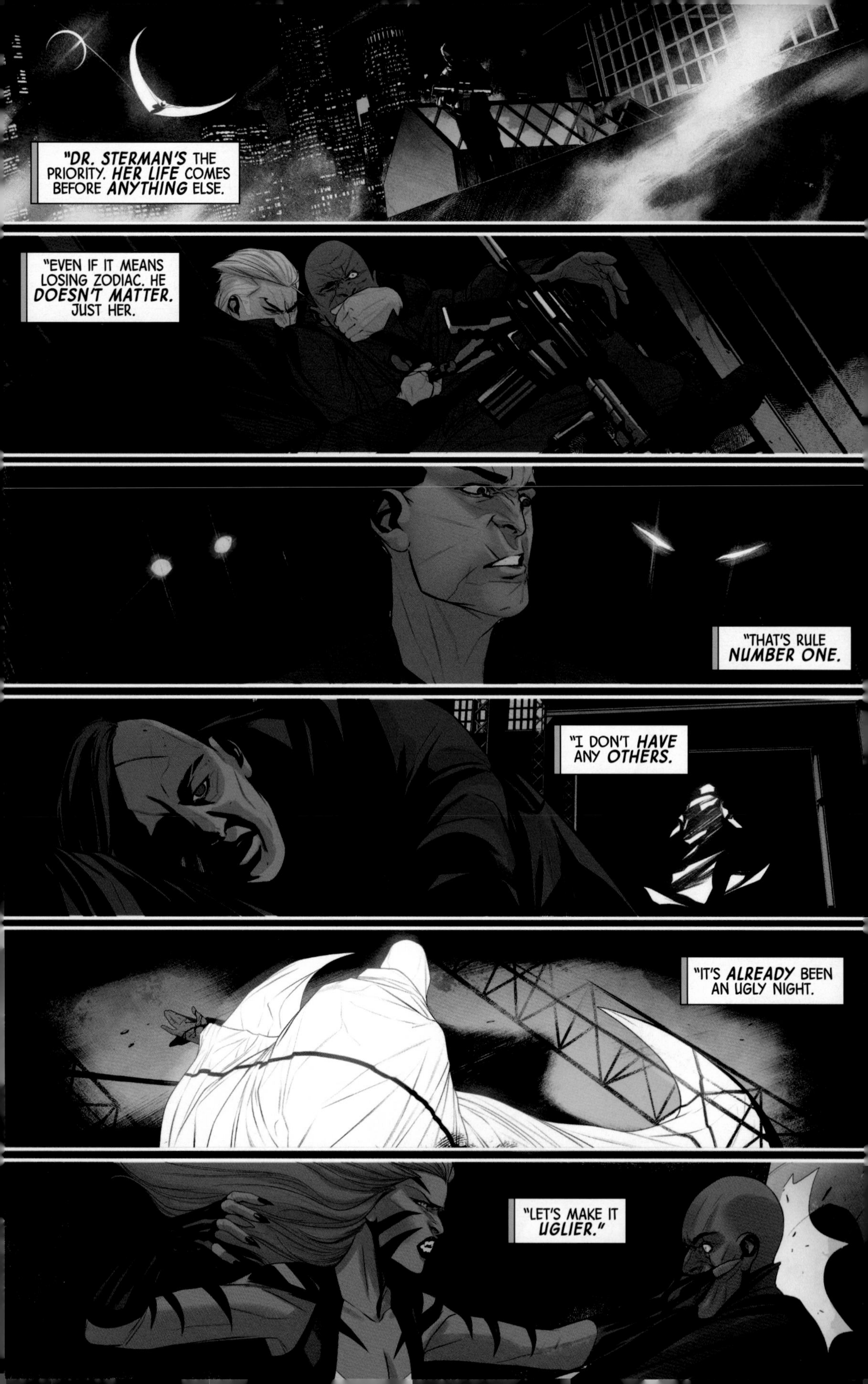
"DR. STERMAN'S THE PRIORITY. HER LIFE COMES BEFORE ANYTHING ELSE.
"EVEN IF IT MEANS LOSING ZODIAC. HE DOESN'T MATTER. JUST HER.
"THAT'S RULE NUMBER ONE.
"I DON'T HAVE ANY OTHERS.
"IT'S ALREADY BEEN AN UGLY NIGHT.
"LET'S MAKE IT UGLIER."

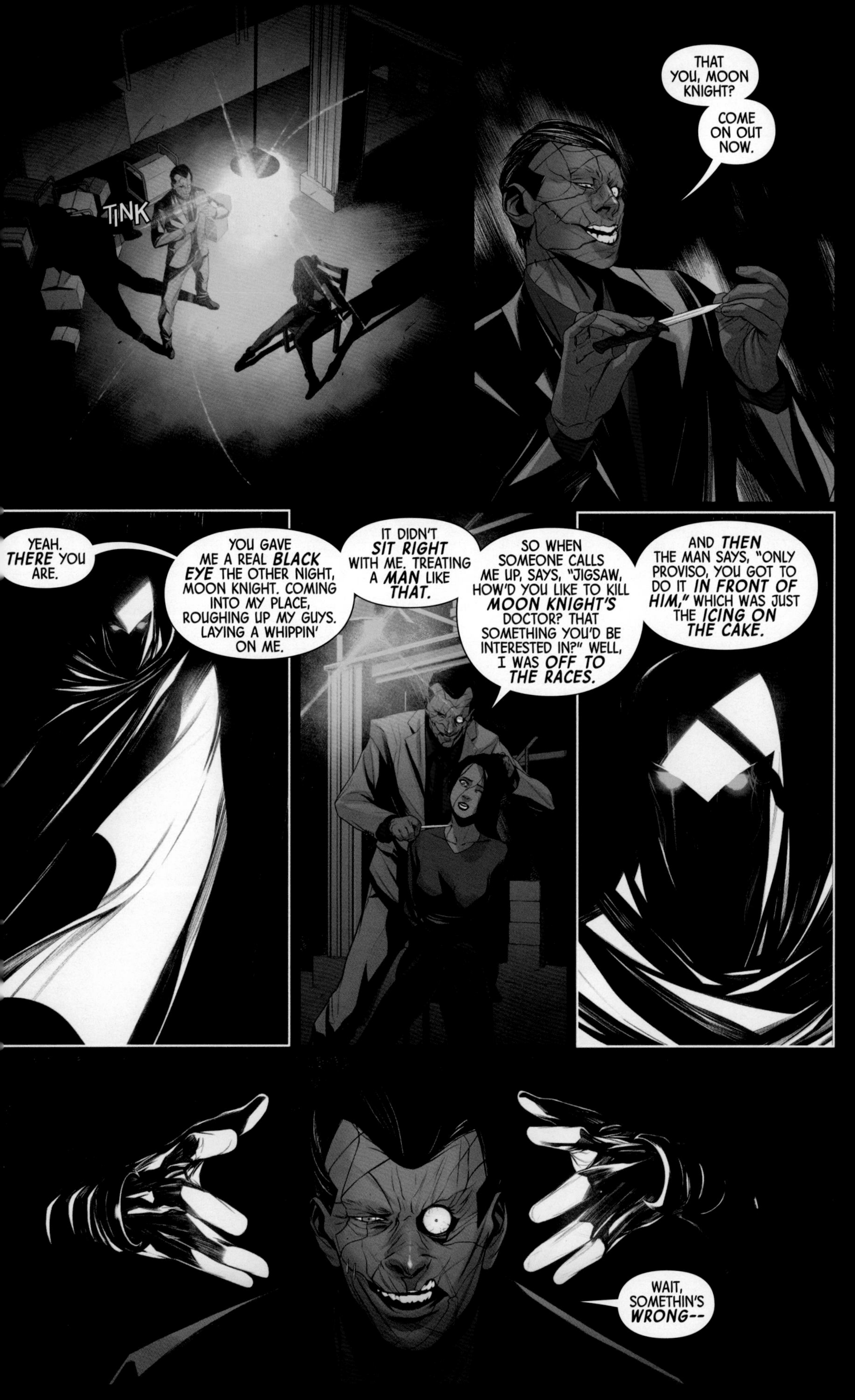
TINK
THAT YOU, MOON KNIGHT?
COME ON OUT NOW.
YEAH. THERE YOU ARE.
YOU GAVE ME A REAL BLACK EYE THE OTHER NIGHT, MOON KNIGHT. COMING INTO MY PLACE, ROUGHING UP MY GUYS. LAYING A WHIPPIN' ON ME.
IT DIDN'T SIT RIGHT WITH ME. TREATING A MAN LIKE THAT.
SO WHEN SOMEONE CALLS ME UP, SAYS, "JIGSAW, HOW'D YOU LIKE TO KILL MOON KNIGHT'S DOCTOR? THAT SOMETHING YOU'D BE INTERESTED IN?" WELL, I WAS OFF TO THE RACES.
AND THEN THE MAN SAYS, "ONLY PROVISO, YOU GOT TO DO IT IN FRONT OF HIM," WHICH WAS JUST THE ICING ON THE CAKE.
WAIT, SOMETHIN'S WRONG--

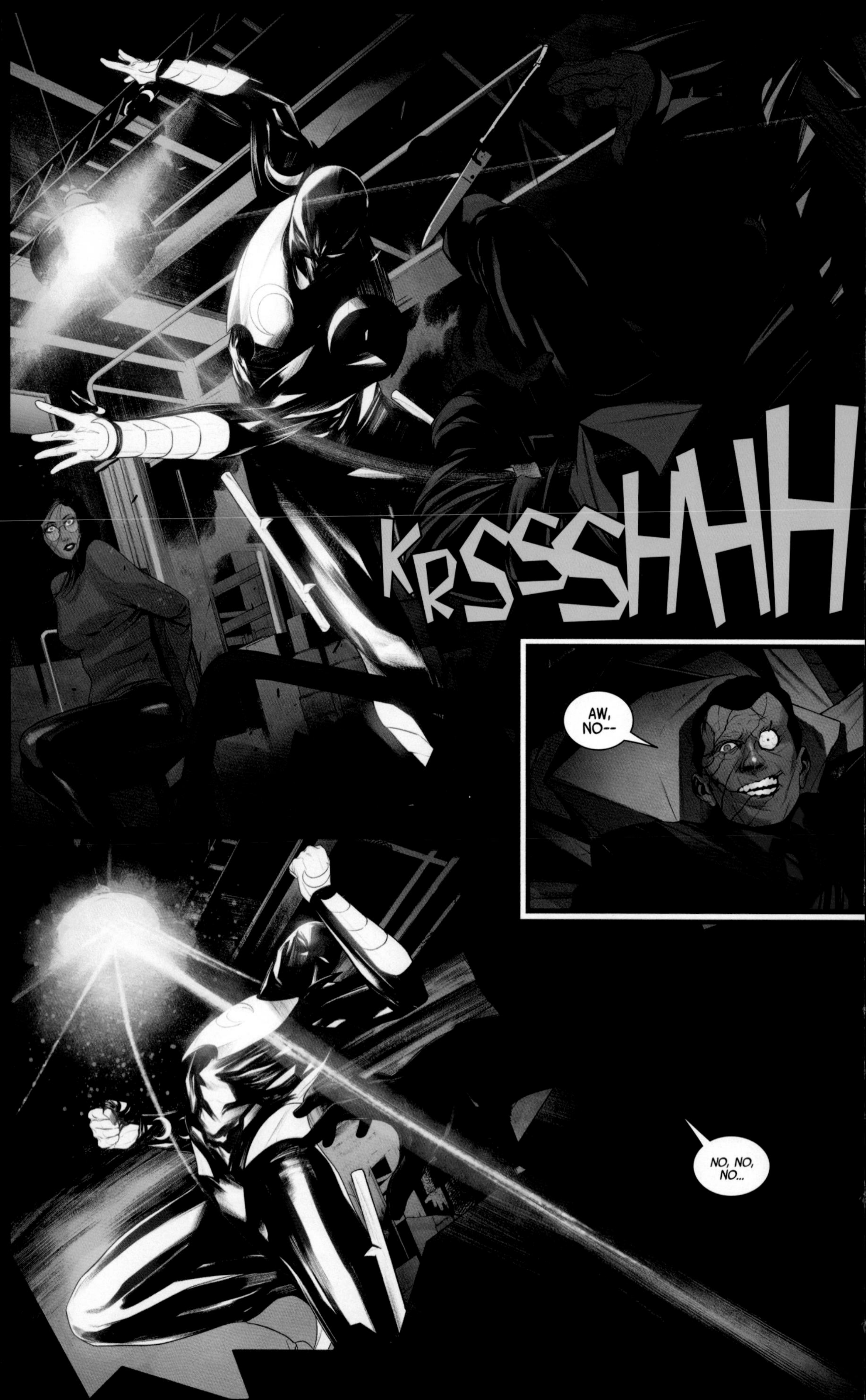
KRSSSHHH
AW, NO--
NO, NO, NO...

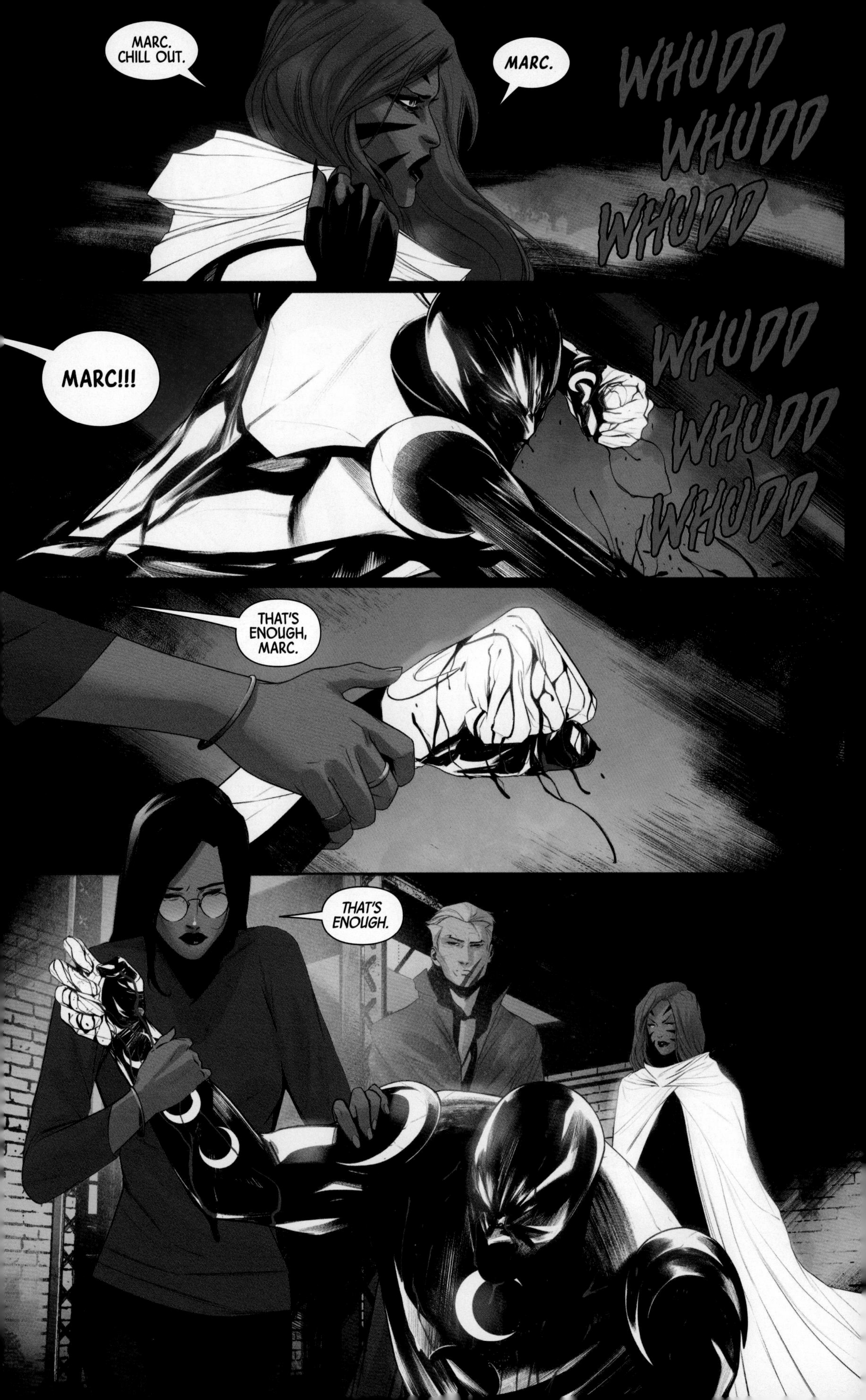
MARC.
CHILL OUT.
MARC.
WHUDD
WHUDD
WHUDD
MARC!!!
WHUDD
WHUDD
WHUDD
THAT'S ENOUGH, MARC.
THAT'S ENOUGH.

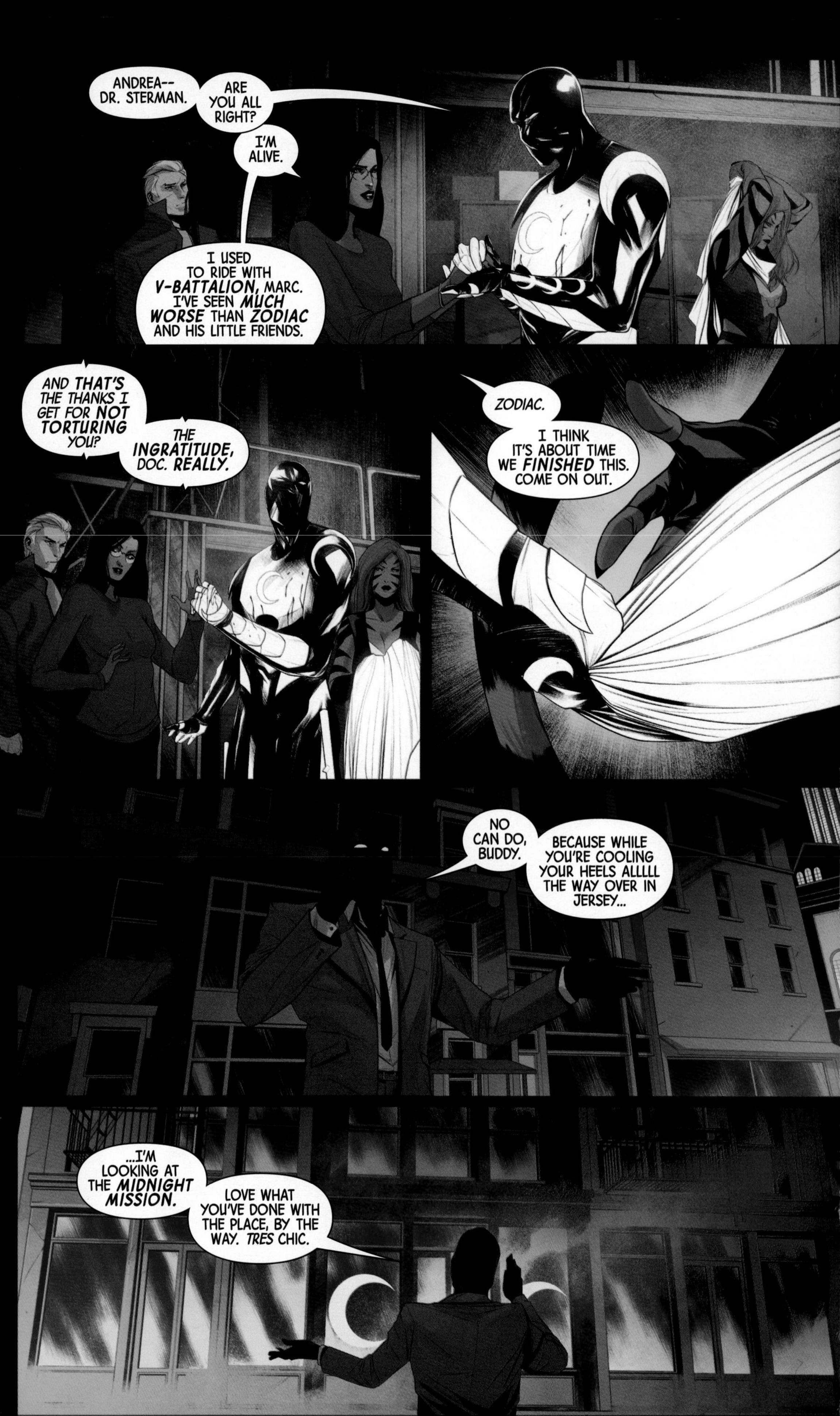
ANDREA-- DR. STERMAN.
ARE YOU ALL RIGHT?
I'M ALIVE.
I USED TO RIDE WITH V-BATTALION, MARC. I'VE SEEN MUCH WORSE THAN ZODIAC AND HIS LITTLE FRIENDS.
AND THAT'S THE THANKS I GET FOR NOT TORTURING YOU?
THE INGRATITUDE, DOC. REALLY.
ZODIAC.
I THINK IT'S ABOUT TIME WE FINISHED THIS. COME ON OUT.
NO CAN DO, BUDDY.
BECAUSE WHILE YOU'RE COOLING YOUR HEELS ALLLLL THE WAY OVER IN JERSEY...
...I'M LOOKING AT THE MIDNIGHT MISSION.
LOVE WHAT YOU'VE DONE WITH THE PLACE, BY THE WAY. TRES CHIC.

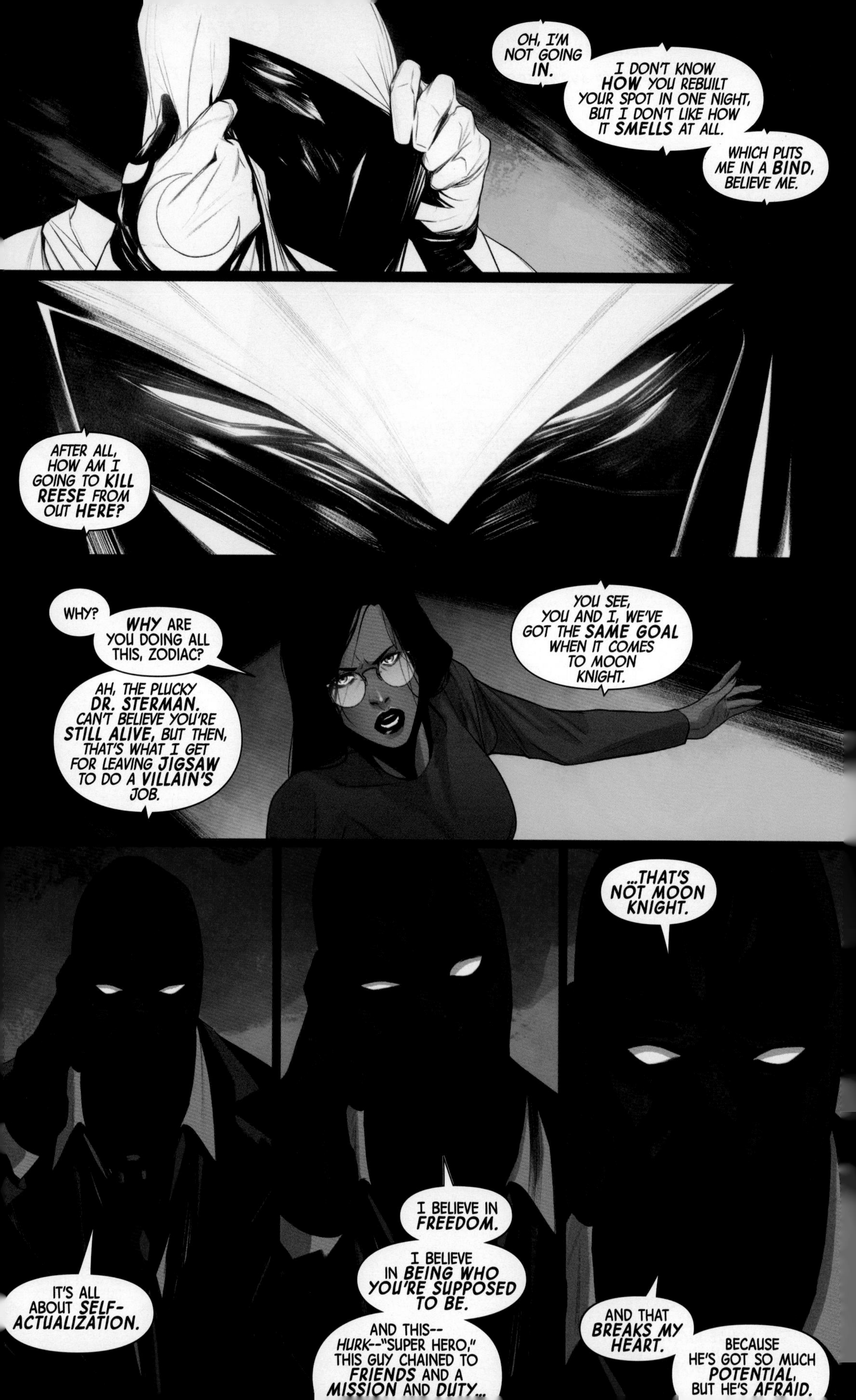
OH, I'M NOT GOING IN.
I DON'T KNOW HOW YOU REBUILT YOUR SPOT IN ONE NIGHT, BUT I DON'T LIKE HOW IT SMELLS AT ALL.
WHICH PUTS ME IN A BIND, BELIEVE ME.
AFTER ALL, HOW AM I GOING TO KILL REESE FROM OUT HERE?
WHY?
WHY ARE YOU DOING ALL THIS, ZODIAC?
AH, THE PLUCKY DR. STERMAN. CAN'T BELIEVE YOU'RE STILL ALIVE, BUT THEN, THAT'S WHAT I GET FOR LEAVING JIGSAW TO DO A VILLAIN'S JOB.
YOU SEE, YOU AND I, WE'VE GOT THE SAME GOAL WHEN IT COMES TO MOON KNIGHT.
IT'S ALL ABOUT SELF-ACTUALIZATION.
I BELIEVE IN FREEDOM.
I BELIEVE IN BEING WHO YOU'RE SUPPOSED TO BE.
AND THIS-- HURK--"SUPER HERO," THIS GUY CHAINED TO FRIENDS AND A MISSION AND DUTY...
...THAT'S NOT MOON KNIGHT.
AND THAT BREAKS MY HEART.
BECAUSE HE'S GOT SO MUCH POTENTIAL, BUT HE'S AFRAID.

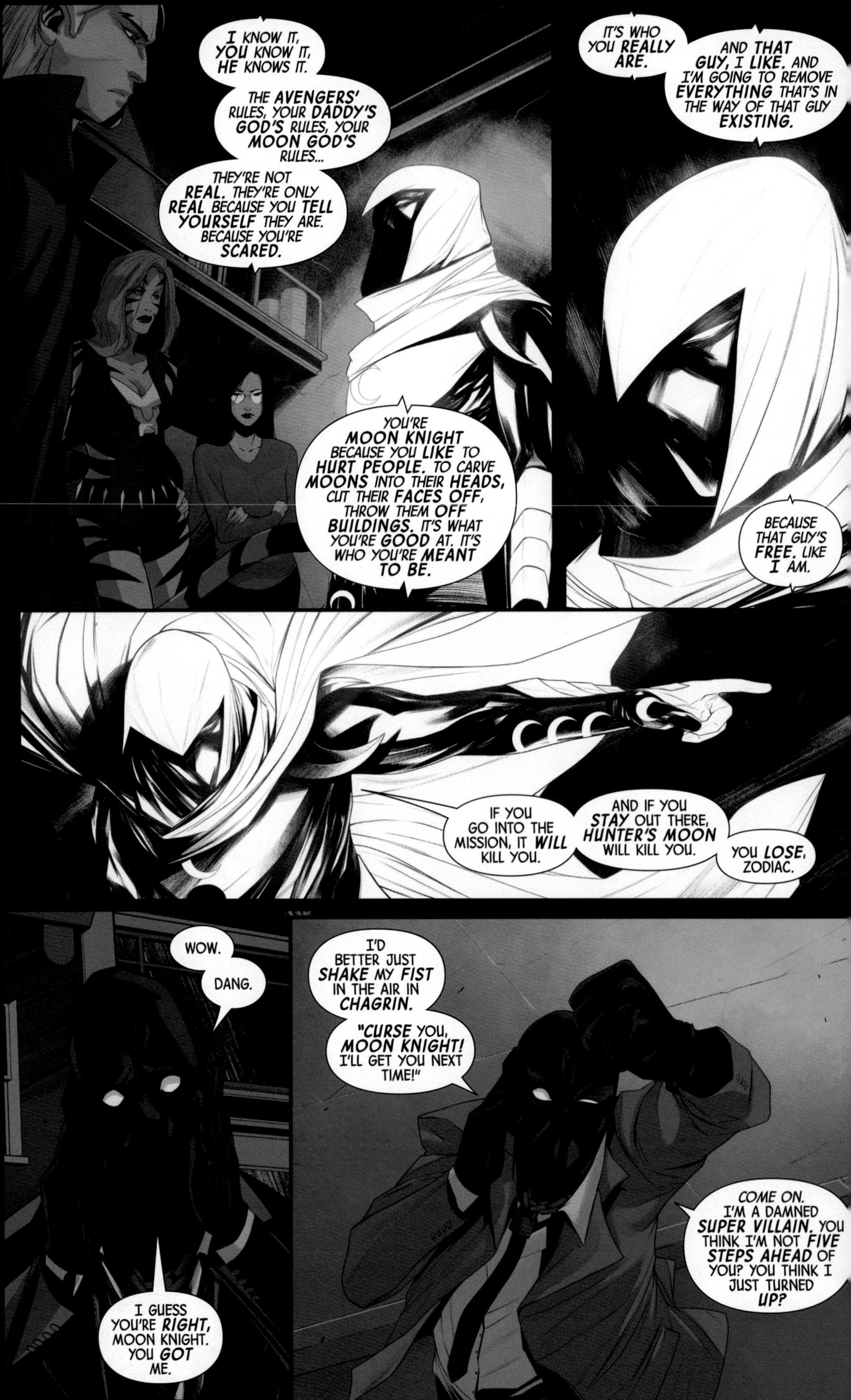
I KNOW IT, YOU KNOW IT, HE KNOWS IT.
THE AVENGERS' RULES, YOUR DADDY'S GOD'S RULES, YOUR MOON GOD'S RULES...
THEY'RE NOT REAL. THEY'RE ONLY REAL BECAUSE YOU TELL YOURSELF THEY ARE. BECAUSE YOU'RE SCARED.
YOU'RE MOON KNIGHT BECAUSE YOU LIKE TO HURT PEOPLE. TO CARVE MOONS INTO THEIR HEADS, CUT THEIR FACES OFF, THROW THEM OFF BUILDINGS. IT'S WHAT YOU'RE GOOD AT. IT'S WHO YOU'RE MEANT TO BE.
IT'S WHO YOU REALLY ARE.
AND THAT GUY, I LIKE. AND I'M GOING TO REMOVE EVERYTHING THAT'S IN THE WAY OF THAT GUY EXISTING.
BECAUSE THAT GUY'S FREE. LIKE I AM.
IF YOU GO INTO THE MISSION, IT WILL KILL YOU.
AND IF YOU STAY OUT THERE, HUNTER'S MOON WILL KILL YOU.
YOU LOSE, ZODIAC.
WOW.
DANG.
I GUESS YOU'RE RIGHT, MOON KNIGHT. YOU GOT ME.
I'D BETTER JUST SHAKE MY FIST IN THE AIR IN CHAGRIN.
"CURSE YOU, MOON KNIGHT! I'LL GET YOU NEXT TIME!"
COME ON. I'M A DAMNED SUPER VILLAIN. YOU THINK I'M NOT FIVE STEPS AHEAD OF YOU? YOU THINK I JUST TURNED UP?

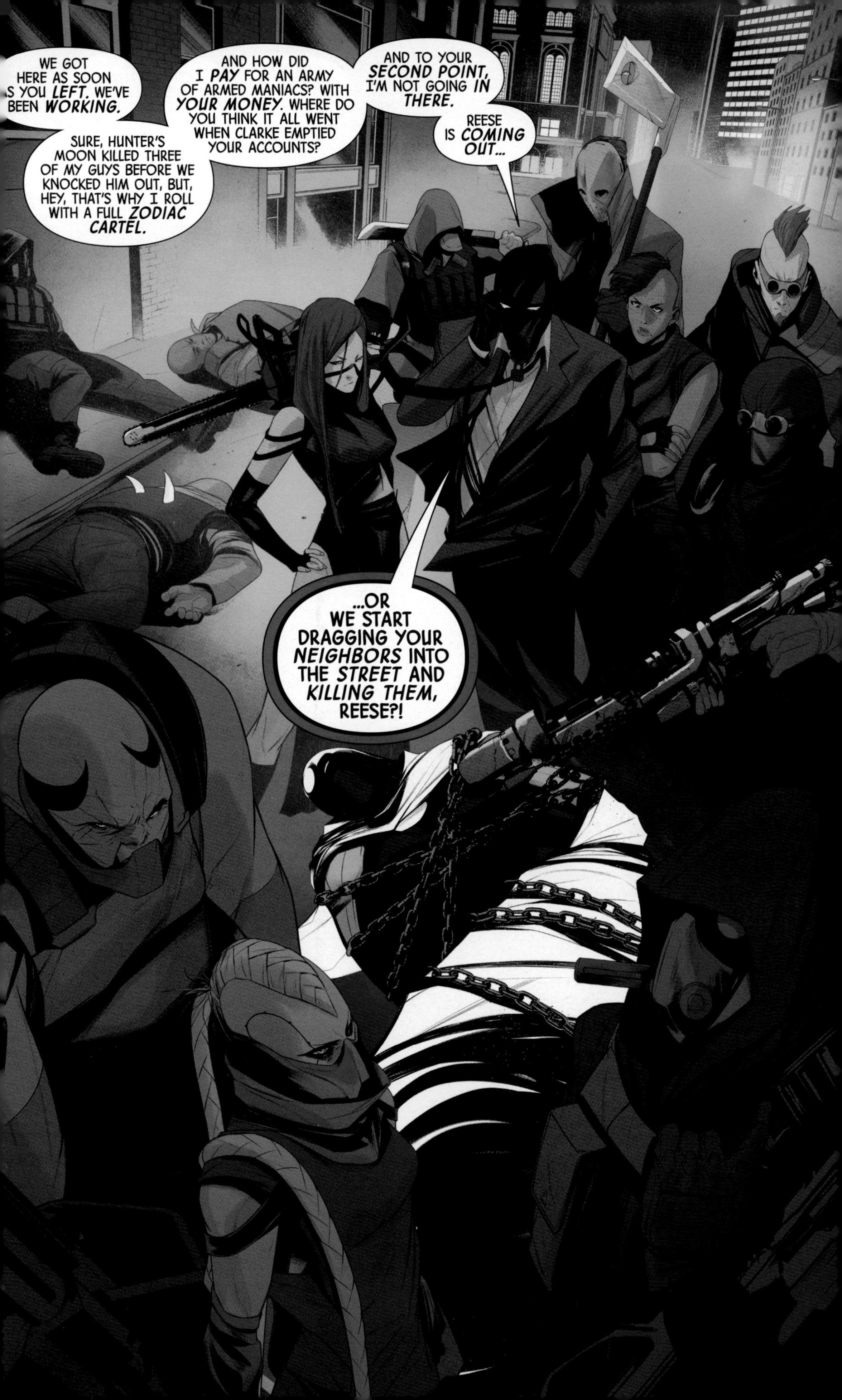
WE GOT HERE AS SOON AS YOU LEFT. WE'VE BEEN WORKING.
SURE, HUNTER'S MOON KILLED THREE OF MY GUYS BEFORE WE KNOCKED HIM OUT, BUT, HEY, THAT'S WHY I ROLL WITH A FULL ZODIAC CARTEL.
AND HOW DID I PAY FOR AN ARMY OF ARMED MANIACS? WITH YOUR MONEY. WHERE DO YOU THINK IT ALL WENT WHEN CLARKE EMPTIED YOUR ACCOUNTS?
AND TO YOUR SECOND POINT, I'M NOT GOING IN THERE.
REESE IS COMING OUT...
...OR WE START DRAGGING YOUR NEIGHBORS INTO THE STREET AND KILLING THEM, REESE?!

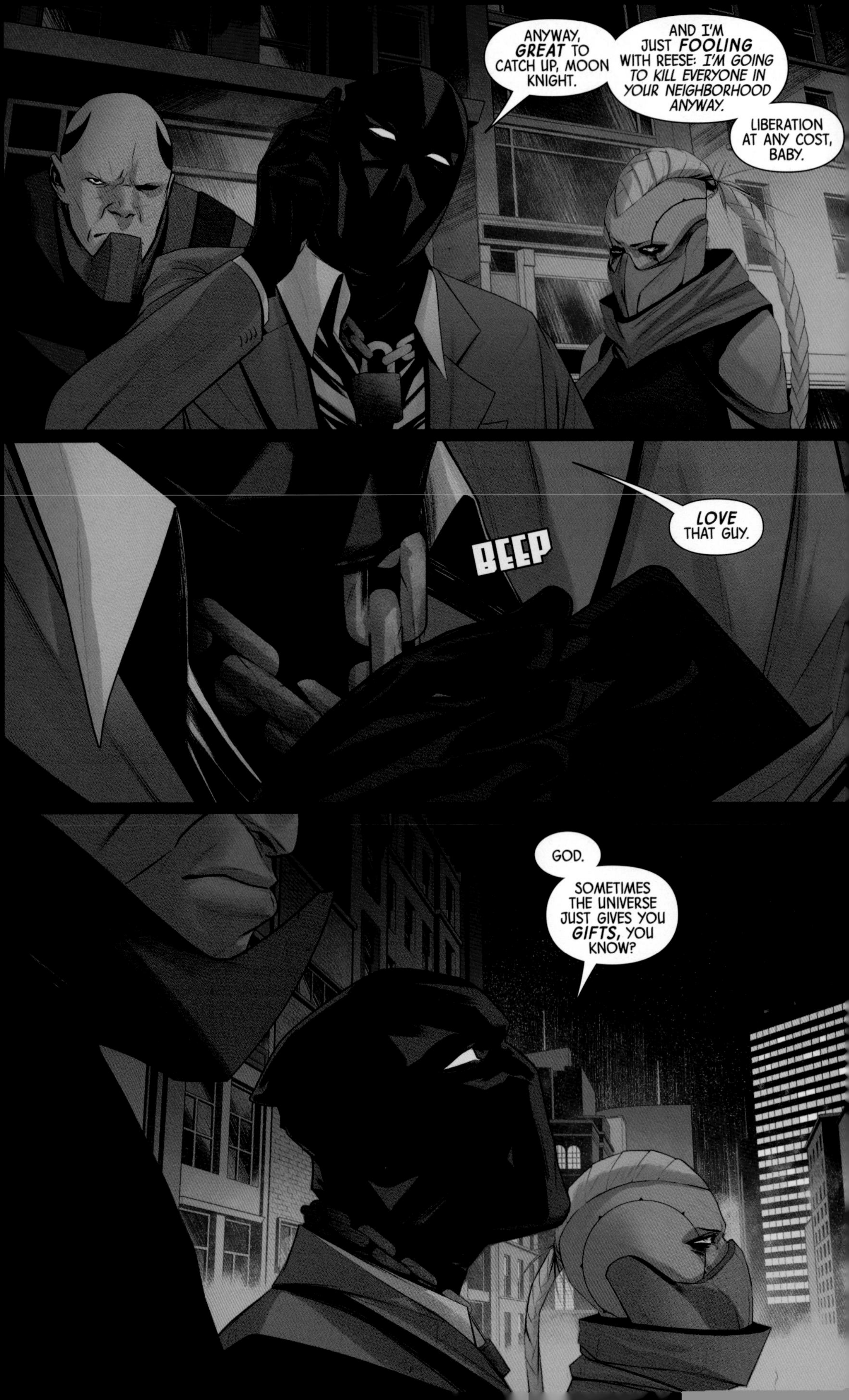
ANYWAY, GREAT TO CATCH UP, MOON KNIGHT.
AND I'M JUST FOOLING WITH REESE: I'M GOING TO KILL EVERYONE IN YOUR NEIGHBORHOOD ANYWAY.
LIBERATION AT ANY COST, BABY.
LOVE THAT GUY.
BEEP
GOD.
SOMETIMES THE UNIVERSE JUST GIVES YOU GIFTS, YOU KNOW?

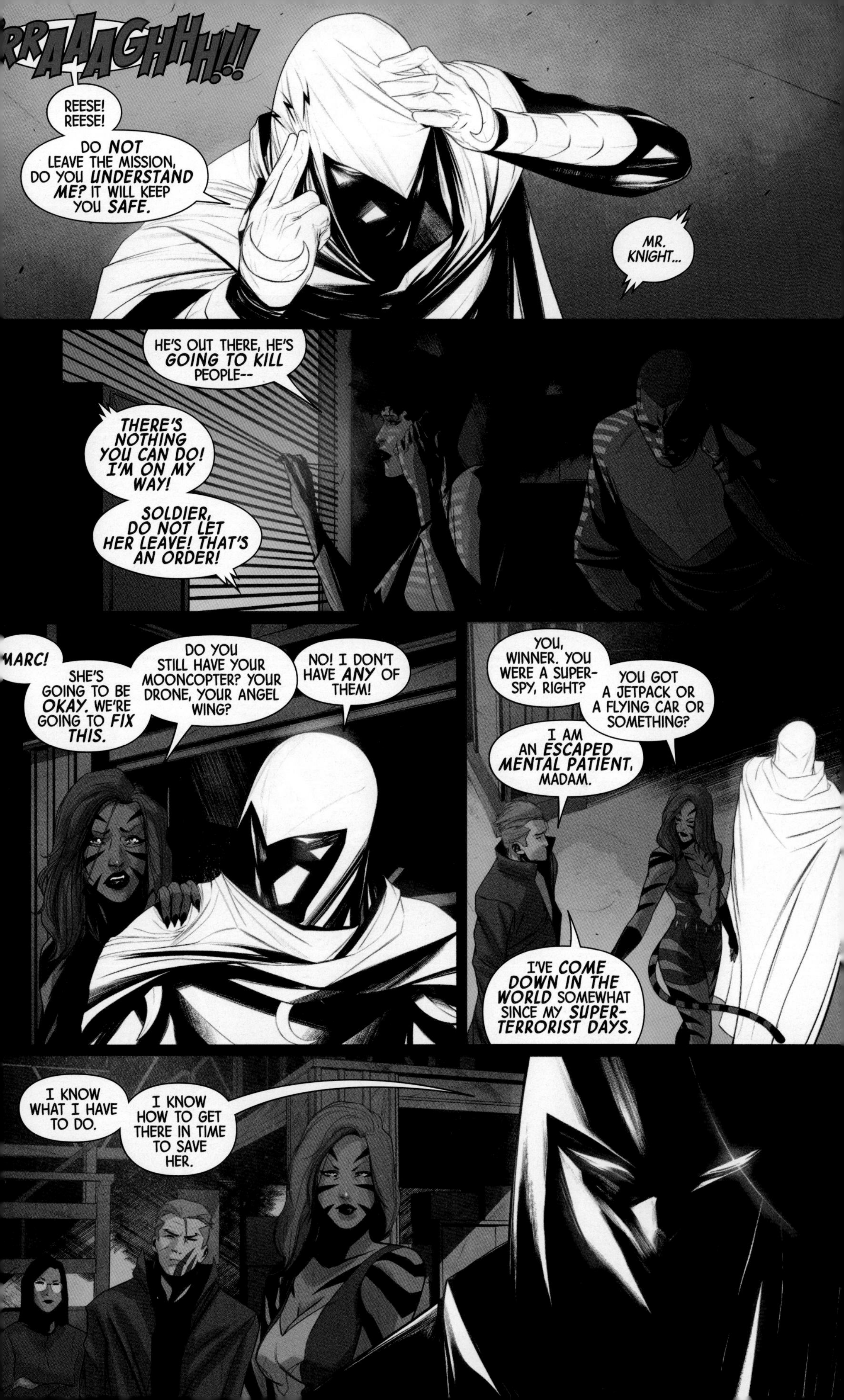

RRAAAAGHHH!!!
REESE! REESE!
DO NOT LEAVE THE MISSION, DO YOU UNDERSTAND ME? IT WILL KEEP YOU SAFE.
MR. KNIGHT...
HE'S OUT THERE, HE'S GOING TO KILL PEOPLE--
THERE'S NOTHING YOU CAN DO! I'M ON MY WAY!
SOLDIER, DO NOT LET HER LEAVE! THAT'S AN ORDER!
MARC!
SHE'S GOING TO BE OKAY. WE'RE GOING TO FIX THIS.
DO YOU STILL HAVE YOUR MOONCOPTER? YOUR DRONE, YOUR ANGEL WING?
NO! I DON'T HAVE ANY OF THEM!
YOU, WINNER. YOU WERE A SUPER-SPY, RIGHT?
YOU GOT A JETPACK OR A FLYING CAR OR SOMETHING?
I AM AN ESCAPED MENTAL PATIENT, MADAM.
I'VE COME DOWN IN THE WORLD SOMEWHAT SINCE MY SUPER-TERRORIST DAYS.
I KNOW WHAT I HAVE TO DO.
I KNOW HOW TO GET THERE IN TIME TO SAVE HER.

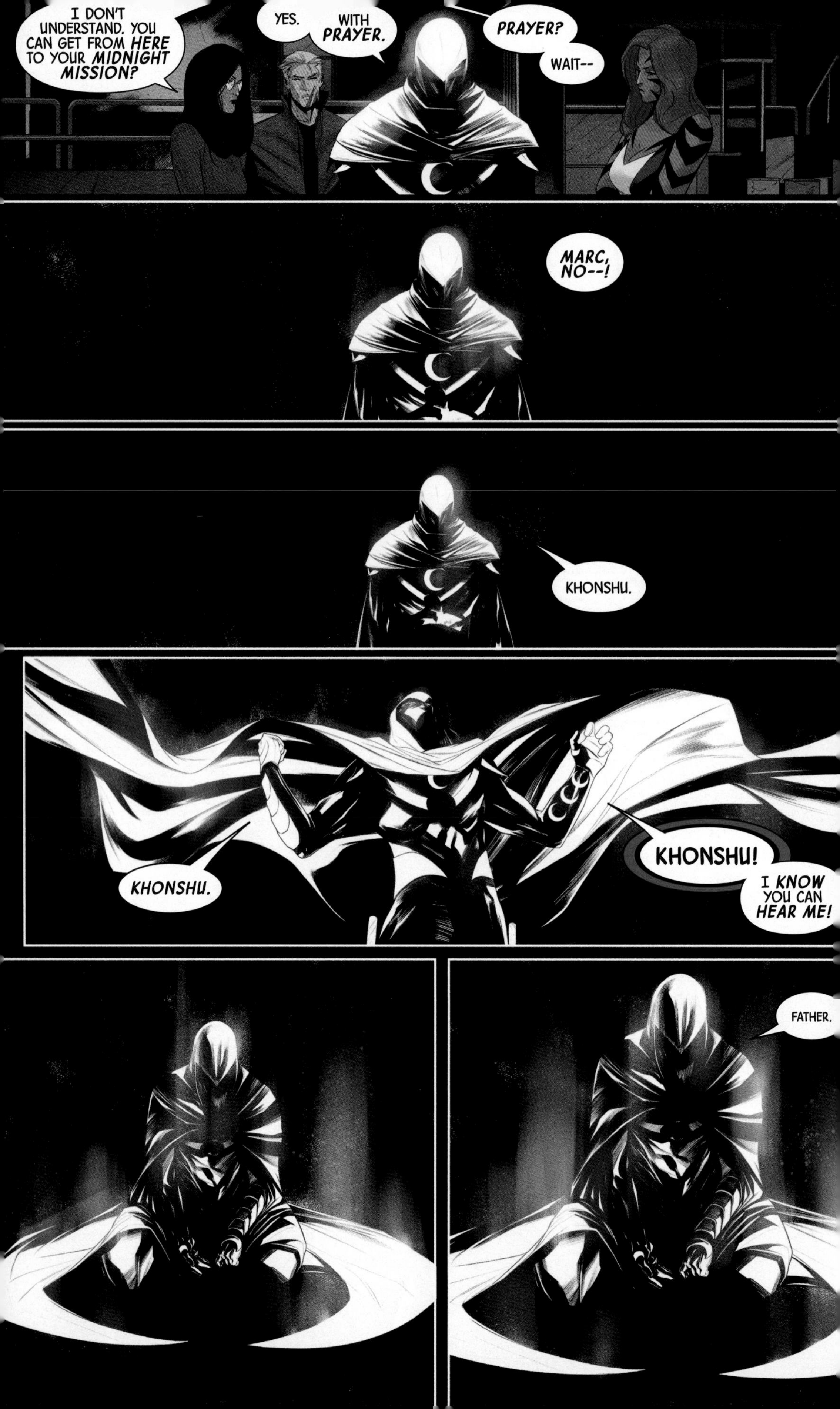

I DON'T UNDERSTAND. YOU CAN GET FROM HERE TO YOUR MIDNIGHT MISSION?
YES.
WITH PRAYER.
PRAYER?
WAIT--
MARC, NO--!
KHONSHU.
KHONSHU.
KHONSHU!
I KNOW YOU CAN HEAR ME!
FATHER.

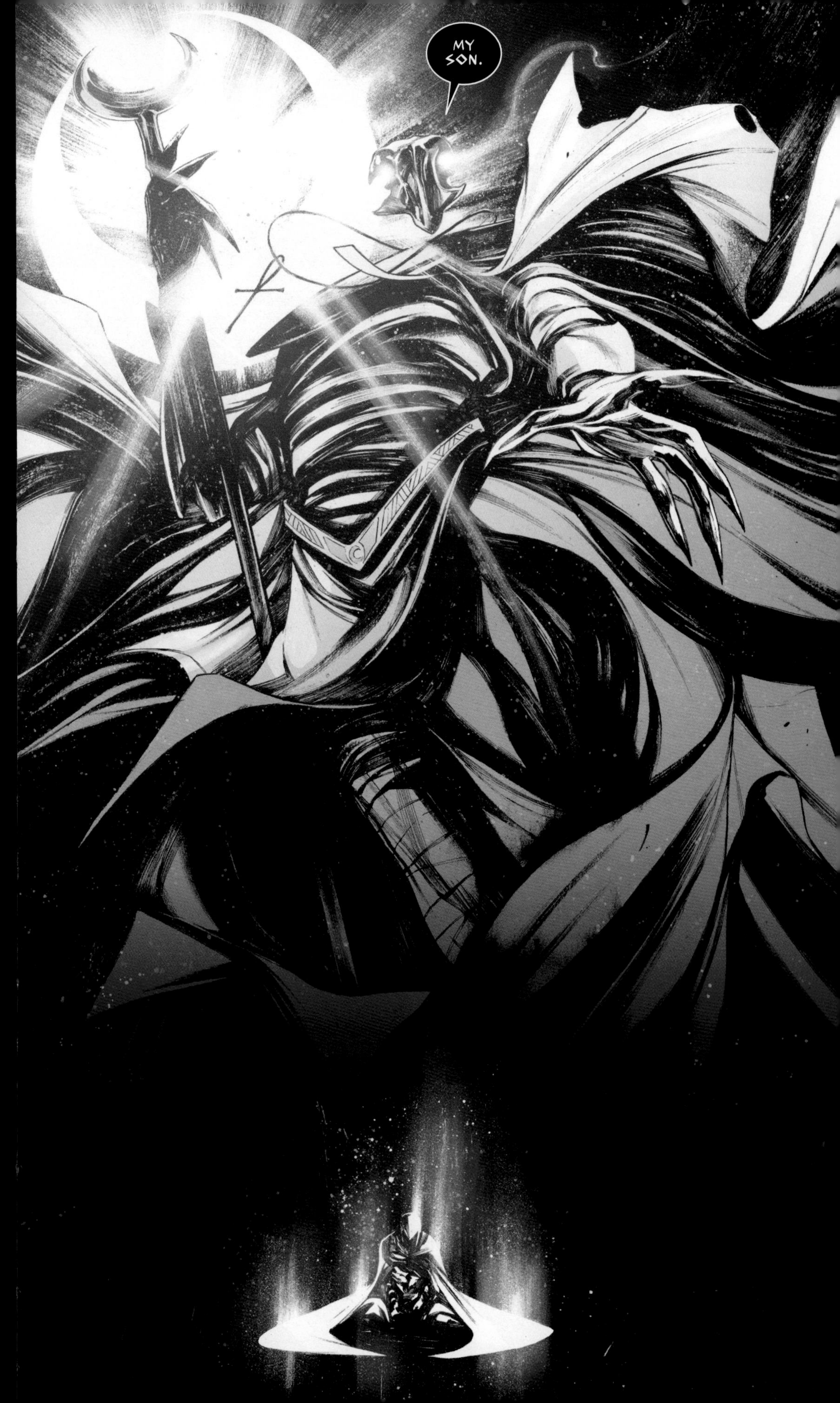
MY SON.

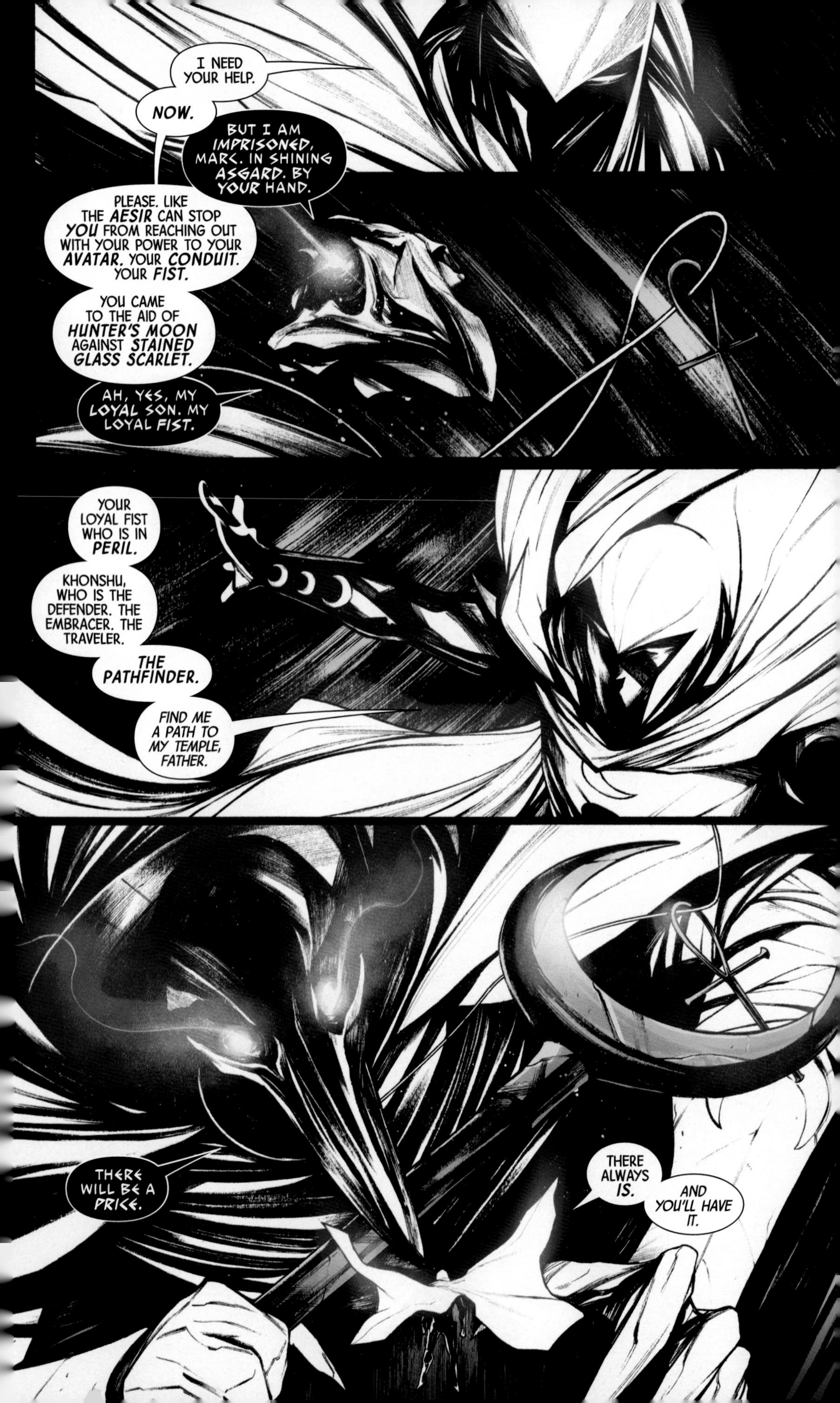
I NEED YOUR HELP.
NOW.
BUT I AM IMPRISONED, MARC. IN SHINING ASGARD. BY YOUR HAND.
PLEASE. LIKE THE AESIR CAN STOP YOU FROM REACHING OUT WITH YOUR POWER TO YOUR AVATAR. YOUR CONDUIT. YOUR FIST.
YOU CAME TO THE AID OF HUNTER'S MOON AGAINST STAINED GLASS SCARLET.
AH, YES, MY LOYAL SON. MY LOYAL FIST.
YOUR LOYAL FIST WHO IS IN PERIL.
KHONSHU, WHO IS THE DEFENDER. THE EMBRACER. THE TRAVELER.
THE PATHFINDER.
FIND ME A PATH TO MY TEMPLE, FATHER.
THERE WILL BE A PRICE.
THERE ALWAYS IS.
AND YOU'LL HAVE IT.

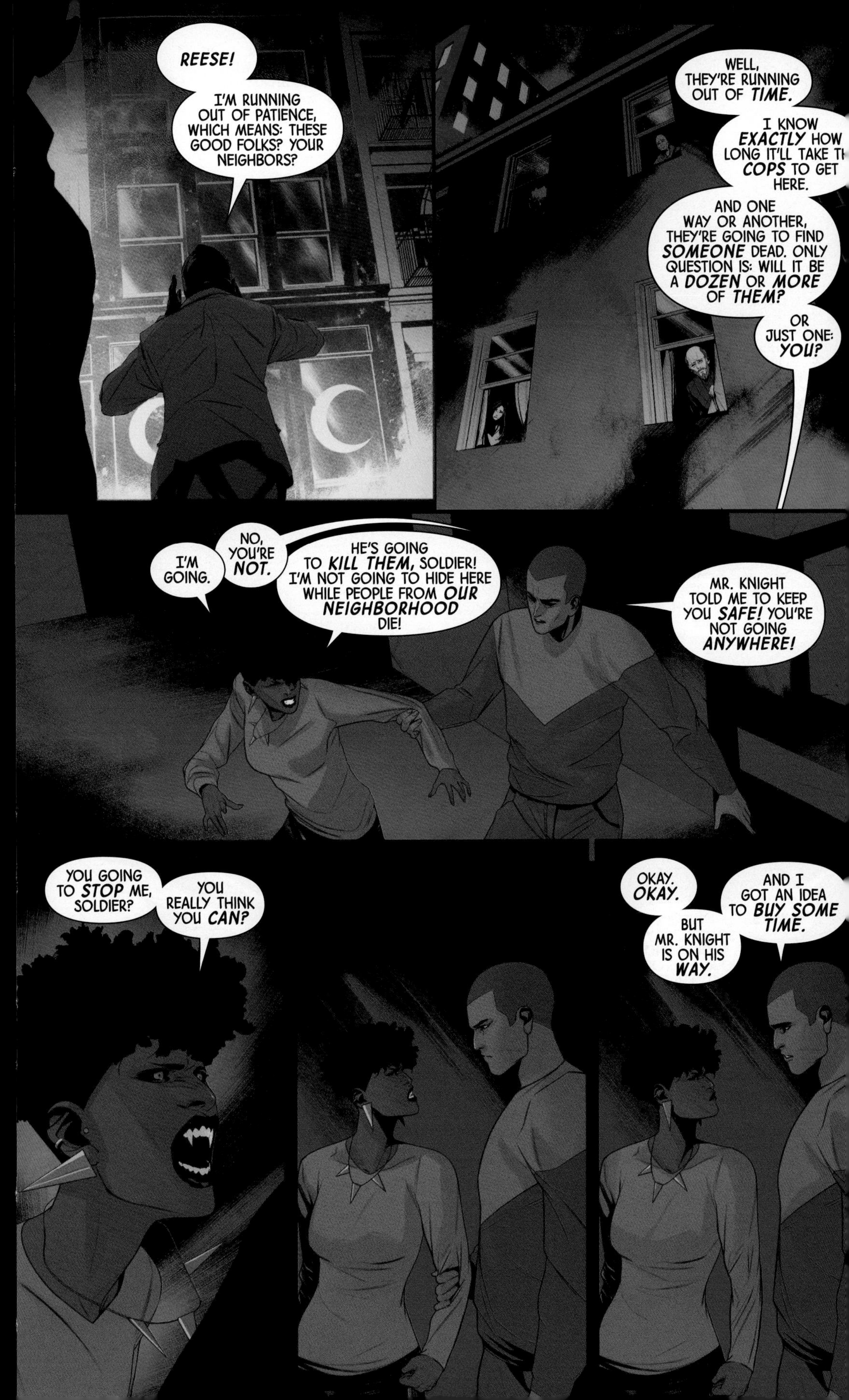
REESE!
I'M RUNNING OUT OF PATIENCE, WHICH MEANS: THESE GOOD FOLKS? YOUR NEIGHBORS?
WELL, THEY'RE RUNNING OUT OF TIME.
I KNOW EXACTLY HOW LONG IT'LL TAKE THE COPS TO GET HERE.
AND ONE WAY OR ANOTHER, THEY'RE GOING TO FIND SOMEONE DEAD. ONLY QUESTION IS: WILL IT BE A DOZEN OR MORE OF THEM?
OR JUST ONE: YOU?
I'M GOING.
NO, YOU'RE NOT.
HE'S GOING TO KILL THEM, SOLDIER! I'M NOT GOING TO HIDE HERE WHILE PEOPLE FROM OUR NEIGHBORHOOD DIE!
MR. KNIGHT TOLD ME TO KEEP YOU SAFE! YOU'RE NOT GOING ANYWHERE!
YOU GOING TO STOP ME, SOLDIER?
YOU REALLY THINK YOU CAN?
OKAY. OKAY.
BUT MR. KNIGHT IS ON HIS WAY.
AND I GOT AN IDEA TO BUY SOME TIME.

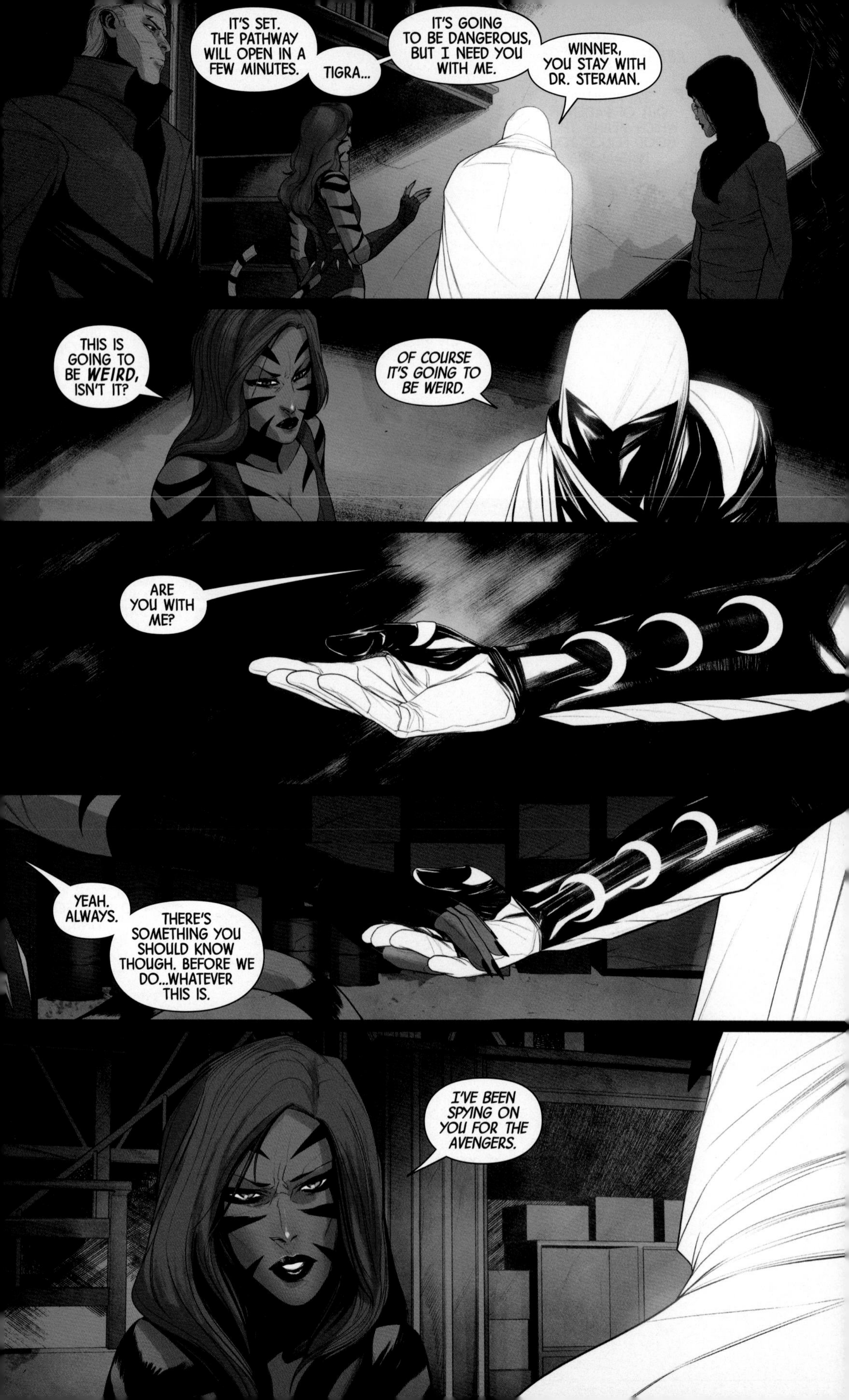
IT'S SET. THE PATHWAY WILL OPEN IN A FEW MINUTES.
TIGRA...
IT'S GOING TO BE DANGEROUS, BUT I NEED YOU WITH ME.
WINNER, YOU STAY WITH DR. STERMAN.
THIS IS GOING TO BE WEIRD, ISN'T IT?
OF COURSE IT'S GOING TO BE WEIRD.
ARE YOU WITH ME?
YEAH. ALWAYS.
THERE'S SOMETHING YOU SHOULD KNOW THOUGH. BEFORE WE DO...WHATEVER THIS IS.
I'VE BEEN SPYING ON YOU FOR THE AVENGERS.

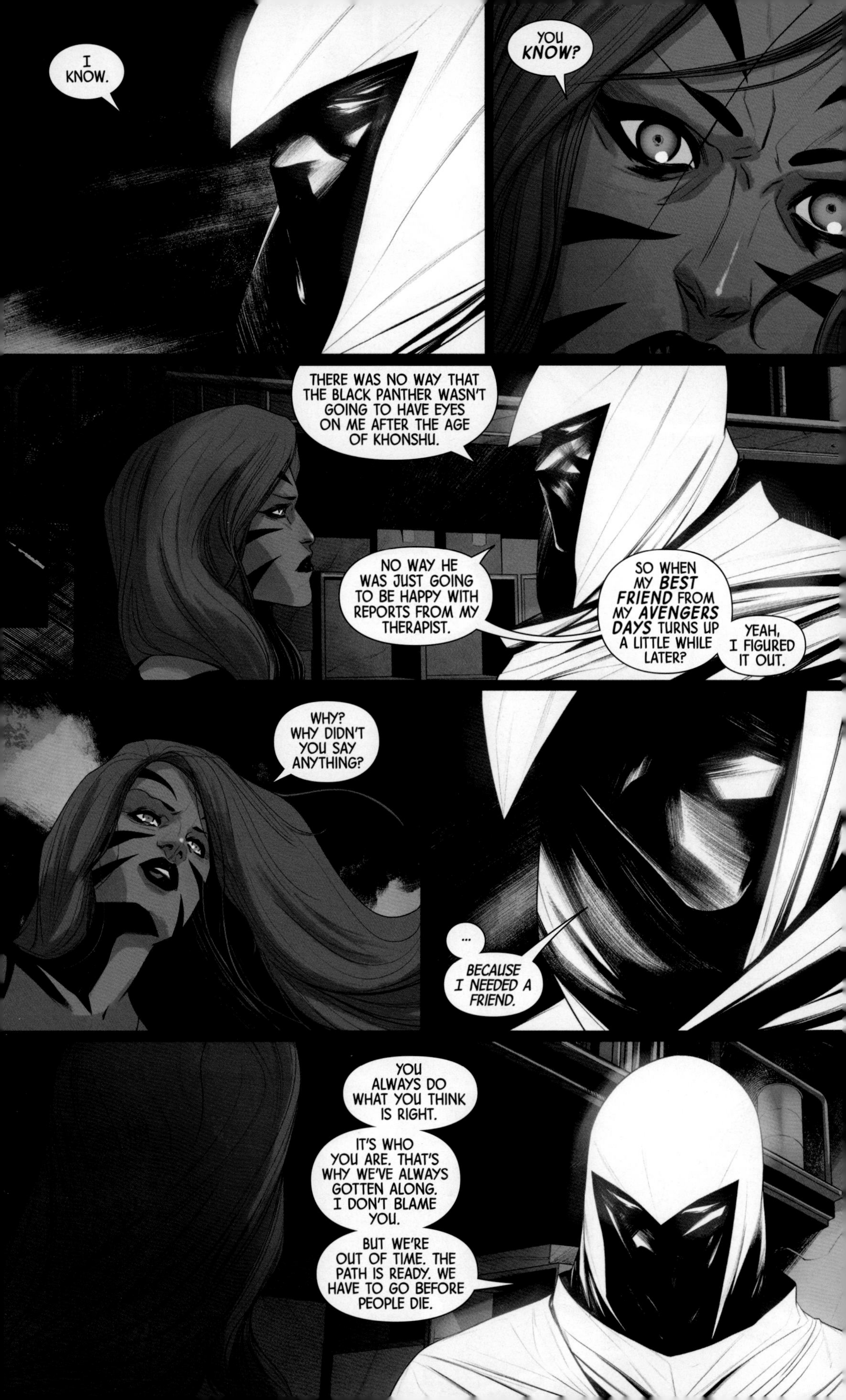
I KNOW.
YOU KNOW?
THERE WAS NO WAY THAT THE BLACK PANTHER WASN'T GOING TO HAVE EYES ON ME AFTER THE AGE OF KHONSHU.
NO WAY HE WAS JUST GOING TO BE HAPPY WITH REPORTS FROM MY THERAPIST.
SO WHEN MY BEST FRIEND FROM MY AVENGERS DAYS TURNS UP A LITTLE WHILE LATER?
YEAH, I FIGURED IT OUT.
WHY? WHY DIDN'T YOU SAY ANYTHING?
...
BECAUSE I NEEDED A FRIEND.
YOU ALWAYS DO WHAT YOU THINK IS RIGHT.
IT'S WHO YOU ARE. THAT'S WHY WE'VE ALWAYS GOTTEN ALONG. I DON'T BLAME YOU.
BUT WE'RE OUT OF TIME. THE PATH IS READY. WE HAVE TO GO BEFORE PEOPLE DIE.

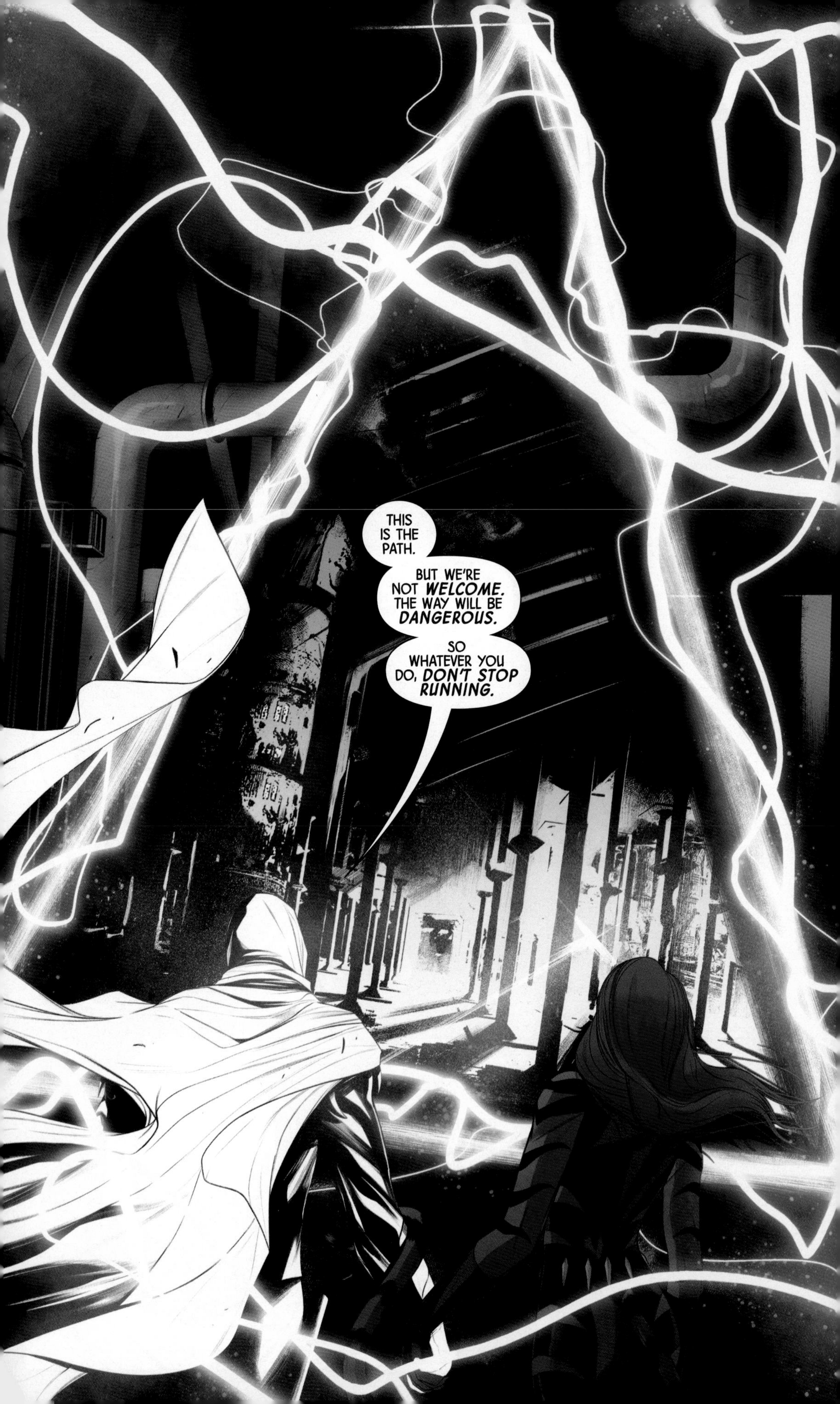
THIS IS THE PATH.
BUT WE'RE NOT WELCOME. THE WAY WILL BE DANGEROUS.
SO WHATEVER YOU DO, DON'T STOP RUNNING.

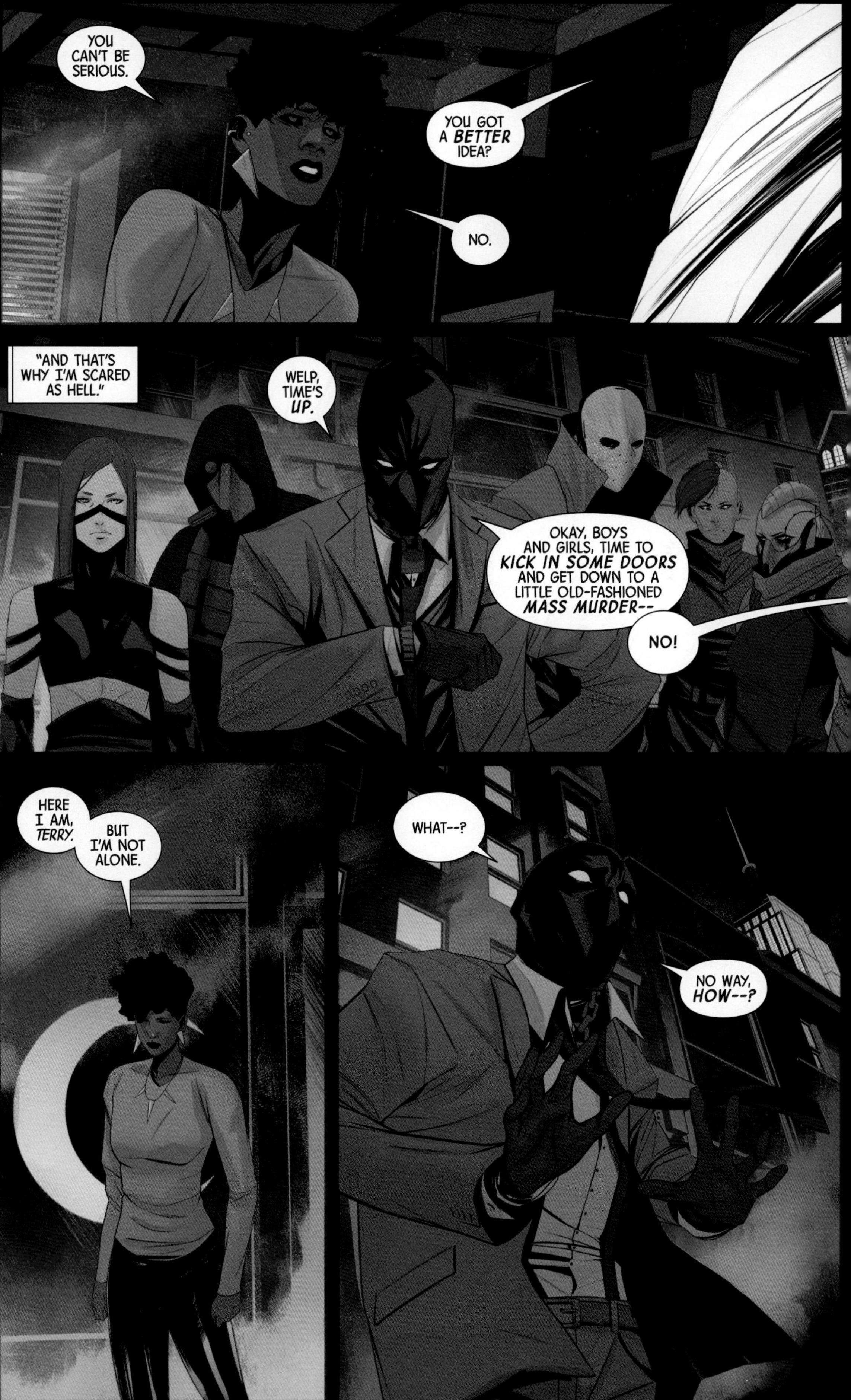
YOU CAN'T BE SERIOUS.
YOU GOT A *BETTER* IDEA?
NO.
"AND THAT'S WHY I'M SCARED AS HELL."
WELP, TIME'S *UP.*
OKAY, BOYS AND GIRLS, TIME TO *KICK IN SOME DOORS* AND GET DOWN TO A LITTLE OLD-FASHIONED *MASS MURDER--*
NO!
HERE I AM, *TERRY.*
BUT I'M NOT ALONE.
WHAT--?
NO WAY, *HOW--?*

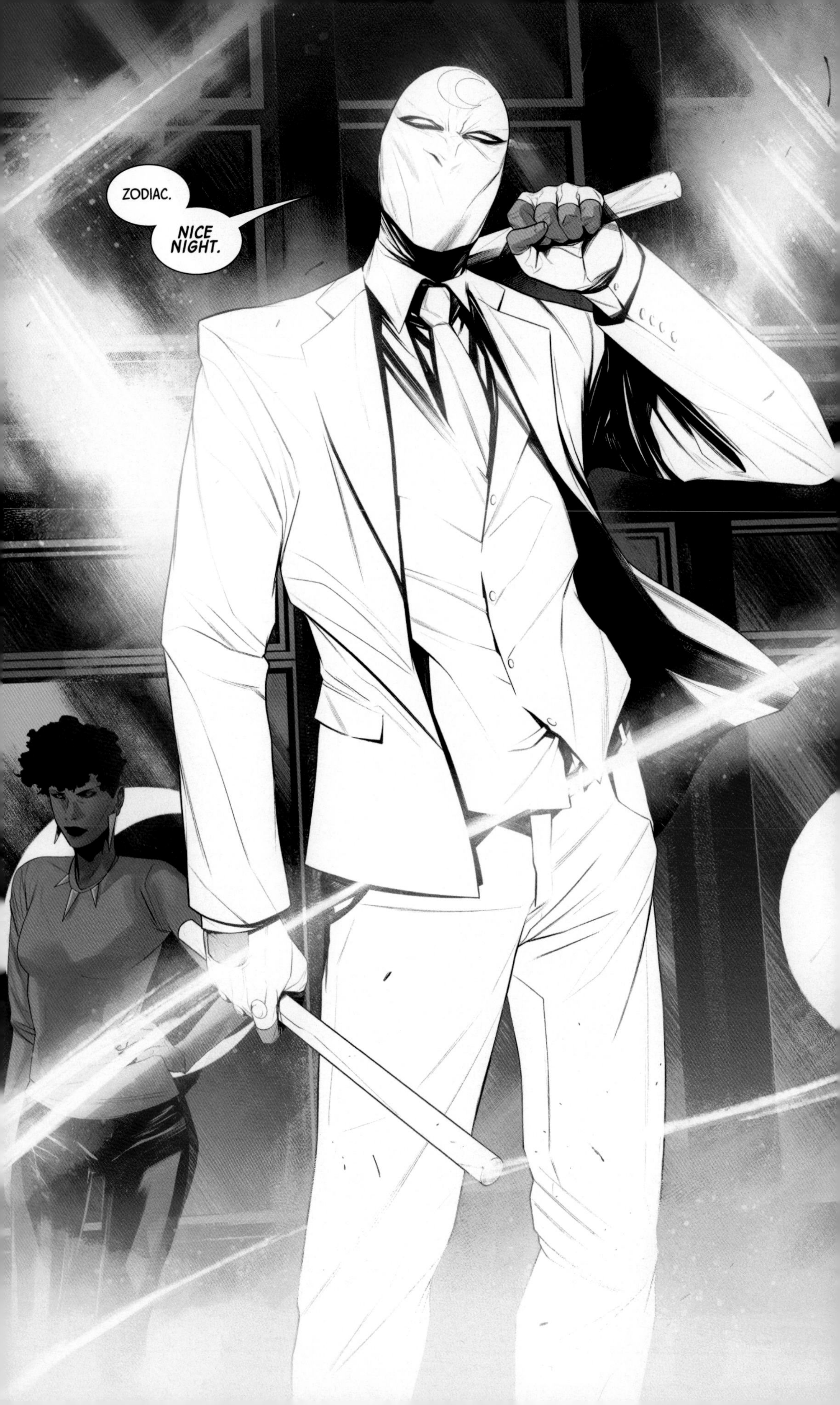
ZODIAC.
NICE NIGHT.

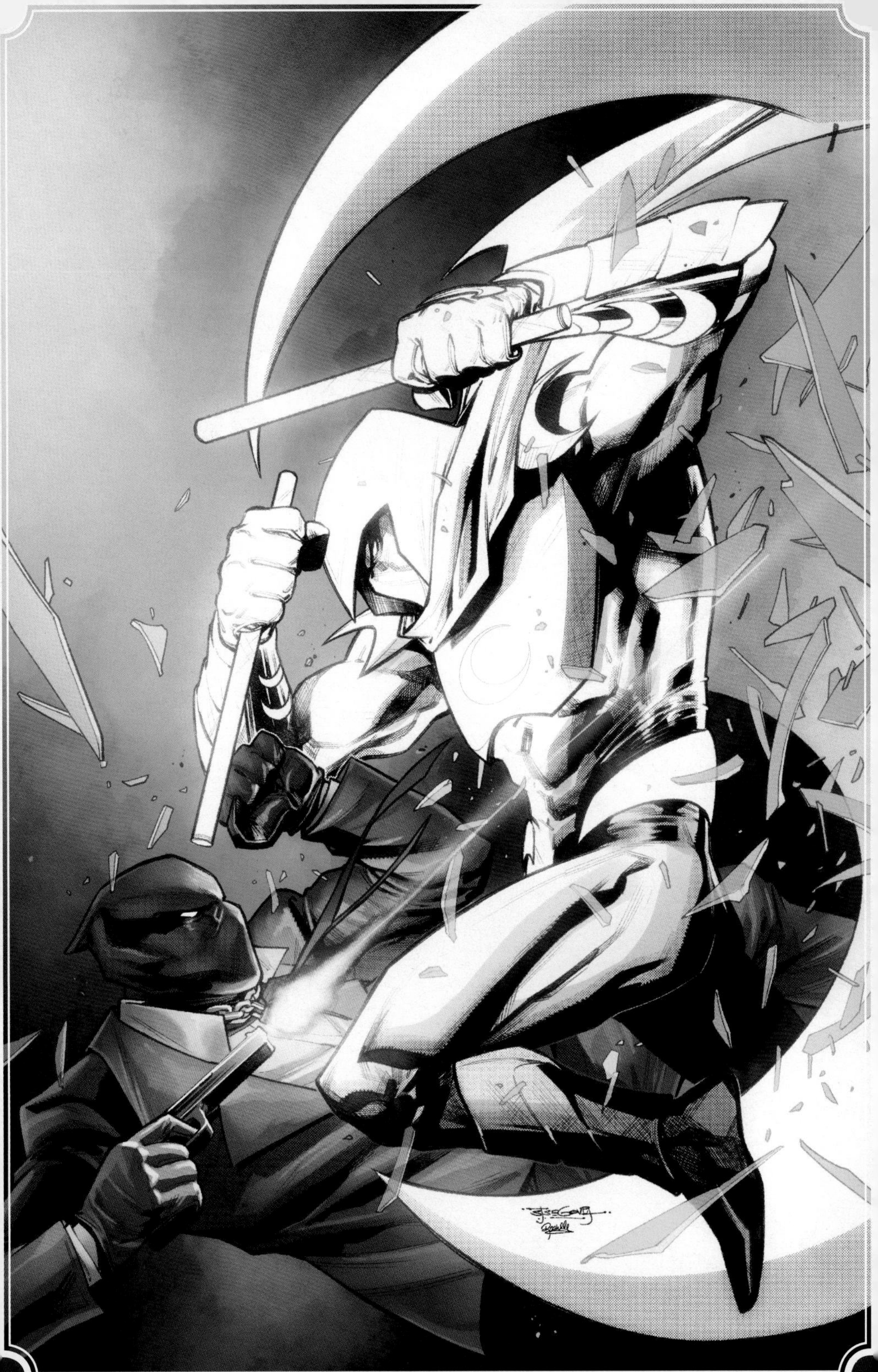

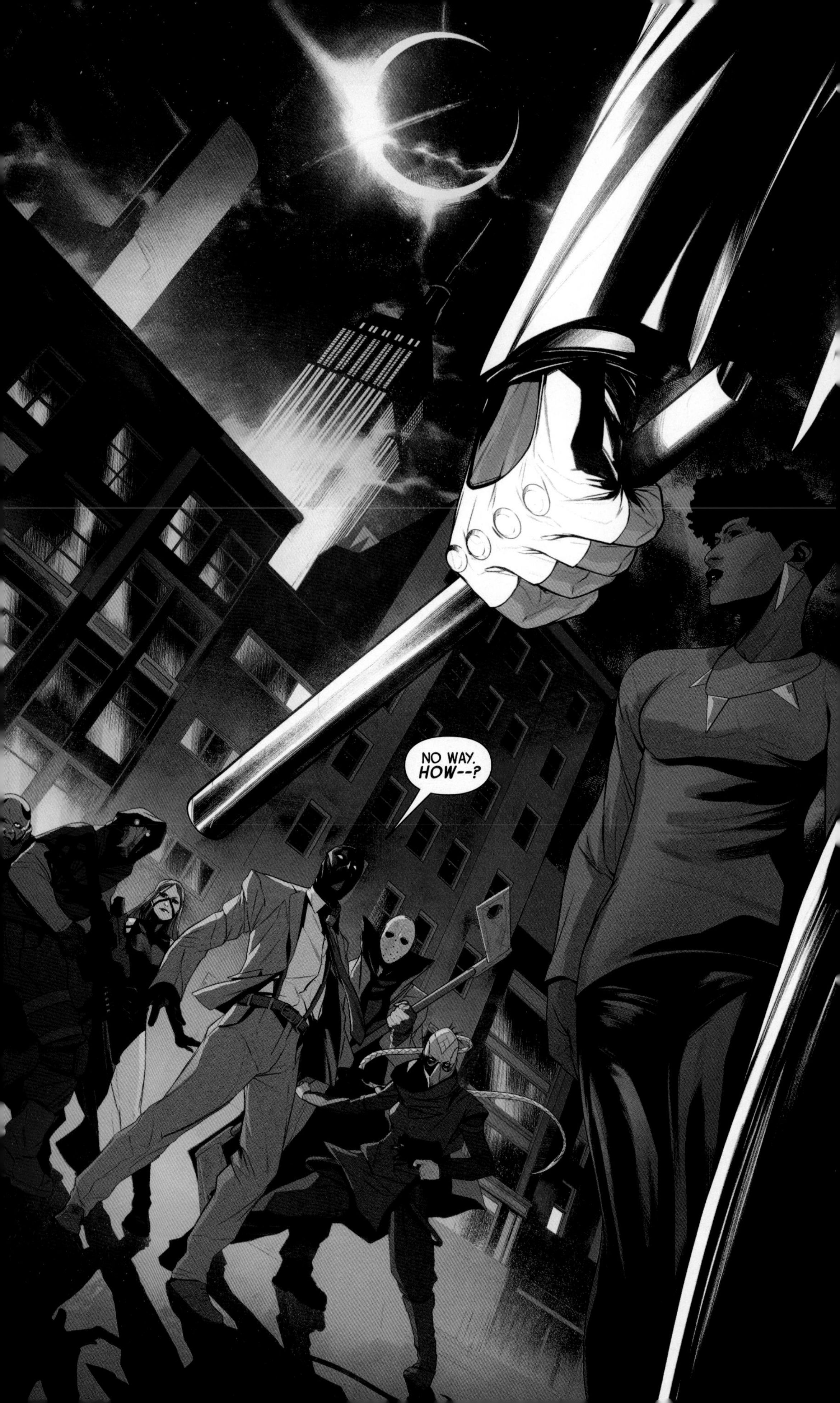
NO WAY. HOW--?

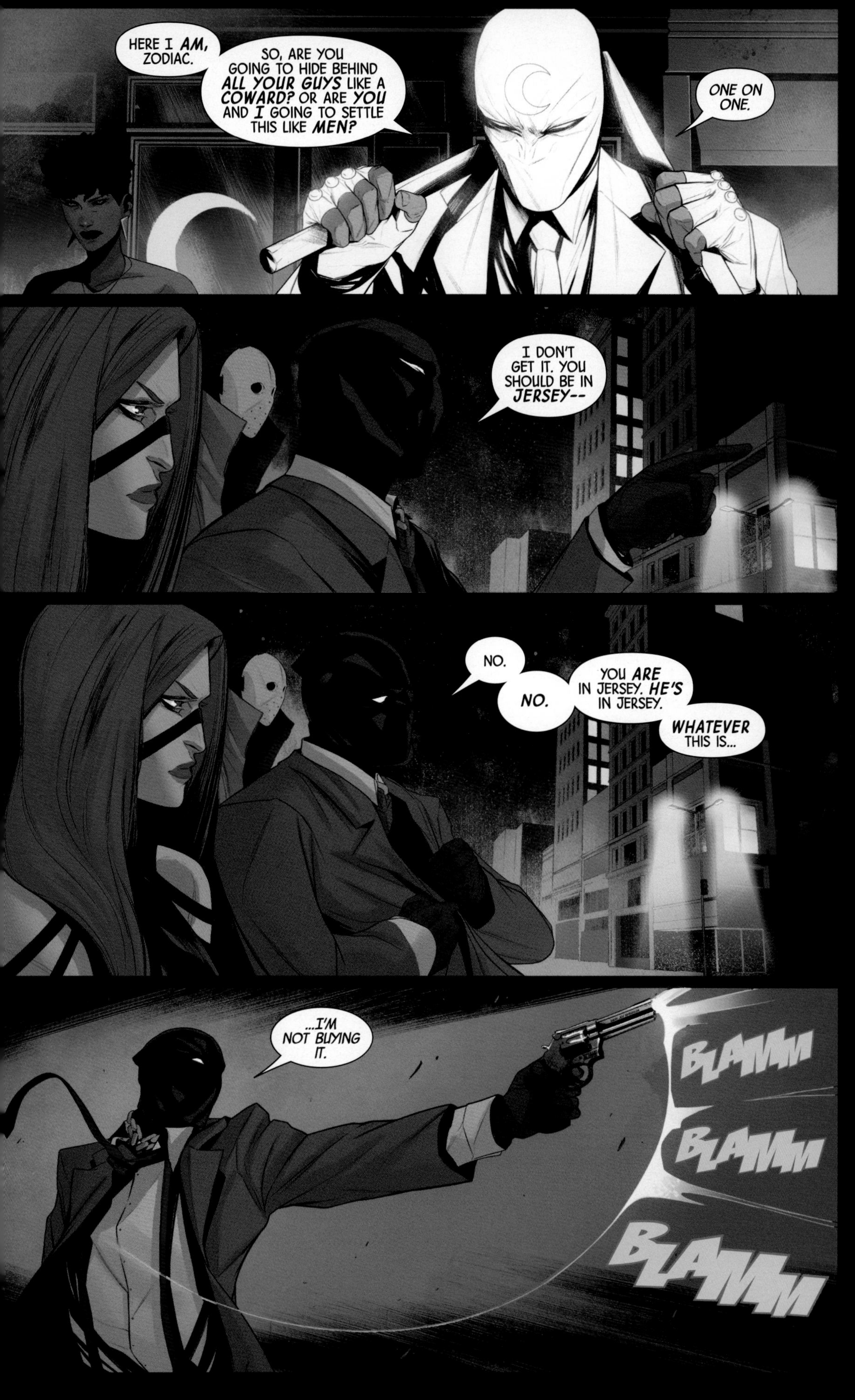
HERE I AM, ZODIAC.
SO, ARE YOU GOING TO HIDE BEHIND ALL YOUR GUYS LIKE A COWARD? OR ARE YOU AND I GOING TO SETTLE THIS LIKE MEN?
ONE ON ONE.
I DON'T GET IT. YOU SHOULD BE IN JERSEY--
NO.
NO.
YOU ARE IN JERSEY. HE'S IN JERSEY.
WHATEVER THIS IS...
...I'M NOT BUYING IT.
BLAMM
BLAMM
BLAMM

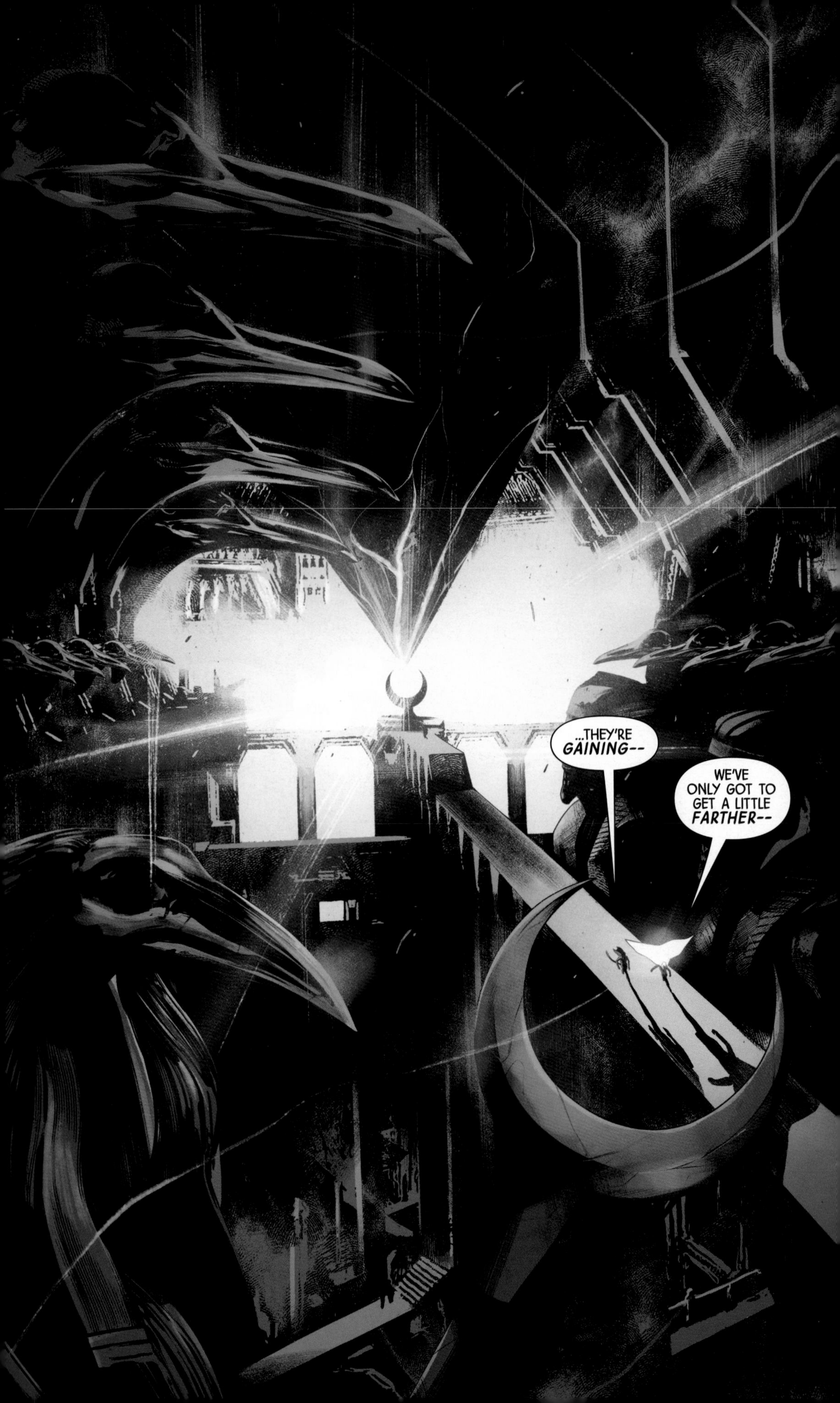
...THEY'RE GAINING--
WE'VE ONLY GOT TO GET A LITTLE FARTHER--

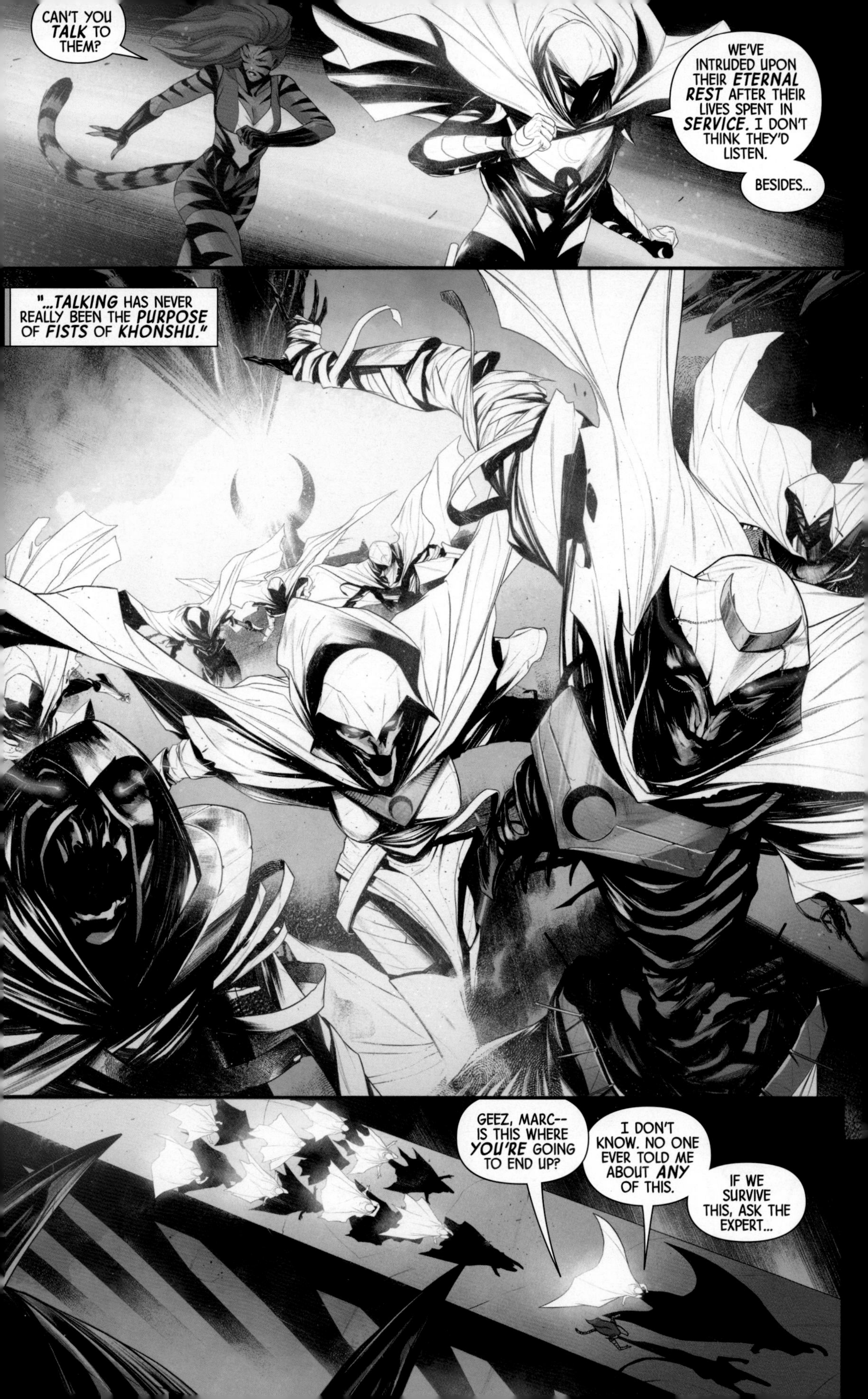
CAN'T YOU TALK TO THEM?
WE'VE INTRUDED UPON THEIR ETERNAL REST AFTER THEIR LIVES SPENT IN SERVICE. I DON'T THINK THEY'D LISTEN.
BESIDES...
"...TALKING HAS NEVER REALLY BEEN THE PURPOSE OF FISTS OF KHONSHU."
GEEZ, MARC-- IS THIS WHERE YOU'RE GOING TO END UP?
I DON'T KNOW. NO ONE EVER TOLD ME ABOUT ANY OF THIS.
IF WE SURVIVE THIS, ASK THE EXPERT...

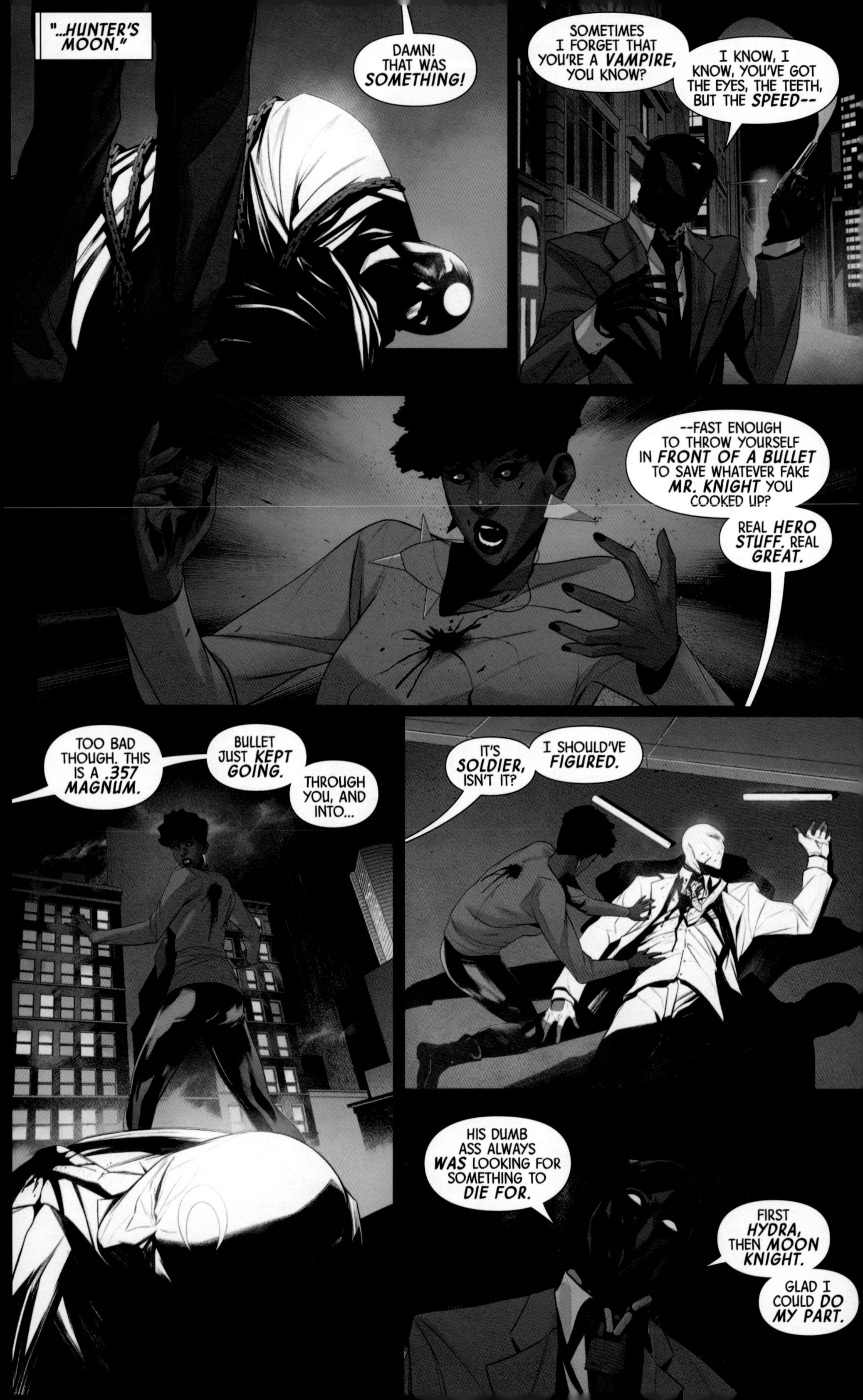
"...HUNTER'S MOON."
DAMN! THAT WAS SOMETHING!
SOMETIMES I FORGET THAT YOU'RE A VAMPIRE, YOU KNOW?
I KNOW, I KNOW, YOU'VE GOT THE EYES, THE TEETH, BUT THE SPEED--
--FAST ENOUGH TO THROW YOURSELF IN FRONT OF A BULLET TO SAVE WHATEVER FAKE MR. KNIGHT YOU COOKED UP?
REAL HERO STUFF. REAL GREAT.
TOO BAD THOUGH. THIS IS A .357 MAGNUM.
BULLET JUST KEPT GOING.
THROUGH YOU, AND INTO...
IT'S SOLDIER, ISN'T IT?
I SHOULD'VE FIGURED.
HIS DUMB ASS ALWAYS WAS LOOKING FOR SOMETHING TO DIE FOR.
FIRST HYDRA, THEN MOON KNIGHT.
GLAD I COULD DO MY PART.

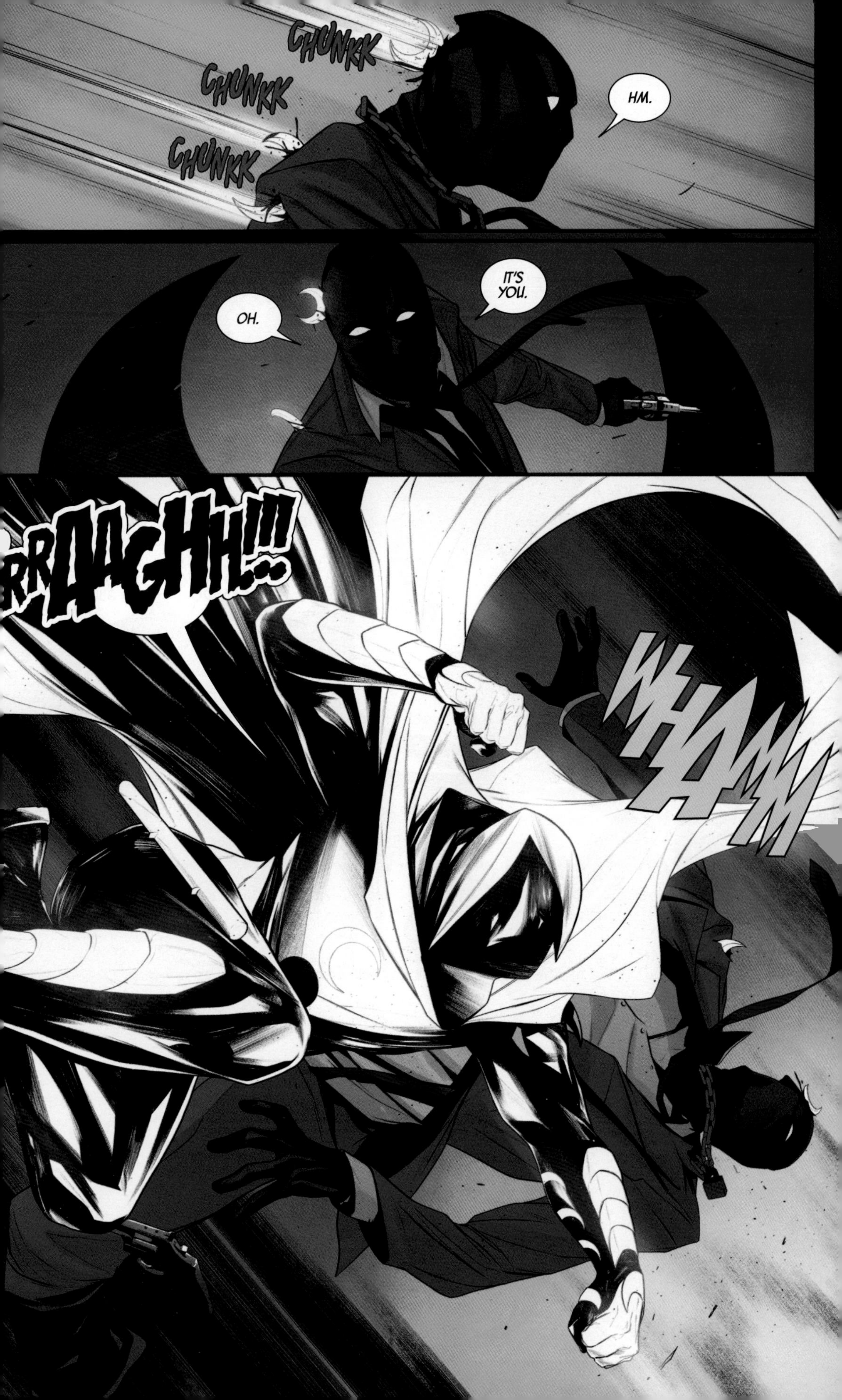
CHUNKK
CHUNKK
CHUNKK
HM.
OH.
IT'S YOU.
RRAAGHH!!!
WHAM

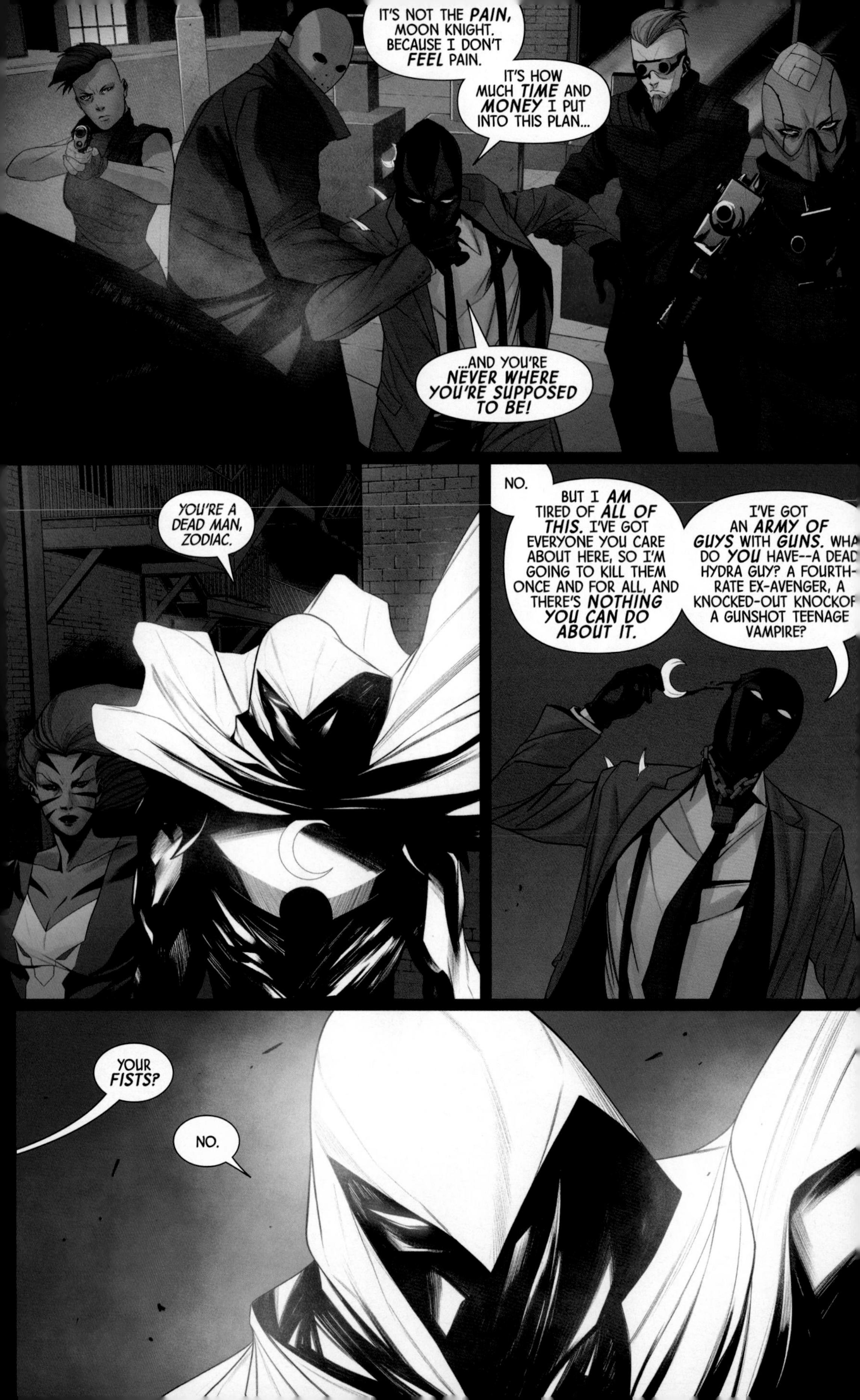
IT'S NOT THE PAIN, MOON KNIGHT. BECAUSE I DON'T FEEL PAIN.
IT'S HOW MUCH TIME AND MONEY I PUT INTO THIS PLAN...
...AND YOU'RE NEVER WHERE YOU'RE SUPPOSED TO BE!
YOU'RE A DEAD MAN, ZODIAC.
NO.
BUT I AM TIRED OF ALL OF THIS. I'VE GOT EVERYONE YOU CARE ABOUT HERE, SO I'M GOING TO KILL THEM ONCE AND FOR ALL, AND THERE'S NOTHING YOU CAN DO ABOUT IT.
I'VE GOT AN ARMY OF GUYS WITH GUNS. WHA DO YOU HAVE--A DEAD HYDRA GUY? A FOURTH-RATE EX-AVENGER, A KNOCKED-OUT KNOCKOF A GUNSHOT TEENAGE VAMPIRE?
YOUR FISTS?
NO.

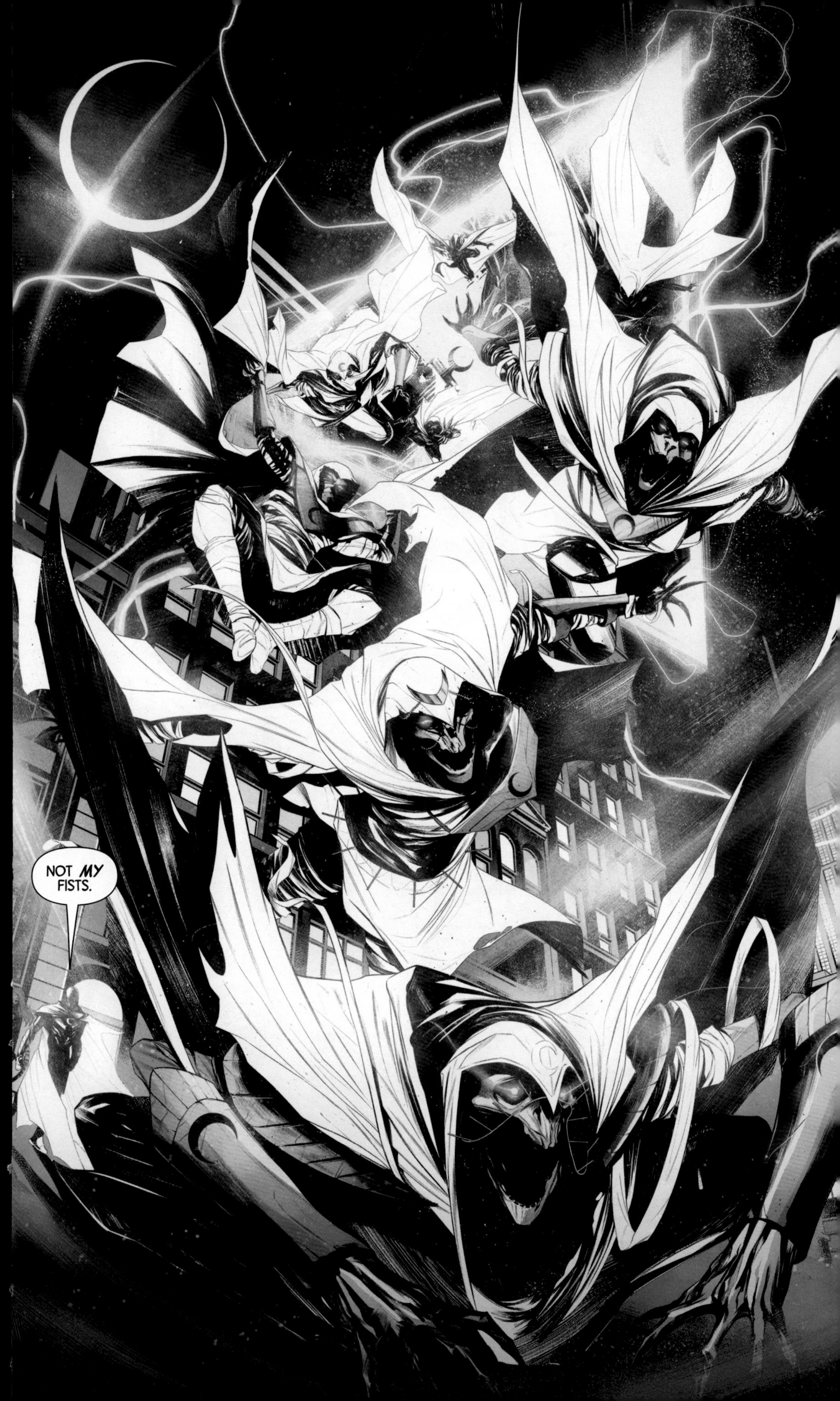
NOT MY FISTS.

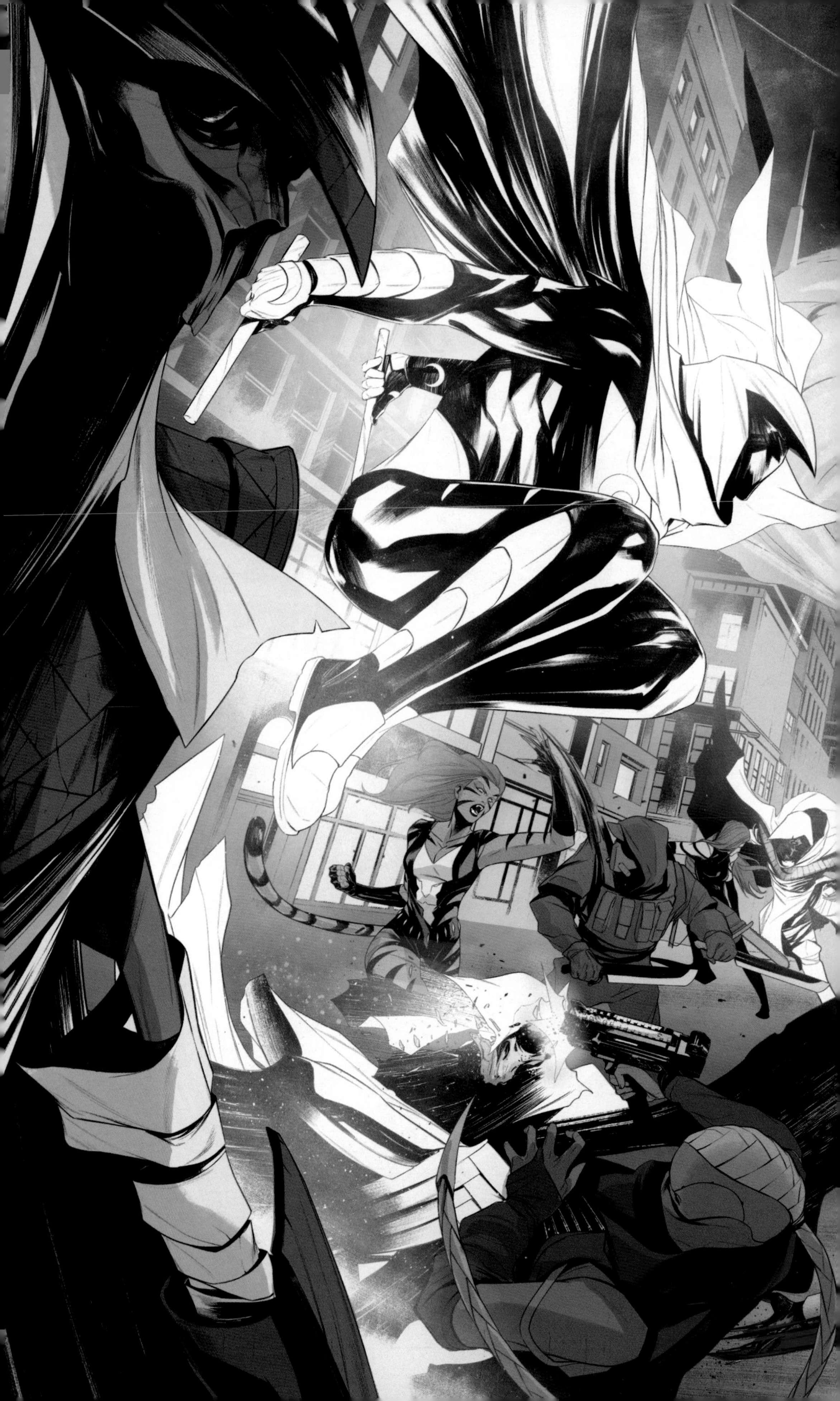

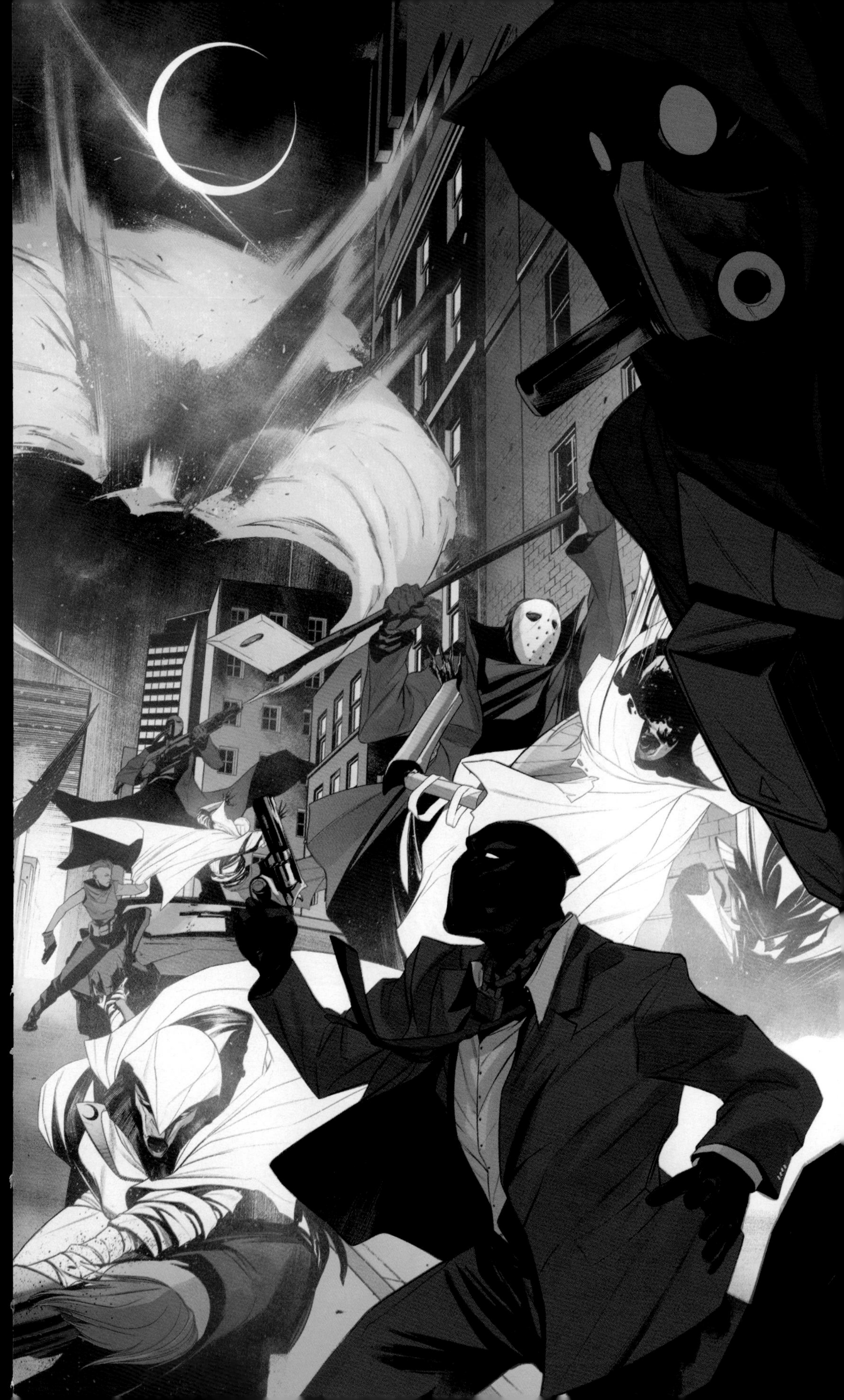

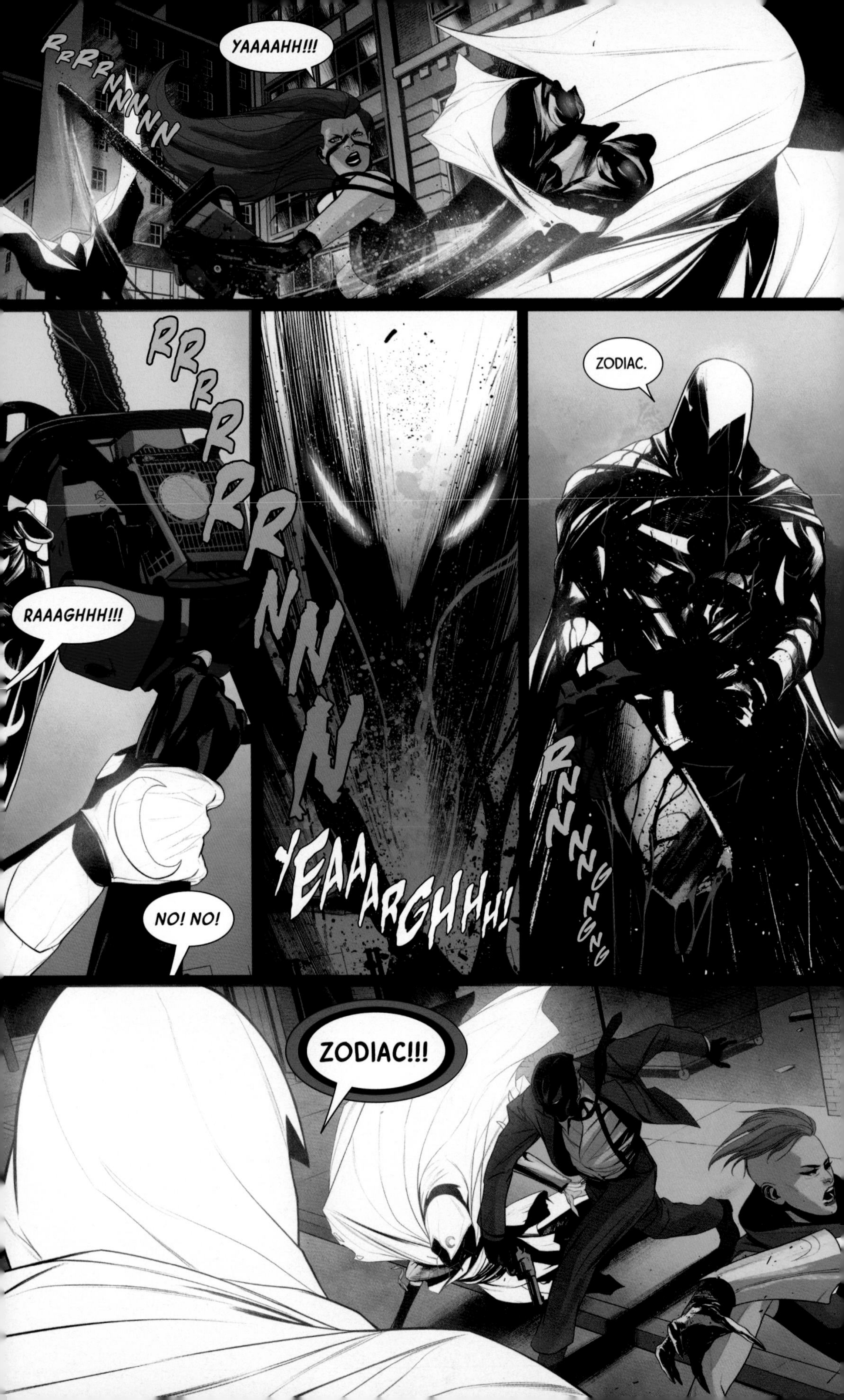
RRRRNNNNNN
YAAAAHH!!!
RRRRRRRRNNN
RAAAGHHH!!!
NO! NO!
YEAAARGHHH!
ZODIAC.
RNNNNGNG
ZODIAC!!!

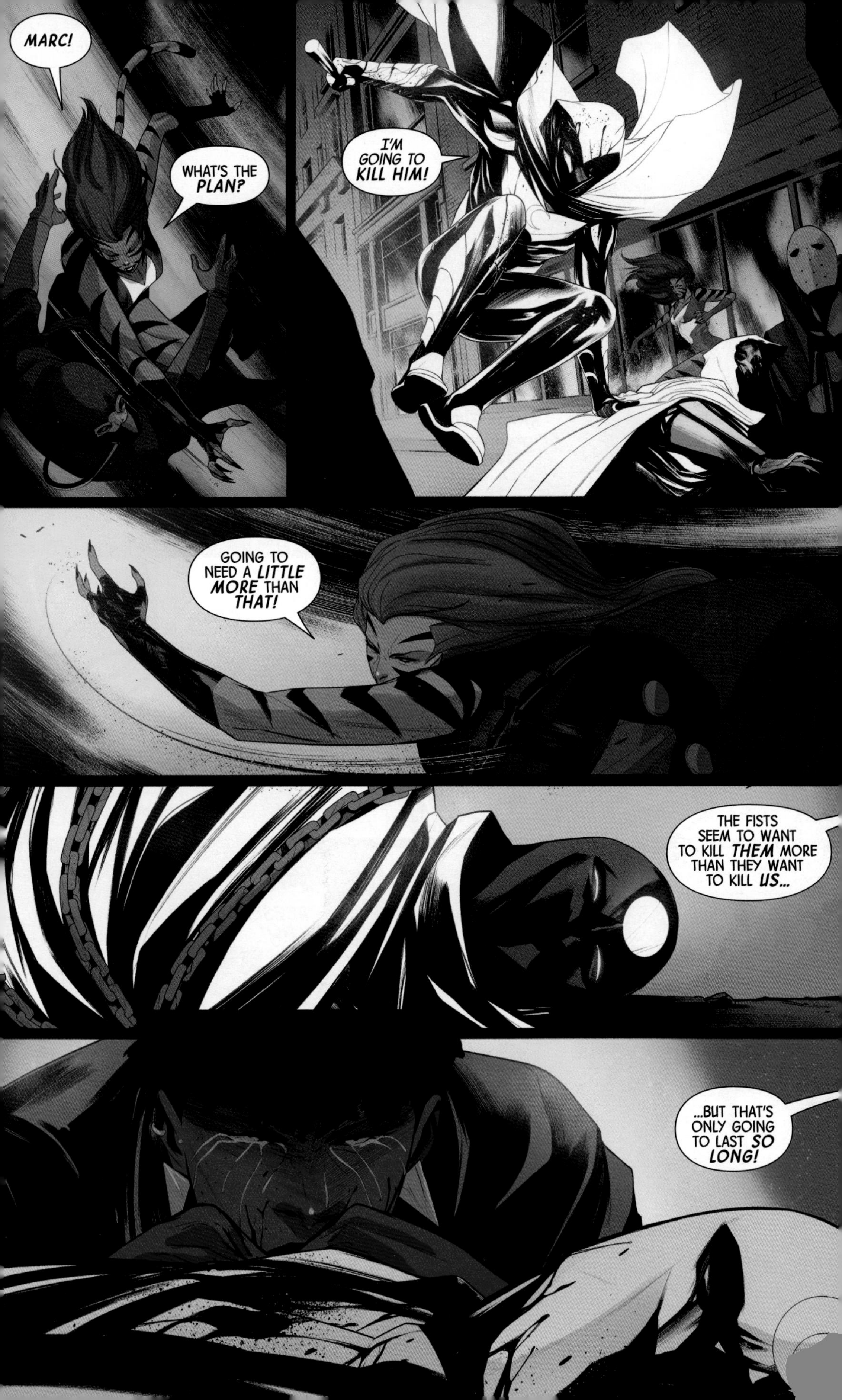

MARC!
WHAT'S THE PLAN?
I'M GOING TO KILL HIM!
GOING TO NEED A LITTLE MORE THAN THAT!
THE FISTS SEEM TO WANT TO KILL THEM MORE THAN THEY WANT TO KILL US...
...BUT THAT'S ONLY GOING TO LAST SO LONG!

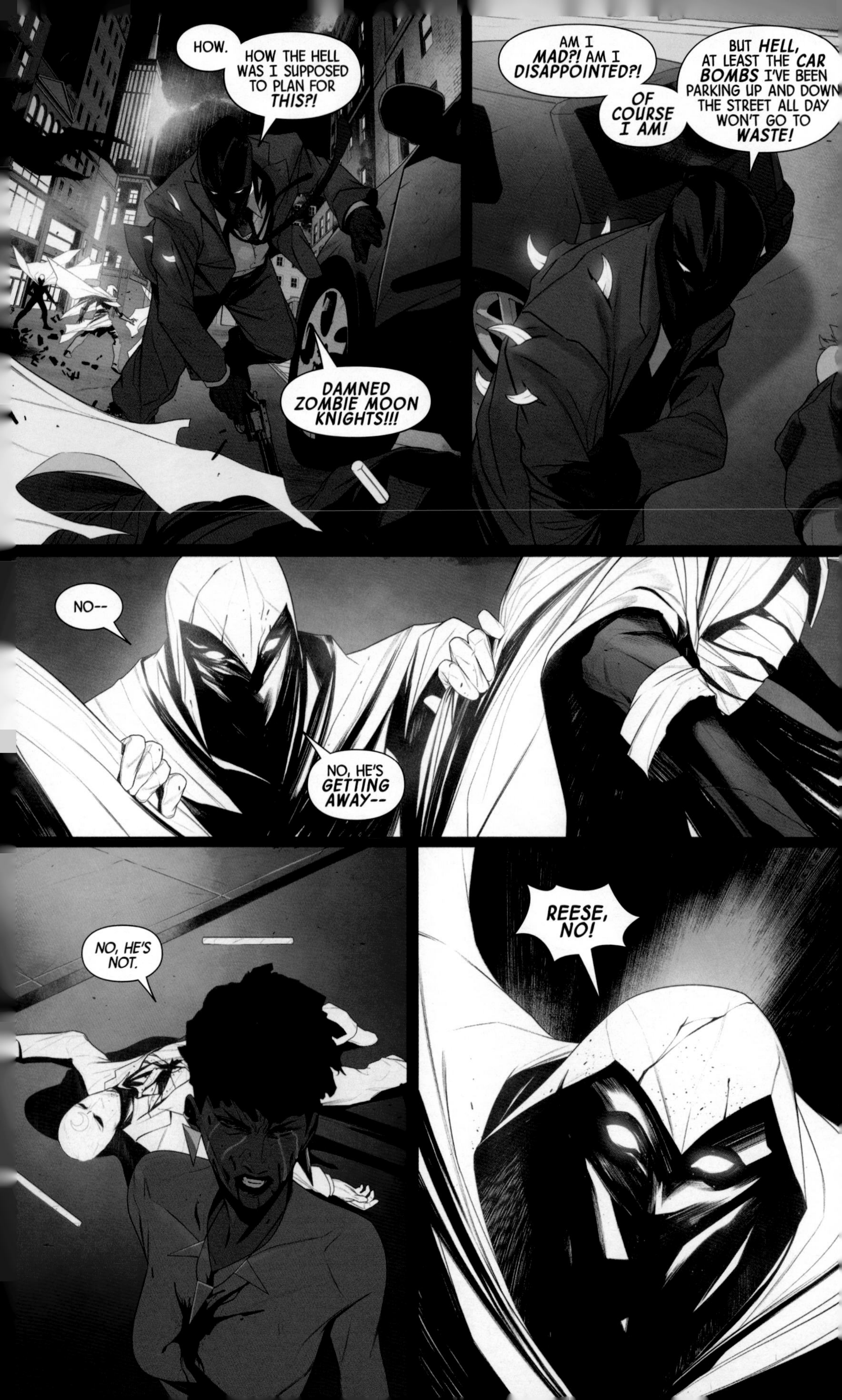

HOW.
HOW THE HELL WAS I SUPPOSED TO PLAN FOR THIS?!
DAMNED ZOMBIE MOON KNIGHTS!!!
AM I MAD?! AM I DISAPPOINTED?!
OF COURSE I AM!
BUT HELL, AT LEAST THE CAR BOMBS I'VE BEEN PARKING UP AND DOWN THE STREET ALL DAY WON'T GO TO WASTE!
NO--
NO, HE'S GETTING AWAY--
NO, HE'S NOT.
REESE, NO!

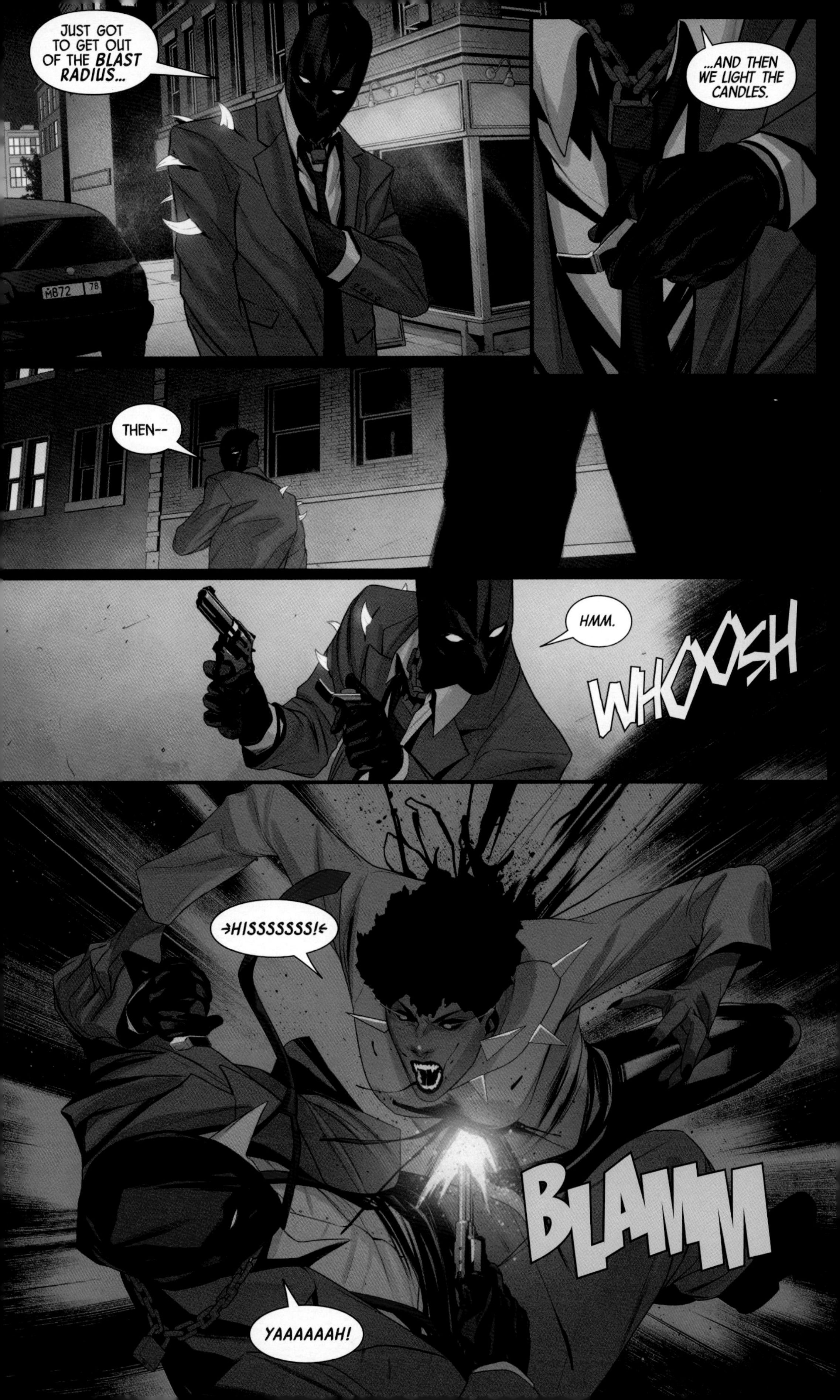
JUST GOT TO GET OUT OF THE BLAST RADIUS...
...AND THEN WE LIGHT THE CANDLES.
THEN--
HMM.
WHOOOSH
>HISSSSSSS!<
BLAMM
YAAAAAAH!

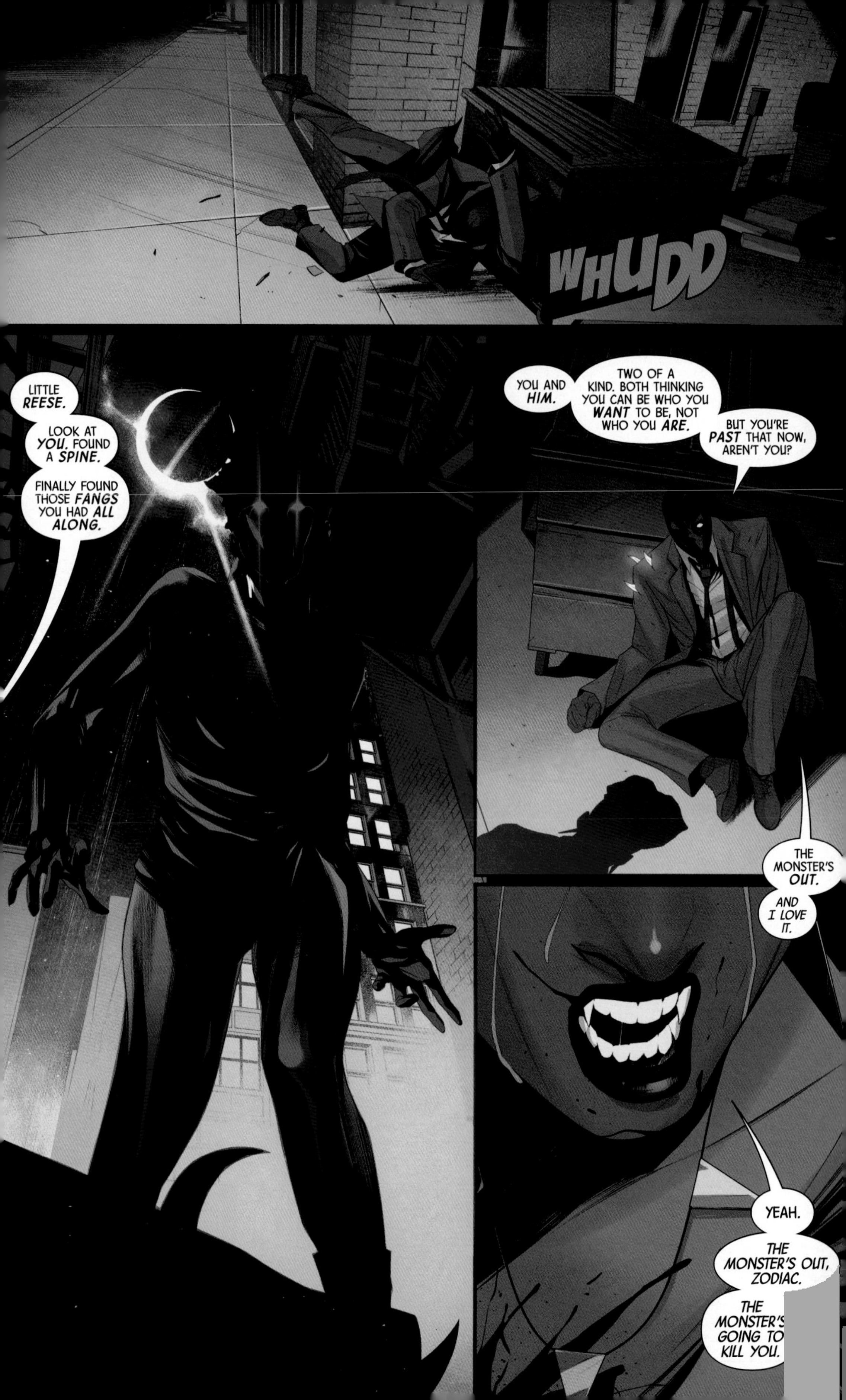
WHUDD
LITTLE REESE.
LOOK AT YOU. FOUND A SPINE.
FINALLY FOUND THOSE FANGS YOU HAD ALL ALONG.
YOU AND HIM.
TWO OF A KIND. BOTH THINKING YOU CAN BE WHO YOU WANT TO BE, NOT WHO YOU ARE.
BUT YOU'RE PAST THAT NOW, AREN'T YOU?
THE MONSTER'S OUT.
AND I LOVE IT.
YEAH.
THE MONSTER'S OUT, ZODIAC.
THE MONSTER'S GOING TO KILL YOU.

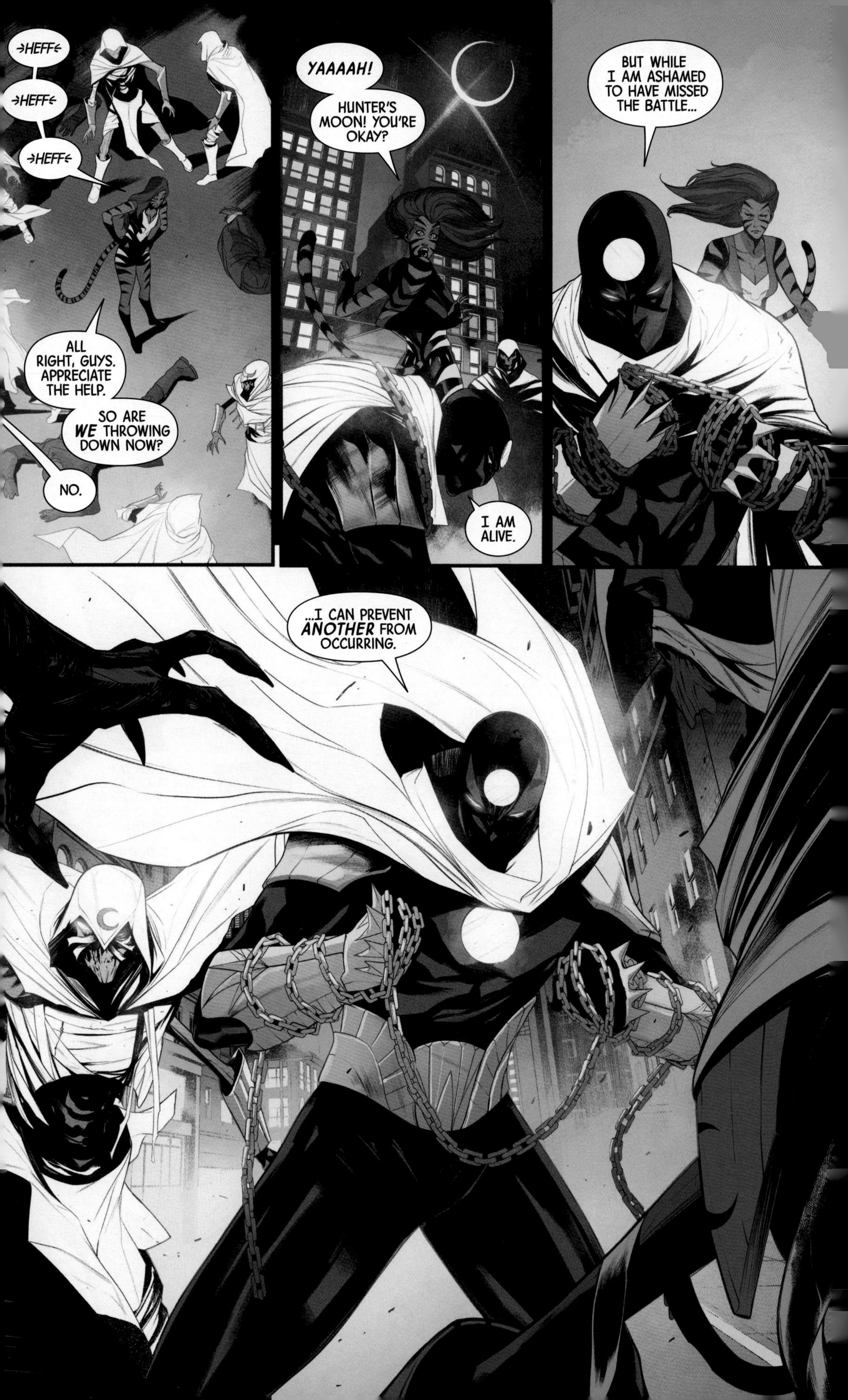

HEFF
HEFF
HEFF
ALL RIGHT, GUYS. APPRECIATE THE HELP.
SO ARE *WE* THROWING DOWN NOW?
NO.
YAAAAH!
HUNTER'S MOON! YOU'RE OKAY?
I AM ALIVE.
BUT WHILE I AM ASHAMED TO HAVE MISSED THE BATTLE...
...I CAN PREVENT *ANOTHER* FROM OCCURRING.

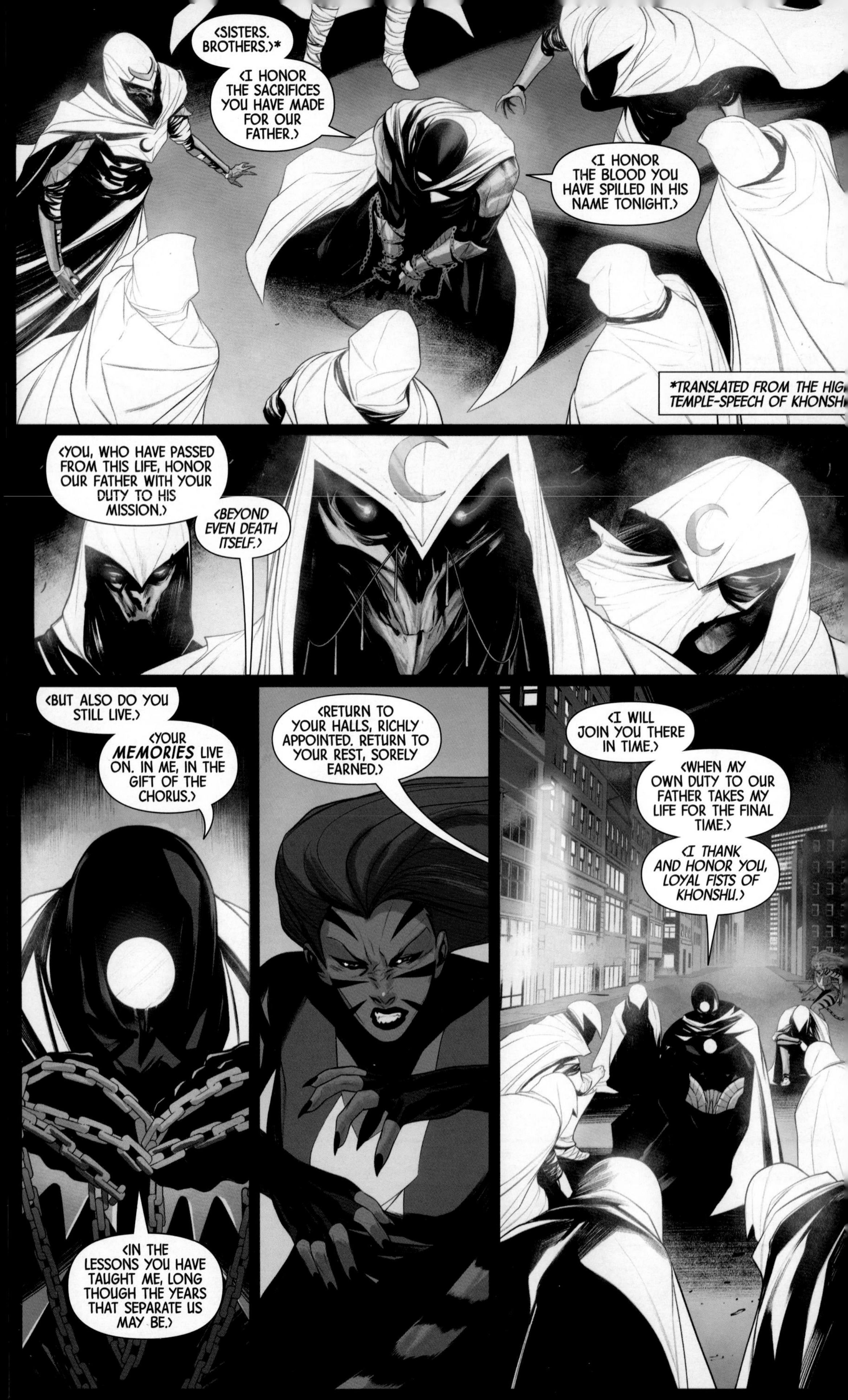
<SISTERS. BROTHERS.>*
<I HONOR THE SACRIFICES YOU HAVE MADE FOR OUR FATHER.>
<I HONOR THE BLOOD YOU HAVE SPILLED IN HIS NAME TONIGHT.>
*TRANSLATED FROM THE HIG
TEMPLE-SPEECH OF KHONSH
<YOU, WHO HAVE PASSED FROM THIS LIFE, HONOR OUR FATHER WITH YOUR DUTY TO HIS MISSION.>
<BEYOND EVEN DEATH ITSELF.>
<BUT ALSO DO YOU STILL LIVE.>
<YOUR MEMORIES LIVE ON. IN ME, IN THE GIFT OF THE CHORUS.>
<IN THE LESSONS YOU HAVE TAUGHT ME, LONG THOUGH THE YEARS THAT SEPARATE US MAY BE.>
<RETURN TO YOUR HALLS, RICHLY APPOINTED. RETURN TO YOUR REST, SORELY EARNED.>
<I WILL JOIN YOU THERE IN TIME.>
<WHEN MY OWN DUTY TO OUR FATHER TAKES MY LIFE FOR THE FINAL TIME.>
<I THANK AND HONOR YOU, LOYAL FISTS OF KHONSHU.>

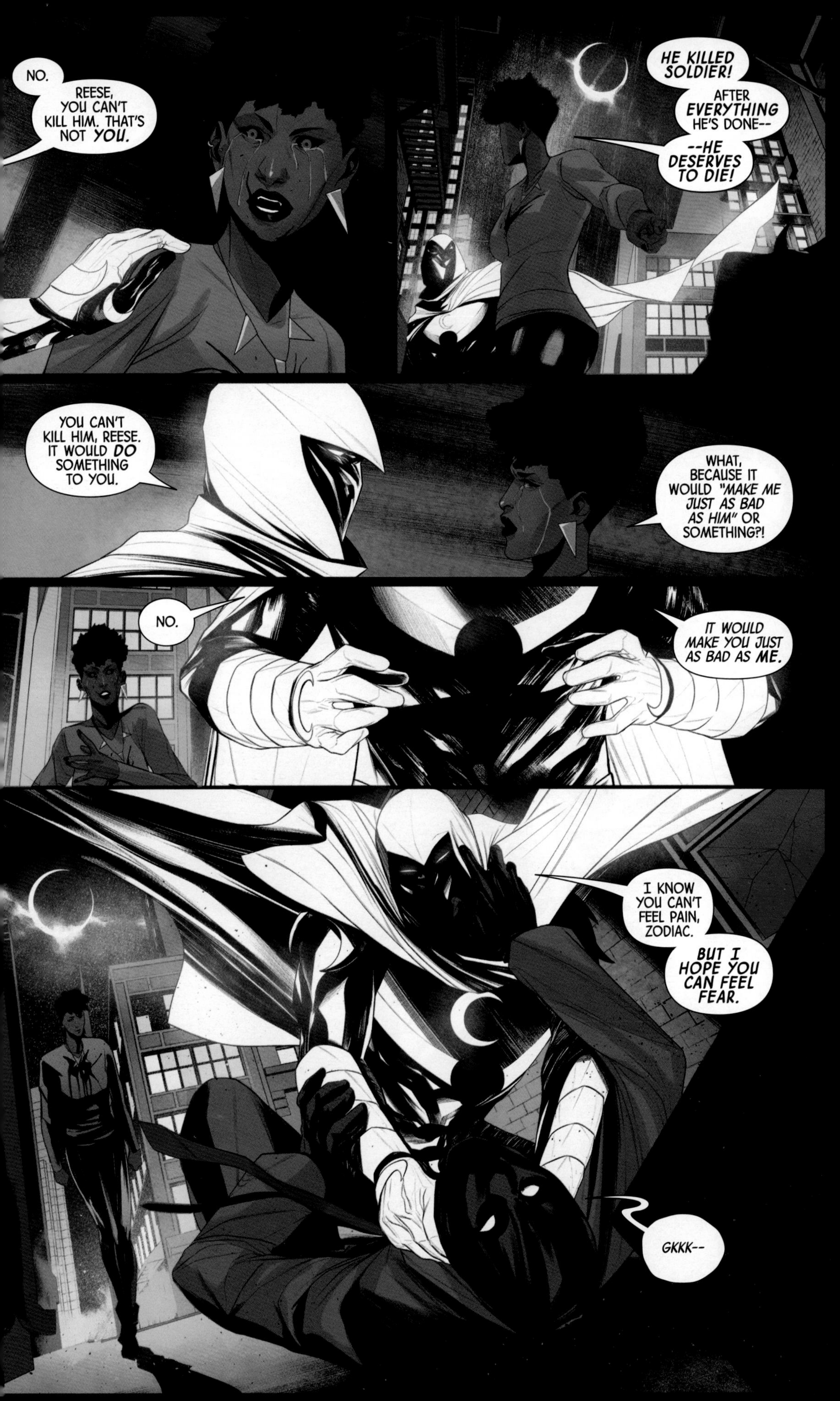

NO.
REESE, YOU CAN'T KILL HIM. THAT'S NOT YOU.
HE KILLED SOLDIER!
AFTER EVERYTHING HE'S DONE--
--HE DESERVES TO DIE!
YOU CAN'T KILL HIM, REESE. IT WOULD DO SOMETHING TO YOU.
WHAT, BECAUSE IT WOULD "MAKE ME JUST AS BAD AS HIM" OR SOMETHING?!
NO.
IT WOULD MAKE YOU JUST AS BAD AS ME.
I KNOW YOU CAN'T FEEL PAIN, ZODIAC.
BUT I HOPE YOU CAN FEEL FEAR.
GKKK--

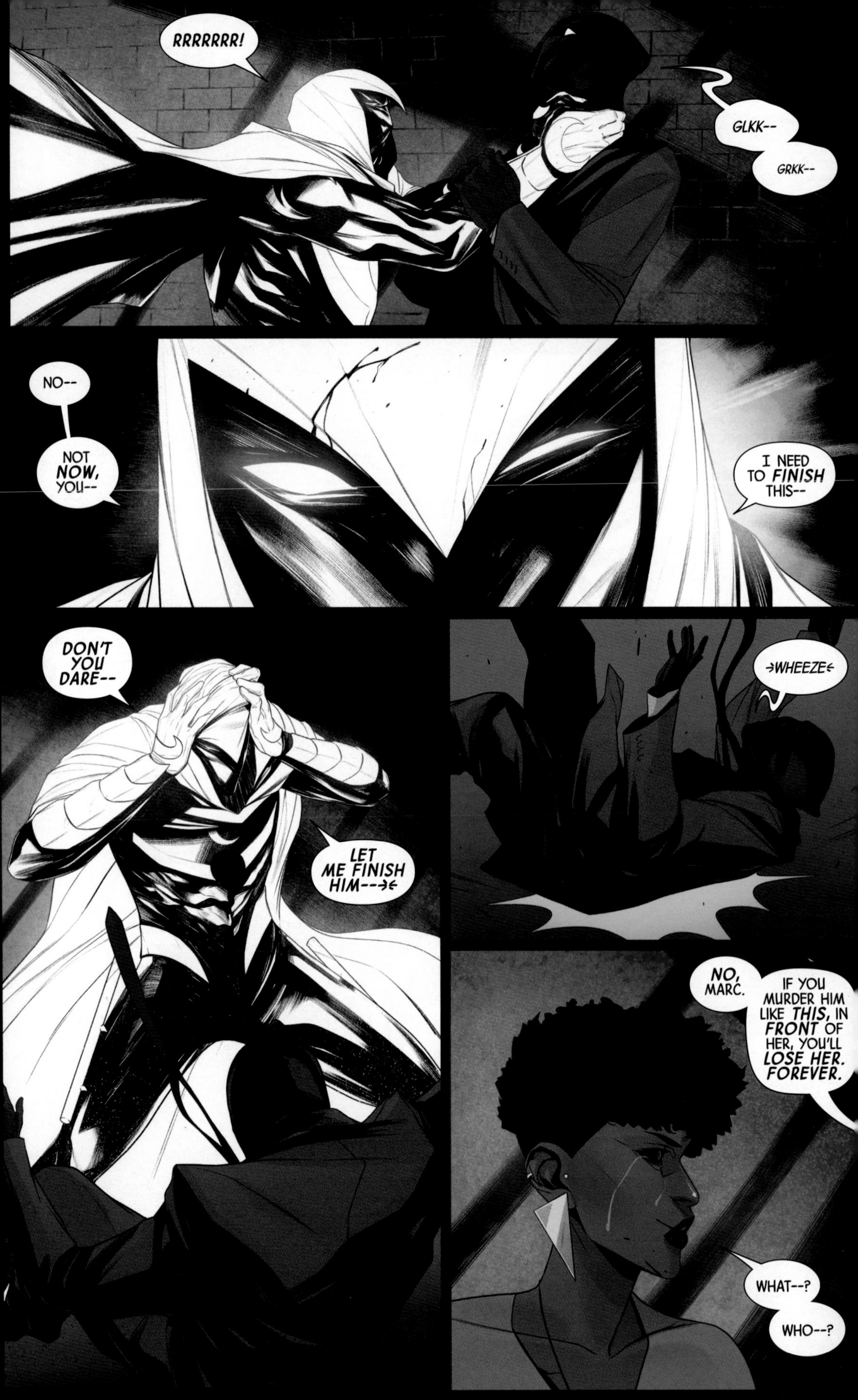
RRRRRRR!
GLKK--
GRKK--
NO--
NOT NOW, YOU--
I NEED TO FINISH THIS--
DON'T YOU DARE--
LET ME FINISH HIM--
→WHEEZE←
NO, MARC.
IF YOU MURDER HIM LIKE THIS, IN FRONT OF HER, YOU'LL LOSE HER. FOREVER.
WHAT--?
WHO--?

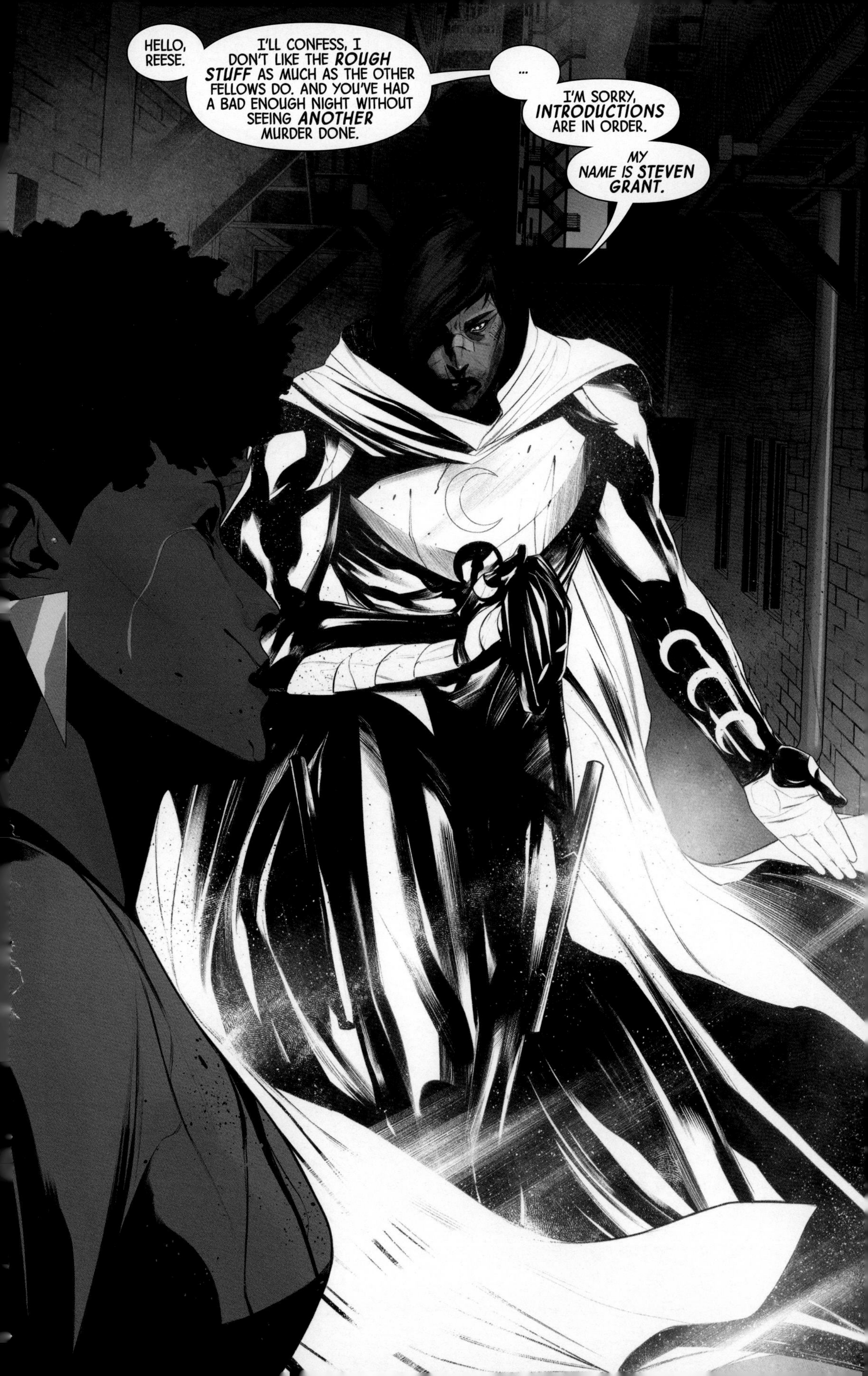
HELLO, REESE.
I'LL CONFESS, I DON'T LIKE THE ROUGH STUFF AS MUCH AS THE OTHER FELLOWS DO. AND YOU'VE HAD A BAD ENOUGH NIGHT WITHOUT SEEING ANOTHER MURDER DONE.
...
I'M SORRY, INTRODUCTIONS ARE IN ORDER.
MY NAME IS STEVEN GRANT.

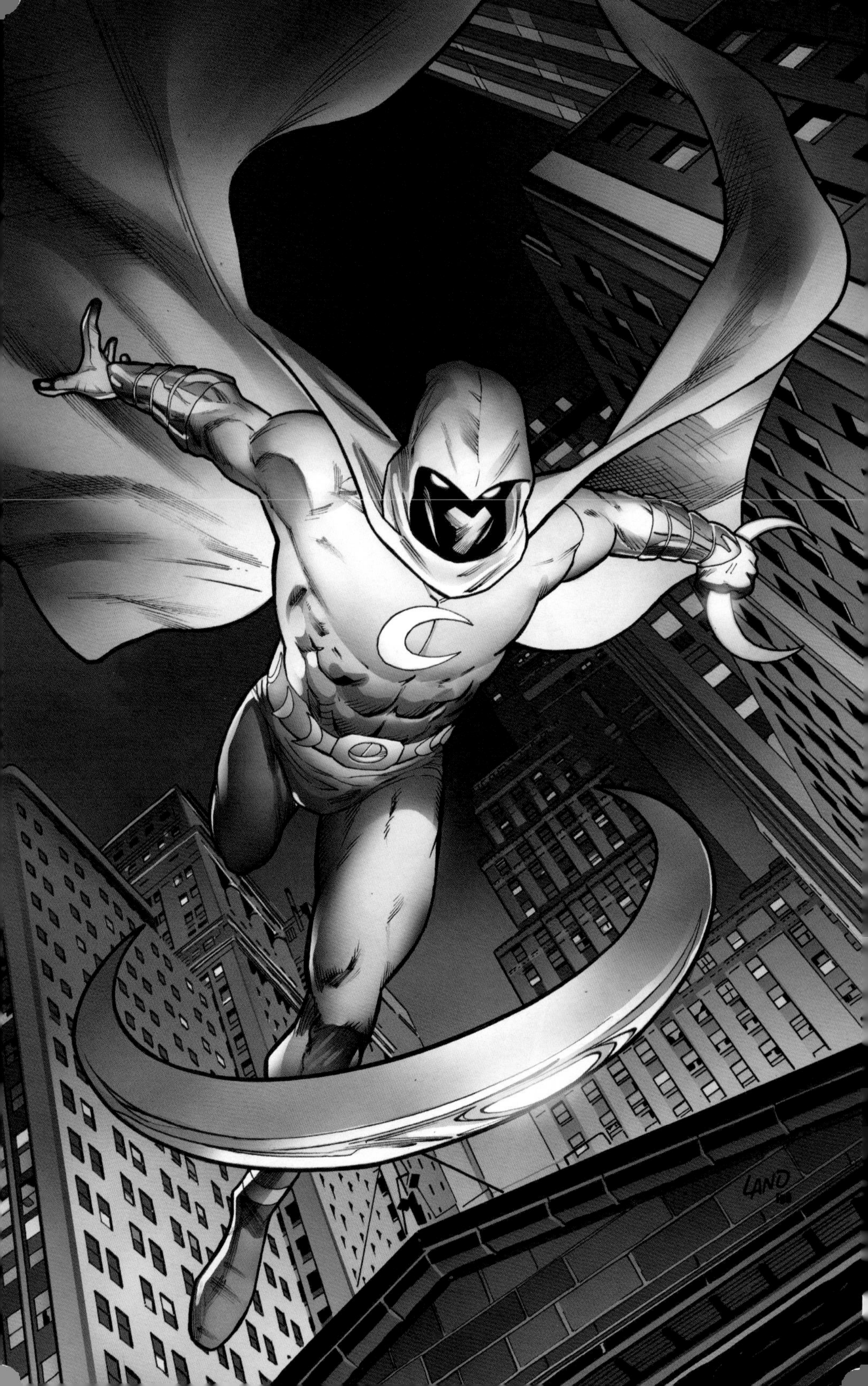
LAND

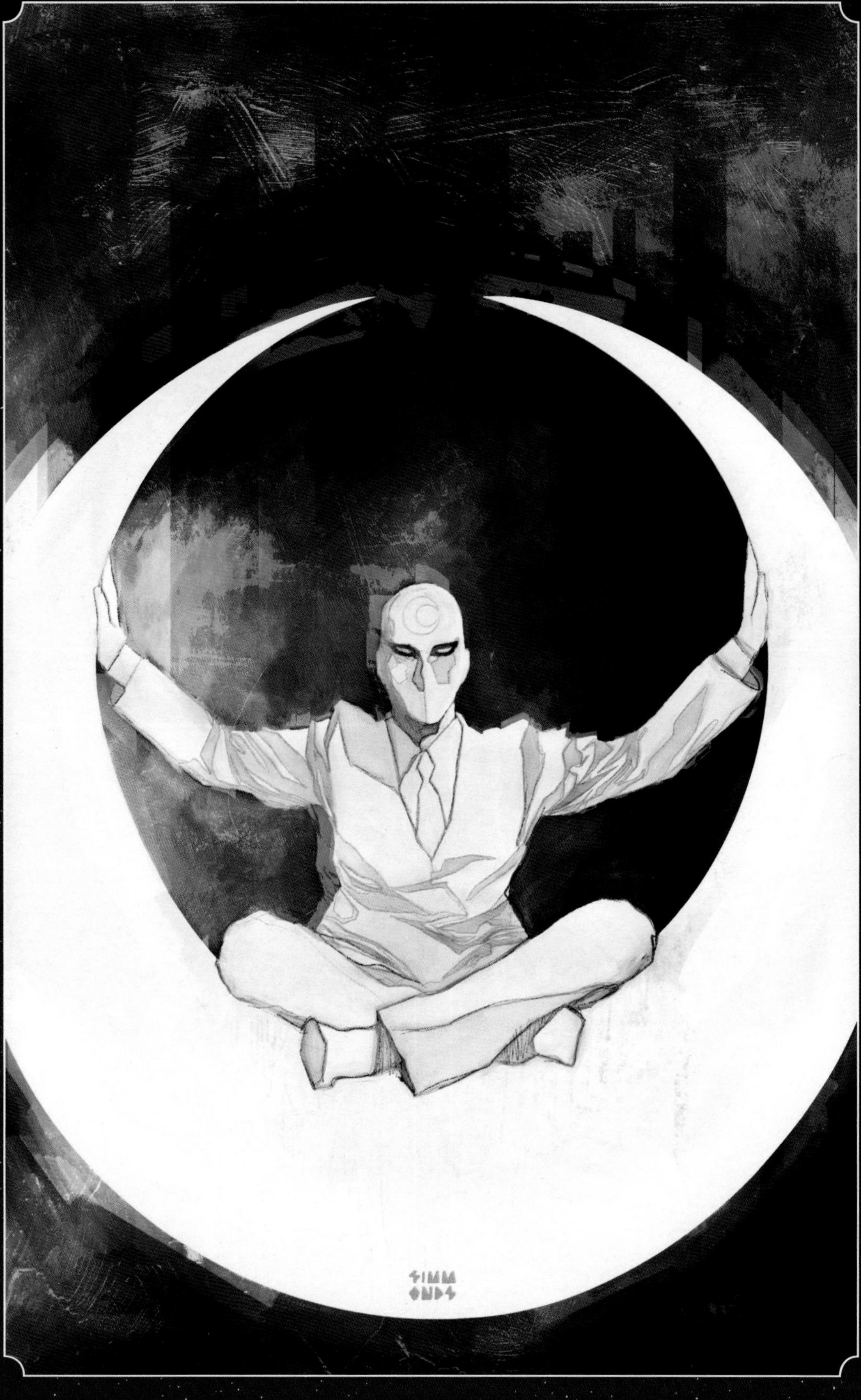
SIMM
ONDS

#9 VARIANT BY **MARTIN SIMMONDS**

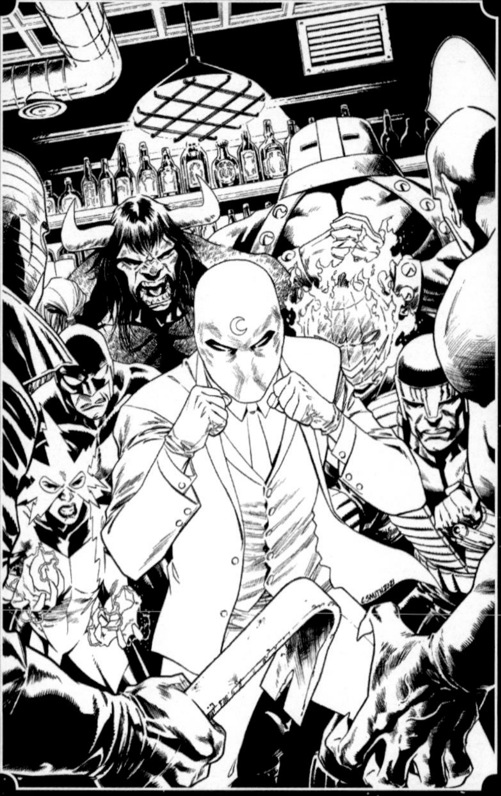

#7 2ND PRINTING VARIANT BY **CORY SMITH**

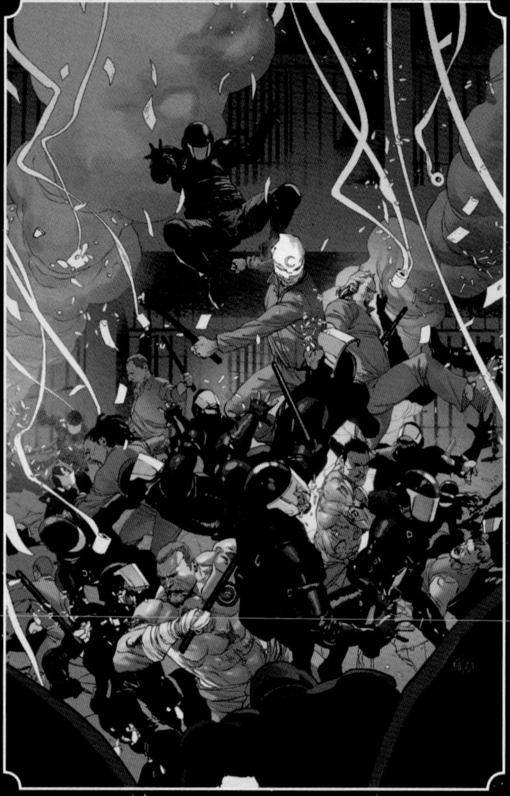

DEVIL'S REIGN: MOON KNIGHT VARIANT BY
LEINIL FRANCIS YU & SUNNY GHO

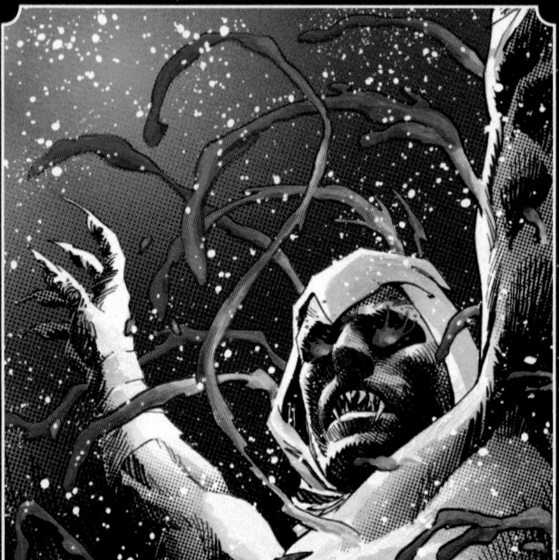

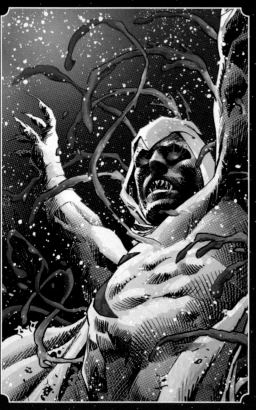

#9 CARNAGE FOREVER VARIANT BY **DAN PANOSIAN**

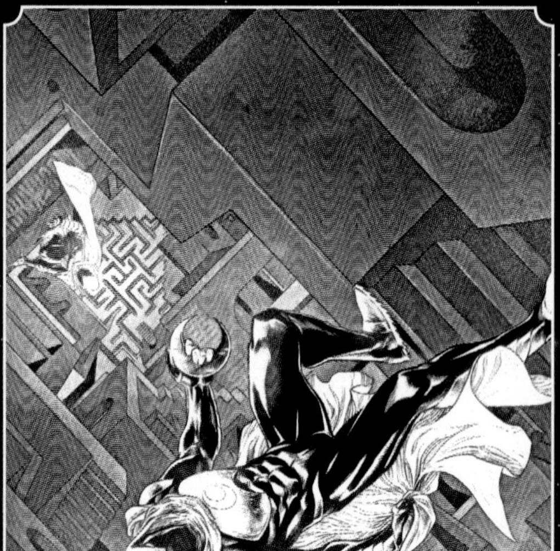

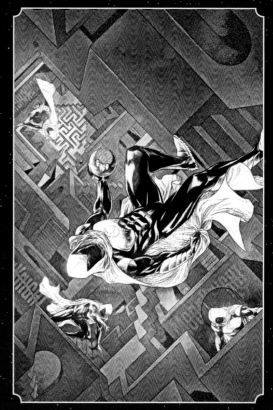

#9 2ND PRINTING VARIANT BY **CORY SMITH**

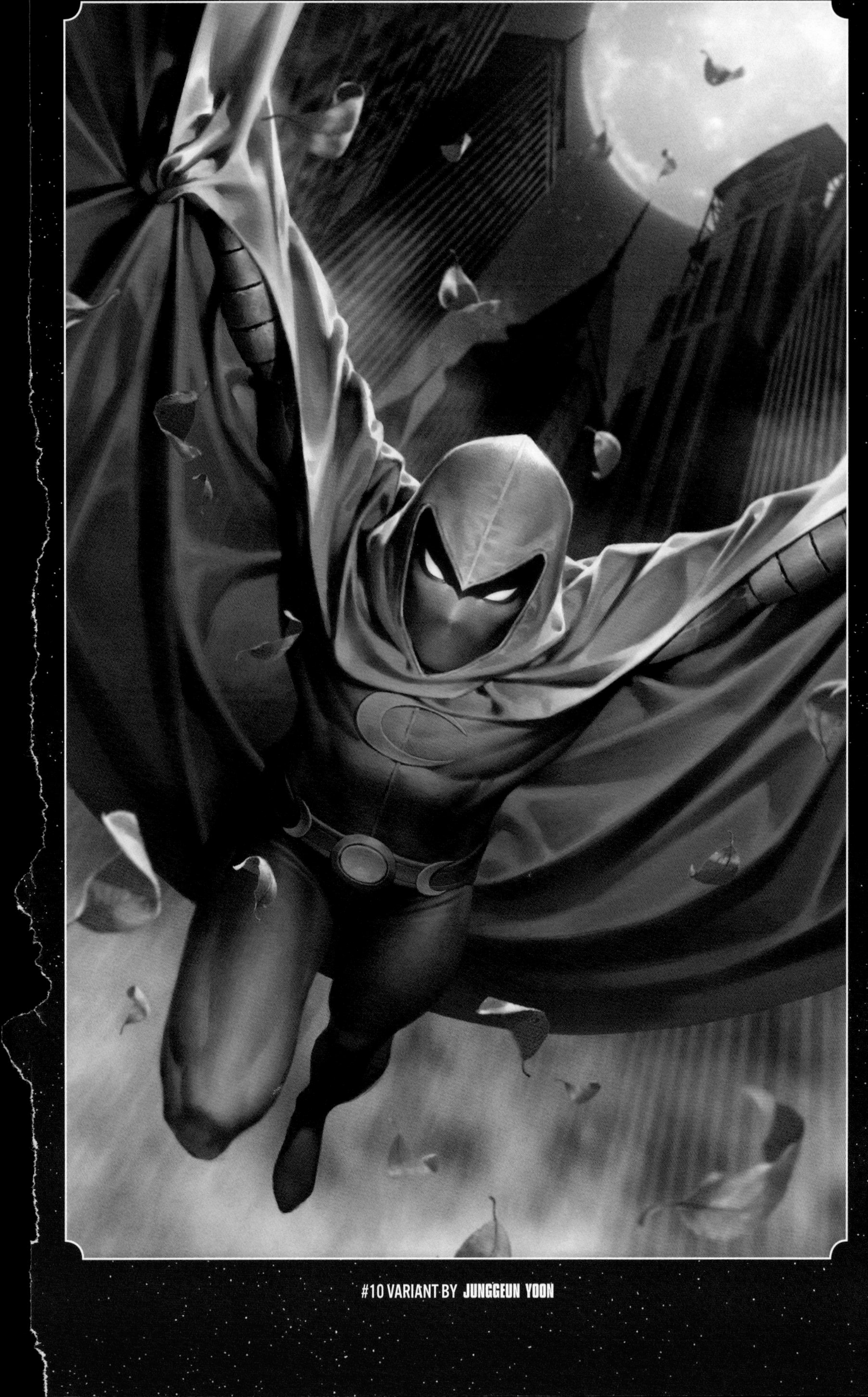

#10 VARIANT BY **JUNGGEUN YOON**

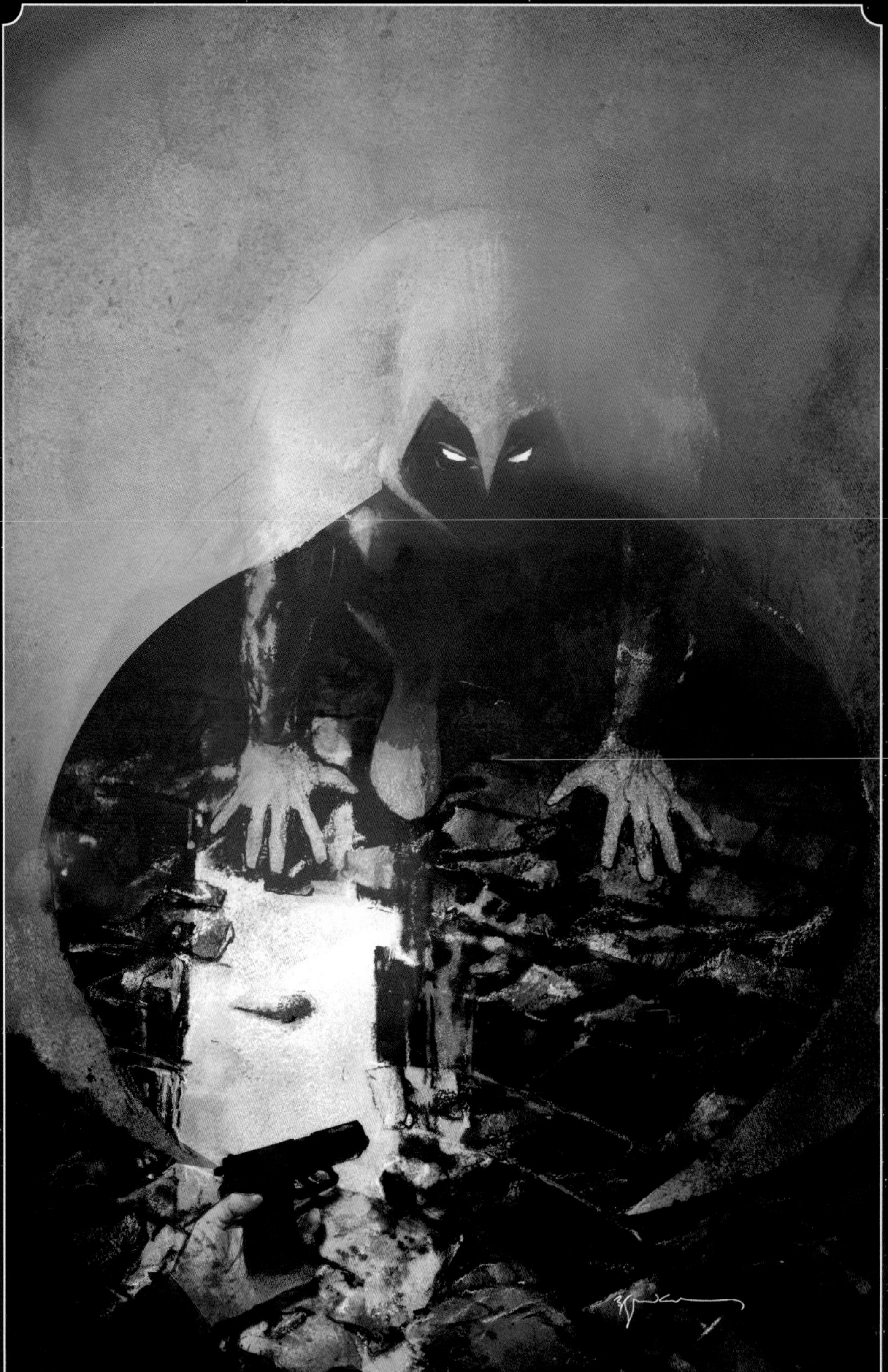

#11 VARIANT BY **BILL SIENKIEWICZ**

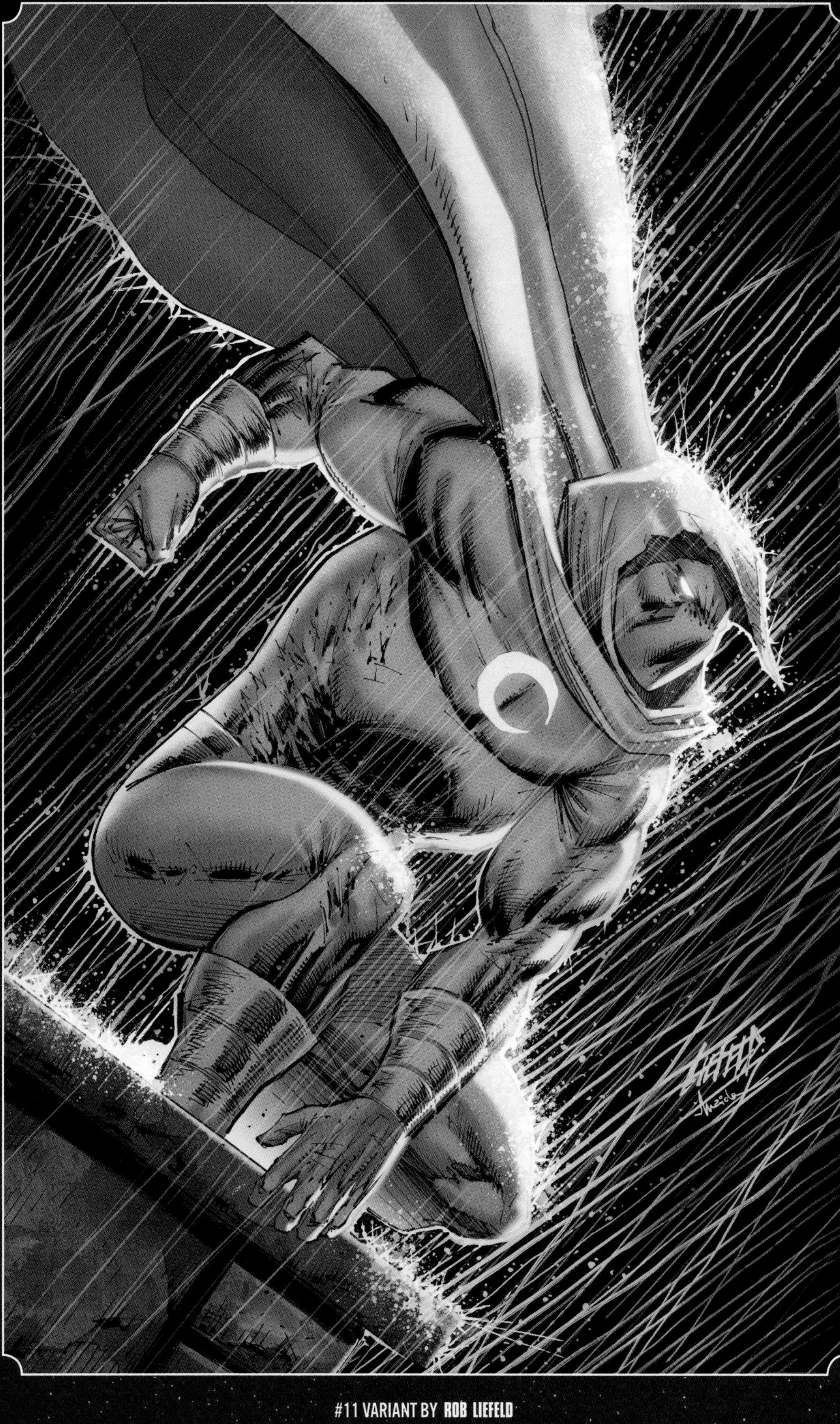
LIEFELD

#11 VARIANT BY **ROB LIEFELD**

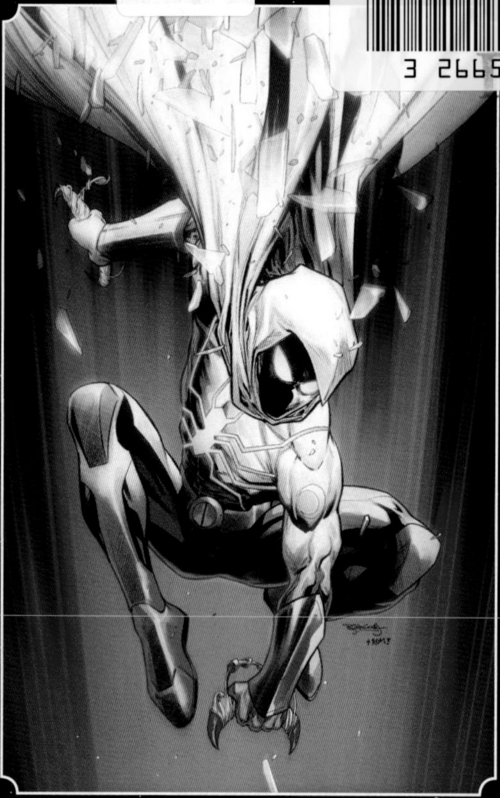

#10 SPIDER-MAN 60TH ANNIVERSARY VARIANT BY **STEPHEN SEGOVIA & ROMULO FAJARDO JR.**

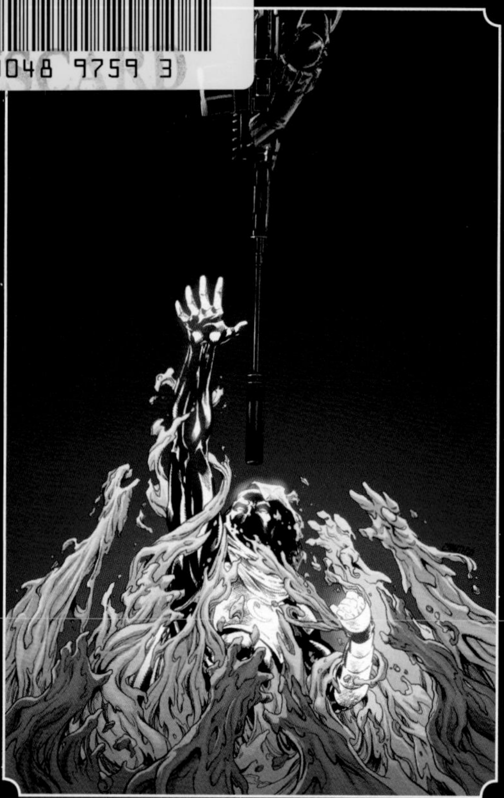

#10 2ND PRINTING VARIANT BY **CORY SMITH**

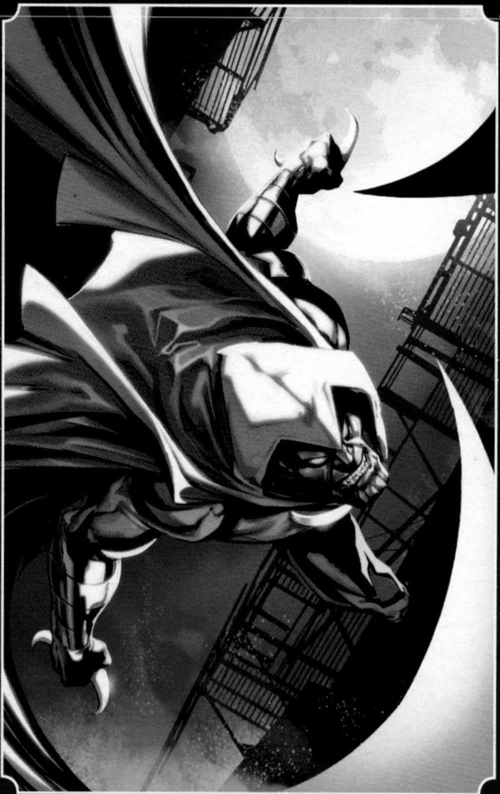

#11 SKRULL VARIANT BY **FRANCESCO MANNA & FLAVIO DISPENZA**

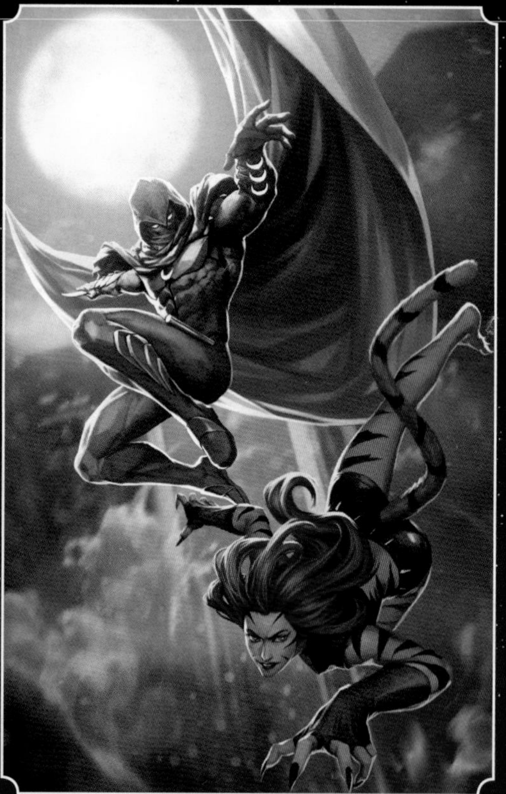

#12 VARIANT BY **SKAN**